Kaze HIKARU

5

Story & Art by
Taeko Watanabe

SB
Shojo Beat

Contents

Story Thus Far

It is the end of the Bakumatsu era, in the third year of Bunkyu (1863), in Kyoto. The Mibu-Roshi (later to become the Shinsengumi) is created to protect the shogun in this chaotic time.

Both Tominaga Sei's father and brother are killed by anti-Shogunate rebels. Sei then joins the Mibu-Roshi Party disguised as a boy, Kamiya Seizaburo, to avenge her family. She comes to regard Okita Soji as her mentor after he saves her from being attacked. Sei aspires to become a true bushi, but she finds herself surrounded by "animals." Further, Soji soon discovers Sei is a girl and keeps her secret while watching over her. Sei considers leaving the troop but stays in order to protect Soji.

The Mibu-Roshi are credited for their efforts and the name "Shinsengumi" is bestowed upon them. At the same time, a secret order is given to eliminate Captain Serizawa for his debauchery. Soji volunteers to carry out those orders.

ISBN : 9781421510187

Characters

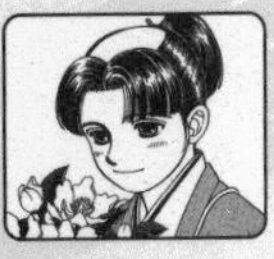

Tominaga Sei
She disguises herself as a boy to enter the Mibu-Roshi. Sei wants to become a warrior so she can avenge her father and brother. She trains under Soji, aspiring to become a true bushi.

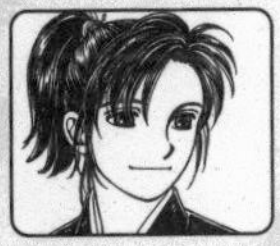

Okita Soji
Assistant vice captain of the Mibu-Roshi and the selected successor of the Ten'nen Rishin-ryu school of sword fighting. He is the only member of the Mibu-Roshi who knows Sei's secret.

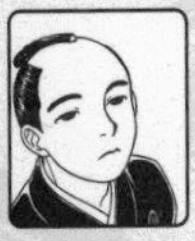

Saito Hajime
Assistant vice captain. He was a friend of Sei's older brother, Yuma, to whom he bears a striking resemblance.

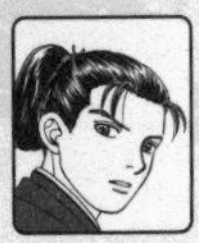

Hijikata Toshizo
Vice captain of the Mibu-Roshi. He commands the Mibu-Roshi with strict authority.

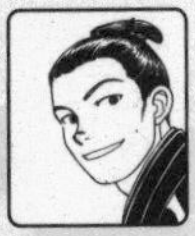

Kondo Isami
Captain of the Mibu-Roshi and fourth master of the Ten'nen Rishin-ryu. Has a very calm temperament and is highly respected.

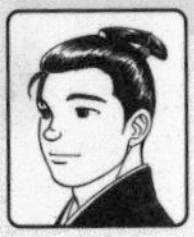

Yamanami Keisuke
Vice captain of the Shinsengumi. Although he is a master of the Hokushin Itto-Ryu, he is kind and well learned.

※Refer to Kaze Hikaru vol. 2.♡

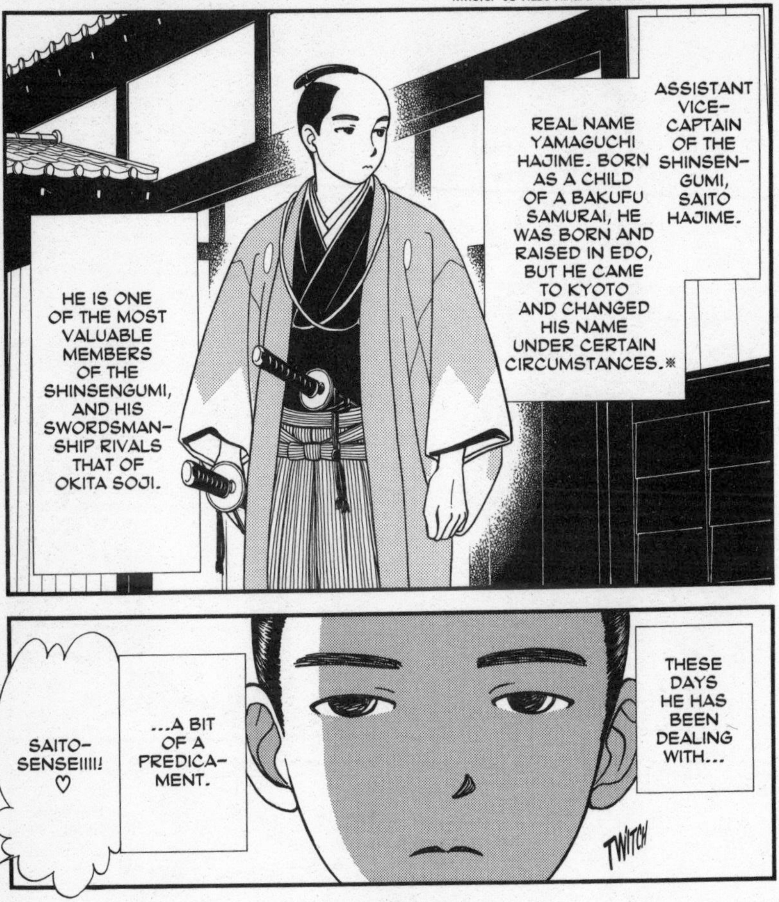
ASSISTANT VICE-CAPTAIN OF THE SHINSEN-GUMI, SAITO HAJIME.
REAL NAME YAMAGUCHI HAJIME. BORN AS A CHILD OF A BAKUFU SAMURAI, HE WAS BORN AND RAISED IN EDO, BUT HE CAME TO KYOTO AND CHANGED HIS NAME UNDER CERTAIN CIRCUMSTANCES.※
HE IS ONE OF THE MOST VALUABLE MEMBERS OF THE SHINSENGUMI, AND HIS SWORDSMAN-SHIP RIVALS THAT OF OKITA SOJI.
THESE DAYS HE HAS BEEN DEALING WITH...
TWITCH
...A BIT OF A PREDICA-MENT.
SAITO-SENSEIIII! ♡

KYOTO "IROHA" KARUTA GAME

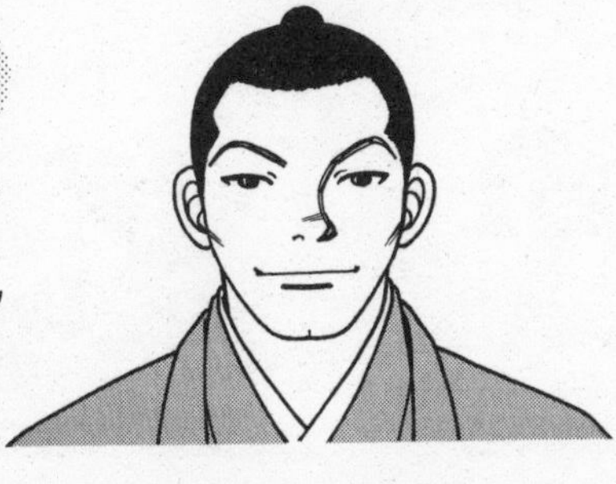

う

"U"

UJI YORI SODACHI

"NO MAN IS BORN A MASTER"

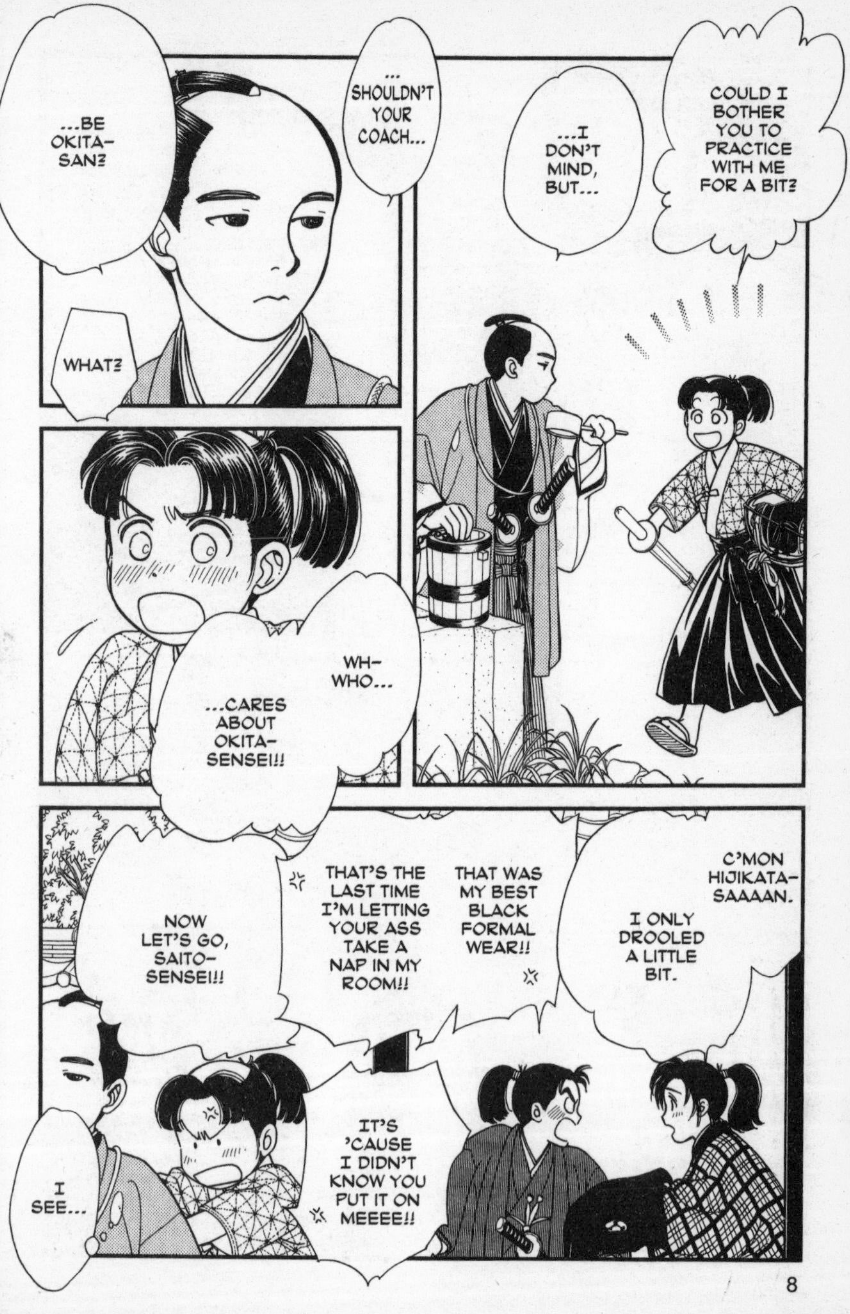
COULD I BOTHER YOU TO PRACTICE WITH ME FOR A BIT?
...I DON'T MIND, BUT...
... SHOULDN'T YOUR COACH...
...BE OKITA-SAN?
WHAT?
WH- WHO...
...CARES ABOUT OKITA-SENSEI!!!
C'MON HIJIKATA-SAAAAN.
I ONLY DROOLED A LITTLE BIT.
THAT WAS MY BEST BLACK FORMAL WEAR!!
THAT'S THE LAST TIME I'M LETTING YOUR ASS TAKE A NAP IN MY ROOM!!
IT'S 'CAUSE I DIDN'T KNOW YOU PUT IT ON MEEEE!!
NOW LET'S GO, SAITO-SENSEI!!!
I SEE...

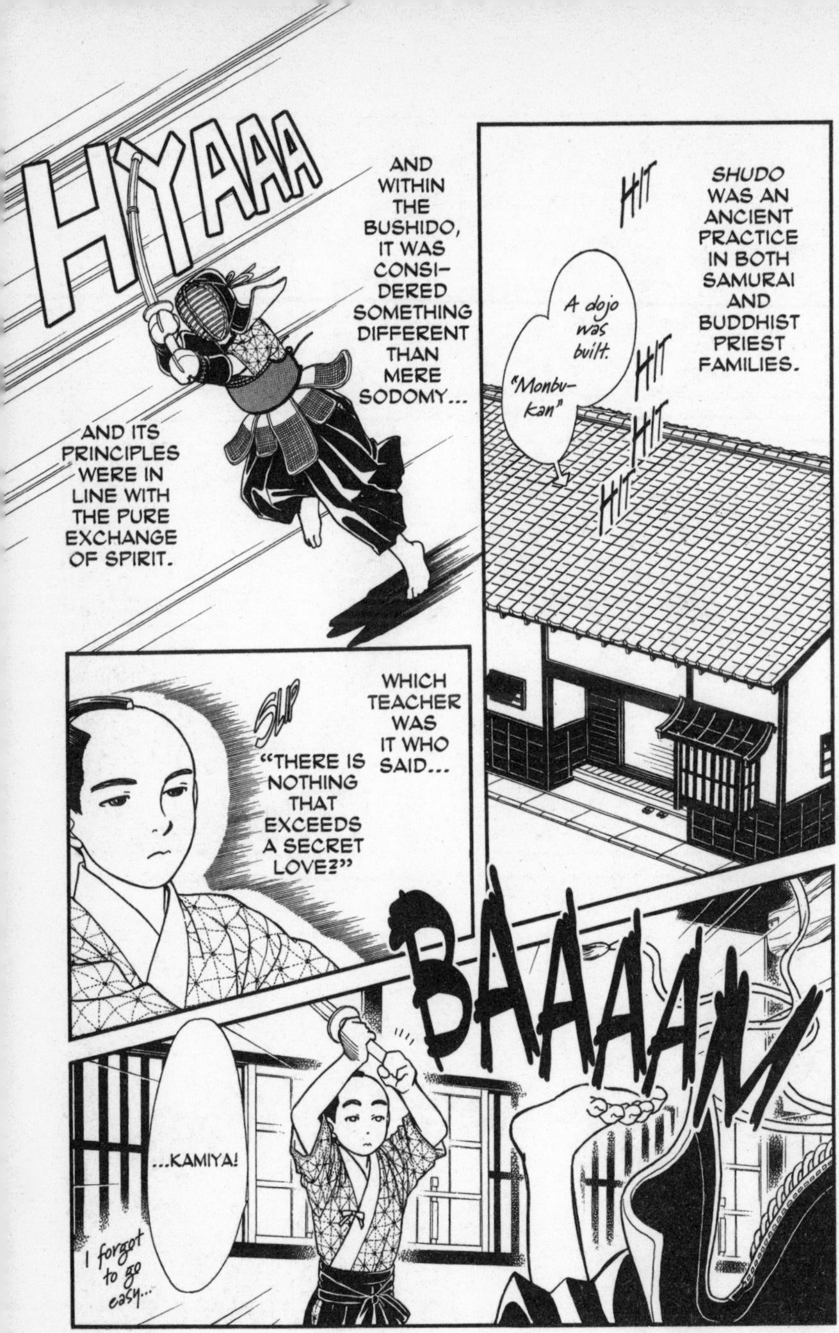
SHUDO WAS AN ANCIENT PRACTICE IN BOTH SAMURAI AND BUDDHIST PRIEST FAMILIES.
HIT HIT HIT HIT
A dojo was built.
"Monbu-kan"
AND WITHIN THE BUSHIDO, IT WAS CONSI-DERED SOMETHING DIFFERENT THAN MERE SODOMY...
HIYAAA
AND ITS PRINCIPLES WERE IN LINE WITH THE PURE EXCHANGE OF SPIRIT.
WHICH TEACHER WAS IT WHO SAID...
"THERE IS NOTHING THAT EXCEEDS A SECRET LOVE?"
SLIP
BAAAAM
...KAMIYA!
I forgot to go easy...

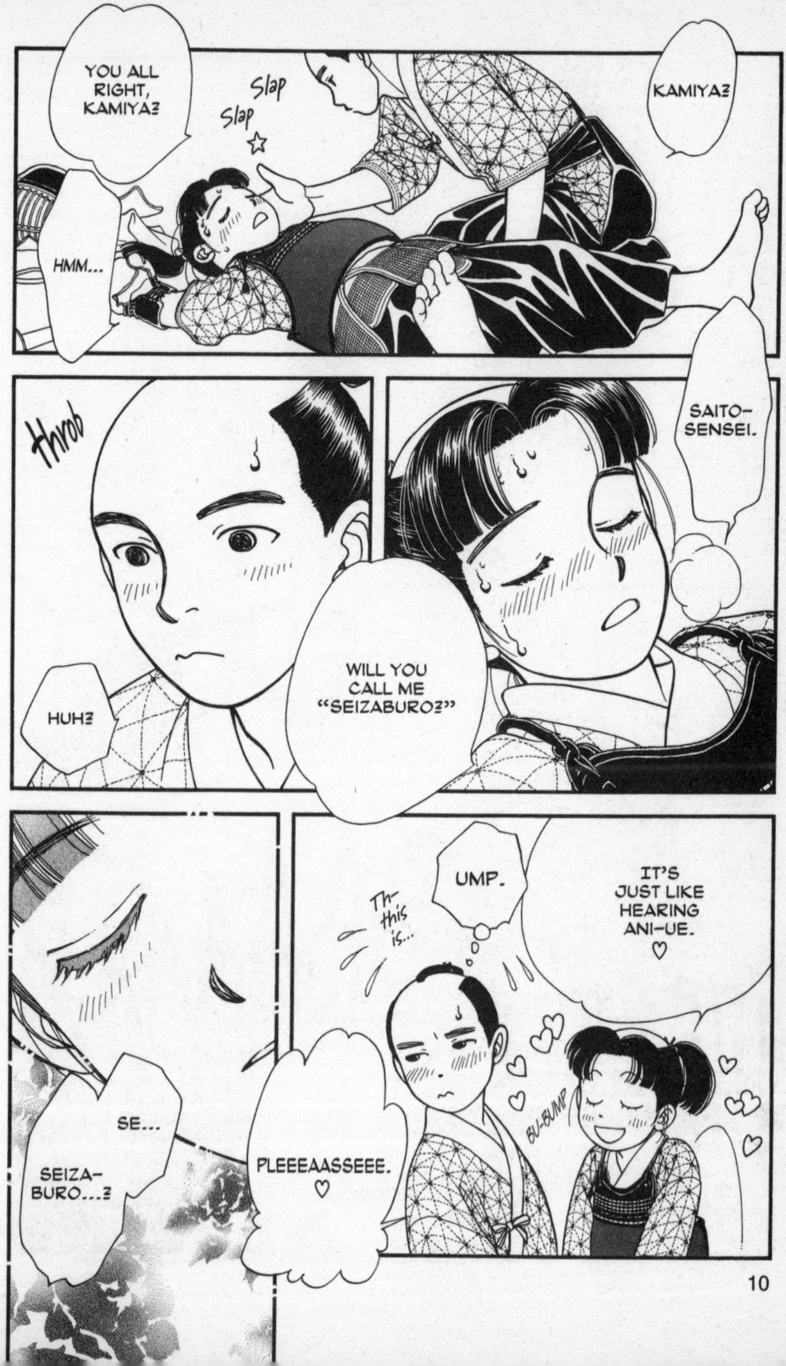
KAMIYA?
Slap
Slap
YOU ALL RIGHT, KAMIYA?
HMM...
SAITO-SENSEI.
WILL YOU CALL ME "SEIZABURO?"
Throb
HUH?
IT'S JUST LIKE HEARING ANI-UE. ♡
UMP.
Th-this is...
BU-BUMP
PLEEEAASSEEE. ♡
SE...
SEIZABURO...?

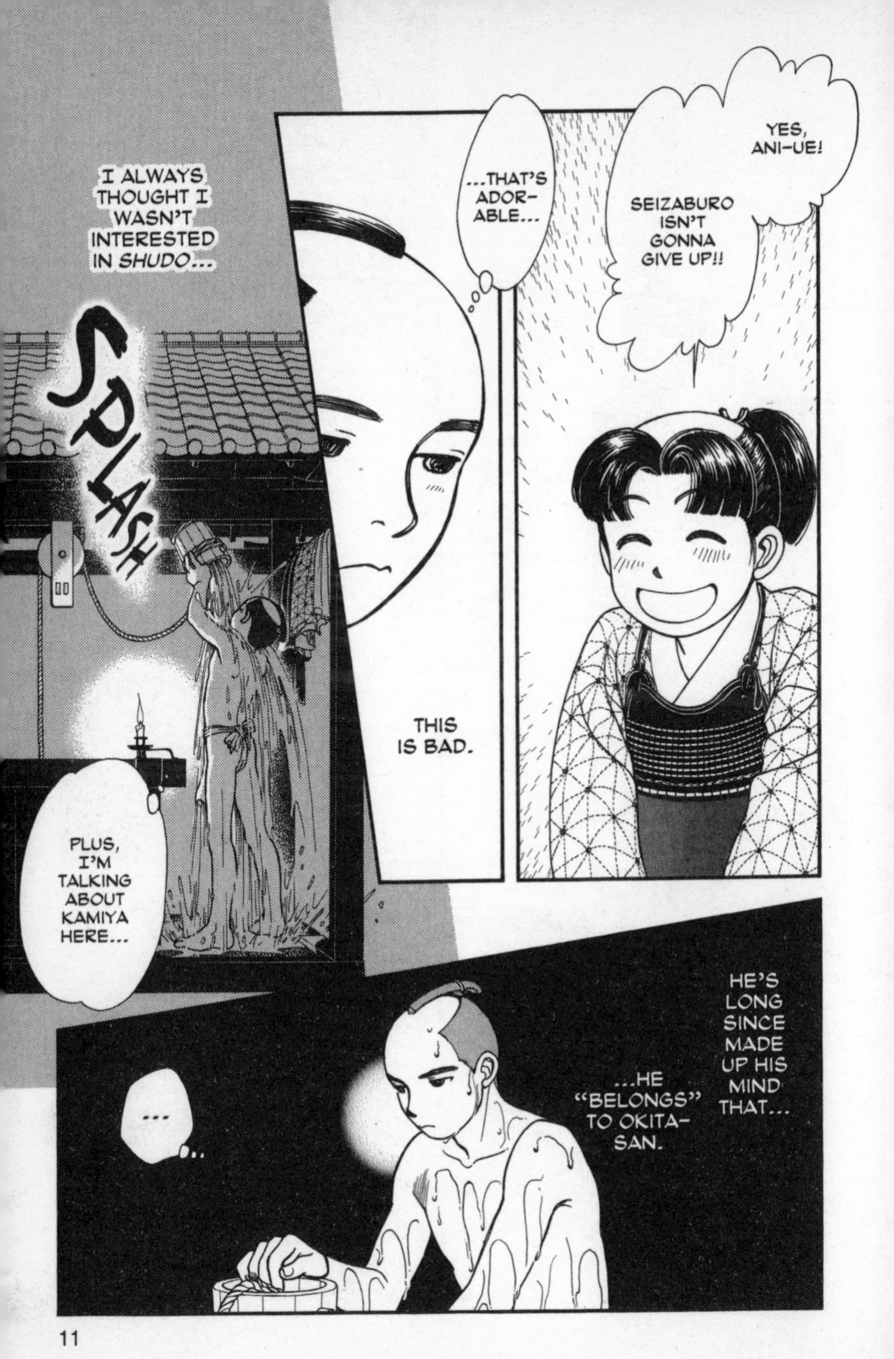
YES, ANI-UE!
SEIZABURO ISN'T GONNA GIVE UP!!
...THAT'S ADORABLE...
THIS IS BAD.
I ALWAYS THOUGHT I WASN'T INTERESTED IN *SHUDO*...
SPLASH
PLUS, I'M TALKING ABOUT KAMIYA HERE...
HE'S LONG SINCE MADE UP HIS MIND THAT...
...HE "BELONGS" TO OKITA-SAN.
...

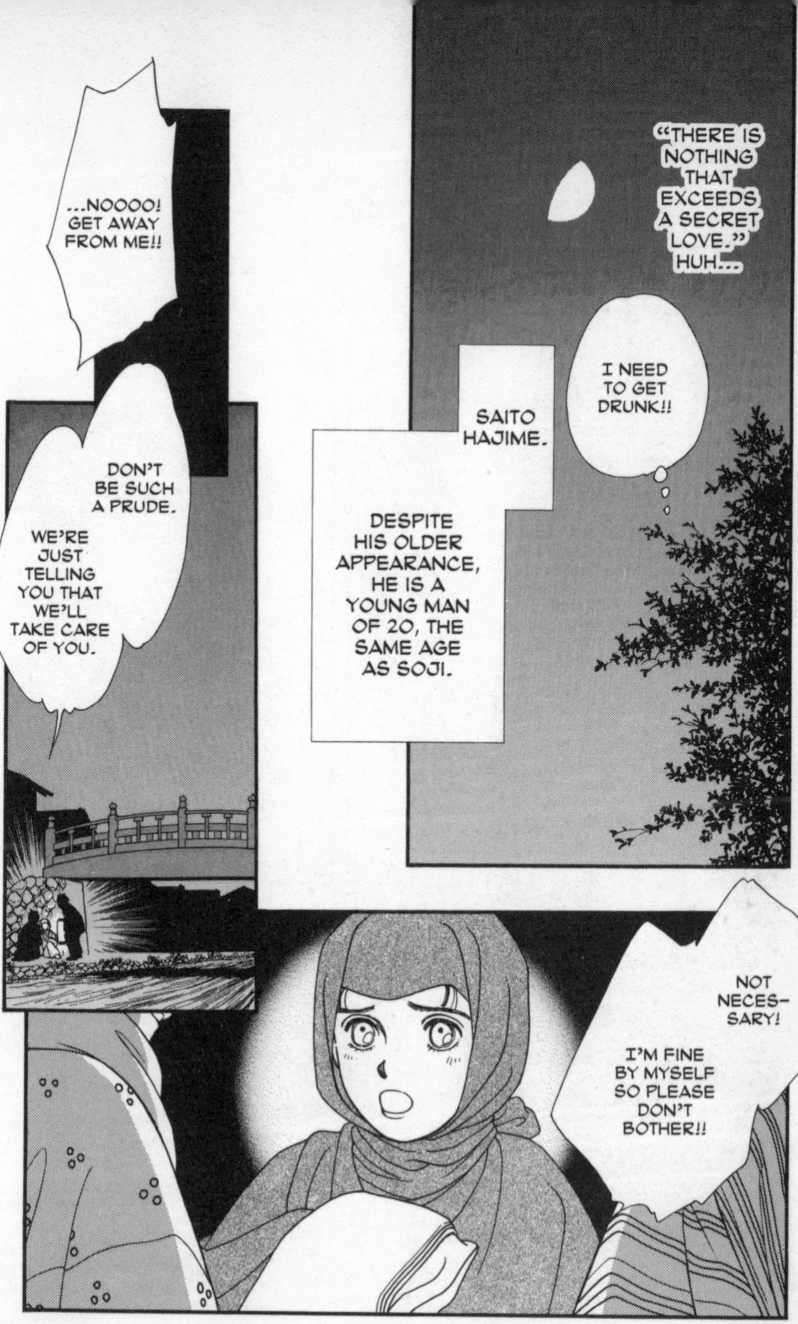
"THERE IS NOTHING THAT EXCEEDS A SECRET LOVE." HUH...
I NEED TO GET DRUNK!!
SAITO HAJIME.
DESPITE HIS OLDER APPEARANCE, HE IS A YOUNG MAN OF 20, THE SAME AGE AS SOJI.
...NOOOO! GET AWAY FROM ME!!
DON'T BE SUCH A PRUDE.
WE'RE JUST TELLING YOU THAT WE'LL TAKE CARE OF YOU.
NOT NECES-SARY!
I'M FINE BY MYSELF SO PLEASE DON'T BOTHER!!

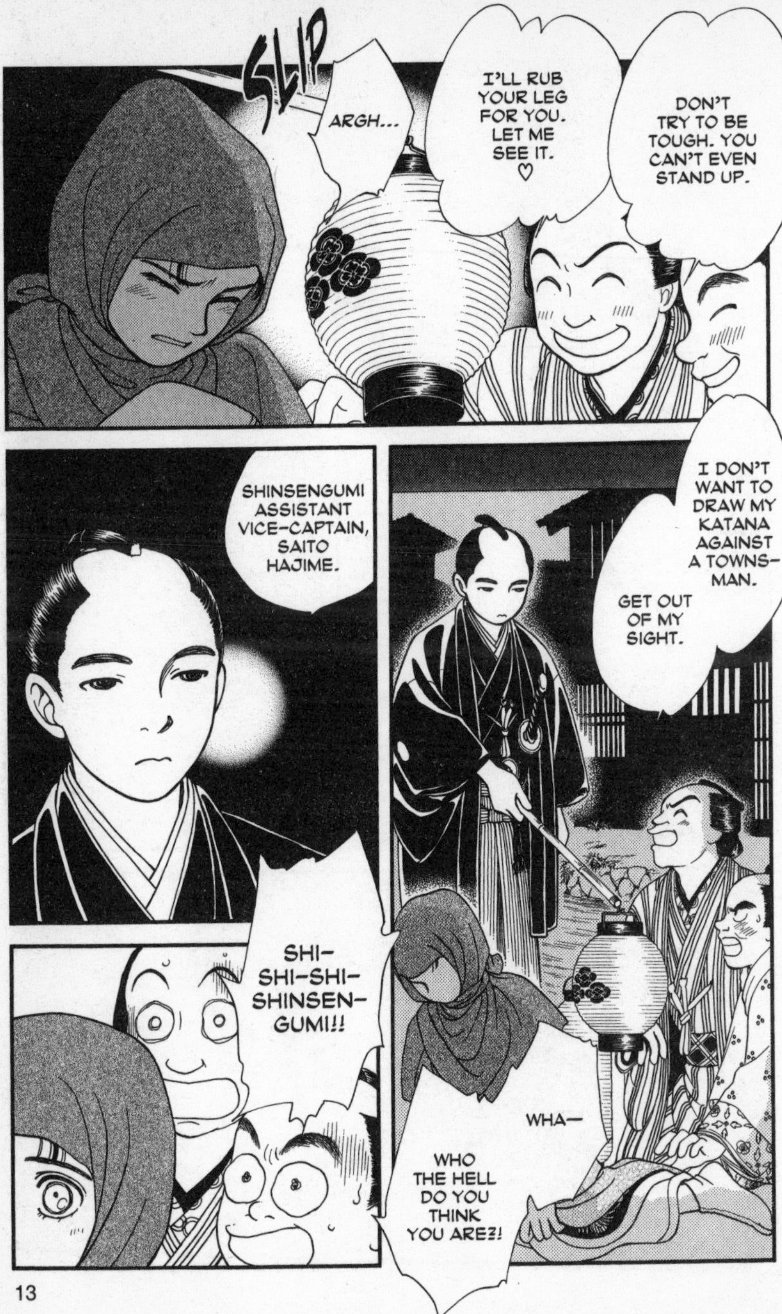
DON'T TRY TO BE TOUGH. YOU CAN'T EVEN STAND UP.
I'LL RUB YOUR LEG FOR YOU. LET ME SEE IT. ♡
SLIP
ARGH...
I DON'T WANT TO DRAW MY KATANA AGAINST A TOWNSMAN.
GET OUT OF MY SIGHT.
WHA—
WHO THE HELL DO YOU THINK YOU ARE?!
SHINSENGUMI ASSISTANT VICE-CAPTAIN, SAITO HAJIME.
SHI-SHI-SHI-SHINSEN-GUMI!!

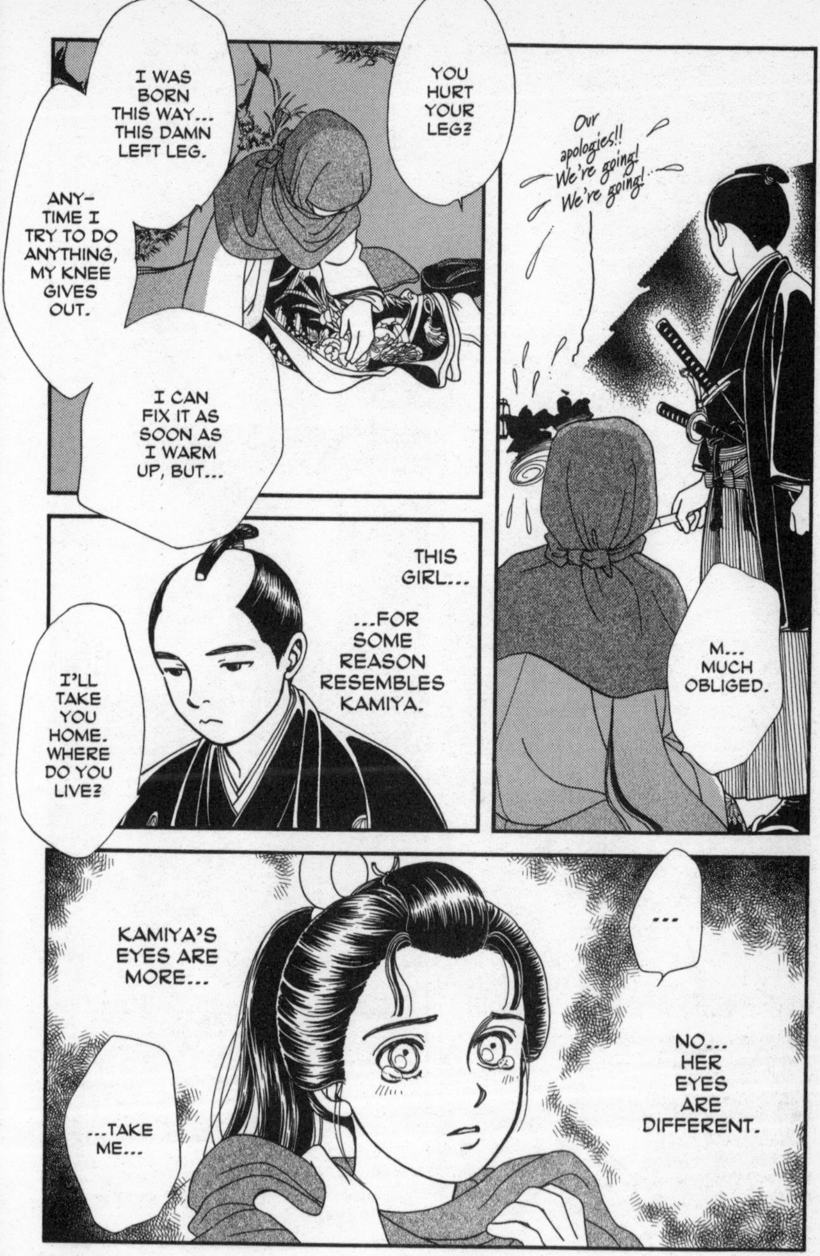
Our apologies!! We're going! We're going!
M... MUCH OBLIGED.
YOU HURT YOUR LEG?
I WAS BORN THIS WAY... THIS DAMN LEFT LEG.
ANY-TIME I TRY TO DO ANYTHING, MY KNEE GIVES OUT.
I CAN FIX IT AS SOON AS I WARM UP, BUT...
THIS GIRL...
...FOR SOME REASON RESEMBLES KAMIYA.
I'LL TAKE YOU HOME. WHERE DO YOU LIVE?
...
NO... HER EYES ARE DIFFERENT.
KAMIYA'S EYES ARE MORE...
...TAKE ME...

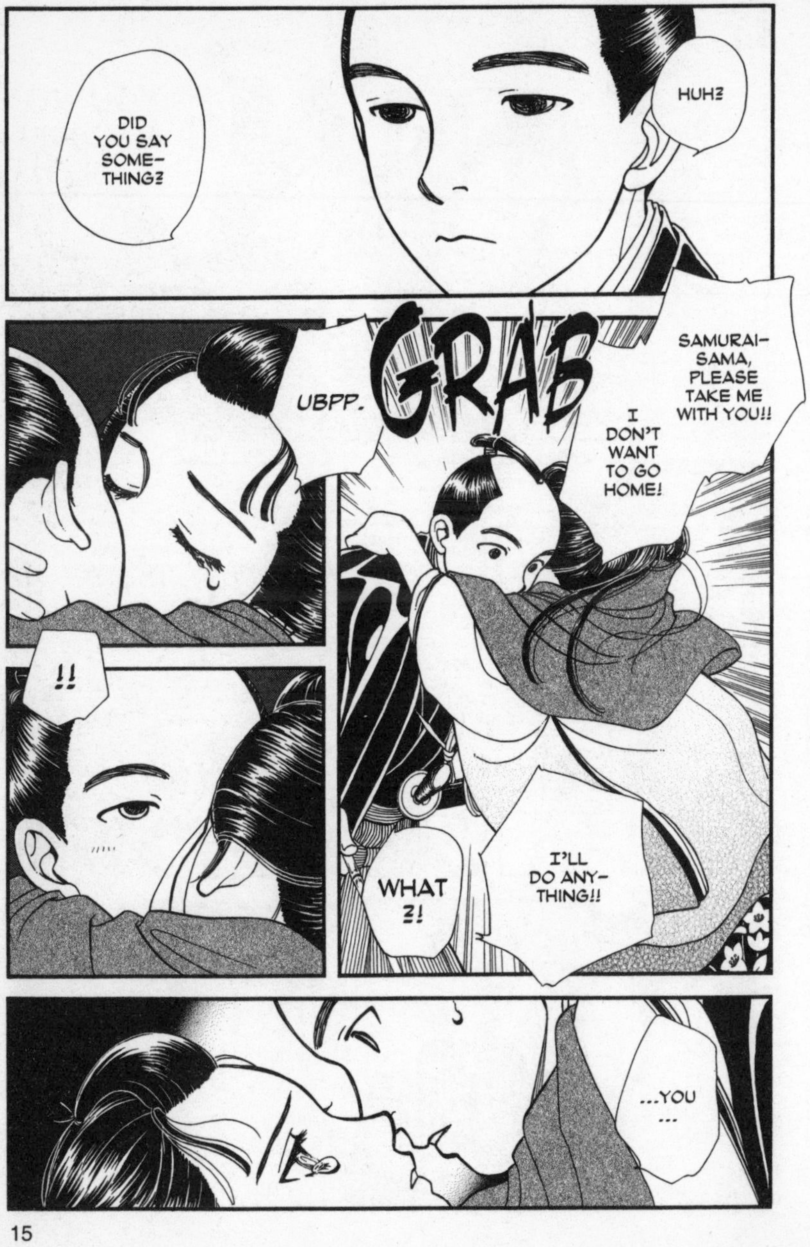
HUH?
DID YOU SAY SOME-THING?
SAMURAI-SAMA, PLEASE TAKE ME WITH YOU!!
GRAB
I DON'T WANT TO GO HOME!
I'LL DO ANY-THING!!
WHAT?!
UBPP.
!!
...YOU ...

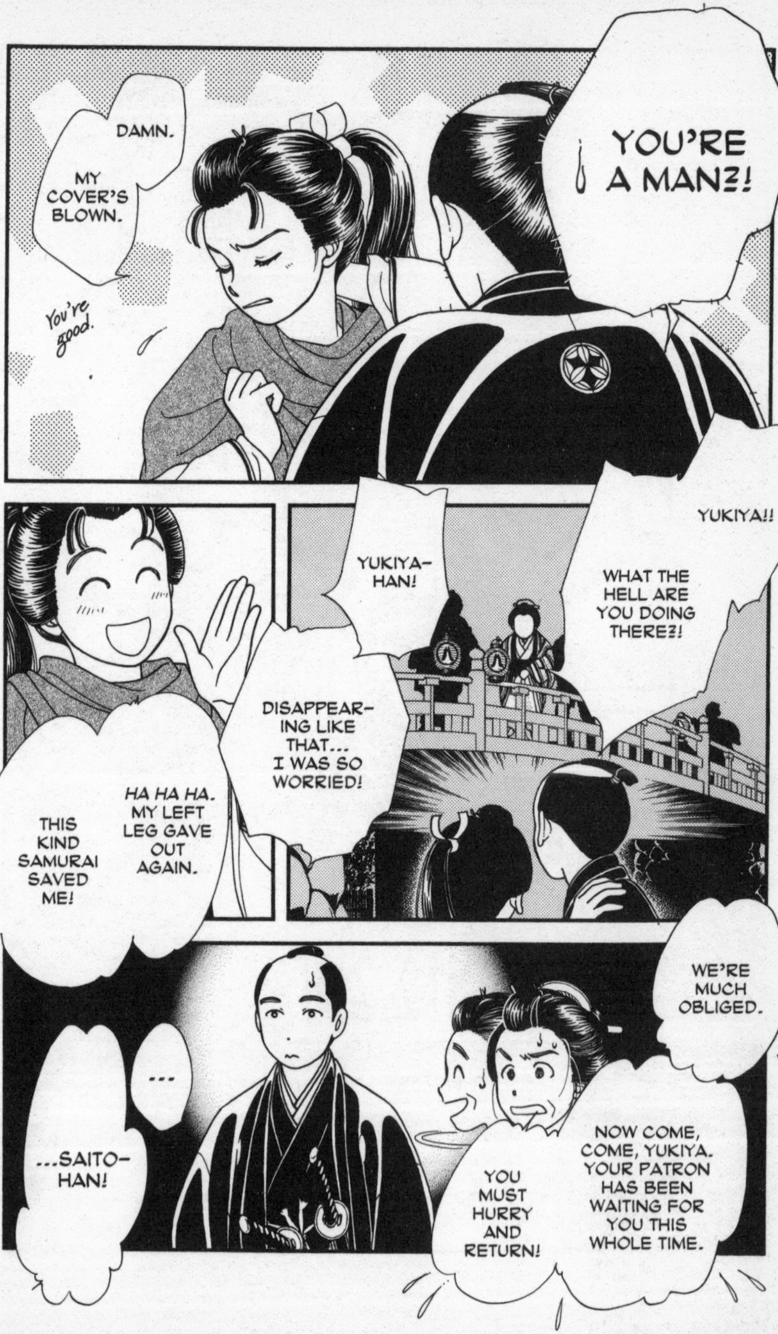
YOU'RE A MAN?!
DAMN. MY COVER'S BLOWN.
You're good.
YUKIYA!!
WHAT THE HELL ARE YOU DOING THERE?!
YUKIYA-HAN!
DISAPPEARING LIKE THAT... I WAS SO WORRIED!
HA HA HA. MY LEFT LEG GAVE OUT AGAIN.
THIS KIND SAMURAI SAVED ME!
WE'RE MUCH OBLIGED.
NOW COME, COME, YUKIYA. YOUR PATRON HAS BEEN WAITING FOR YOU THIS WHOLE TIME.
YOU MUST HURRY AND RETURN!
...
...SAITO-HAN!

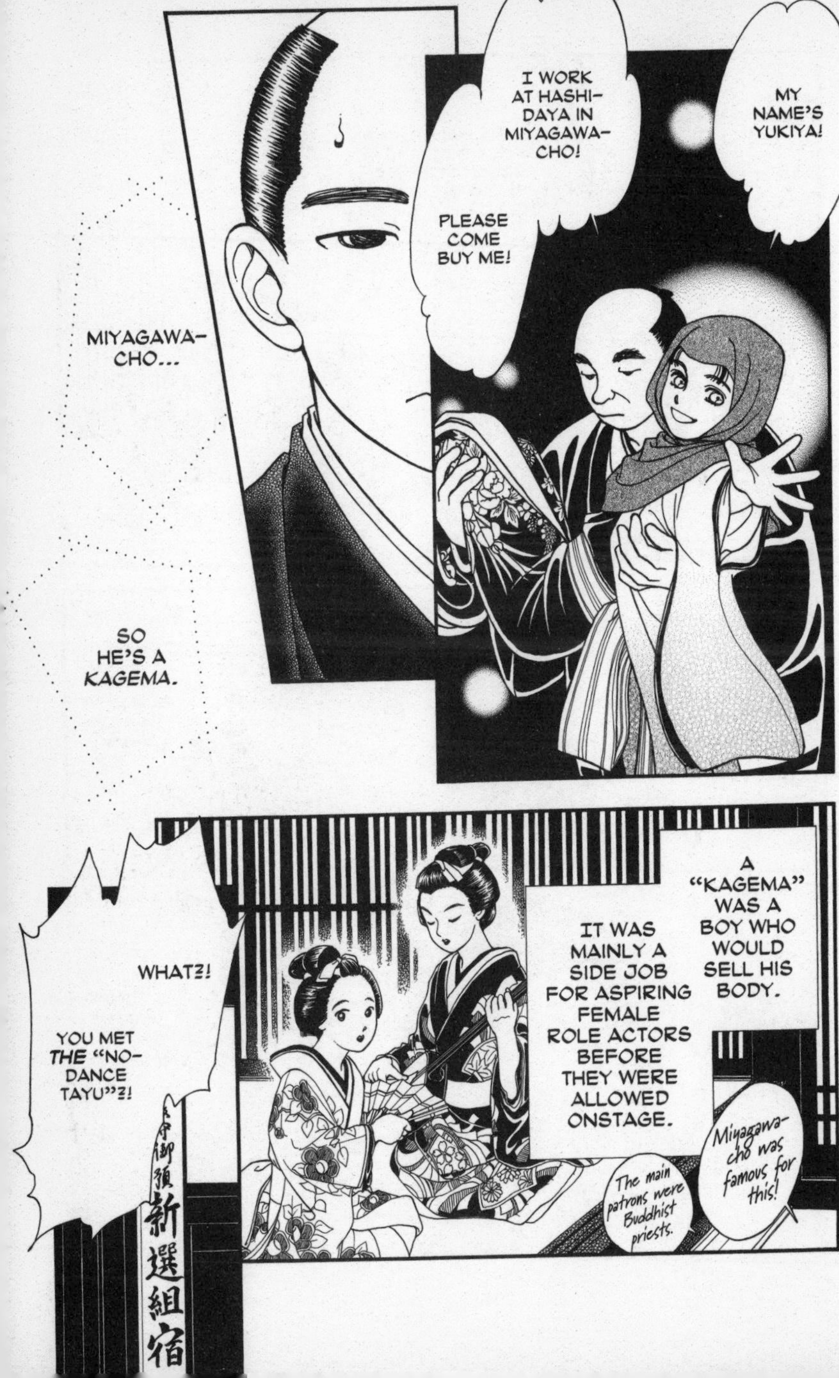
MY NAME'S YUKIYA!
I WORK AT HASHI-DAYA IN MIYAGAWA-CHO!
PLEASE COME BUY ME!
MIYAGAWA-CHO...
SO HE'S A KAGEMA.
A "KAGEMA" WAS A BOY WHO WOULD SELL HIS BODY.
IT WAS MAINLY A SIDE JOB FOR ASPIRING FEMALE ROLE ACTORS BEFORE THEY WERE ALLOWED ONSTAGE.
Miyagawa-cho was famous for this!
The main patrons were Buddhist priests.
WHAT?!
YOU MET THE "NO-DANCE TAYU"?!
新選組宿

※A Tayu was a high-ranking actor, or the highest rank among prostitutes.

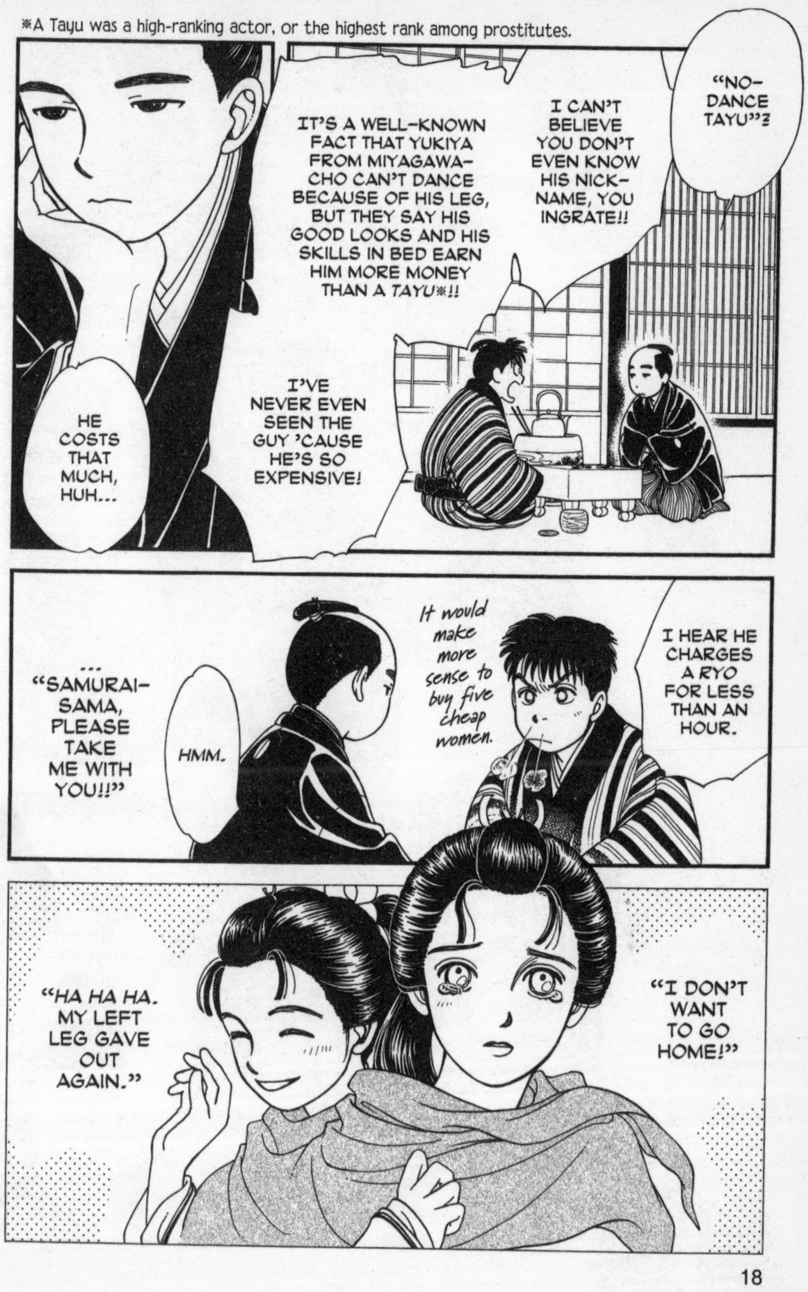
"NO-DANCE TAYU"?
I CAN'T BELIEVE YOU DON'T EVEN KNOW HIS NICK-NAME, YOU INGRATE!!
IT'S A WELL-KNOWN FACT THAT YUKIYA FROM MIYAGAWA-CHO CAN'T DANCE BECAUSE OF HIS LEG, BUT THEY SAY HIS GOOD LOOKS AND HIS SKILLS IN BED EARN HIM MORE MONEY THAN A *TAYU*※!!
I'VE NEVER EVEN SEEN THE GUY 'CAUSE HE'S SO EXPENSIVE!
HE COSTS THAT MUCH, HUH...
I HEAR HE CHARGES A *RYO* FOR LESS THAN AN HOUR.
It would make more sense to buy five cheap women.
HMM.
... "SAMURAI-SAMA, PLEASE TAKE ME WITH YOU!!"
"I DON'T WANT TO GO HOME!"
"*HA HA HA.* MY LEFT LEG GAVE OUT AGAIN."

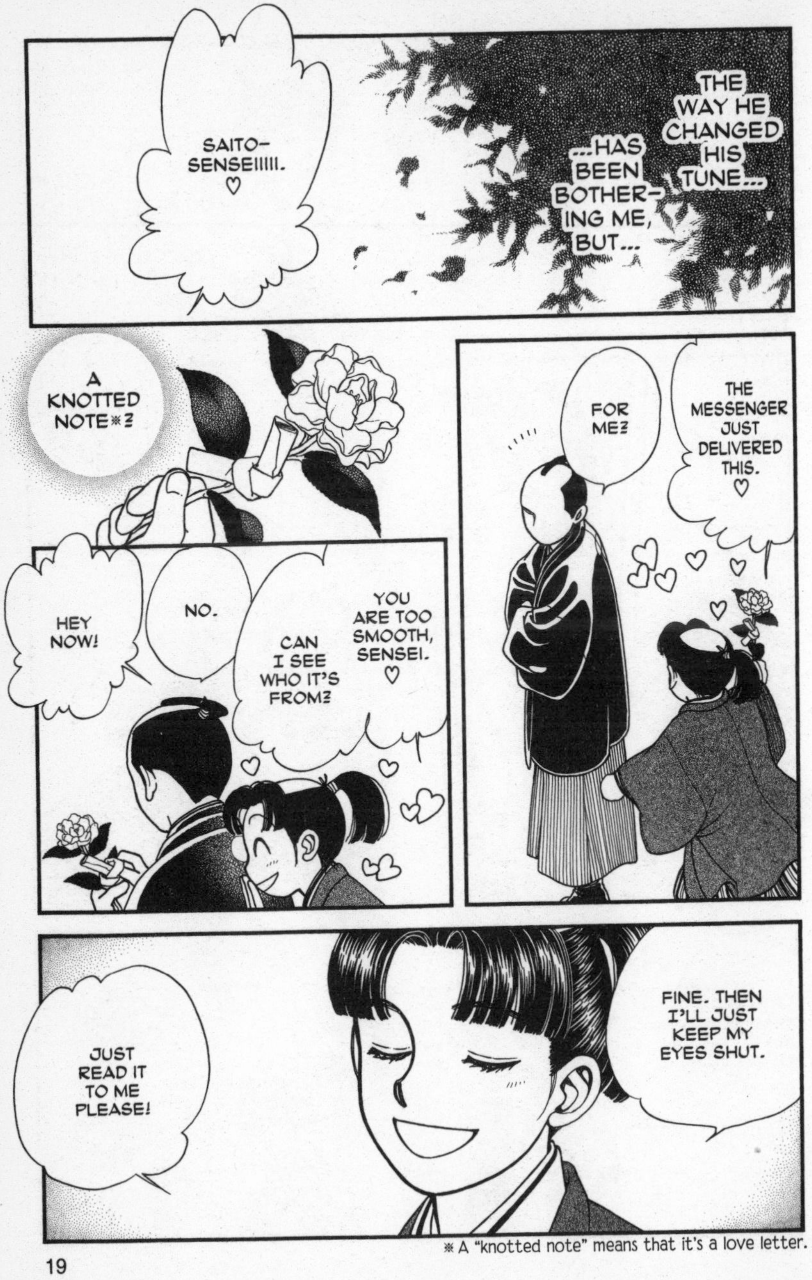
THE WAY HE CHANGED HIS TUNE...
...HAS BEEN BOTHERING ME, BUT...
SAITO-SENSEI!!!!!. ♡
THE MESSENGER JUST DELIVERED THIS. ♡
FOR ME?
A KNOTTED NOTE※?
YOU ARE TOO SMOOTH, SENSEI. ♡
CAN I SEE WHO IT'S FROM?
NO.
HEY NOW!
FINE. THEN I'LL JUST KEEP MY EYES SHUT.
JUST READ IT TO ME PLEASE!

※ A "knotted note" means that it's a love letter.

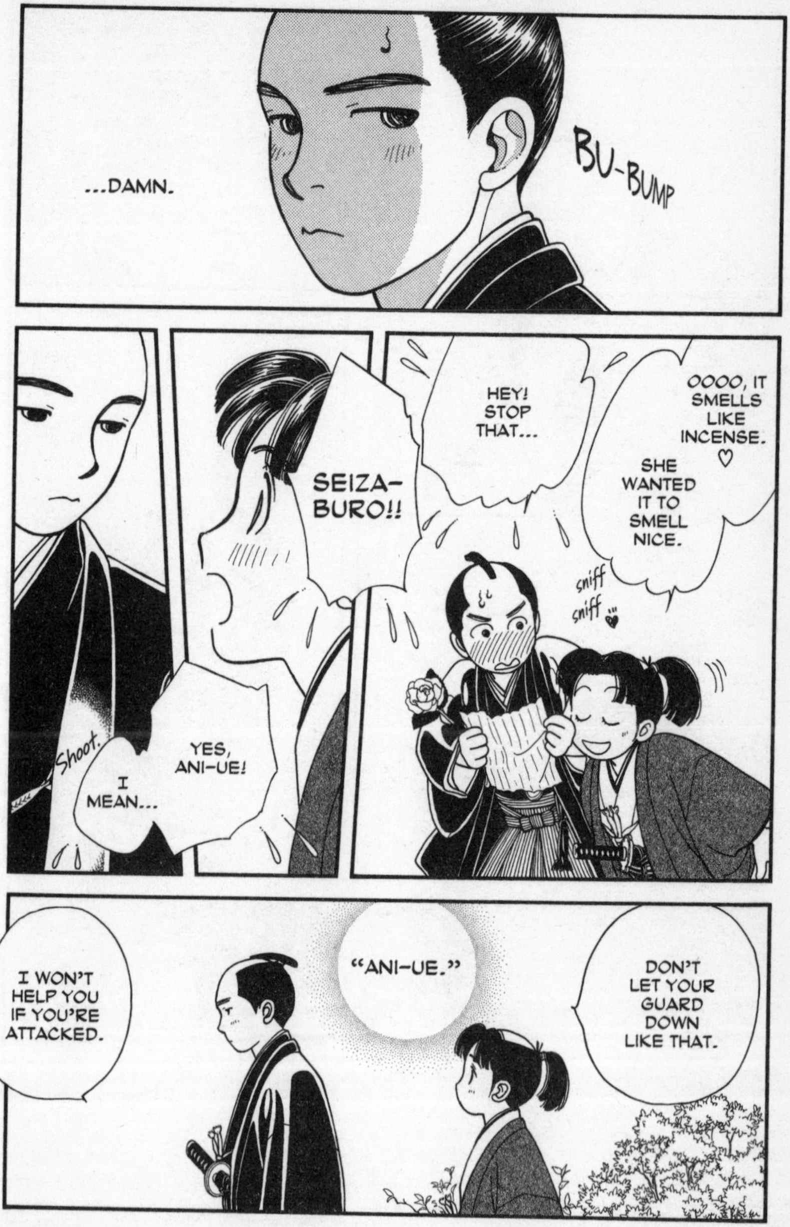
BU-BUMP
...DAMN.
OOOO, IT SMELLS LIKE INCENSE. ♡
SHE WANTED IT TO SMELL NICE.
sniff sniff
HEY! STOP THAT...
SEIZA-BURO!!
YES, ANI-UE!
I MEAN...
Shoot.
DON'T LET YOUR GUARD DOWN LIKE THAT.
"ANI-UE."
I WON'T HELP YOU IF YOU'RE ATTACKED.

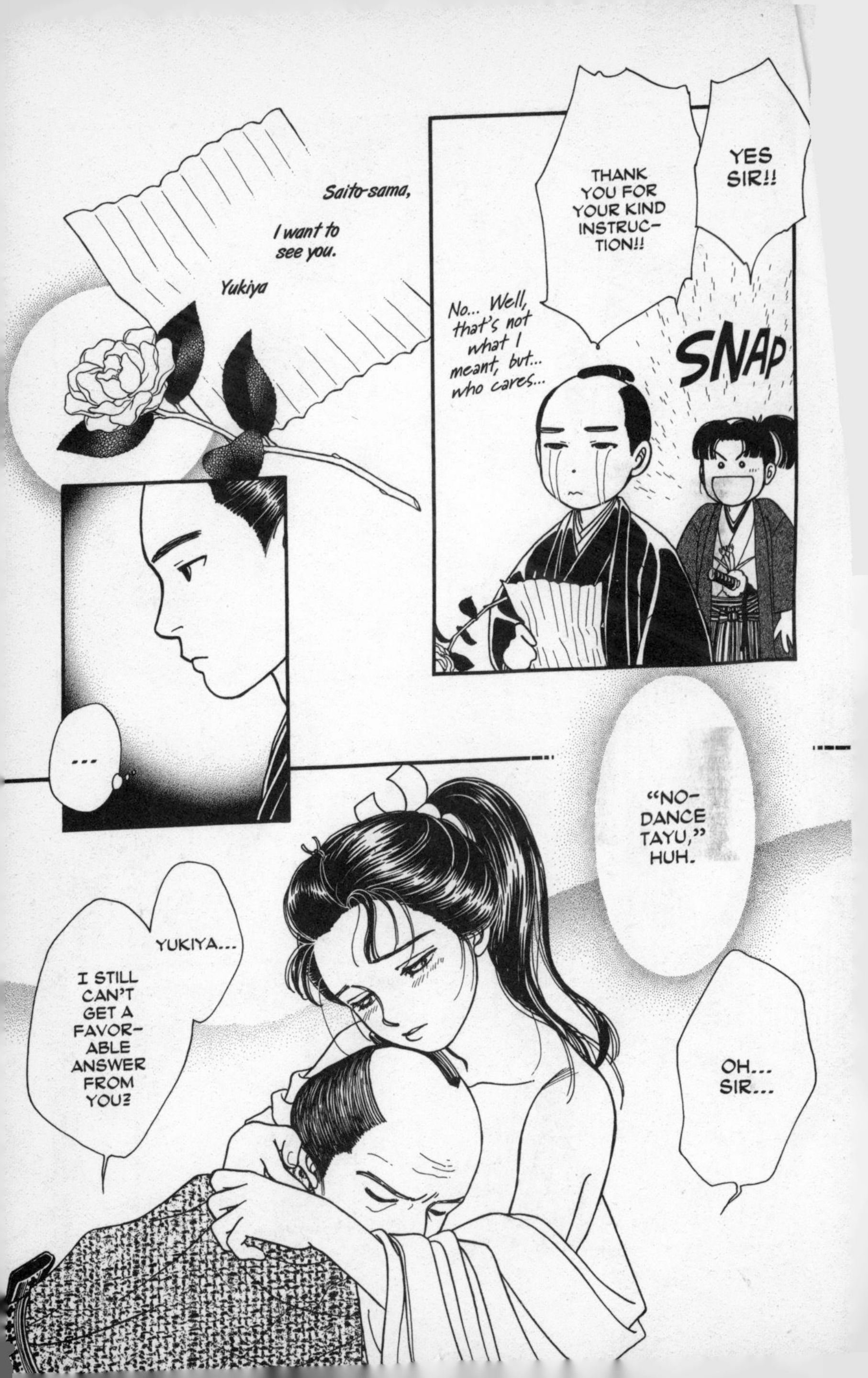
YES SIR!!
THANK YOU FOR YOUR KIND INSTRUCTION!!
SNAP
No... Well, that's not what I meant, but... who cares...
Saito-sama,
I want to see you.
Yukiya
...
"NO-DANCE TAYU," HUH.
OH... SIR...
YUKIYA...
I STILL CAN'T GET A FAVORABLE ANSWER FROM YOU?

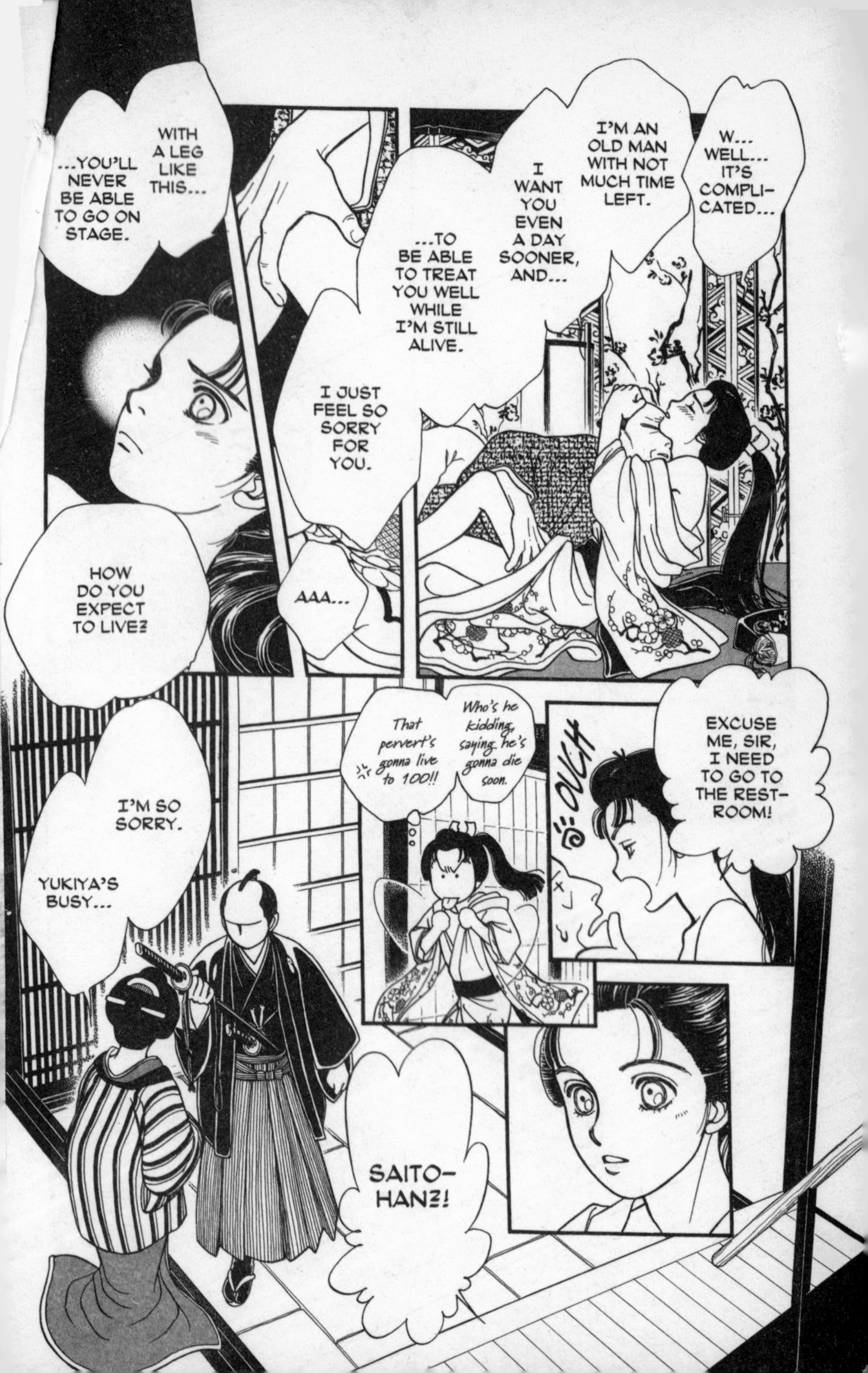
W... WELL... IT'S COMPLICATED...
I'M AN OLD MAN WITH NOT MUCH TIME LEFT.
I WANT YOU EVEN A DAY SOONER, AND...
...TO BE ABLE TO TREAT YOU WELL WHILE I'M STILL ALIVE.
I JUST FEEL SO SORRY FOR YOU.
AAA...
WITH A LEG LIKE THIS...
...YOU'LL NEVER BE ABLE TO GO ON STAGE.
HOW DO YOU EXPECT TO LIVE?
EXCUSE ME, SIR, I NEED TO GO TO THE REST-ROOM!
OUCH
Who's he kidding, saying he's gonna die soon.
That pervert's gonna live to 100!!
I'M SO SORRY.
YUKIYA'S BUSY...
SAITO-HAN?!

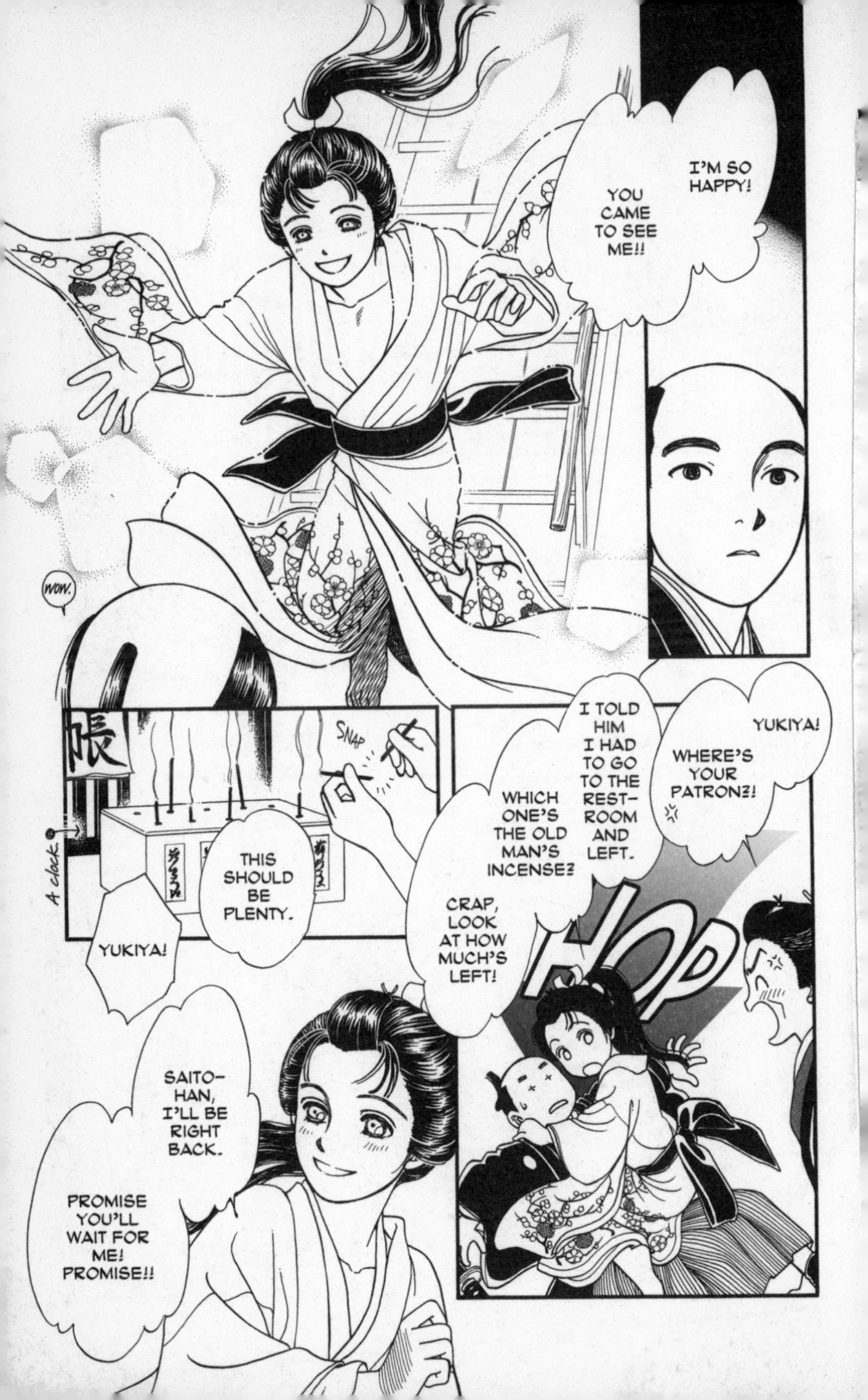
I'M SO HAPPY!
YOU CAME TO SEE ME!!
WOW.
YUKIYA!
WHERE'S YOUR PATRON?!
I TOLD HIM I HAD TO GO TO THE REST-ROOM AND LEFT.
HOP
WHICH ONE'S THE OLD MAN'S INCENSE?
CRAP, LOOK AT HOW MUCH'S LEFT!
SNAP
帳
THIS SHOULD BE PLENTY.
A clock.
YUKIYA!
SAITO-HAN, I'LL BE RIGHT BACK.
PROMISE YOU'LL WAIT FOR ME! PROMISE!!

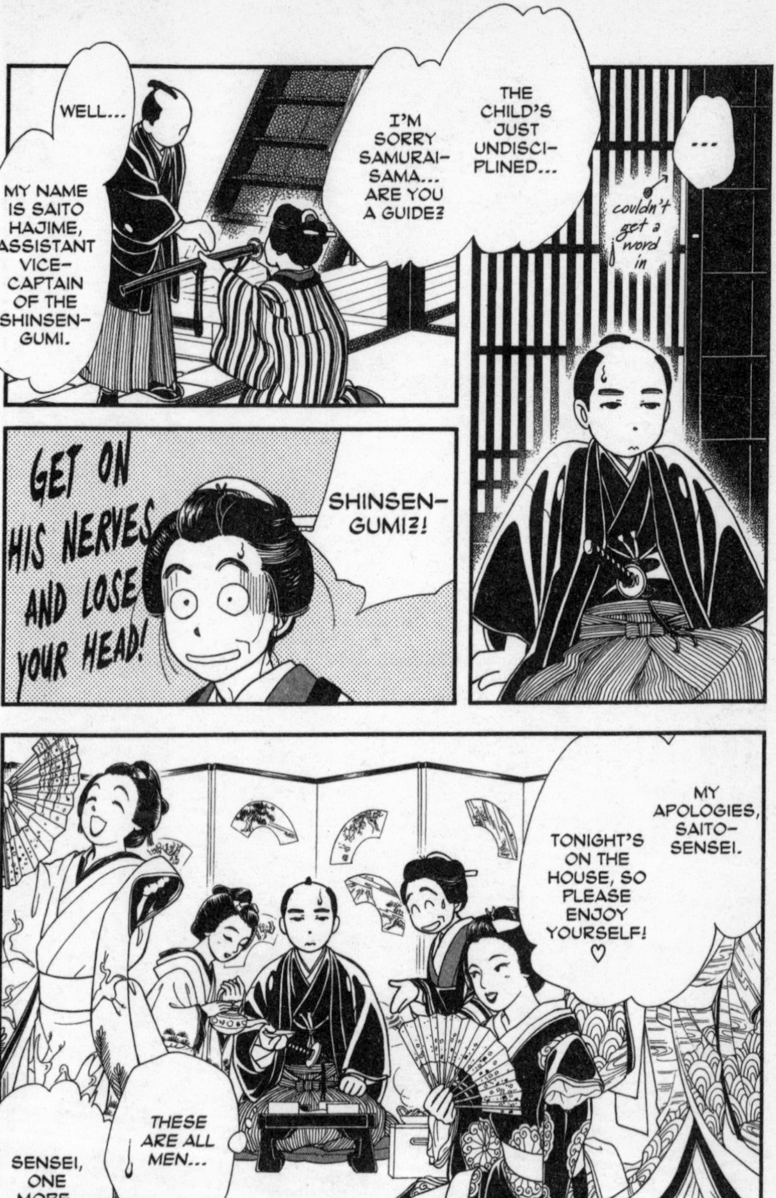
...
couldn't get a word in
THE CHILD'S JUST UNDISCIPLINED...
I'M SORRY SAMURAI-SAMA... ARE YOU A GUIDE?
WELL...
MY NAME IS SAITO HAJIME, ASSISTANT VICE-CAPTAIN OF THE SHINSEN-GUMI.
SHINSEN-GUMI?!
GET ON HIS NERVES AND LOSE YOUR HEAD!
MY APOLOGIES, SAITO-SENSEI.
TONIGHT'S ON THE HOUSE, SO PLEASE ENJOY YOURSELF! ♡
THESE ARE ALL MEN...
SENSEI, ONE MORE. ♡

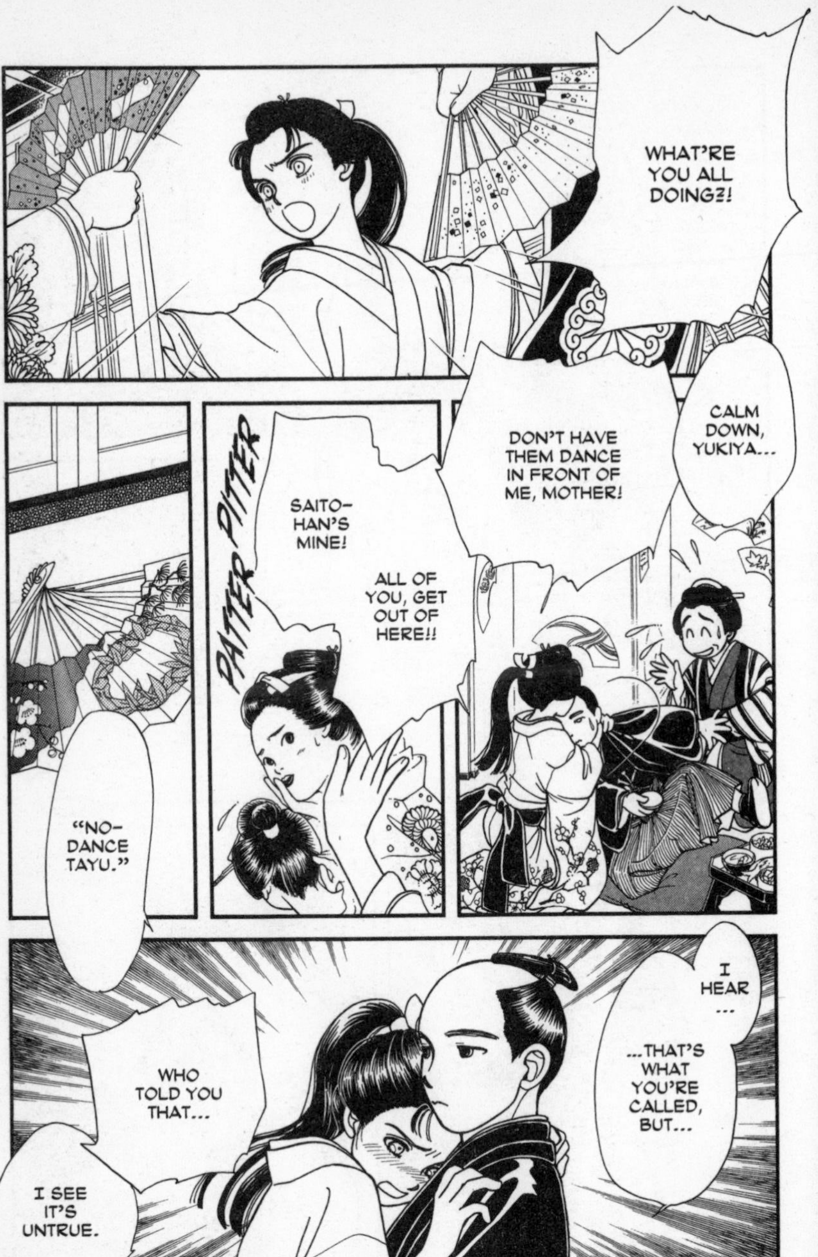
WHAT'RE YOU ALL DOING?!
CALM DOWN, YUKIYA...
DON'T HAVE THEM DANCE IN FRONT OF ME, MOTHER!
SAITO-HAN'S MINE!
PITTER PATTER
ALL OF YOU, GET OUT OF HERE!!
"NO-DANCE TAYU."
I HEAR ...
...THAT'S WHAT YOU'RE CALLED, BUT...
WHO TOLD YOU THAT...
I SEE IT'S UNTRUE.

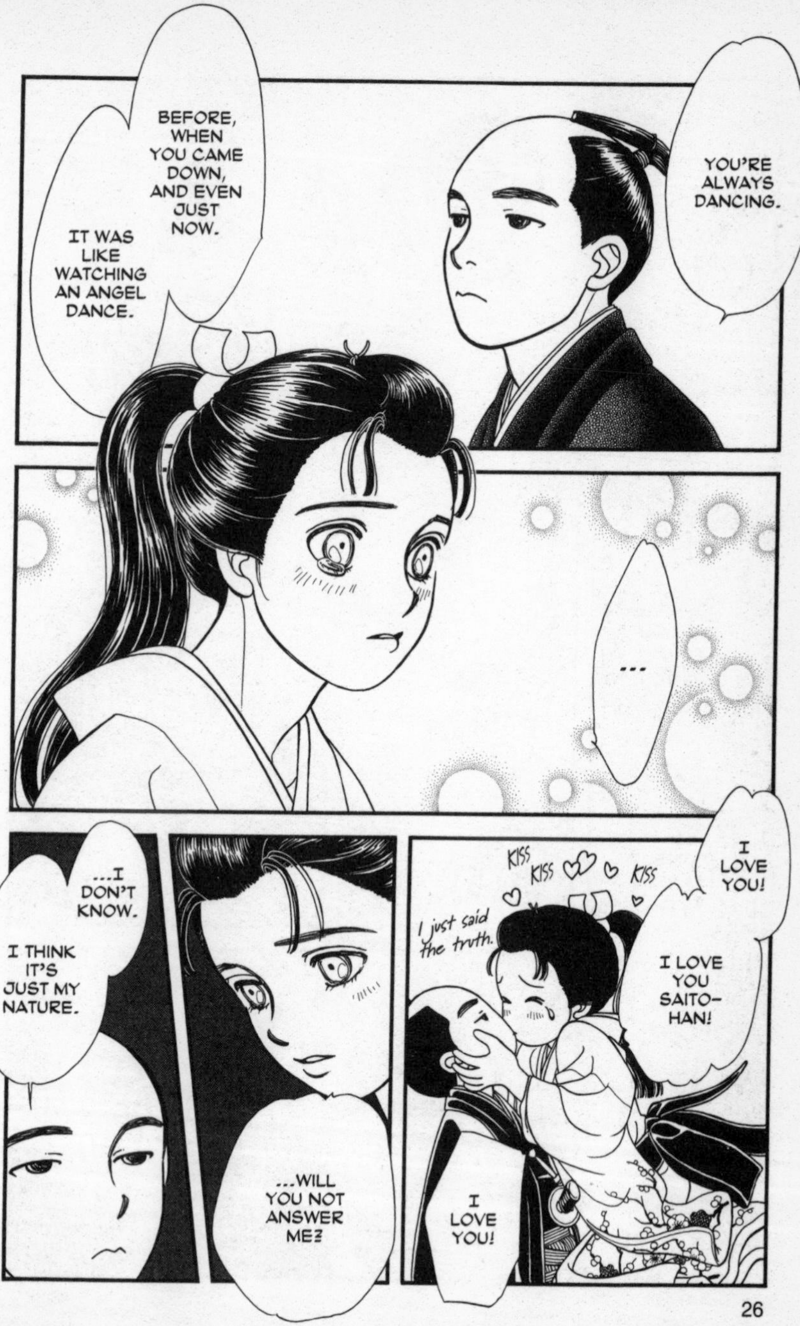
YOU'RE ALWAYS DANCING.
BEFORE, WHEN YOU CAME DOWN, AND EVEN JUST NOW.
IT WAS LIKE WATCHING AN ANGEL DANCE.
...
I LOVE YOU!
I LOVE YOU SAITO-HAN!
KISS KISS KISS
I just said the truth.
I LOVE YOU!
...WILL YOU NOT ANSWER ME?
...I DON'T KNOW.
I THINK IT'S JUST MY NATURE.

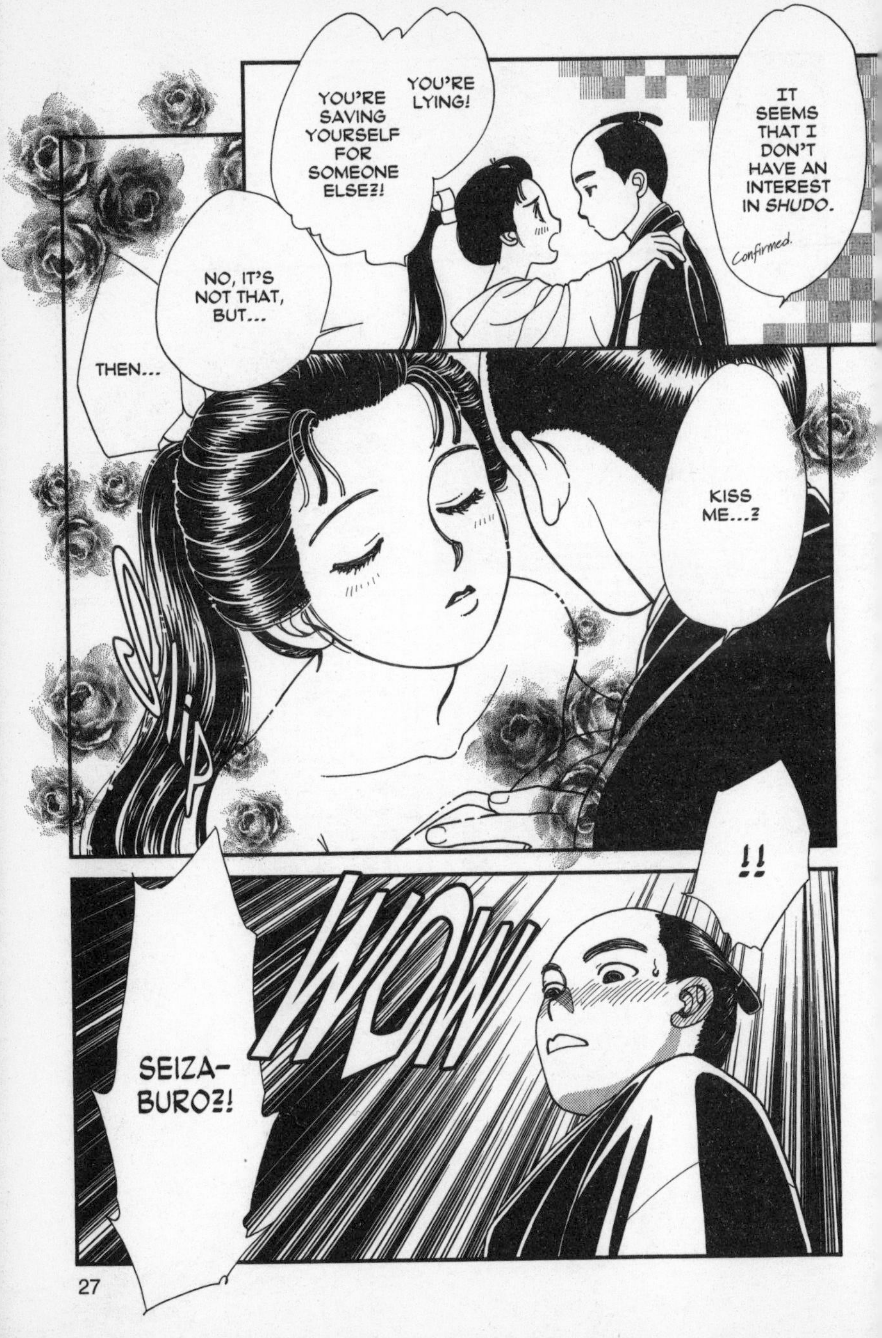
IT SEEMS THAT I DON'T HAVE AN INTEREST IN *SHUDO*.
Confirmed.
YOU'RE LYING!
YOU'RE SAVING YOURSELF FOR SOMEONE ELSE?!
NO, IT'S NOT THAT, BUT...
THEN...
KISS ME...?
SLIP
!!
WOW
SEIZA-BURO?!

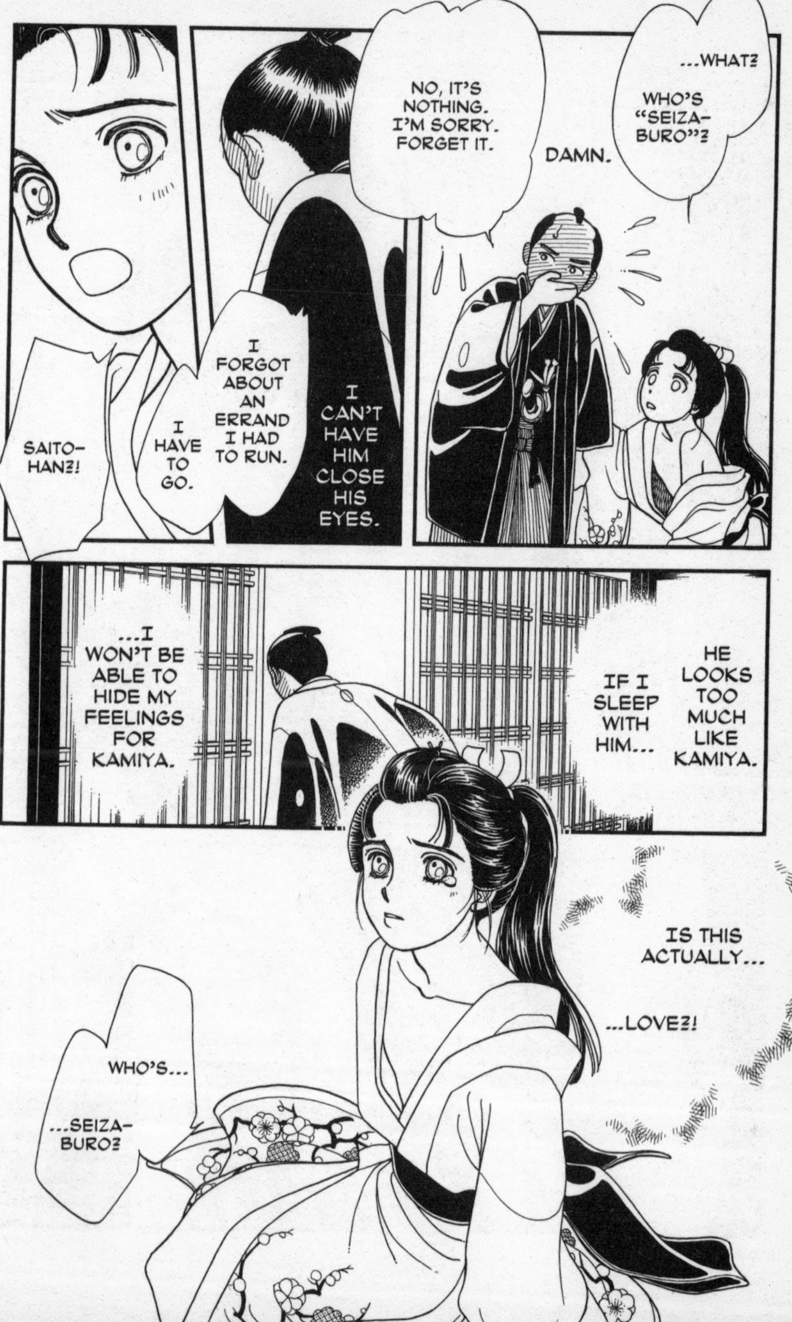
...WHAT?
WHO'S "SEIZABURO"?
DAMN.
NO, IT'S NOTHING. I'M SORRY. FORGET IT.
I CAN'T HAVE HIM CLOSE HIS EYES.
I FORGOT ABOUT AN ERRAND I HAD TO RUN.
I HAVE TO GO.
SAITO-HAN?!
HE LOOKS TOO MUCH LIKE KAMIYA.
IF I SLEEP WITH HIM...
...I WON'T BE ABLE TO HIDE MY FEELINGS FOR KAMIYA.
IS THIS ACTUALLY...
...LOVE?!
WHO'S...
...SEIZABURO?

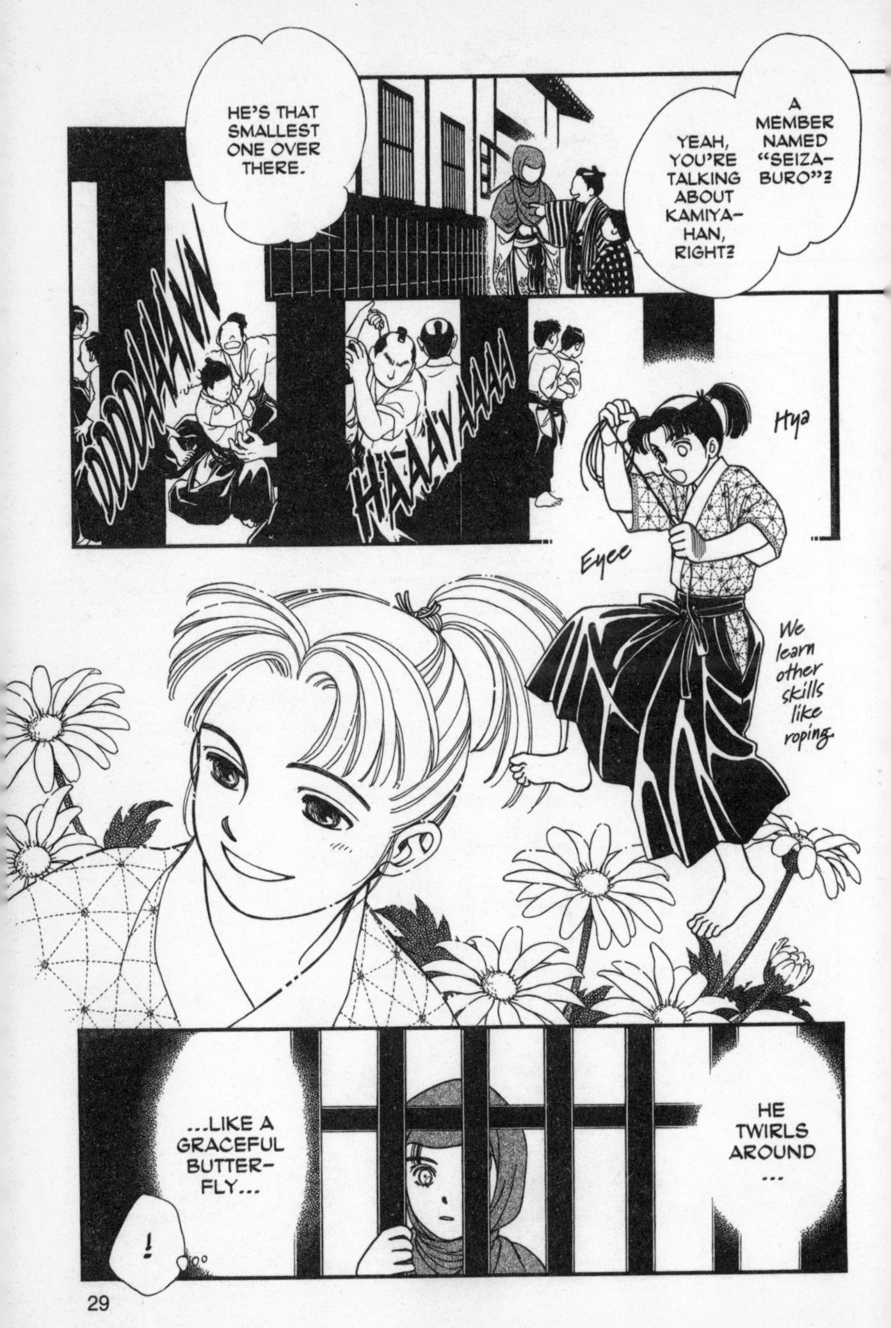
A MEMBER NAMED "SEIZABURO"?
YEAH, YOU'RE TALKING ABOUT KAMIYA-HAN, RIGHT?
HE'S THAT SMALLEST ONE OVER THERE.
Hya
Eyee
HAAAAAA
DOOAAANN
We learn other skills like roping.
HE TWIRLS AROUND...
...LIKE A GRACEFUL BUTTERFLY...
!

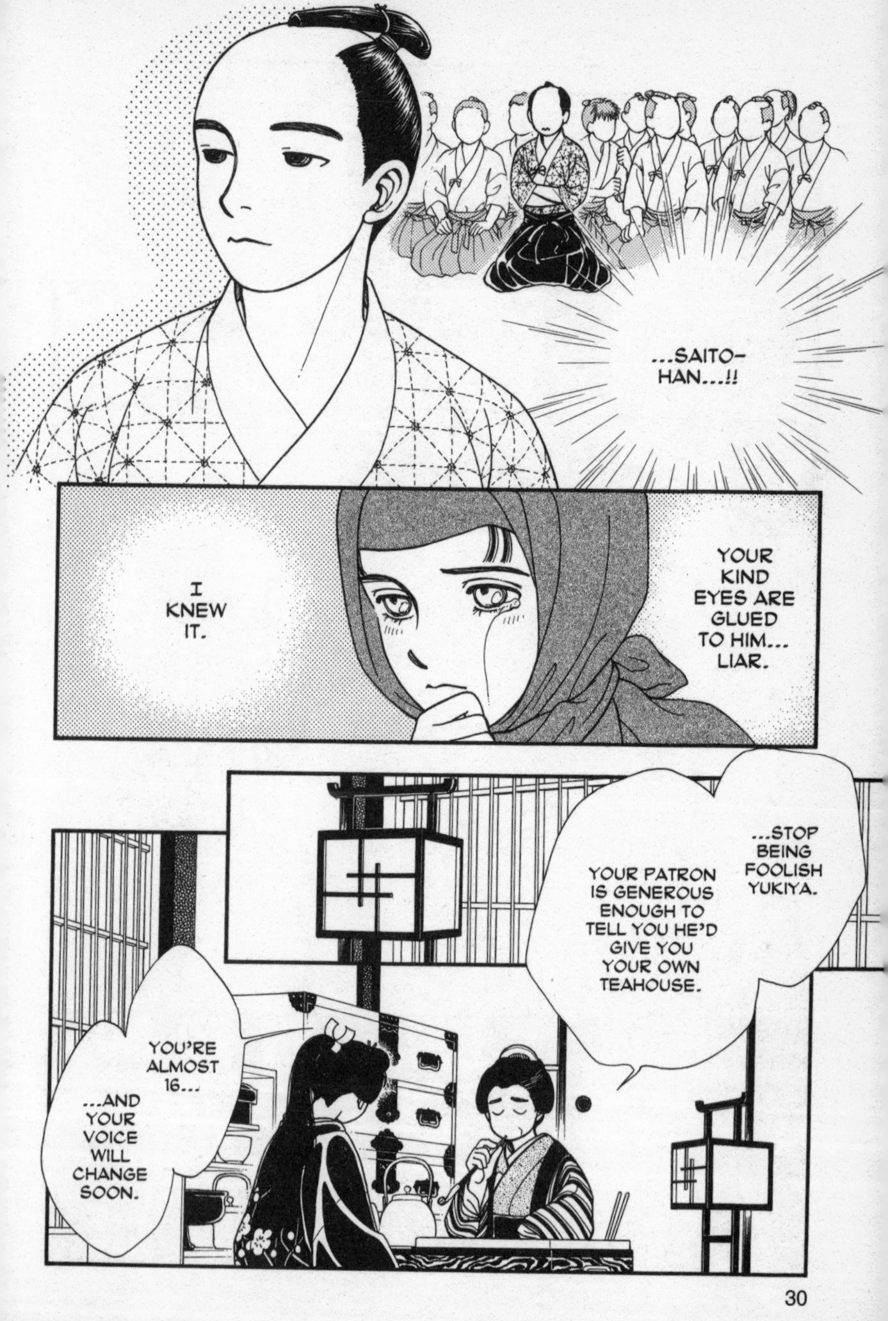
...SAITO-HAN...!!
YOUR KIND EYES ARE GLUED TO HIM... LIAR.
I KNEW IT.
...STOP BEING FOOLISH YUKIYA.
YOUR PATRON IS GENEROUS ENOUGH TO TELL YOU HE'D GIVE YOU YOUR OWN TEAHOUSE.
YOU'RE ALMOST 16...
...AND YOUR VOICE WILL CHANGE SOON.

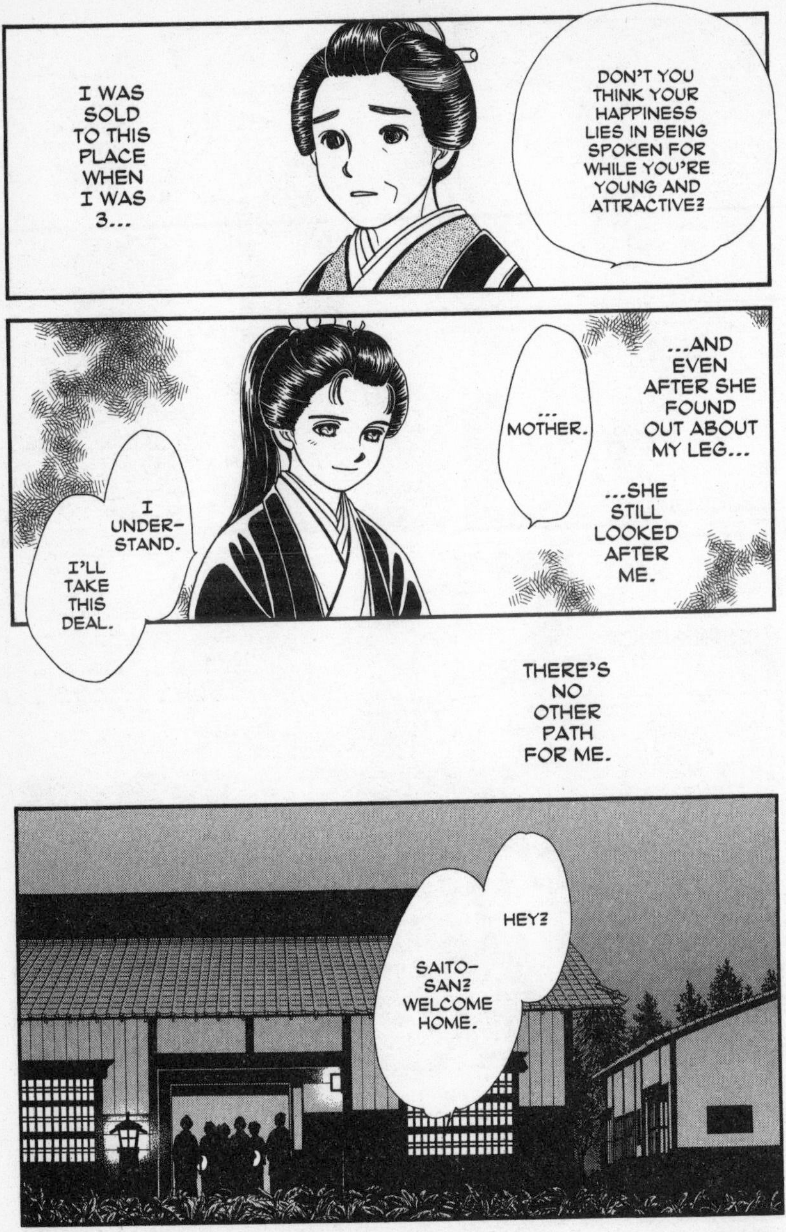
DON'T YOU THINK YOUR HAPPINESS LIES IN BEING SPOKEN FOR WHILE YOU'RE YOUNG AND ATTRACTIVE?
I WAS SOLD TO THIS PLACE WHEN I WAS 3...
...AND EVEN AFTER SHE FOUND OUT ABOUT MY LEG...
...SHE STILL LOOKED AFTER ME.
... MOTHER.
I UNDERSTAND.
I'LL TAKE THIS DEAL.
THERE'S NO OTHER PATH FOR ME.
HEY?
SAITO-SAN? WELCOME HOME.

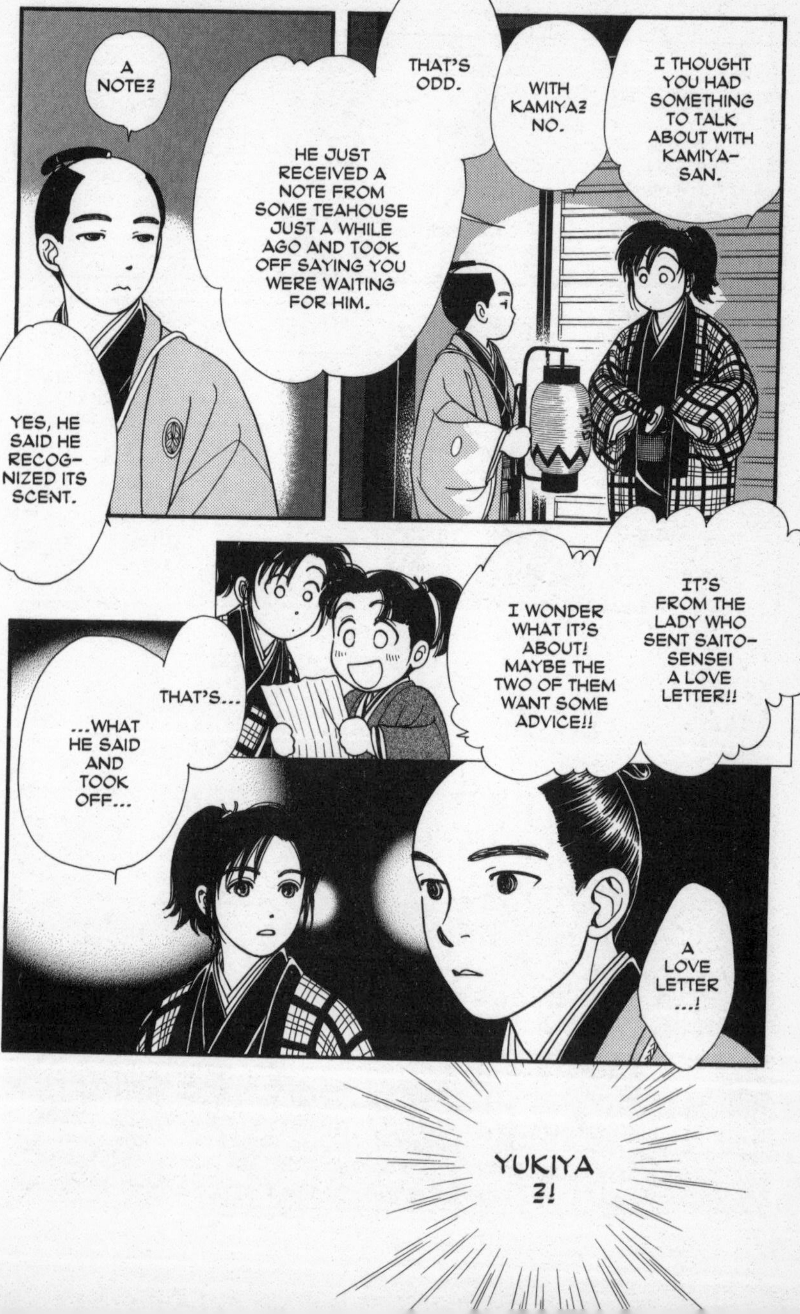
I THOUGHT YOU HAD SOMETHING TO TALK ABOUT WITH KAMIYA-SAN.
WITH KAMIYA? NO.
THAT'S ODD.
HE JUST RECEIVED A NOTE FROM SOME TEAHOUSE JUST A WHILE AGO AND TOOK OFF SAYING YOU WERE WAITING FOR HIM.
A NOTE?
YES, HE SAID HE RECOG-NIZED ITS SCENT.
IT'S FROM THE LADY WHO SENT SAITO-SENSEI A LOVE LETTER!!
I WONDER WHAT IT'S ABOUT! MAYBE THE TWO OF THEM WANT SOME ADVICE!!
THAT'S...
...WHAT HE SAID AND TOOK OFF...
A LOVE LETTER ...!
YUKIYA ?!

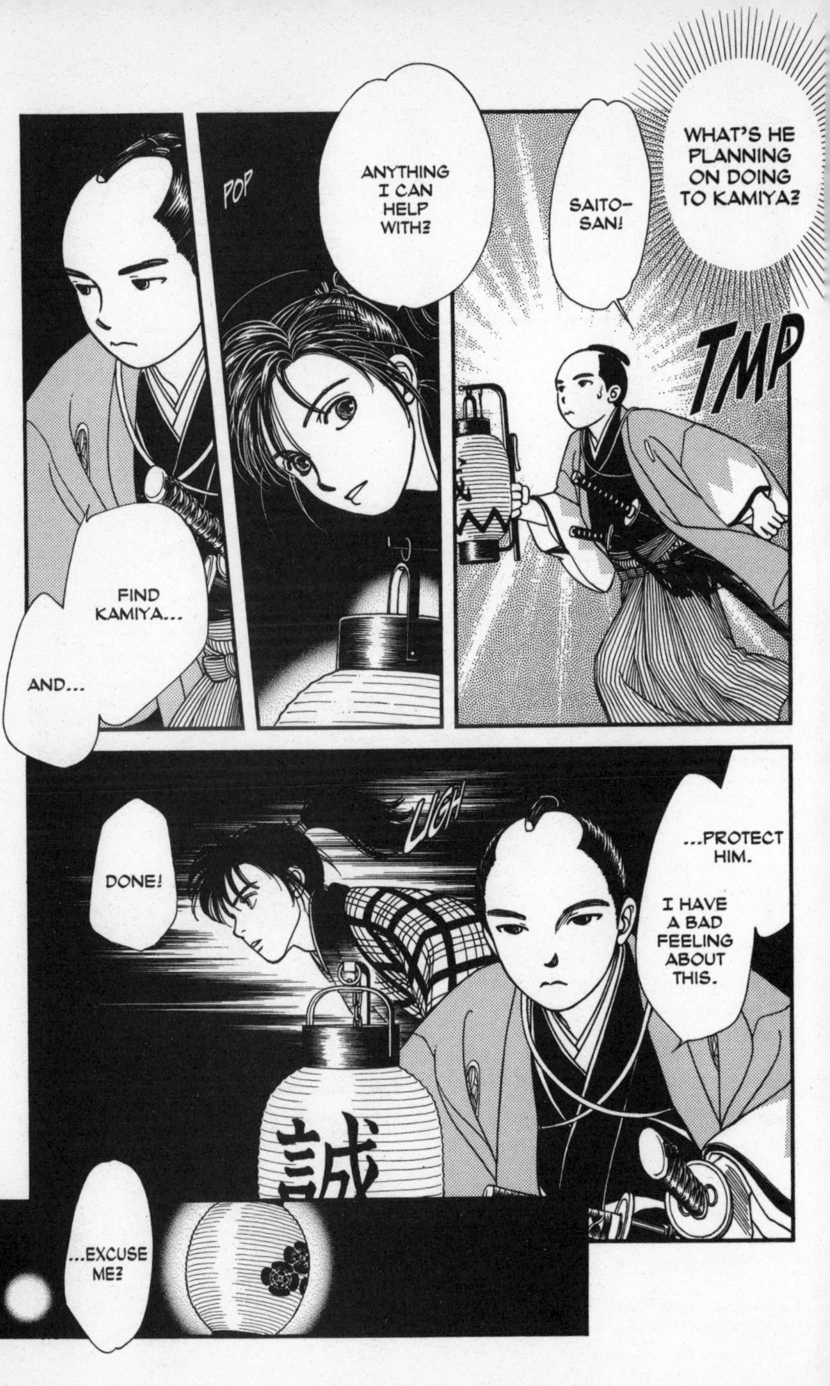
WHAT'S HE PLANNING ON DOING TO KAMIYA?
SAITO-SAN!
TMP
POP
ANYTHING I CAN HELP WITH?
FIND KAMIYA...
AND...
...PROTECT HIM.
I HAVE A BAD FEELING ABOUT THIS.
UGH
DONE!
...EXCUSE ME?

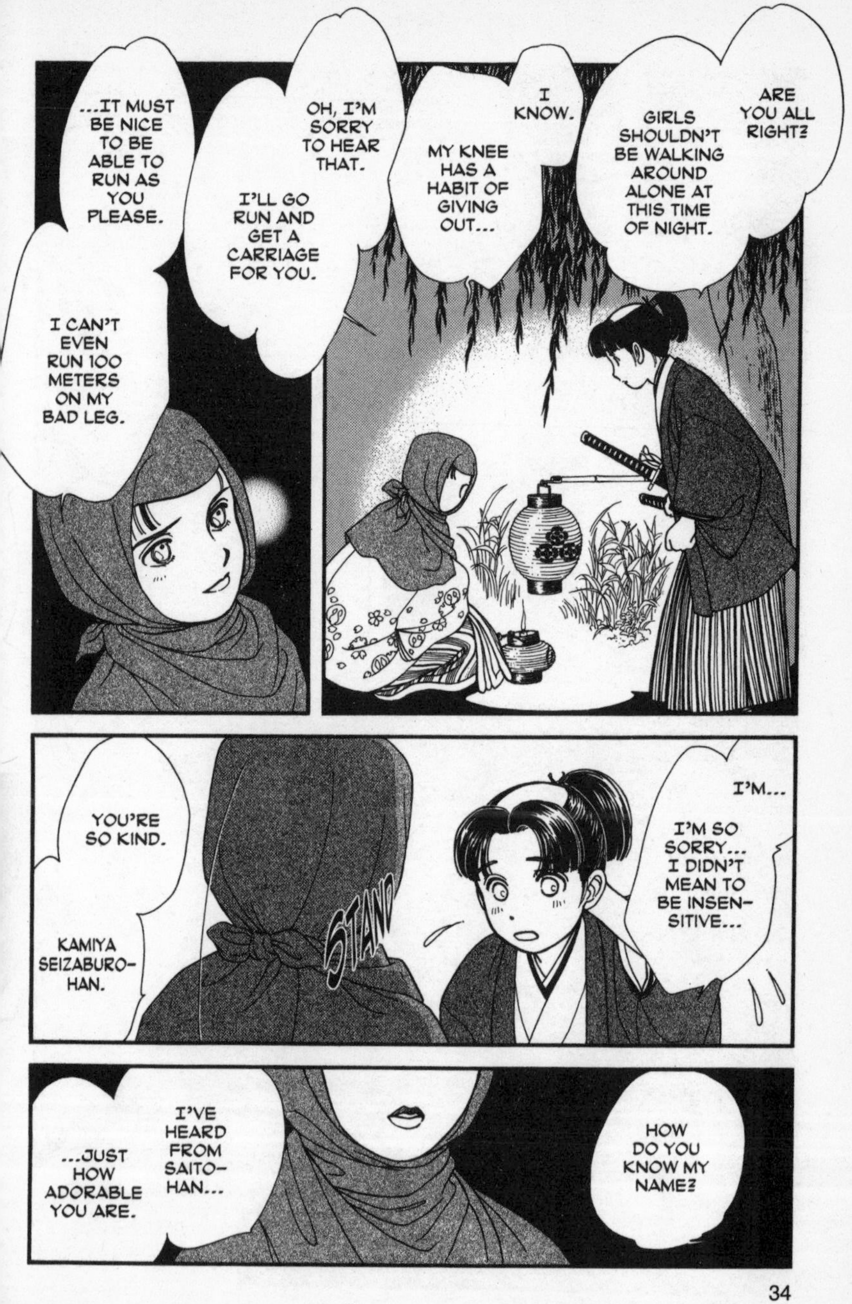
ARE YOU ALL RIGHT?
GIRLS SHOULDN'T BE WALKING AROUND ALONE AT THIS TIME OF NIGHT.
I KNOW.
MY KNEE HAS A HABIT OF GIVING OUT...
OH, I'M SORRY TO HEAR THAT.
I'LL GO RUN AND GET A CARRIAGE FOR YOU.
...IT MUST BE NICE TO BE ABLE TO RUN AS YOU PLEASE.
I CAN'T EVEN RUN 100 METERS ON MY BAD LEG.
I'M...
I'M SO SORRY... I DIDN'T MEAN TO BE INSEN-SITIVE...
STAND
YOU'RE SO KIND.
KAMIYA SEIZABURO-HAN.
HOW DO YOU KNOW MY NAME?
I'VE HEARD FROM SAITO-HAN...
...JUST HOW ADORABLE YOU ARE.

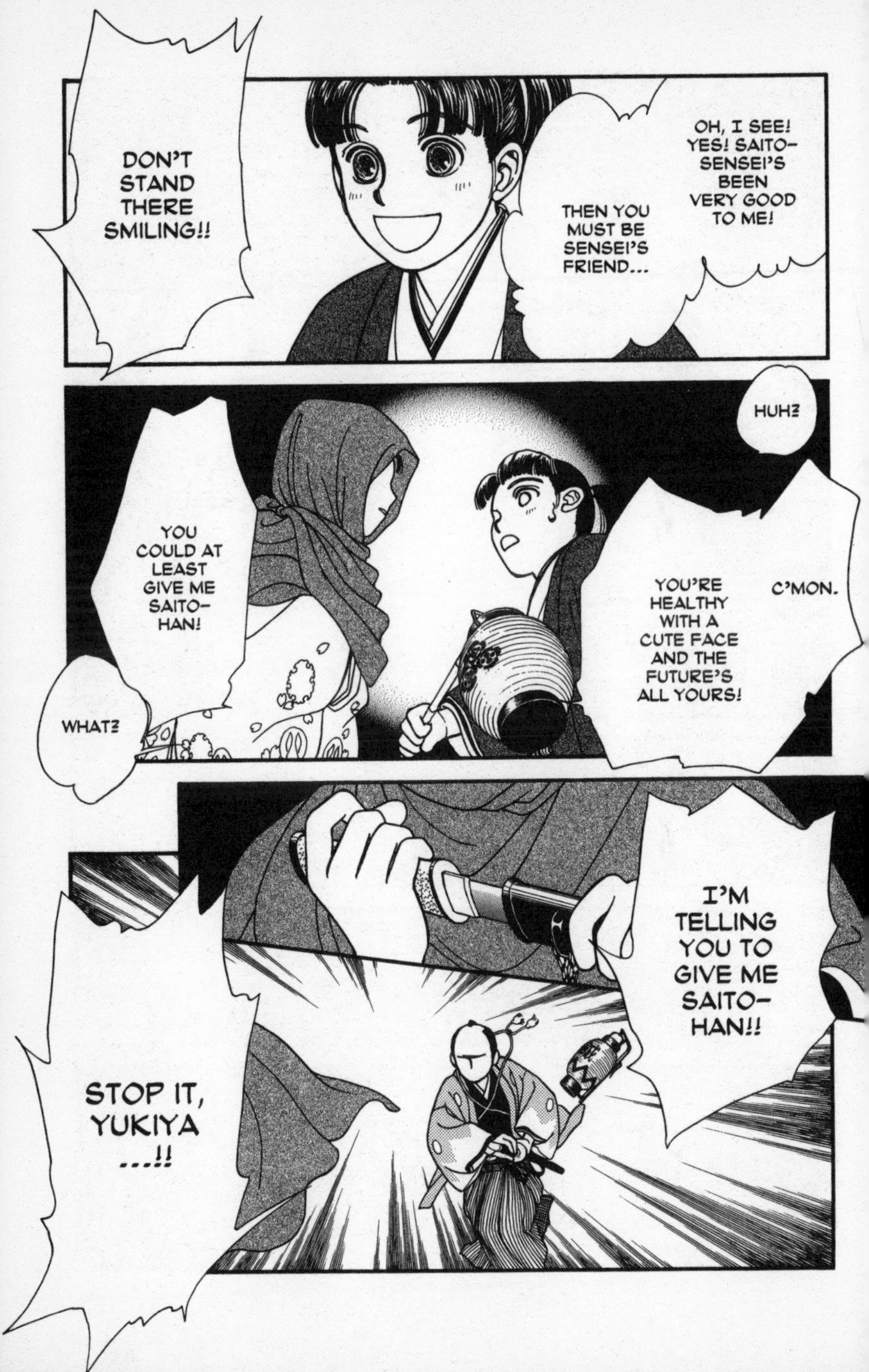

OH, I SEE! YES! SAITO-SENSEI'S BEEN VERY GOOD TO ME!
THEN YOU MUST BE SENSEI'S FRIEND...
DON'T STAND THERE SMILING!!
HUH?
C'MON.
YOU'RE HEALTHY WITH A CUTE FACE AND THE FUTURE'S ALL YOURS!
YOU COULD AT LEAST GIVE ME SAITO-HAN!
WHAT?
I'M TELLING YOU TO GIVE ME SAITO-HAN!!
STOP IT, YUKIYA ...!!

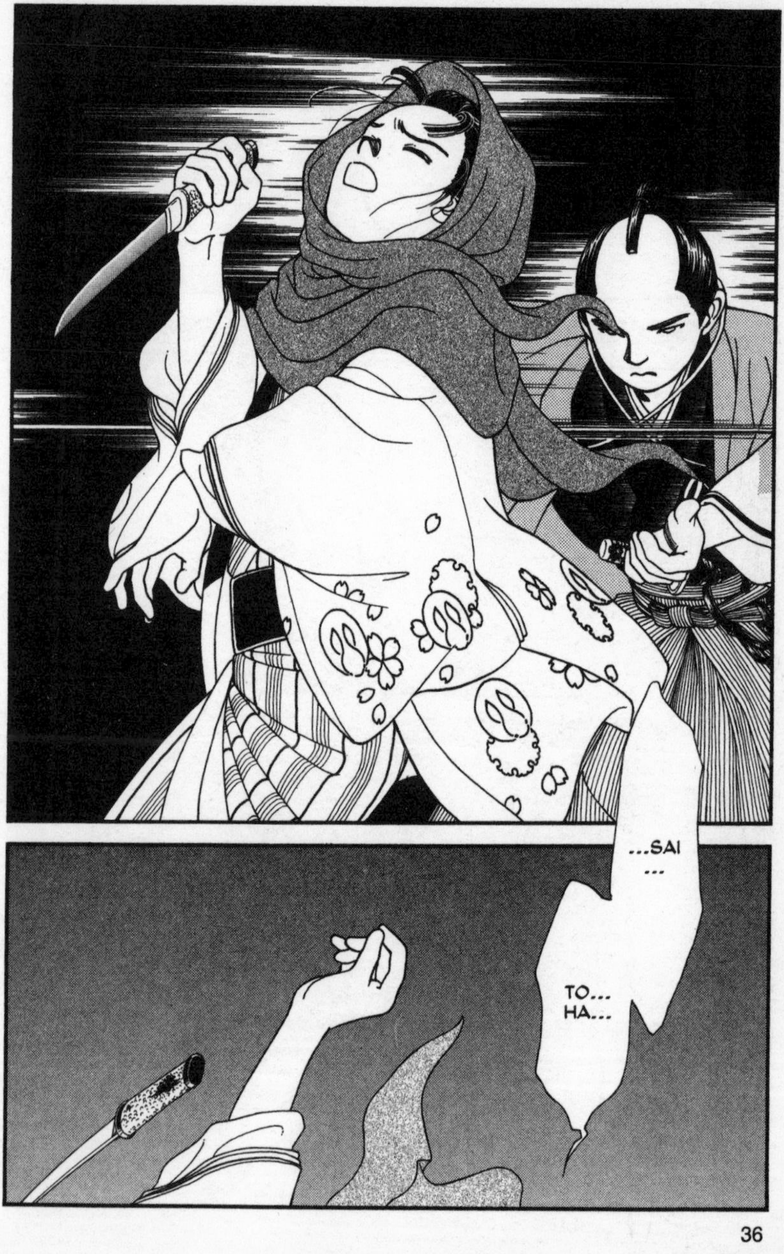
...SAI
...
TO...
HA...

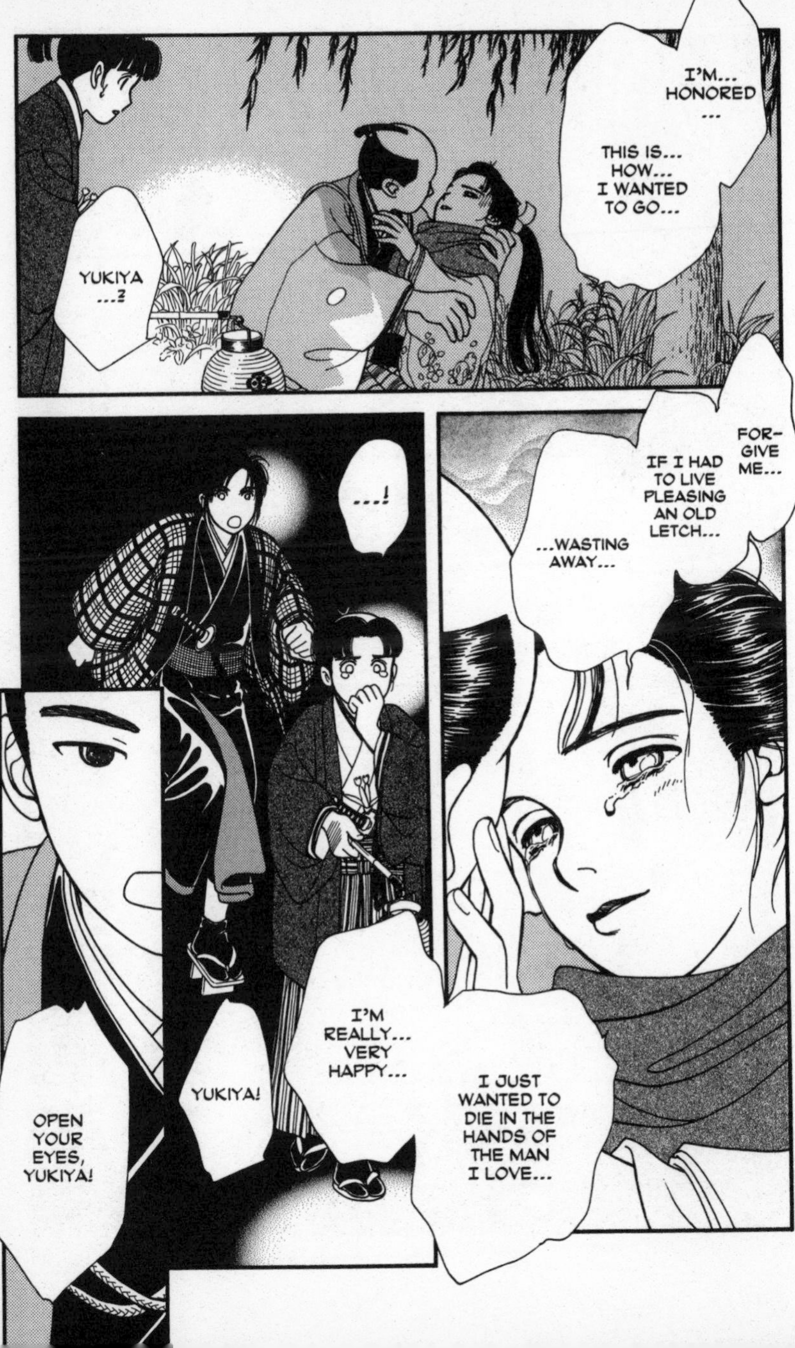
I'M... HONORED ...
THIS IS... HOW... I WANTED TO GO...
YUKIYA ...?
FOR-GIVE ME...
IF I HAD TO LIVE PLEASING AN OLD LETCH...
...WASTING AWAY...
I JUST WANTED TO DIE IN THE HANDS OF THE MAN I LOVE...
I'M REALLY... VERY HAPPY...
...!
YUKIYA!
OPEN YOUR EYES, YUKIYA!

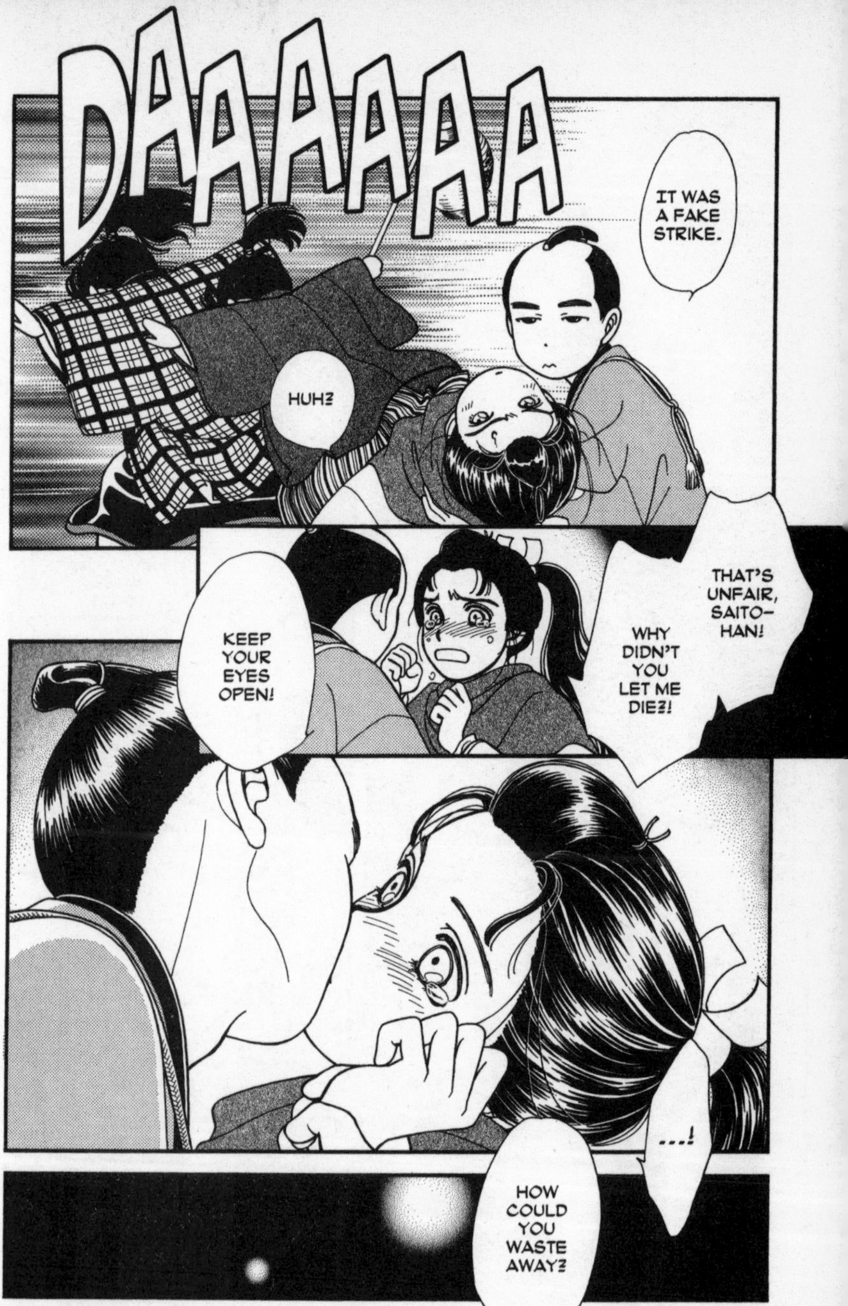
DAAAAAA
IT WAS A FAKE STRIKE.
HUH?
THAT'S UNFAIR, SAITO-HAN!
WHY DIDN'T YOU LET ME DIE?!
KEEP YOUR EYES OPEN!
...!
HOW COULD YOU WASTE AWAY?

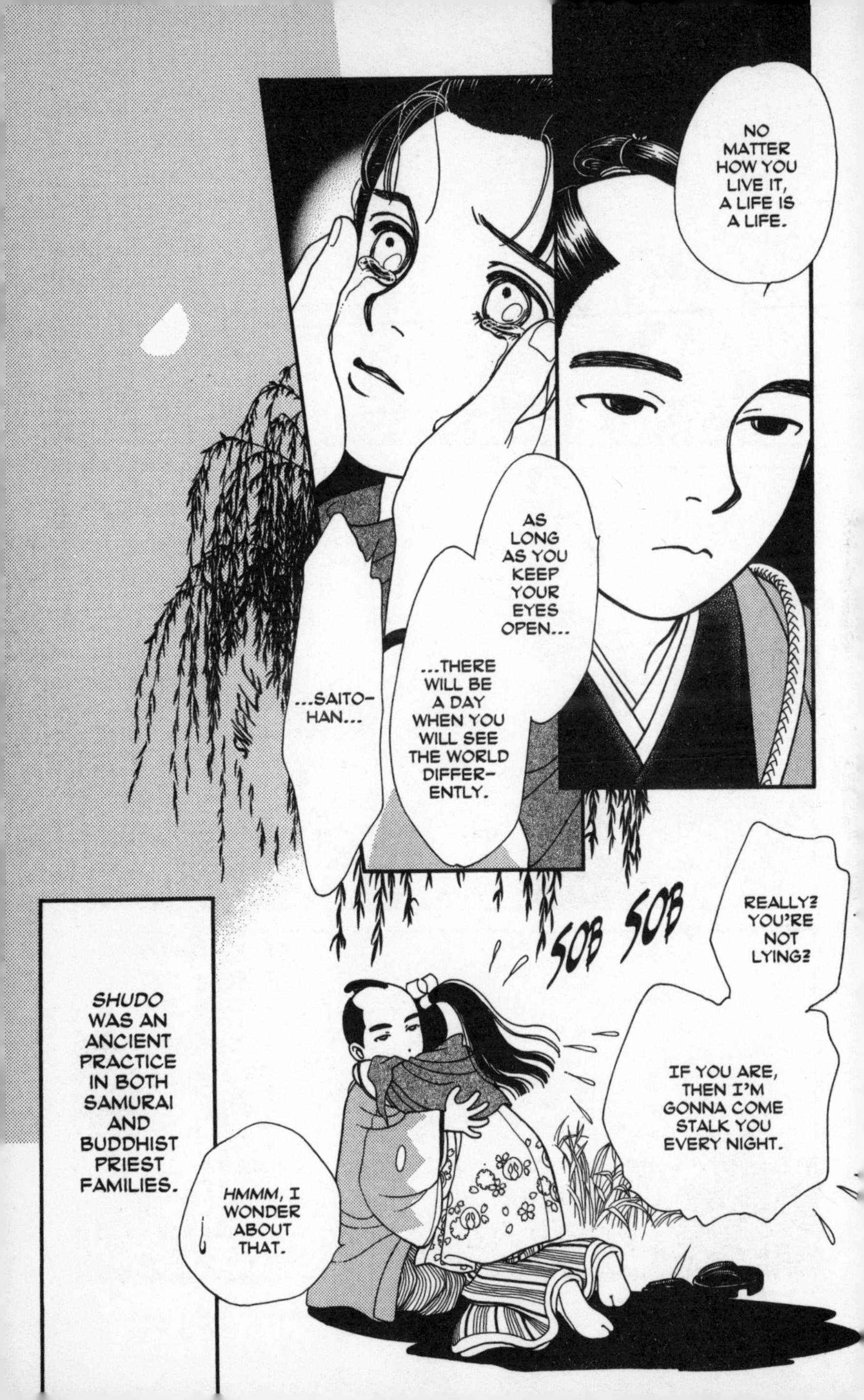
NO MATTER HOW YOU LIVE IT, A LIFE IS A LIFE.
AS LONG AS YOU KEEP YOUR EYES OPEN...
...THERE WILL BE A DAY WHEN YOU WILL SEE THE WORLD DIFFER-ENTLY.
...SAITO-HAN...
REALLY? YOU'RE NOT LYING?
SOB SOB
IF YOU ARE, THEN I'M GONNA COME STALK YOU EVERY NIGHT.
HMMM, I WONDER ABOUT THAT.
SHUDO WAS AN ANCIENT PRACTICE IN BOTH SAMURAI AND BUDDHIST PRIEST FAMILIES.

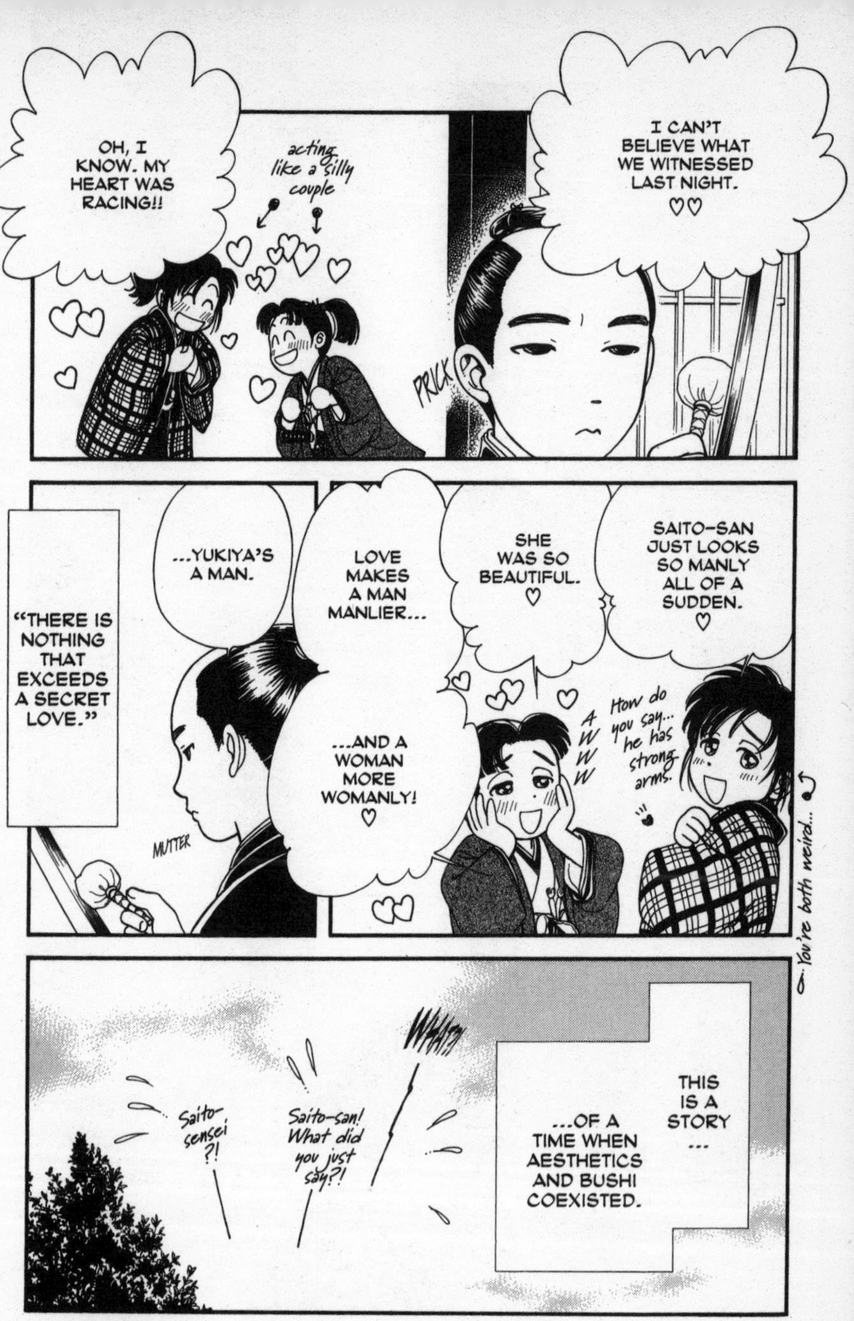
I CAN'T BELIEVE WHAT WE WITNESSED LAST NIGHT. ♡♡
PRICK
OH, I KNOW. MY HEART WAS RACING!!
acting like a silly couple
SAITO-SAN JUST LOOKS SO MANLY ALL OF A SUDDEN. ♡
How do you say... he has strong arms.
SHE WAS SO BEAUTIFUL. ♡
AWWW
LOVE MAKES A MAN MANLIER...
...AND A WOMAN MORE WOMANLY! ♡
You're both weird...
"THERE IS NOTHING THAT EXCEEDS A SECRET LOVE."
...YUKIYA'S A MAN.
MUTTER
THIS IS A STORY ...
...OF A TIME WHEN AESTHETICS AND BUSHI COEXISTED.
Saito-san! What did you just say?!
Saito-sensei?!

KYOTO "IROHA" KARUTA GAME

ゐ

"I"
IWASHI NO ATAMA MO SHINJIN KARA
"MIRACLES HAPPEN TO THOSE WHO BELIEVE IN THEM"

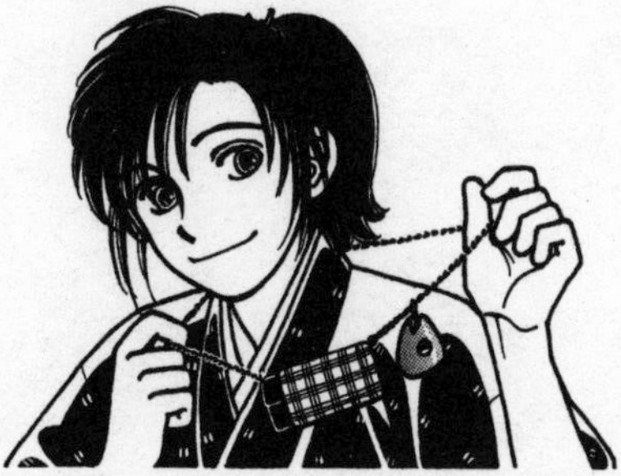

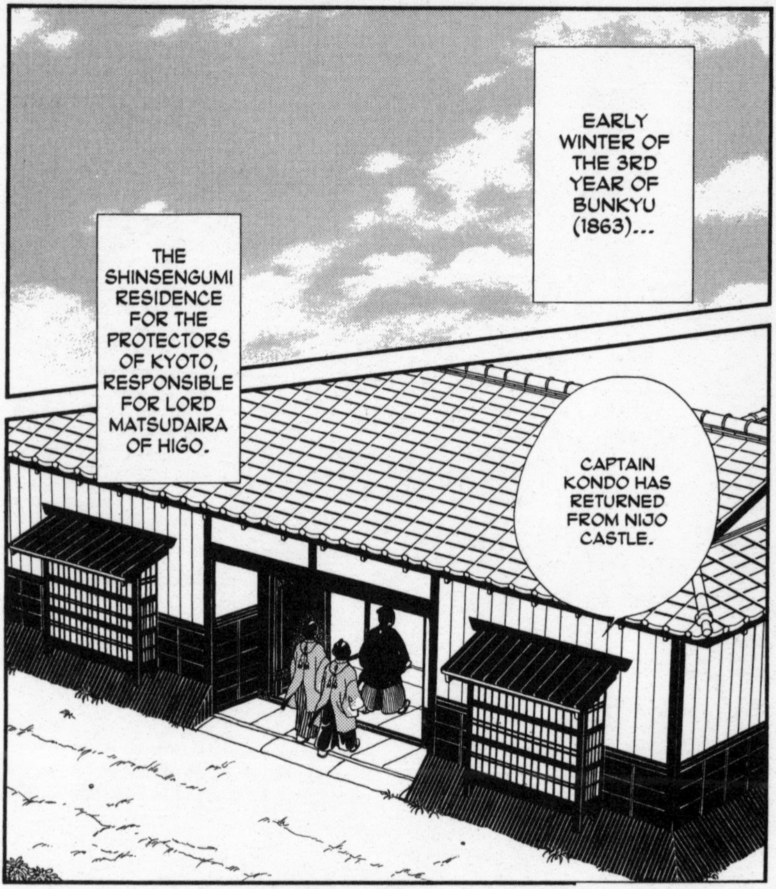
EARLY WINTER OF THE 3RD YEAR OF BUNKYU (1863)...
THE SHINSENGUMI RESIDENCE FOR THE PROTECTORS OF KYOTO, RESPONSIBLE FOR LORD MATSUDAIRA OF HIGO.
CAPTAIN KONDO HAS RETURNED FROM NIJO CASTLE.

KYOTO "IROHA" KARUTA GAME

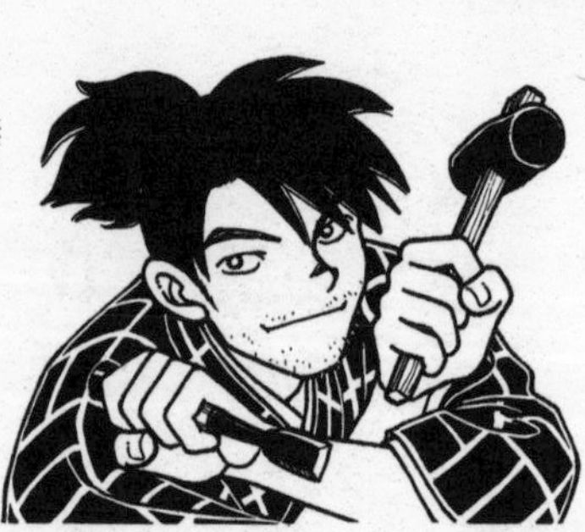

の

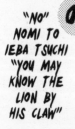

"NO"
NOMI TO IEBA TSUCHI
"YOU MAY KNOW THE LION BY HIS CLAW"

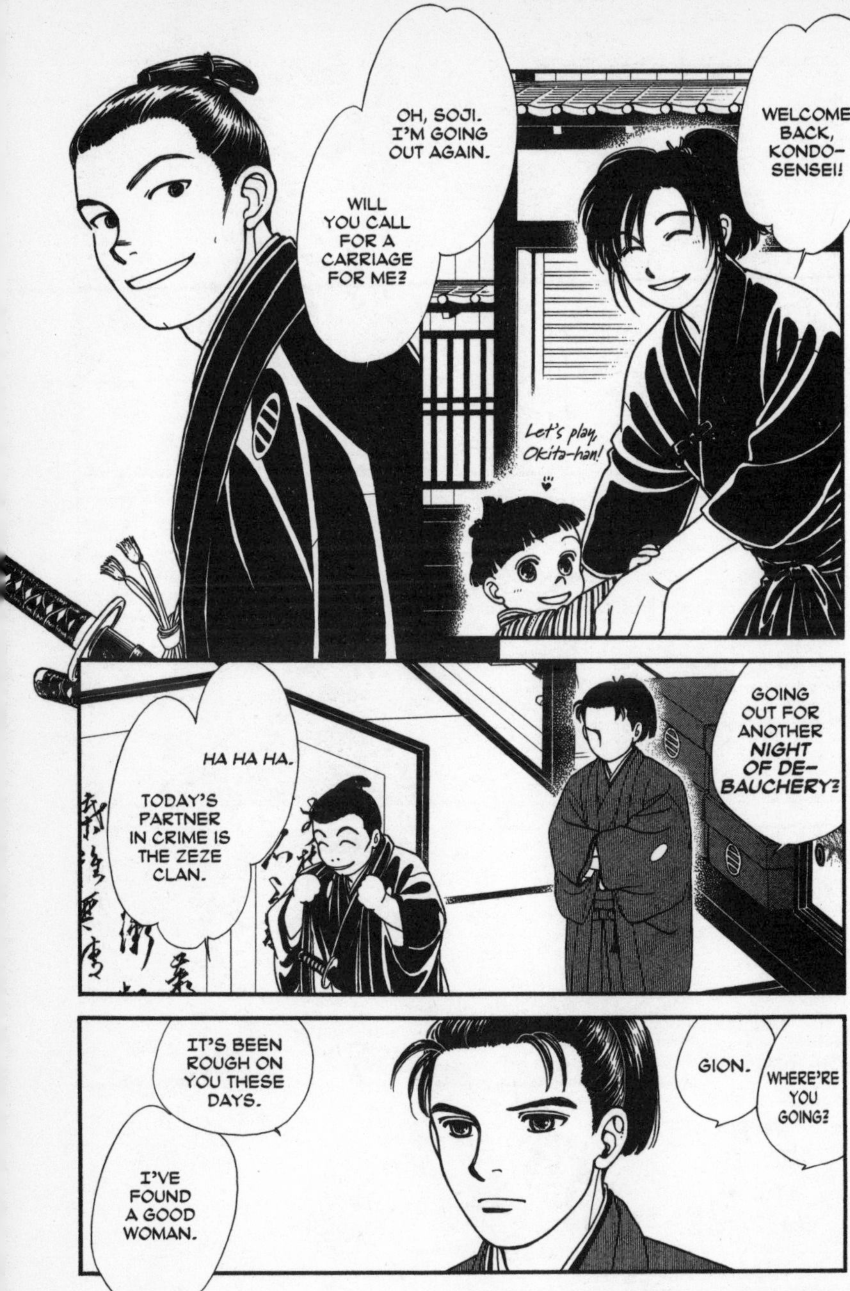
WELCOME BACK, KONDO-SENSEI!
Let's play, Okita-han!
OH, SOJI. I'M GOING OUT AGAIN.
WILL YOU CALL FOR A CARRIAGE FOR ME?
GOING OUT FOR ANOTHER NIGHT OF DE-BAUCHERY?
HA HA HA.
TODAY'S PARTNER IN CRIME IS THE ZEZE CLAN.
WHERE'RE YOU GOING?
GION.
IT'S BEEN ROUGH ON YOU THESE DAYS.
I'VE FOUND A GOOD WOMAN.

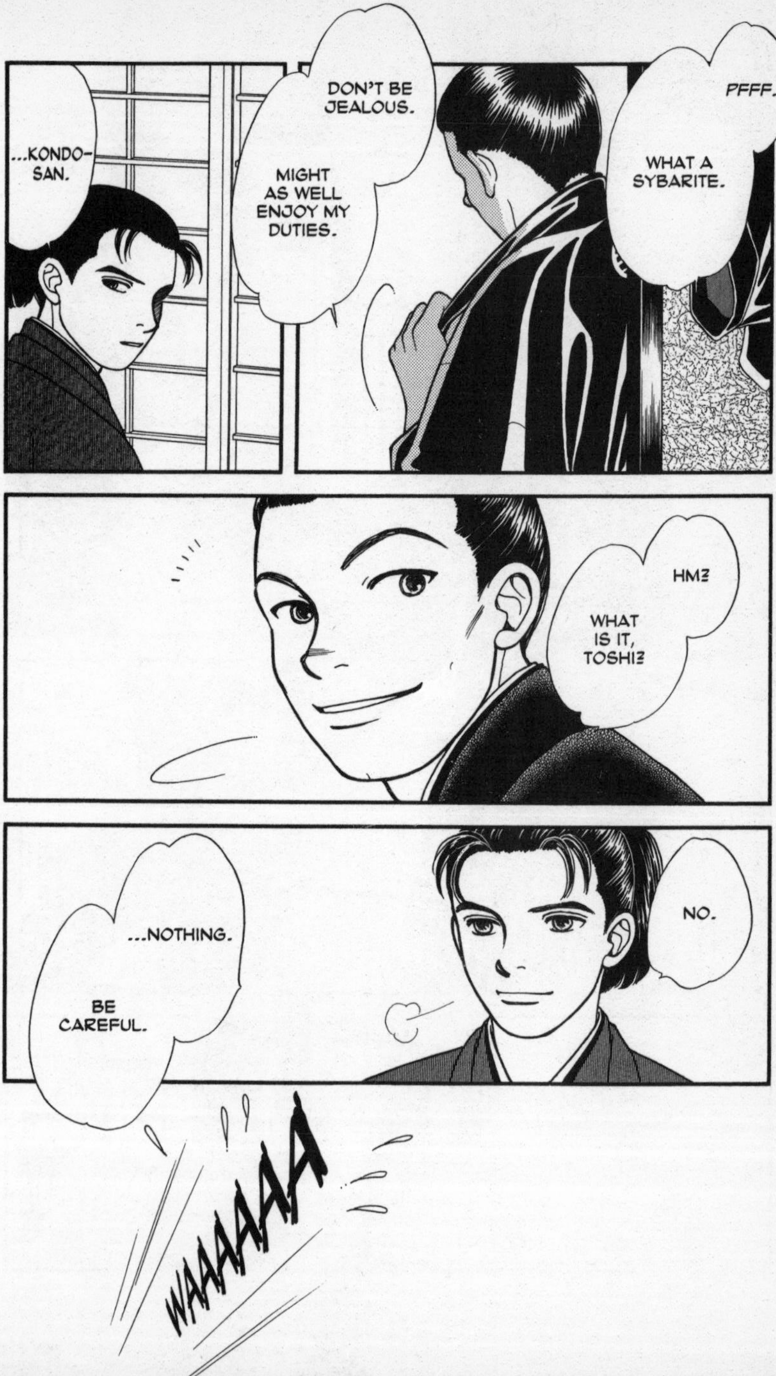
PFFF.
WHAT A SYBARITE.
DON'T BE JEALOUS.
MIGHT AS WELL ENJOY MY DUTIES.
...KONDO-SAN.
HM?
WHAT IS IT, TOSHI?
NO.
...NOTHING.
BE CAREFUL.
WAAAAAA

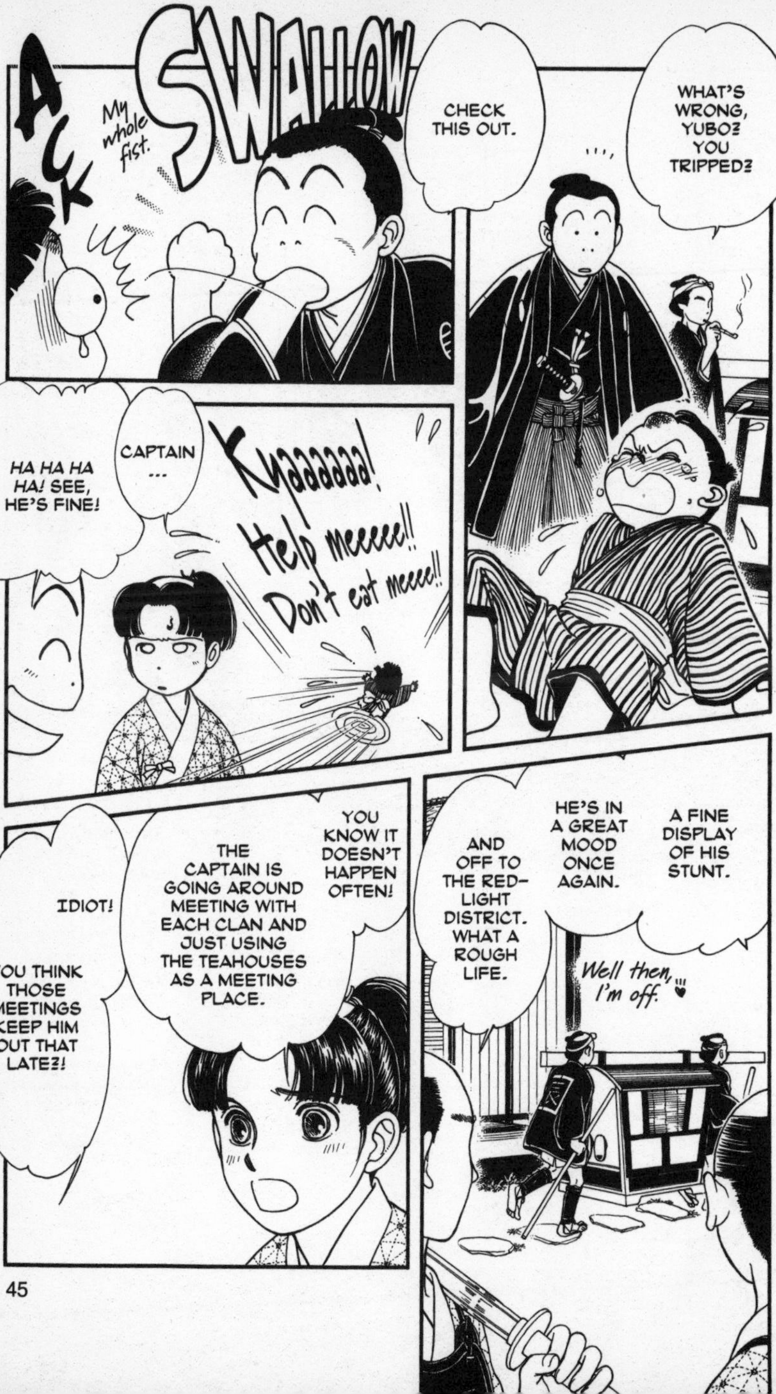
WHAT'S WRONG, YUBO? YOU TRIPPED?
CHECK THIS OUT.
ACK
SWALLOW
My whole fist.
Kyaaaaaa! Help meeeee!! Don't eat meeee!!
CAPTAIN ...
HA HA HA HA! SEE, HE'S FINE!
A FINE DISPLAY OF HIS STUNT.
HE'S IN A GREAT MOOD ONCE AGAIN.
AND OFF TO THE RED-LIGHT DISTRICT. WHAT A ROUGH LIFE.
Well then, I'm off.
YOU KNOW IT DOESN'T HAPPEN OFTEN!
THE CAPTAIN IS GOING AROUND MEETING WITH EACH CLAN AND JUST USING THE TEAHOUSES AS A MEETING PLACE.
IDIOT!
YOU THINK THOSE MEETINGS KEEP HIM OUT THAT LATE?!

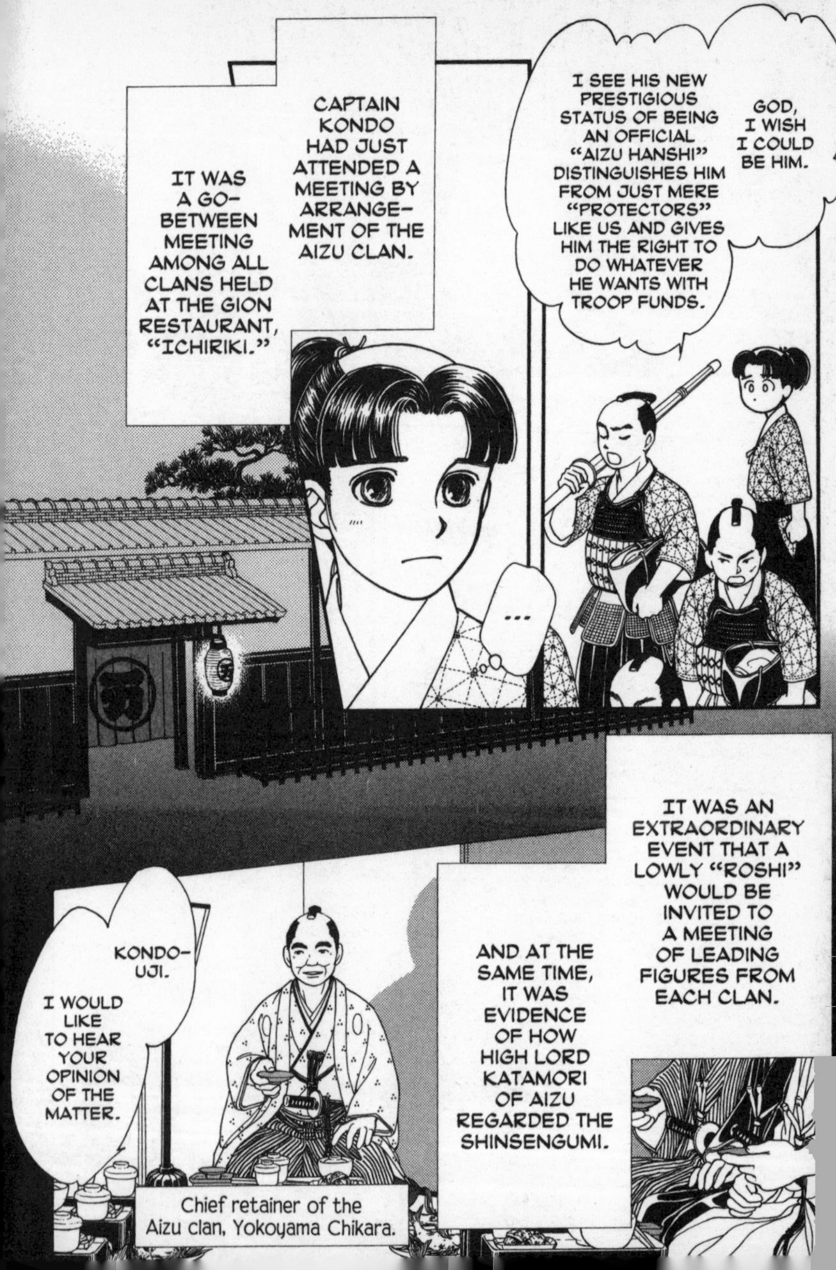
I SEE HIS NEW PRESTIGIOUS STATUS OF BEING AN OFFICIAL "AIZU HANSHI" DISTINGUISHES HIM FROM JUST MERE "PROTECTORS" LIKE US AND GIVES HIM THE RIGHT TO DO WHATEVER HE WANTS WITH TROOP FUNDS.
GOD, I WISH I COULD BE HIM.
CAPTAIN KONDO HAD JUST ATTENDED A MEETING BY ARRANGE-MENT OF THE AIZU CLAN.
IT WAS A GO-BETWEEN MEETING AMONG ALL CLANS HELD AT THE GION RESTAURANT, "ICHIRIKI."
...
IT WAS AN EXTRAORDINARY EVENT THAT A LOWLY "ROSHI" WOULD BE INVITED TO A MEETING OF LEADING FIGURES FROM EACH CLAN.
AND AT THE SAME TIME, IT WAS EVIDENCE OF HOW HIGH LORD KATAMORI OF AIZU REGARDED THE SHINSENGUMI.
KONDO-UJI.
I WOULD LIKE TO HEAR YOUR OPINION OF THE MATTER.
Chief retainer of the Aizu clan, Yokoyama Chikara.

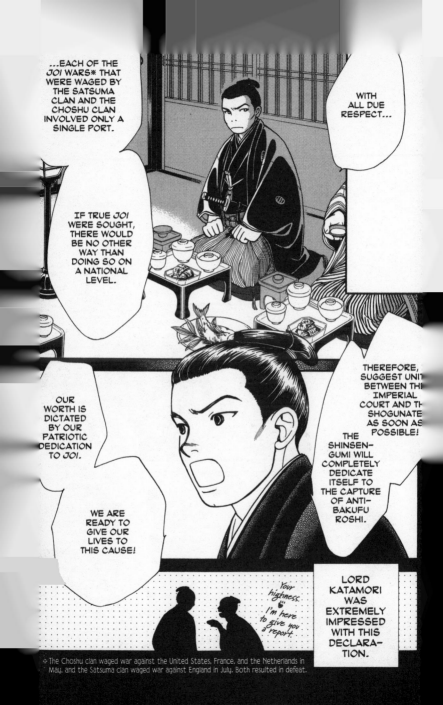

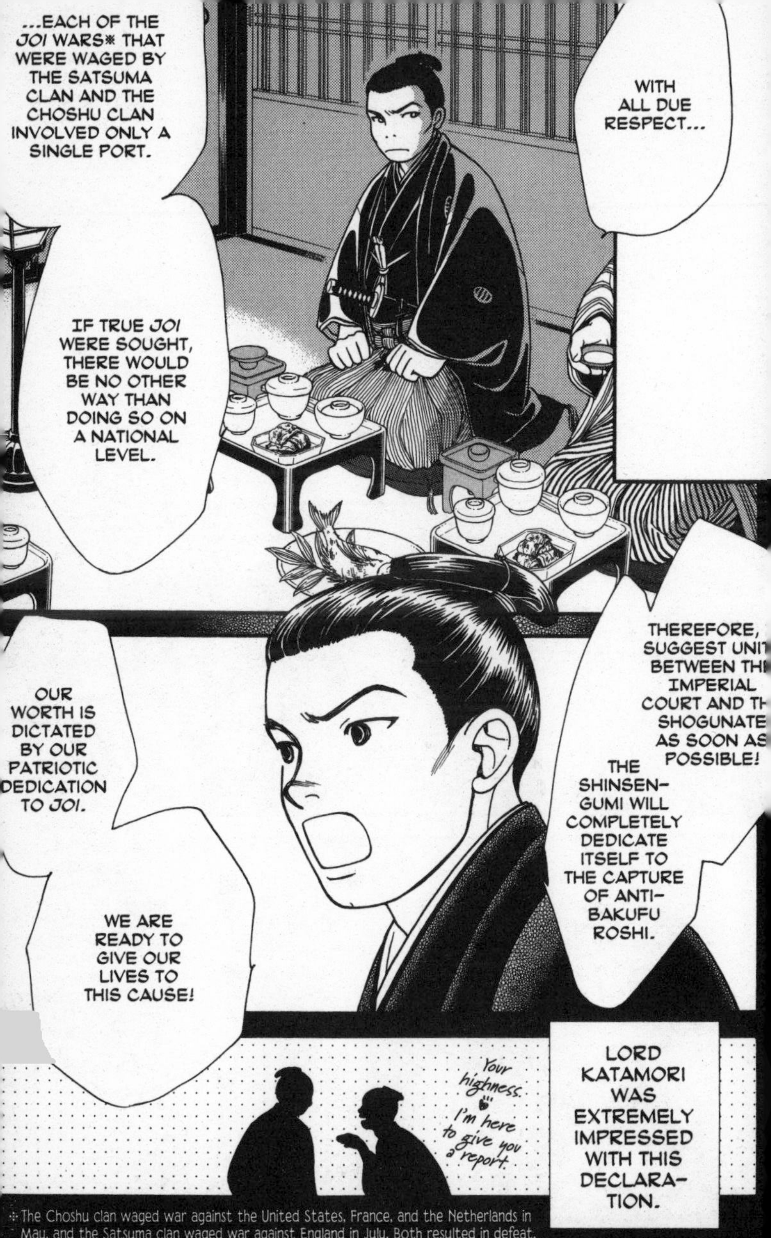
WITH ALL DUE RESPECT...
...EACH OF THE JOI WARS* THAT WERE WAGED BY THE SATSUMA CLAN AND THE CHOSHU CLAN INVOLVED ONLY A SINGLE PORT.
IF TRUE JOI WERE SOUGHT, THERE WOULD BE NO OTHER WAY THAN DOING SO ON A NATIONAL LEVEL.
THEREFORE, SUGGEST UNIT BETWEEN TH IMPERIAL COURT AND TH SHOGUNATE AS SOON AS POSSIBLE!
THE SHINSEN-GUMI WILL COMPLETELY DEDICATE ITSELF TO THE CAPTURE OF ANTI-BAKUFU ROSHI.
OUR WORTH IS DICTATED BY OUR PATRIOTIC DEDICATION TO JOI.
WE ARE READY TO GIVE OUR LIVES TO THIS CAUSE!
LORD KATAMORI WAS EXTREMELY IMPRESSED WITH THIS DECLARATION.
Your highness. I'm here to give you a report.

* The Choshu clan waged war against the United States, France, and the Netherlands in May, and the Satsuma clan waged war against England in July. Both resulted in defeat.

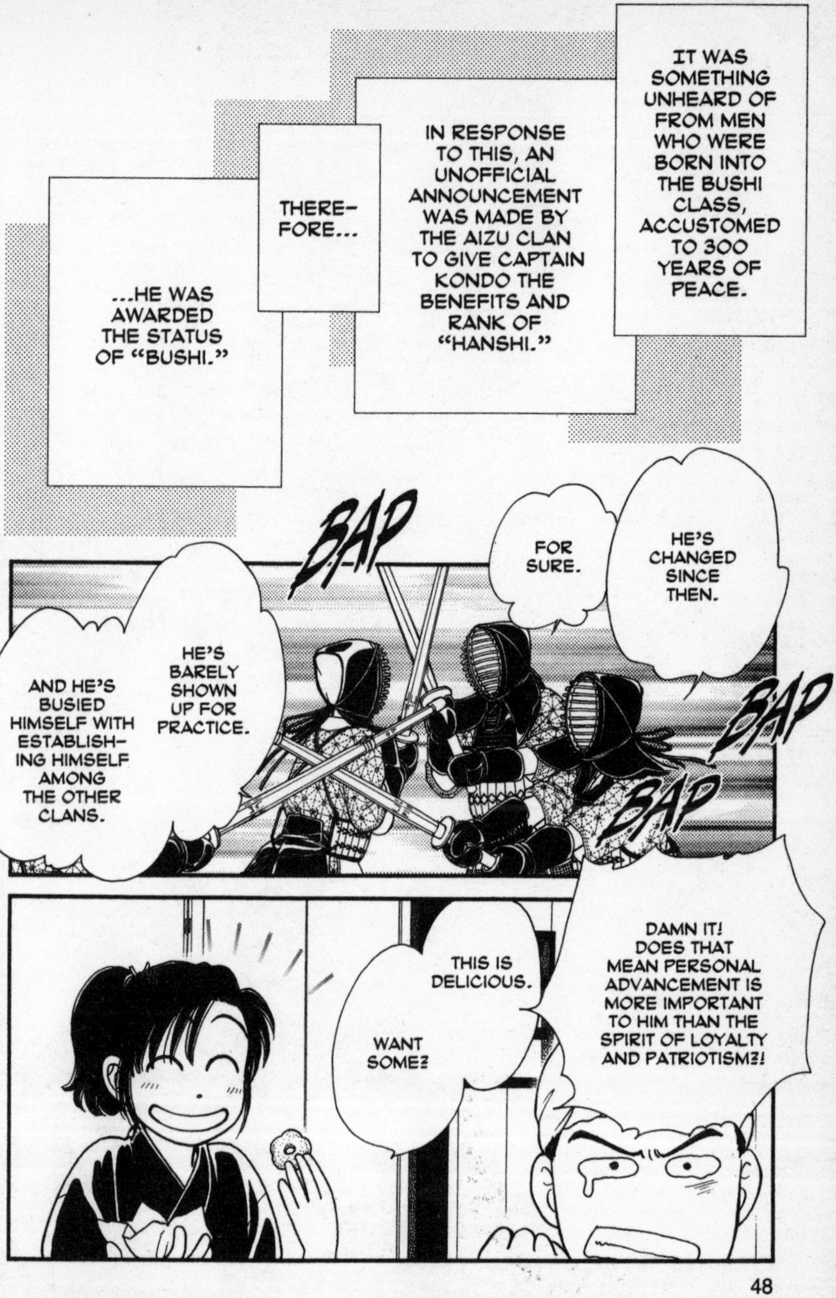
IT WAS SOMETHING UNHEARD OF FROM MEN WHO WERE BORN INTO THE BUSHI CLASS, ACCUSTOMED TO 300 YEARS OF PEACE.
IN RESPONSE TO THIS, AN UNOFFICIAL ANNOUNCEMENT WAS MADE BY THE AIZU CLAN TO GIVE CAPTAIN KONDO THE BENEFITS AND RANK OF "HANSHI."
THERE-FORE...
...HE WAS AWARDED THE STATUS OF "BUSHI."
HE'S CHANGED SINCE THEN.
FOR SURE.
BAP
BAP
BAP
HE'S BARELY SHOWN UP FOR PRACTICE.
AND HE'S BUSIED HIMSELF WITH ESTABLISH-ING HIMSELF AMONG THE OTHER CLANS.
DAMN IT! DOES THAT MEAN PERSONAL ADVANCEMENT IS MORE IMPORTANT TO HIM THAN THE SPIRIT OF LOYALTY AND PATRIOTISM?!
THIS IS DELICIOUS.
WANT SOME?

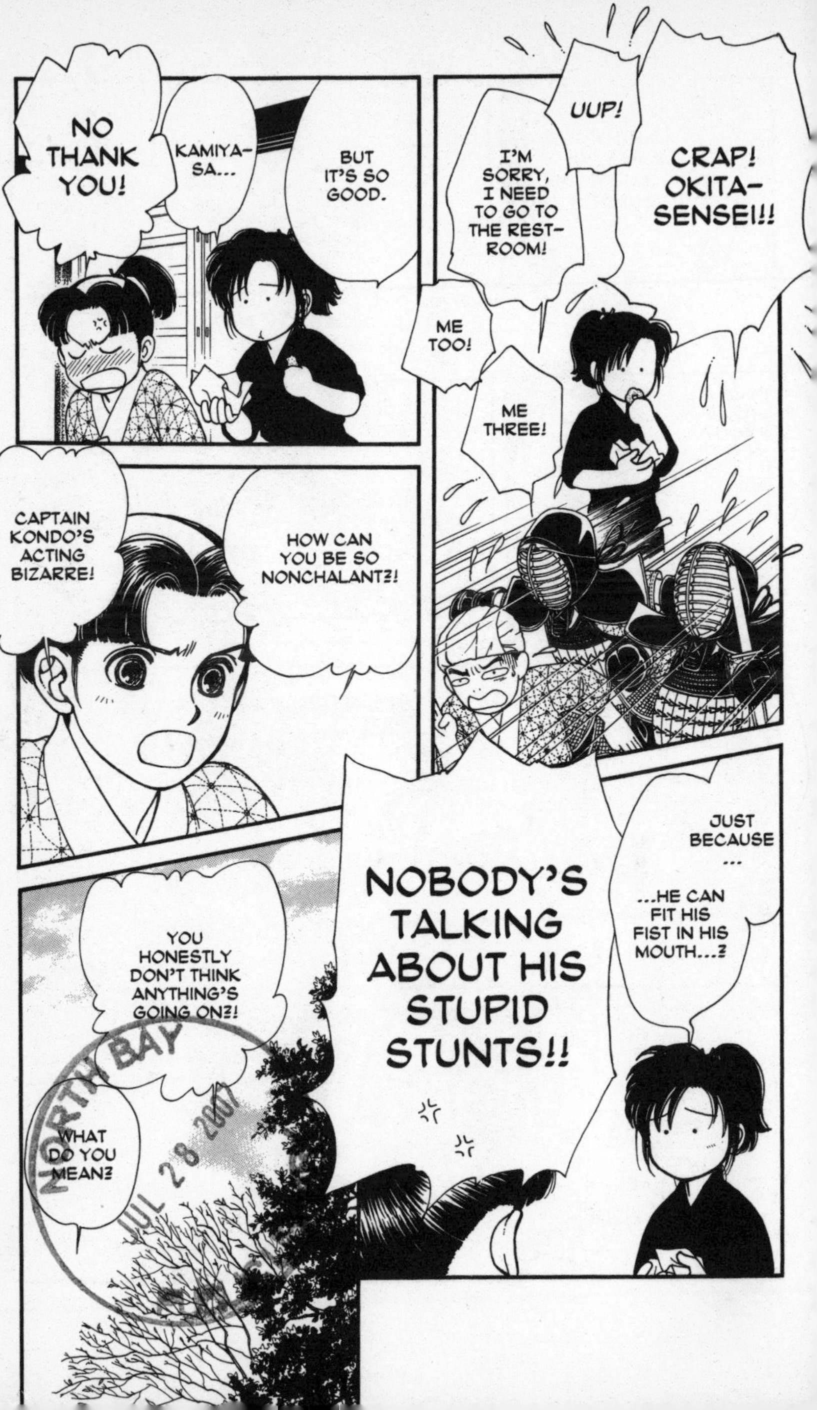
UUP!
CRAP! OKITA-SENSEI!!!
I'M SORRY, I NEED TO GO TO THE REST-ROOM!
ME TOO!
ME THREE!
BUT IT'S SO GOOD.
KAMIYA-SA...
NO THANK YOU!
HOW CAN YOU BE SO NONCHALANT?!
CAPTAIN KONDO'S ACTING BIZARRE!
JUST BECAUSE...
...HE CAN FIT HIS FIST IN HIS MOUTH...?
NOBODY'S TALKING ABOUT HIS STUPID STUNTS!!
YOU HONESTLY DON'T THINK ANYTHING'S GOING ON?!
WHAT DO YOU MEAN?

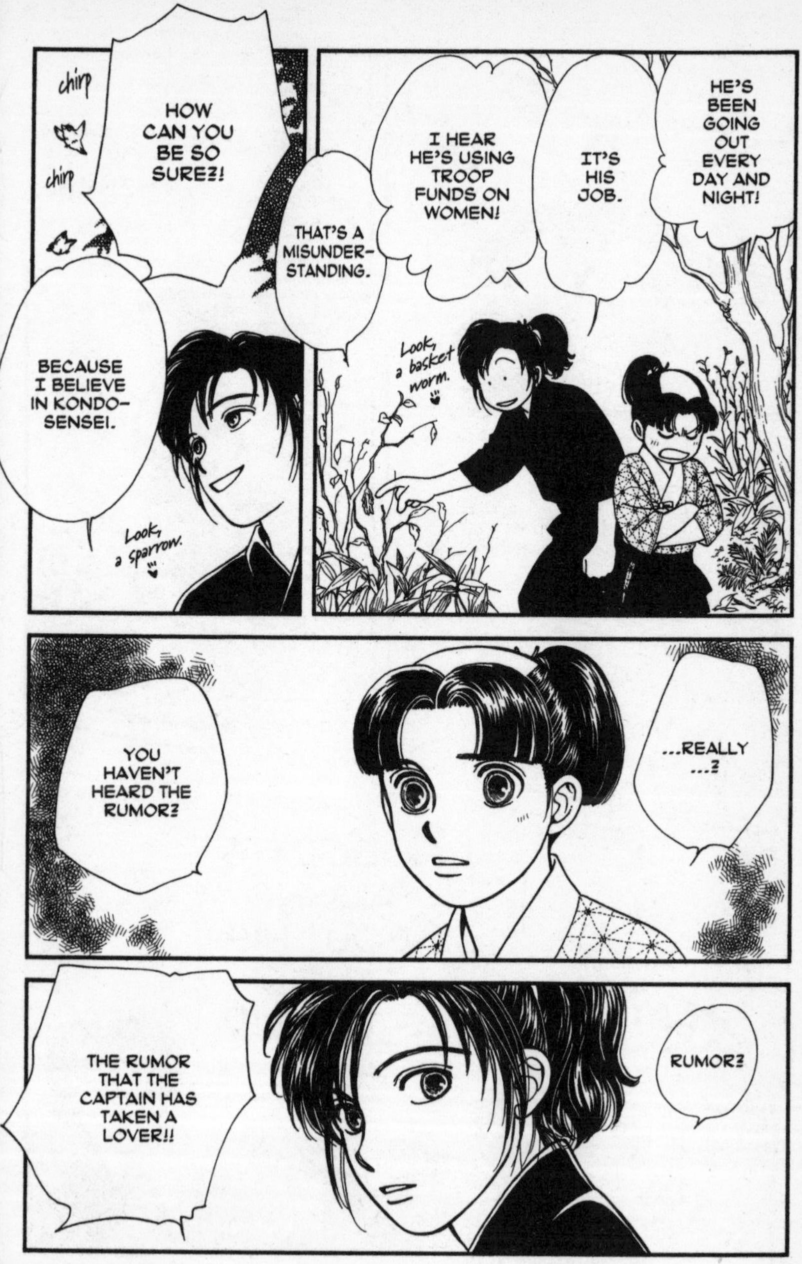
HE'S BEEN GOING OUT EVERY DAY AND NIGHT!
IT'S HIS JOB.
I HEAR HE'S USING TROOP FUNDS ON WOMEN!
THAT'S A MISUNDERSTANDING.
Look, a basket worm.
HOW CAN YOU BE SO SURE?!
chirp
chirp
BECAUSE I BELIEVE IN KONDO-SENSEI.
Look, a sparrow.
...REALLY...?
YOU HAVEN'T HEARD THE RUMOR?
RUMOR?
THE RUMOR THAT THE CAPTAIN HAS TAKEN A LOVER!!

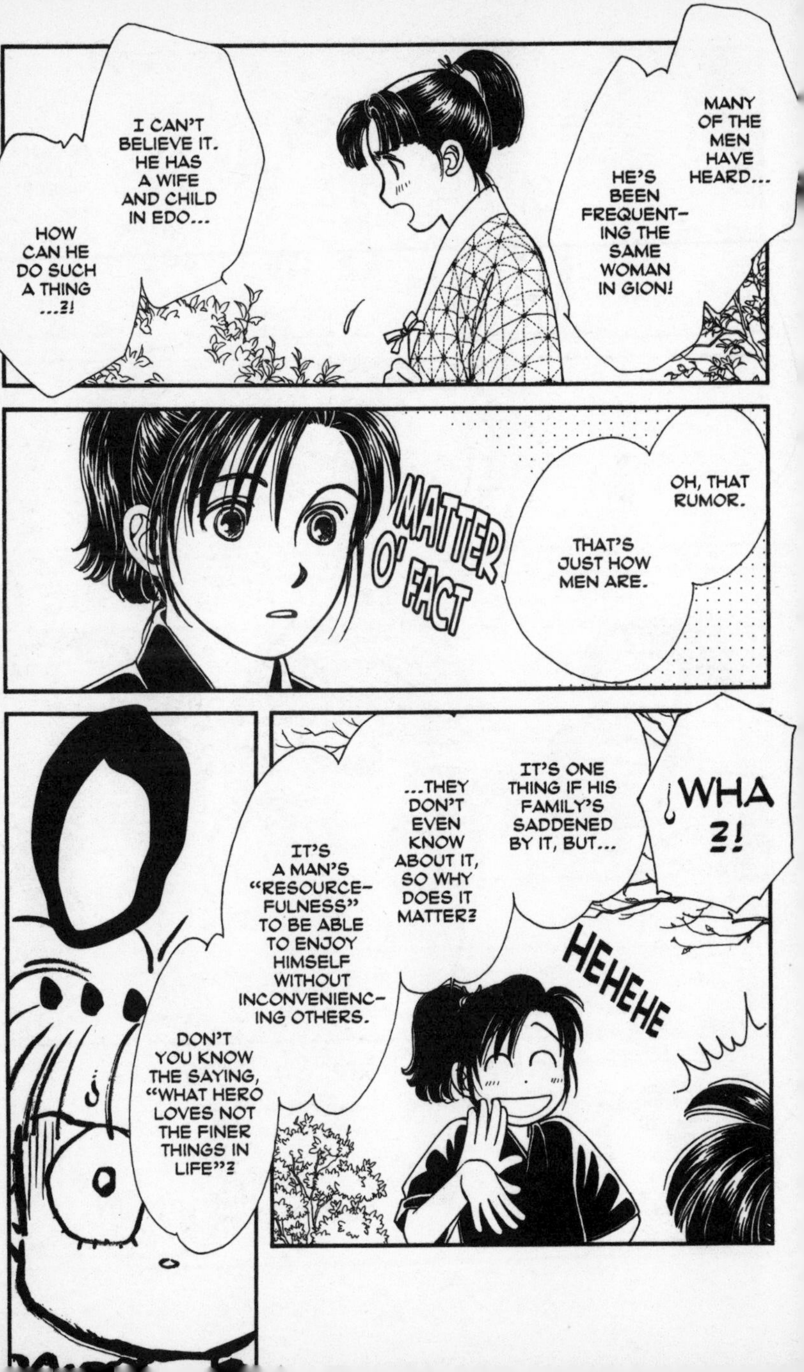
MANY OF THE MEN HAVE HEARD...
HE'S BEEN FREQUENTING THE SAME WOMAN IN GION!
I CAN'T BELIEVE IT. HE HAS A WIFE AND CHILD IN EDO...
HOW CAN HE DO SUCH A THING ...?!
MATTER O' FACT
OH, THAT RUMOR.
THAT'S JUST HOW MEN ARE.
WHA ?!
IT'S ONE THING IF HIS FAMILY'S SADDENED BY IT, BUT...
...THEY DON'T EVEN KNOW ABOUT IT, SO WHY DOES IT MATTER?
IT'S A MAN'S "RESOURCEFULNESS" TO BE ABLE TO ENJOY HIMSELF WITHOUT INCONVENIENCING OTHERS.
DON'T YOU KNOW THE SAYING, "WHAT HERO LOVES NOT THE FINER THINGS IN LIFE"?
HEHEHE

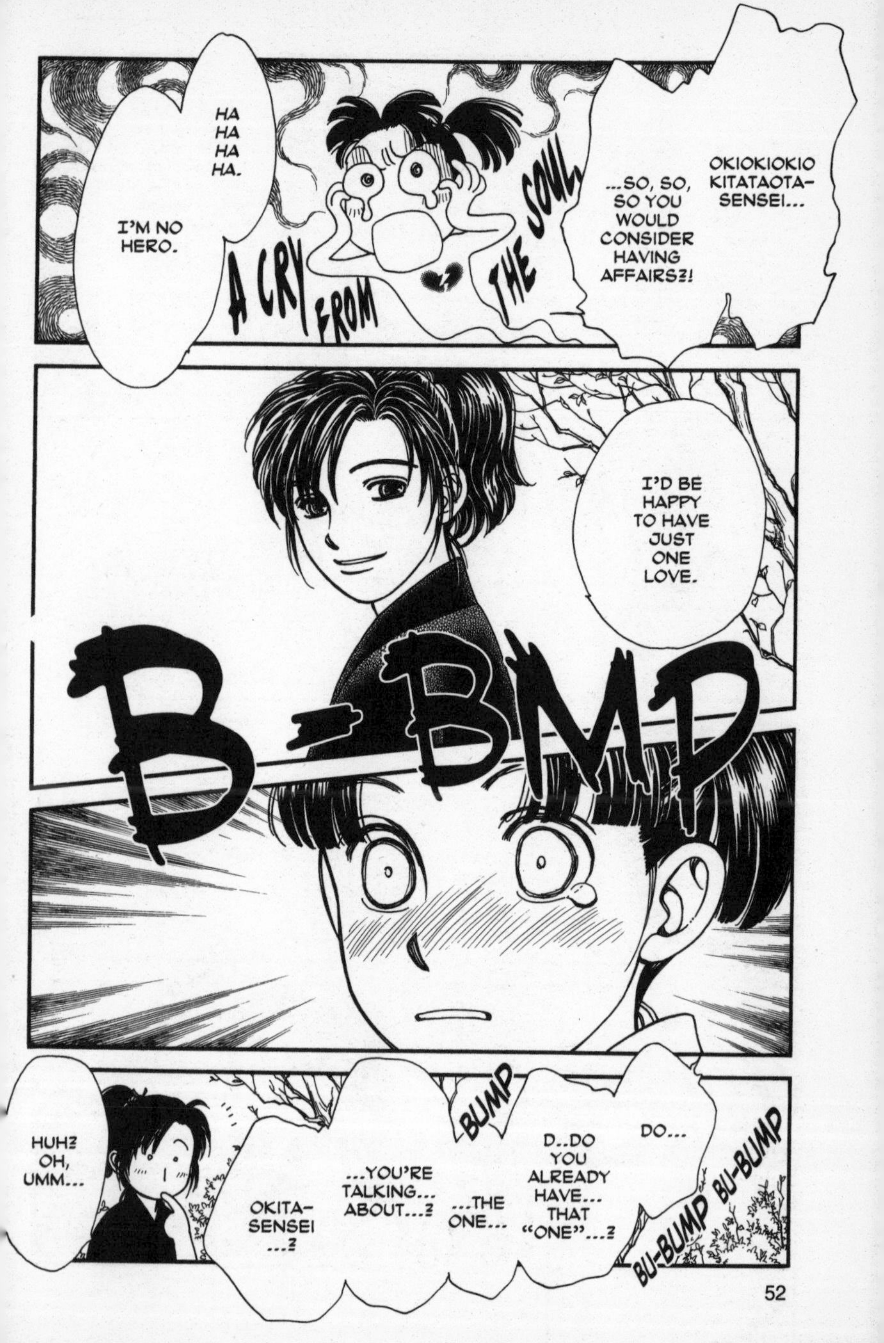
OKIOKIOKIO KITATAOTA-SENSEI...
...SO, SO, SO YOU WOULD CONSIDER HAVING AFFAIRS?!
A CRY FROM THE SOUL
HA HA HA HA.
I'M NO HERO.
I'D BE HAPPY TO HAVE JUST ONE LOVE.
B-BMP
BU-BUMP BU-BUMP
DO...
D..DO YOU ALREADY HAVE... THAT "ONE"...?
...THE ONE...
BUMP
...YOU'RE TALKING... ABOUT...?
OKITA-SENSEI ...?
HUH? OH, UMM...

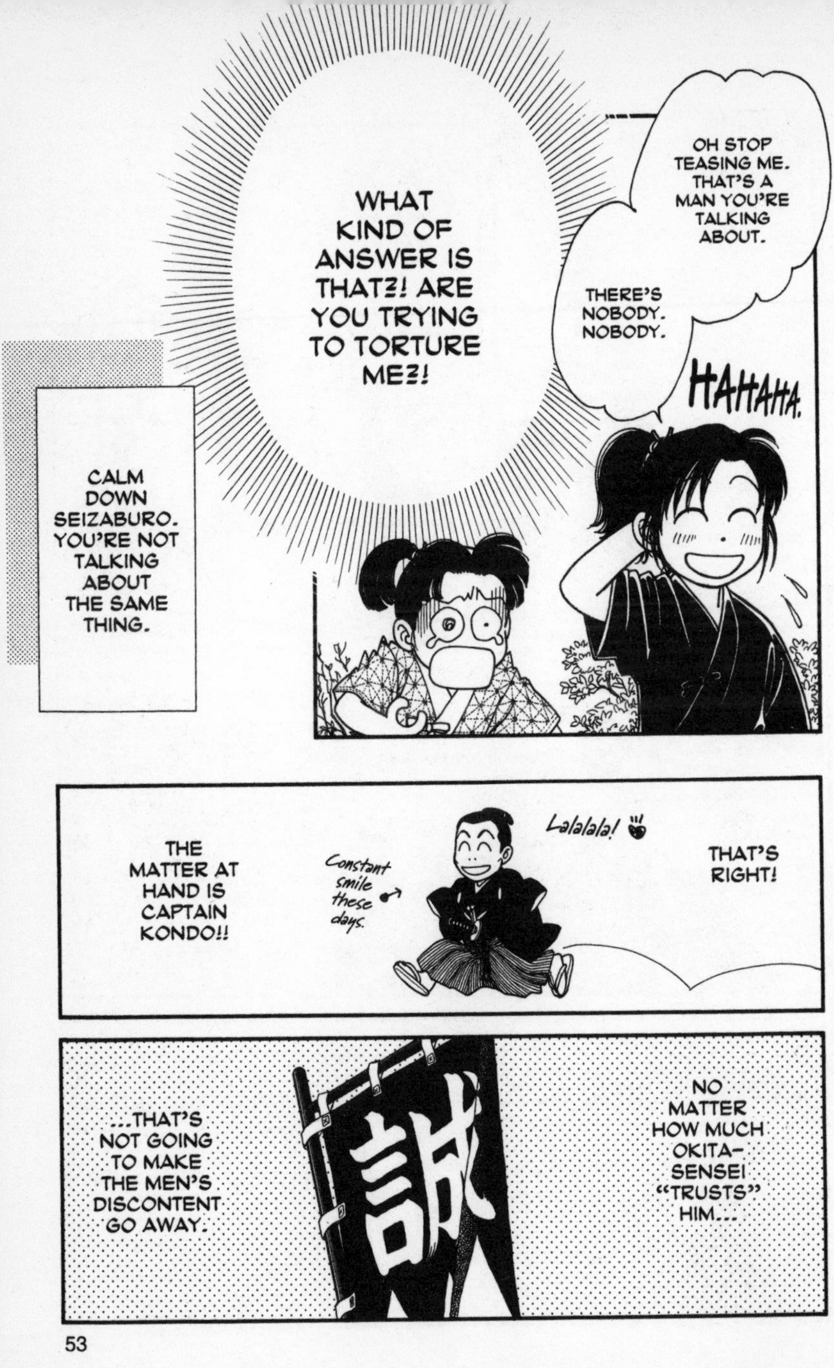
OH STOP TEASING ME. THAT'S A MAN YOU'RE TALKING ABOUT.
THERE'S NOBODY. NOBODY.
HAHAHA.
WHAT KIND OF ANSWER IS THAT?! ARE YOU TRYING TO TORTURE ME?!
CALM DOWN SEIZABURO. YOU'RE NOT TALKING ABOUT THE SAME THING.
THAT'S RIGHT!
Lalalala!
Constant smile these days.
THE MATTER AT HAND IS CAPTAIN KONDO!!
NO MATTER HOW MUCH OKITA-SENSEI "TRUSTS" HIM...
誠
...THAT'S NOT GOING TO MAKE THE MEN'S DISCONTENT GO AWAY.

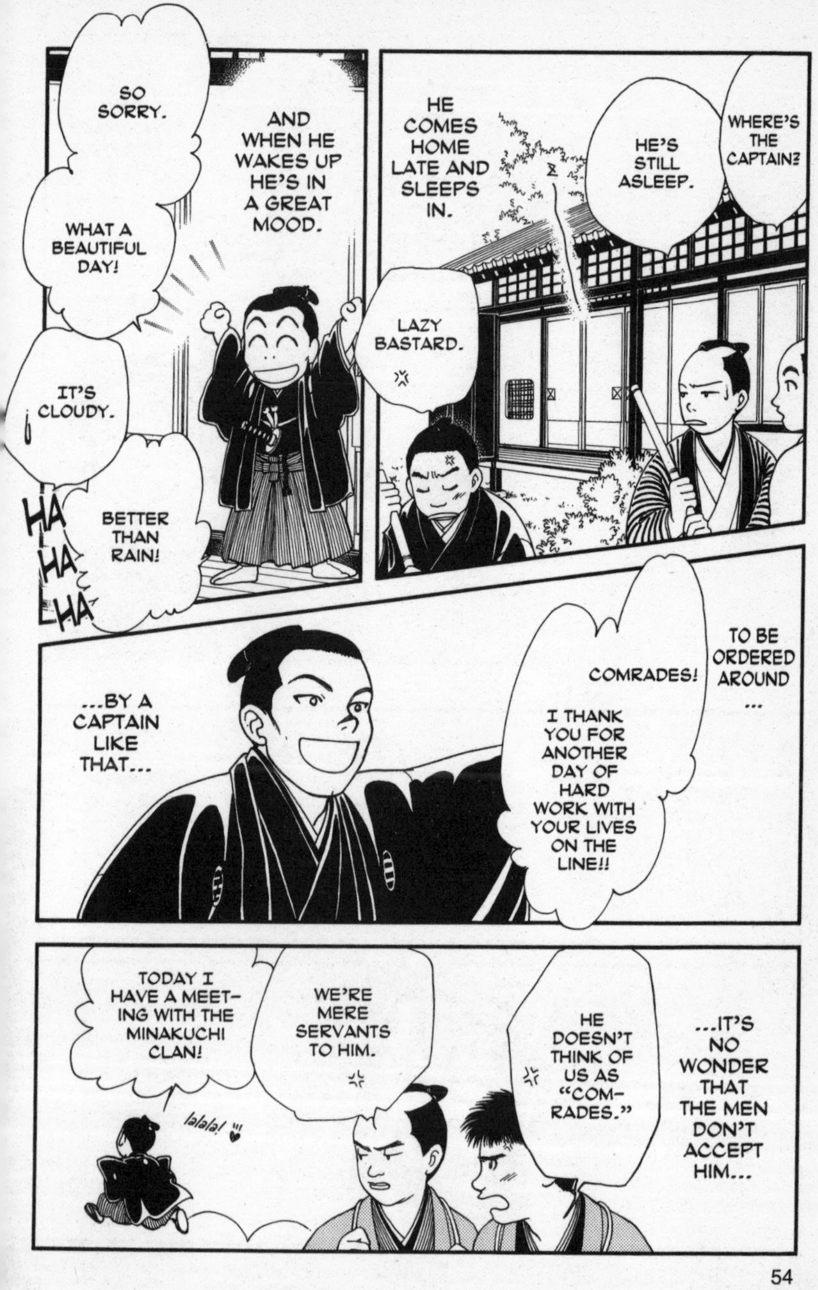
WHERE'S THE CAPTAIN?
HE'S STILL ASLEEP.
HE COMES HOME LATE AND SLEEPS IN.
LAZY BASTARD.
AND WHEN HE WAKES UP HE'S IN A GREAT MOOD.
SO SORRY.
WHAT A BEAUTIFUL DAY!
IT'S CLOUDY.
BETTER THAN RAIN!
HA HA HA
TO BE ORDERED AROUND...
COMRADES!
I THANK YOU FOR ANOTHER DAY OF HARD WORK WITH YOUR LIVES ON THE LINE!!
...BY A CAPTAIN LIKE THAT...
...IT'S NO WONDER THAT THE MEN DON'T ACCEPT HIM...
HE DOESN'T THINK OF US AS "COM-RADES."
WE'RE MERE SERVANTS TO HIM.
TODAY I HAVE A MEET-ING WITH THE MINAKUCHI CLAN!
lalala!

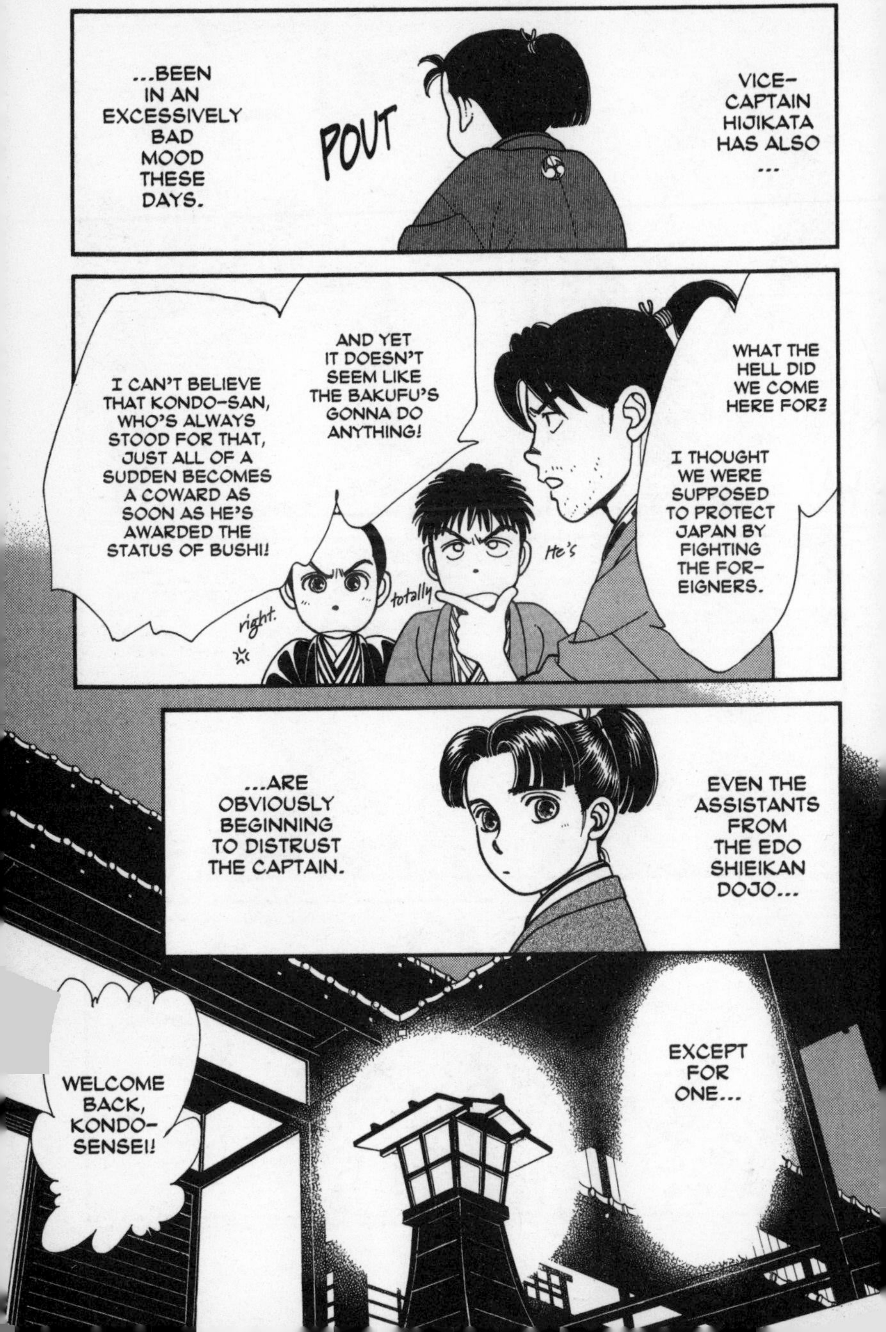
VICE-CAPTAIN HIJIKATA HAS ALSO...
POUT
...BEEN IN AN EXCESSIVELY BAD MOOD THESE DAYS.
WHAT THE HELL DID WE COME HERE FOR?
I THOUGHT WE WERE SUPPOSED TO PROTECT JAPAN BY FIGHTING THE FOR-EIGNERS.
AND YET IT DOESN'T SEEM LIKE THE BAKUFU'S GONNA DO ANYTHING!
I CAN'T BELIEVE THAT KONDO-SAN, WHO'S ALWAYS STOOD FOR THAT, JUST ALL OF A SUDDEN BECOMES A COWARD AS SOON AS HE'S AWARDED THE STATUS OF BUSHI!
He's totally right.
EVEN THE ASSISTANTS FROM THE EDO SHIEIKAN DOJO...
...ARE OBVIOUSLY BEGINNING TO DISTRUST THE CAPTAIN.
EXCEPT FOR ONE...
WELCOME BACK, KONDO-SENSEI!

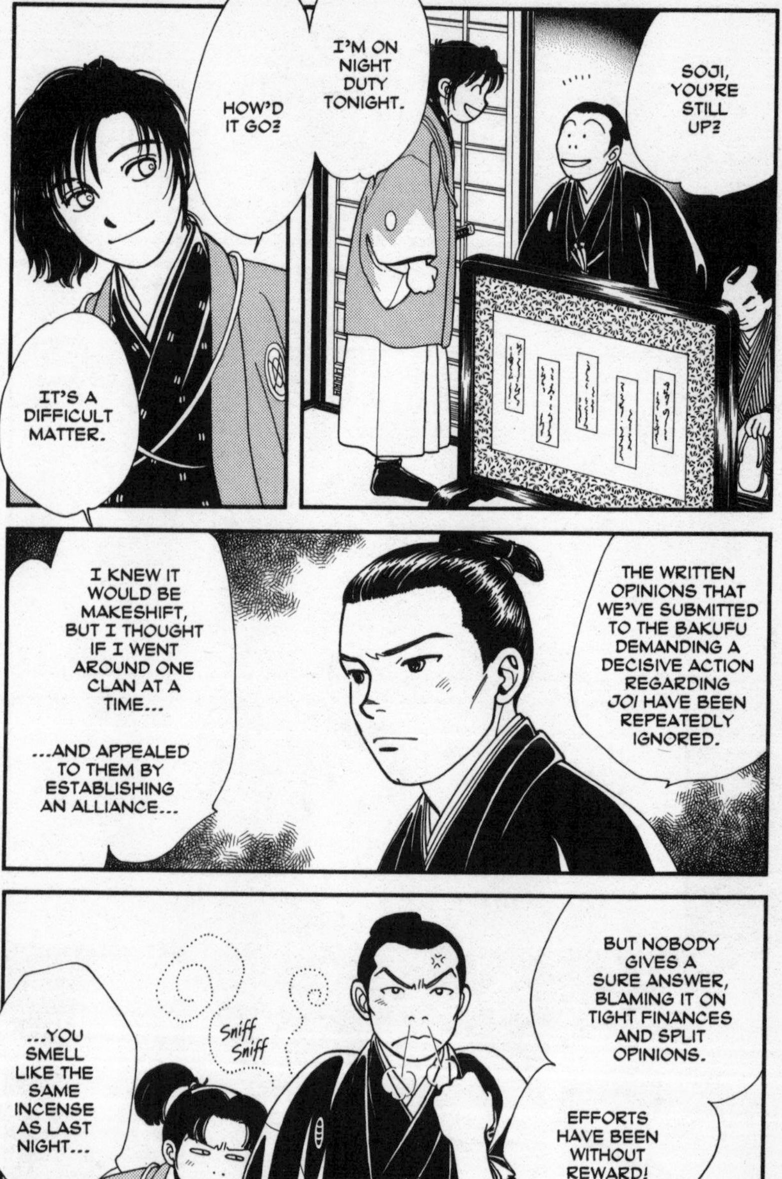
SOJI, YOU'RE STILL UP?
.....
I'M ON NIGHT DUTY TONIGHT.
HOW'D IT GO?
IT'S A DIFFICULT MATTER.
THE WRITTEN OPINIONS THAT WE'VE SUBMITTED TO THE BAKUFU DEMANDING A DECISIVE ACTION REGARDING *JOI* HAVE BEEN REPEATEDLY IGNORED.
I KNEW IT WOULD BE MAKESHIFT, BUT I THOUGHT IF I WENT AROUND ONE CLAN AT A TIME...
...AND APPEALED TO THEM BY ESTABLISHING AN ALLIANCE...
BUT NOBODY GIVES A SURE ANSWER, BLAMING IT ON TIGHT FINANCES AND SPLIT OPINIONS.
EFFORTS HAVE BEEN WITHOUT REWARD!
Sniff Sniff
...YOU SMELL LIKE THE SAME INCENSE AS LAST NIGHT...

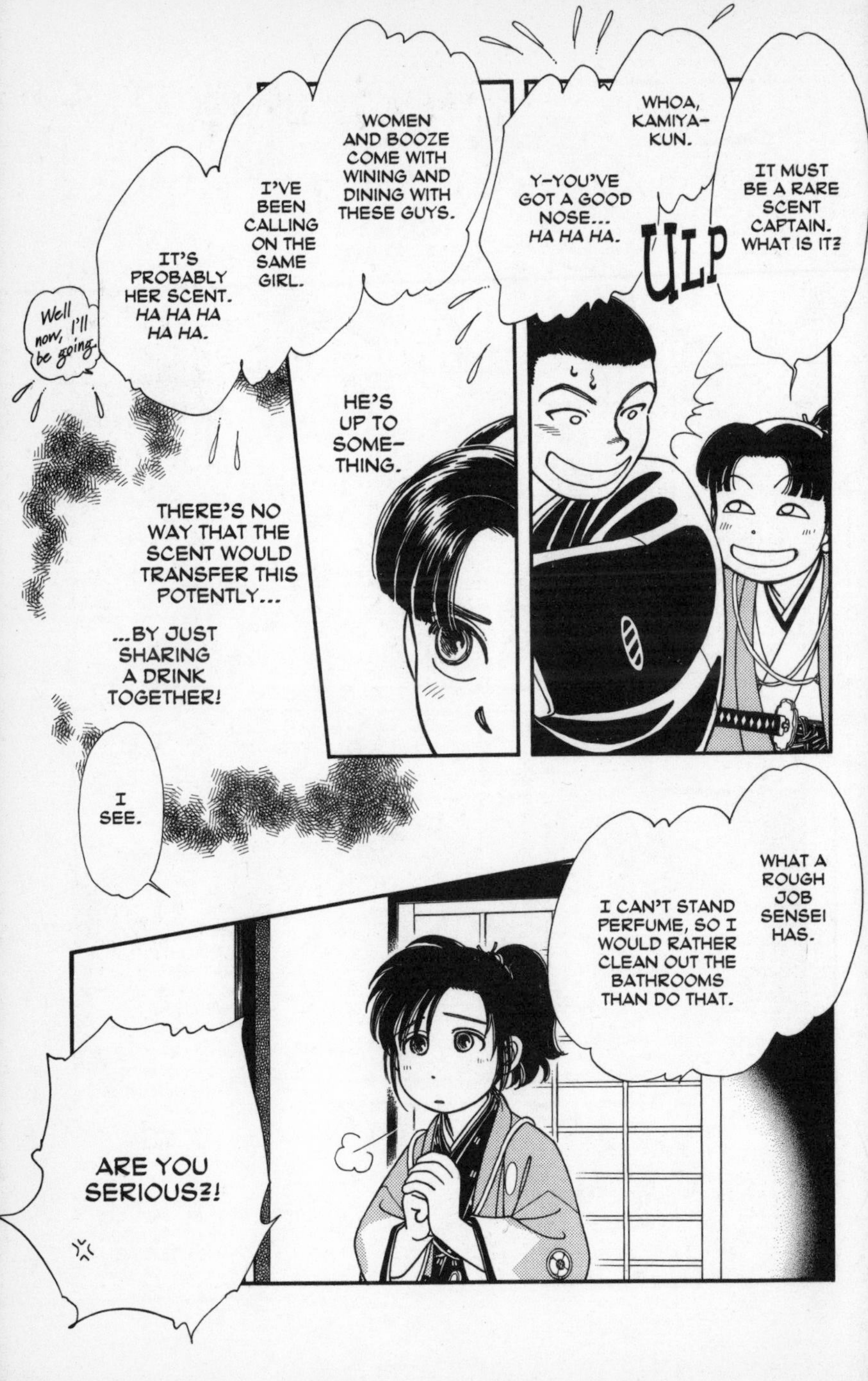
IT MUST BE A RARE SCENT CAPTAIN. WHAT IS IT?
WHOA, KAMIYA-KUN.
Y-YOU'VE GOT A GOOD NOSE... HA HA HA.
ULP
WOMEN AND BOOZE COME WITH WINING AND DINING WITH THESE GUYS.
I'VE BEEN CALLING ON THE SAME GIRL.
IT'S PROBABLY HER SCENT. HA HA HA HA HA.
Well now, I'll be going.
HE'S UP TO SOMETHING.
THERE'S NO WAY THAT THE SCENT WOULD TRANSFER THIS POTENTLY...
...BY JUST SHARING A DRINK TOGETHER!
I SEE.
WHAT A ROUGH JOB SENSEI HAS.
I CAN'T STAND PERFUME, SO I WOULD RATHER CLEAN OUT THE BATHROOMS THAN DO THAT.
ARE YOU SERIOUS?!

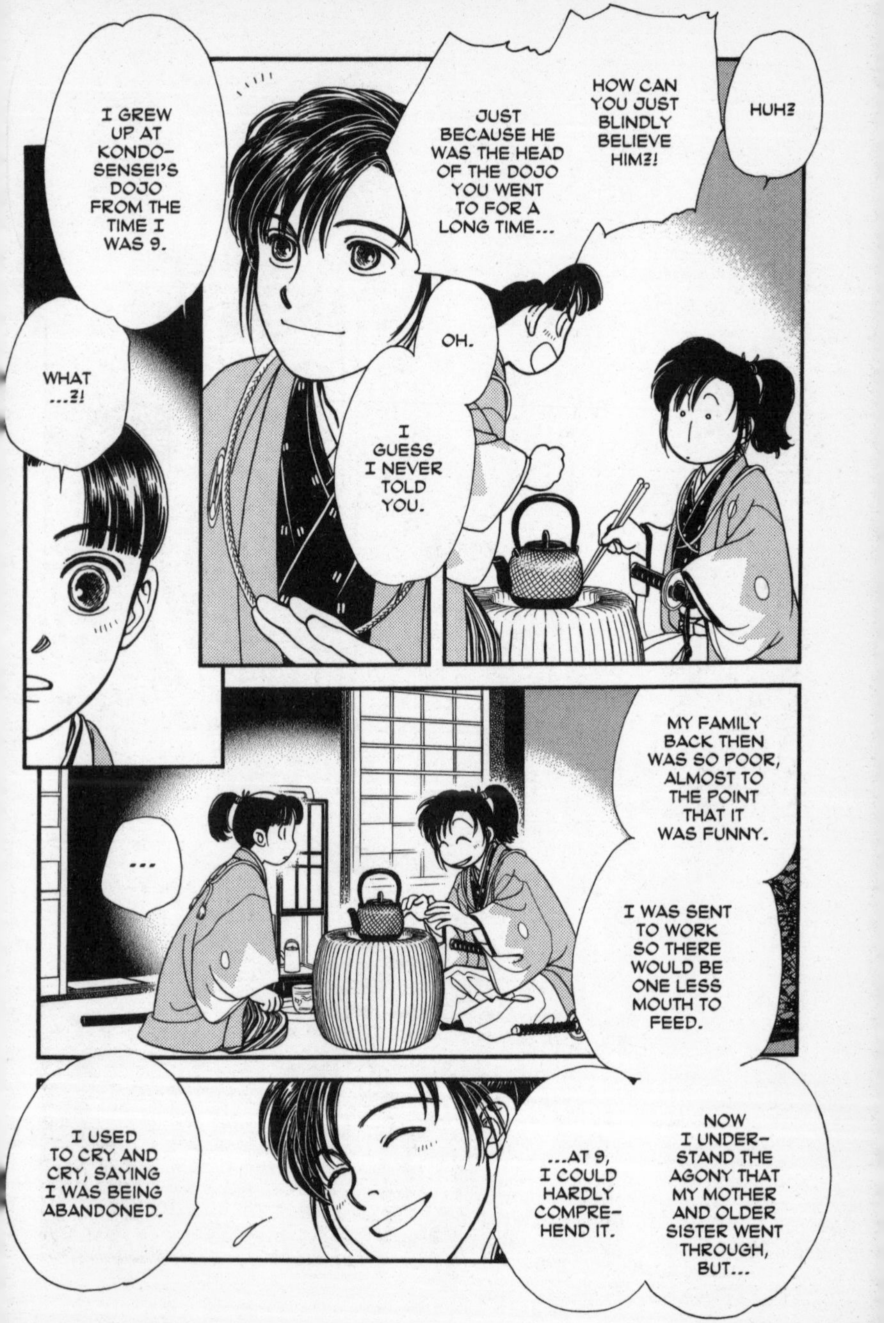
HUH?
HOW CAN YOU JUST BLINDLY BELIEVE HIM?!
JUST BECAUSE HE WAS THE HEAD OF THE DOJO YOU WENT TO FOR A LONG TIME...
OH.
I GUESS I NEVER TOLD YOU.
I GREW UP AT KONDO-SENSEI'S DOJO FROM THE TIME I WAS 9.
WHAT ...?!
MY FAMILY BACK THEN WAS SO POOR, ALMOST TO THE POINT THAT IT WAS FUNNY.
I WAS SENT TO WORK SO THERE WOULD BE ONE LESS MOUTH TO FEED.
...
NOW I UNDER-STAND THE AGONY THAT MY MOTHER AND OLDER SISTER WENT THROUGH, BUT...
...AT 9, I COULD HARDLY COMPRE-HEND IT.
I USED TO CRY AND CRY, SAYING I WAS BEING ABANDONED.

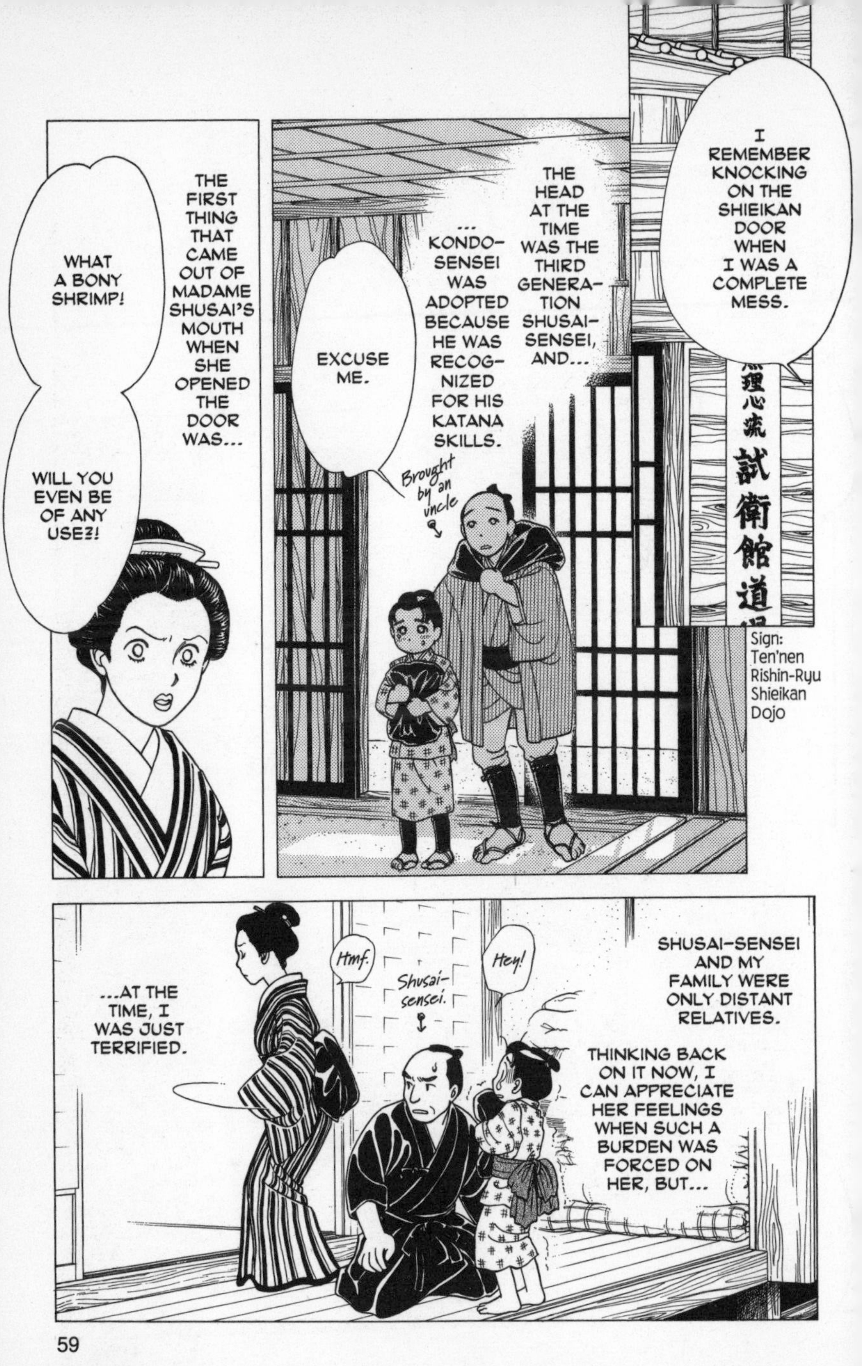
I REMEMBER KNOCKING ON THE SHIEIKAN DOOR WHEN I WAS A COMPLETE MESS.
理心流
試衛館道
Sign: Ten'nen Rishin-Ryu Shieikan Dojo
THE HEAD AT THE TIME WAS THE THIRD GENERATION SHUSAI-SENSEI, AND...
...KONDO-SENSEI WAS ADOPTED BECAUSE HE WAS RECOGNIZED FOR HIS KATANA SKILLS.
EXCUSE ME.
Brought by an uncle
THE FIRST THING THAT CAME OUT OF MADAME SHUSAI'S MOUTH WHEN SHE OPENED THE DOOR WAS...
WHAT A BONY SHRIMP!
WILL YOU EVEN BE OF ANY USE?!
SHUSAI-SENSEI AND MY FAMILY WERE ONLY DISTANT RELATIVES.
THINKING BACK ON IT NOW, I CAN APPRECIATE HER FEELINGS WHEN SUCH A BURDEN WAS FORCED ON HER, BUT...
Hey!
Shusai-sensei.
Hmf.
...AT THE TIME, I WAS JUST TERRIFIED.

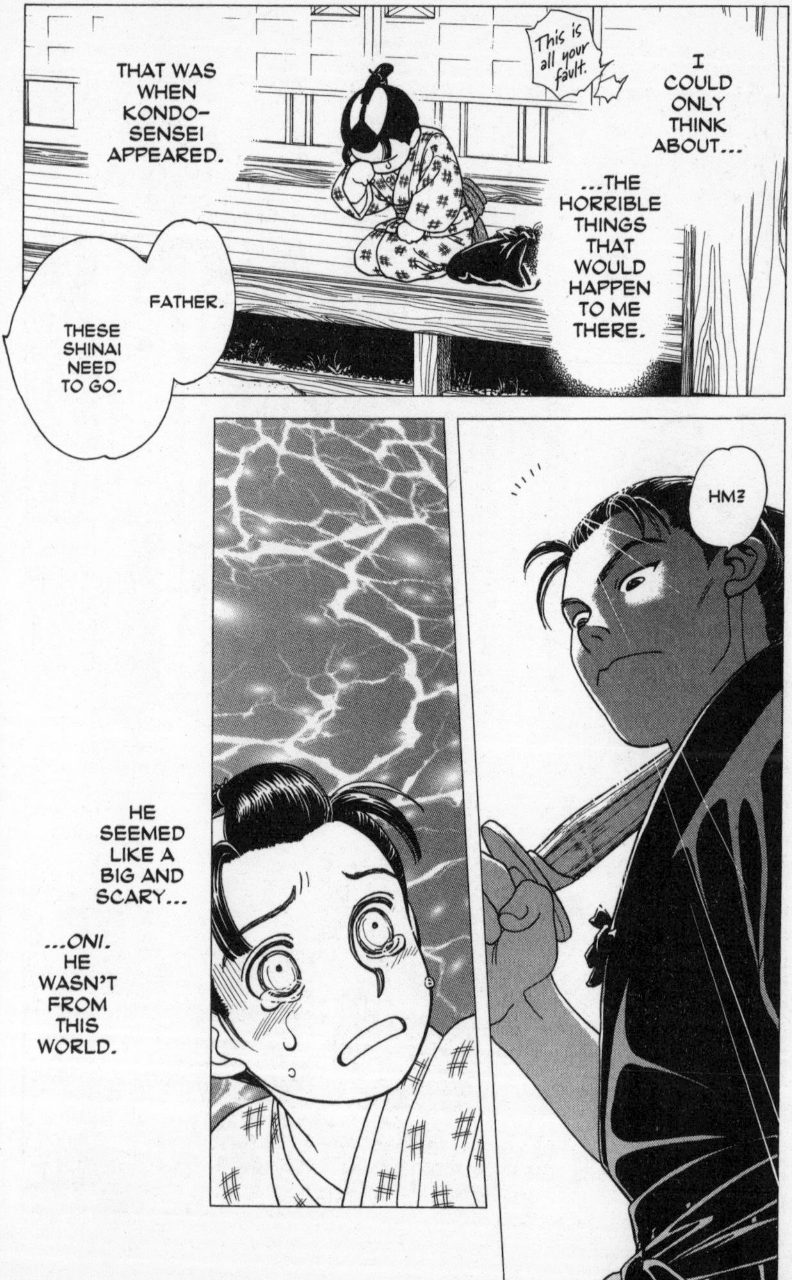
This is all your fault.
I COULD ONLY THINK ABOUT...
...THE HORRIBLE THINGS THAT WOULD HAPPEN TO ME THERE.
THAT WAS WHEN KONDO-SENSEI APPEARED.
FATHER.
THESE SHINAI NEED TO GO.
HM?
HE SEEMED LIKE A BIG AND SCARY...
...ONI. HE WASN'T FROM THIS WORLD.

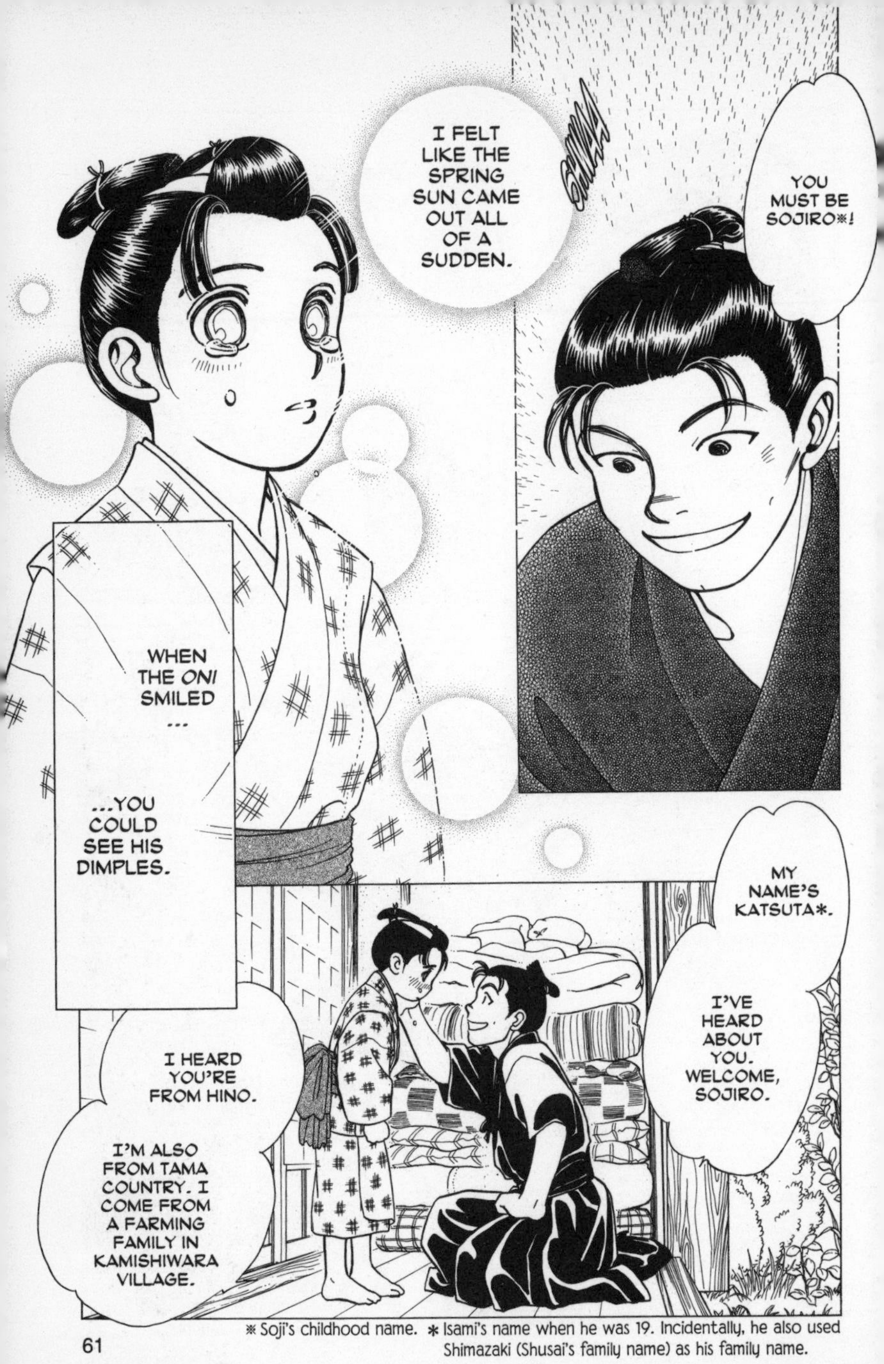
YOU MUST BE SOJIRO※!
I FELT LIKE THE SPRING SUN CAME OUT ALL OF A SUDDEN.
WHEN THE *ONI* SMILED ...
...YOU COULD SEE HIS DIMPLES.
MY NAME'S KATSUTA*.
I'VE HEARD ABOUT YOU. WELCOME, SOJIRO.
I HEARD YOU'RE FROM HINO.
I'M ALSO FROM TAMA COUNTRY. I COME FROM A FARMING FAMILY IN KAMISHIWARA VILLAGE.

※ Soji's childhood name. * Isami's name when he was 19. Incidentally, he also used Shimazaki (Shusai's family name) as his family name.

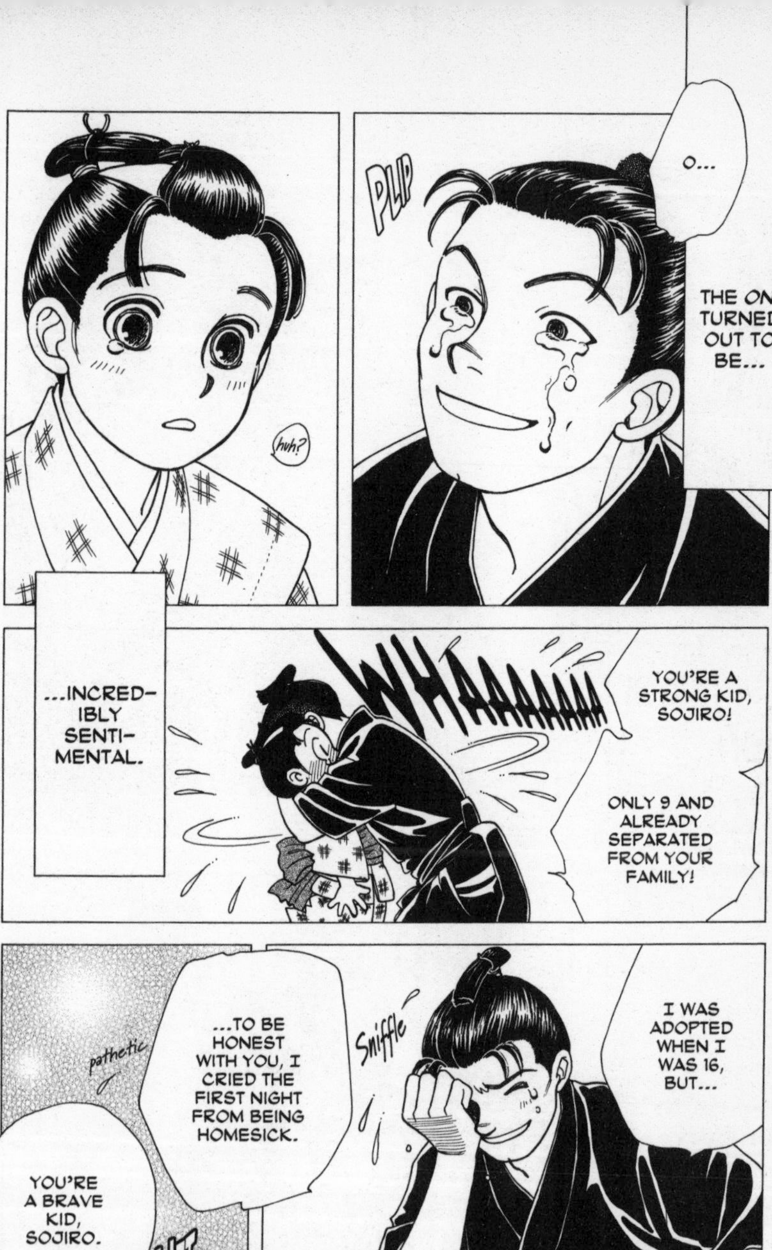
O...
THE *ONI* TURNED OUT TO BE...
PLIP
huh?
YOU'RE A STRONG KID, SOJIRO!
ONLY 9 AND ALREADY SEPARATED FROM YOUR FAMILY!
...INCRED- IBLY SENTI- MENTAL.
I WAS ADOPTED WHEN I WAS 16, BUT...
Sniffle
...TO BE HONEST WITH YOU, I CRIED THE FIRST NIGHT FROM BEING HOMESICK.
pathetic
YOU'RE A BRAVE KID, SOJIRO.
LIFT

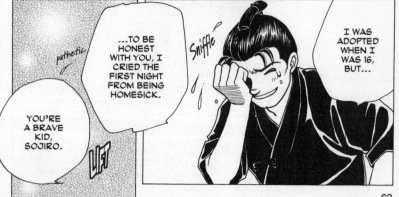

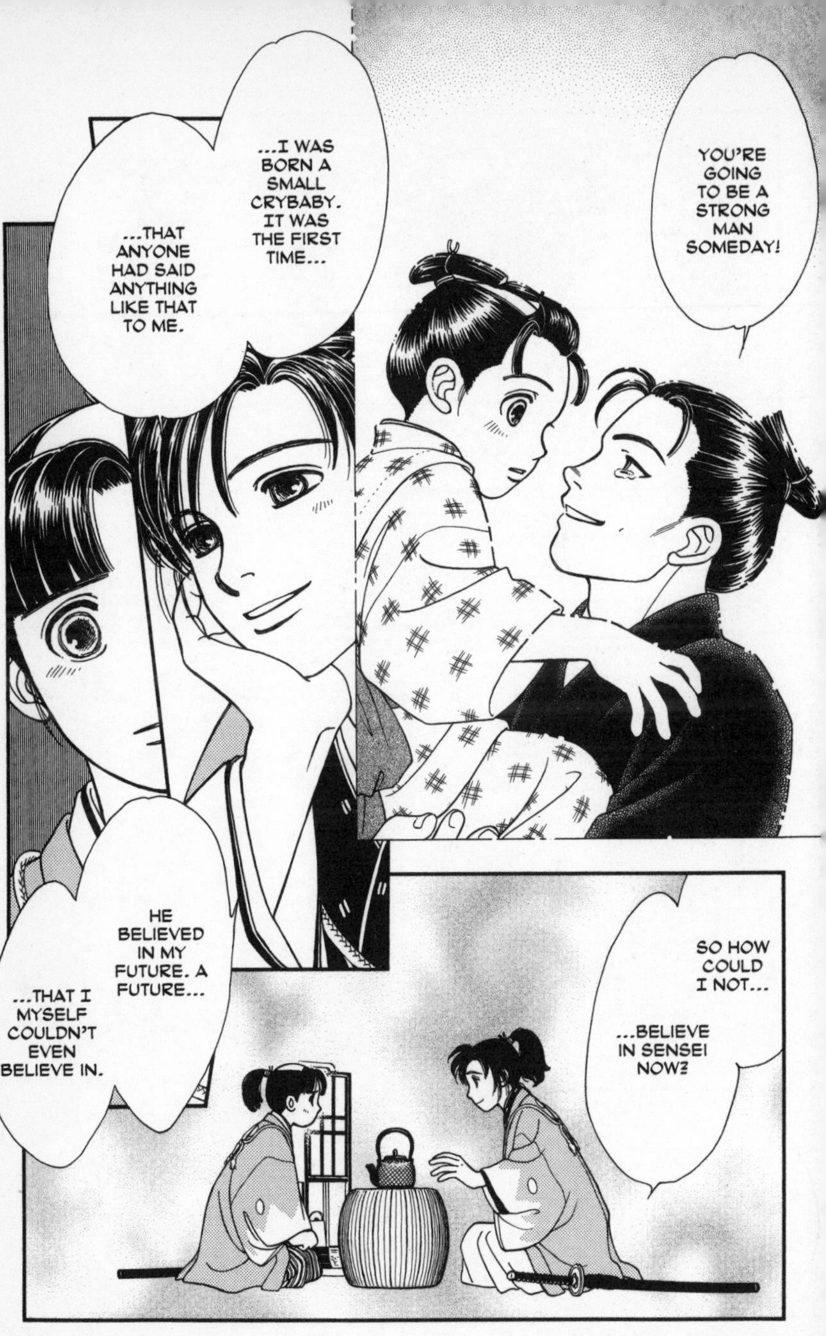
YOU'RE GOING TO BE A STRONG MAN SOMEDAY!
...I WAS BORN A SMALL CRYBABY. IT WAS THE FIRST TIME...
...THAT ANYONE HAD SAID ANYTHING LIKE THAT TO ME.
HE BELIEVED IN MY FUTURE. A FUTURE...
...THAT I MYSELF COULDN'T EVEN BELIEVE IN.
SO HOW COULD I NOT...
...BELIEVE IN SENSEI NOW?

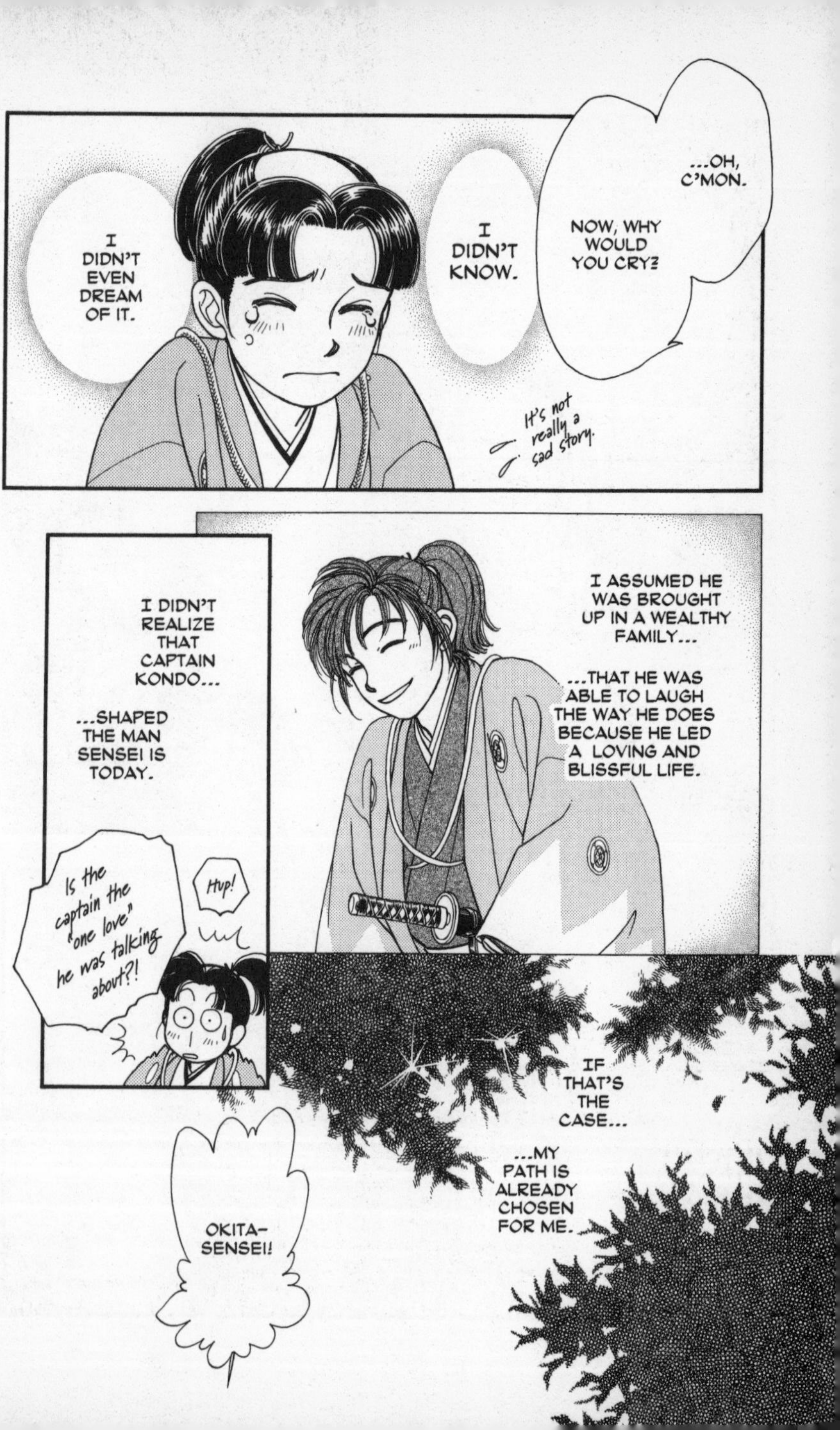

...OH, C'MON.
NOW, WHY WOULD YOU CRY?
I DIDN'T KNOW.
I DIDN'T EVEN DREAM OF IT.
It's not really a sad story.
I ASSUMED HE WAS BROUGHT UP IN A WEALTHY FAMILY...
...THAT HE WAS ABLE TO LAUGH THE WAY HE DOES BECAUSE HE LED A LOVING AND BLISSFUL LIFE.
I DIDN'T REALIZE THAT CAPTAIN KONDO...
...SHAPED THE MAN SENSEI IS TODAY.
Hup!
Is the captain the "one love" he was talking about?!
IF THAT'S THE CASE...
...MY PATH IS ALREADY CHOSEN FOR ME.
OKITA-SENSEI!

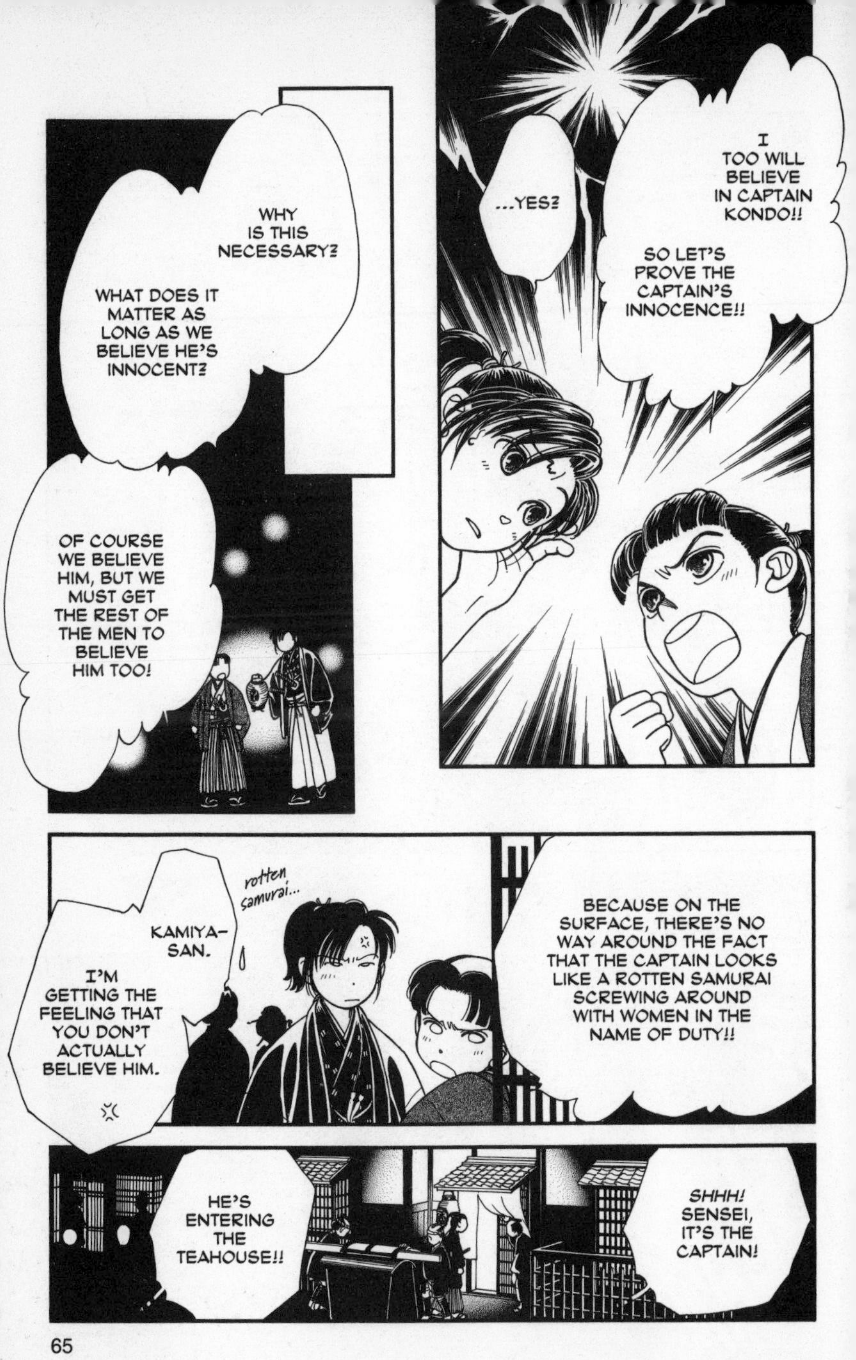
I TOO WILL BELIEVE IN CAPTAIN KONDO!!
SO LET'S PROVE THE CAPTAIN'S INNOCENCE!!
...YES?
WHY IS THIS NECESSARY?
WHAT DOES IT MATTER AS LONG AS WE BELIEVE HE'S INNOCENT?
OF COURSE WE BELIEVE HIM, BUT WE MUST GET THE REST OF THE MEN TO BELIEVE HIM TOO!
BECAUSE ON THE SURFACE, THERE'S NO WAY AROUND THE FACT THAT THE CAPTAIN LOOKS LIKE A ROTTEN SAMURAI SCREWING AROUND WITH WOMEN IN THE NAME OF DUTY!!
rotten samurai...
KAMIYA-SAN.
I'M GETTING THE FEELING THAT YOU DON'T ACTUALLY BELIEVE HIM.
SHHH! SENSEI, IT'S THE CAPTAIN!
HE'S ENTERING THE TEAHOUSE!!

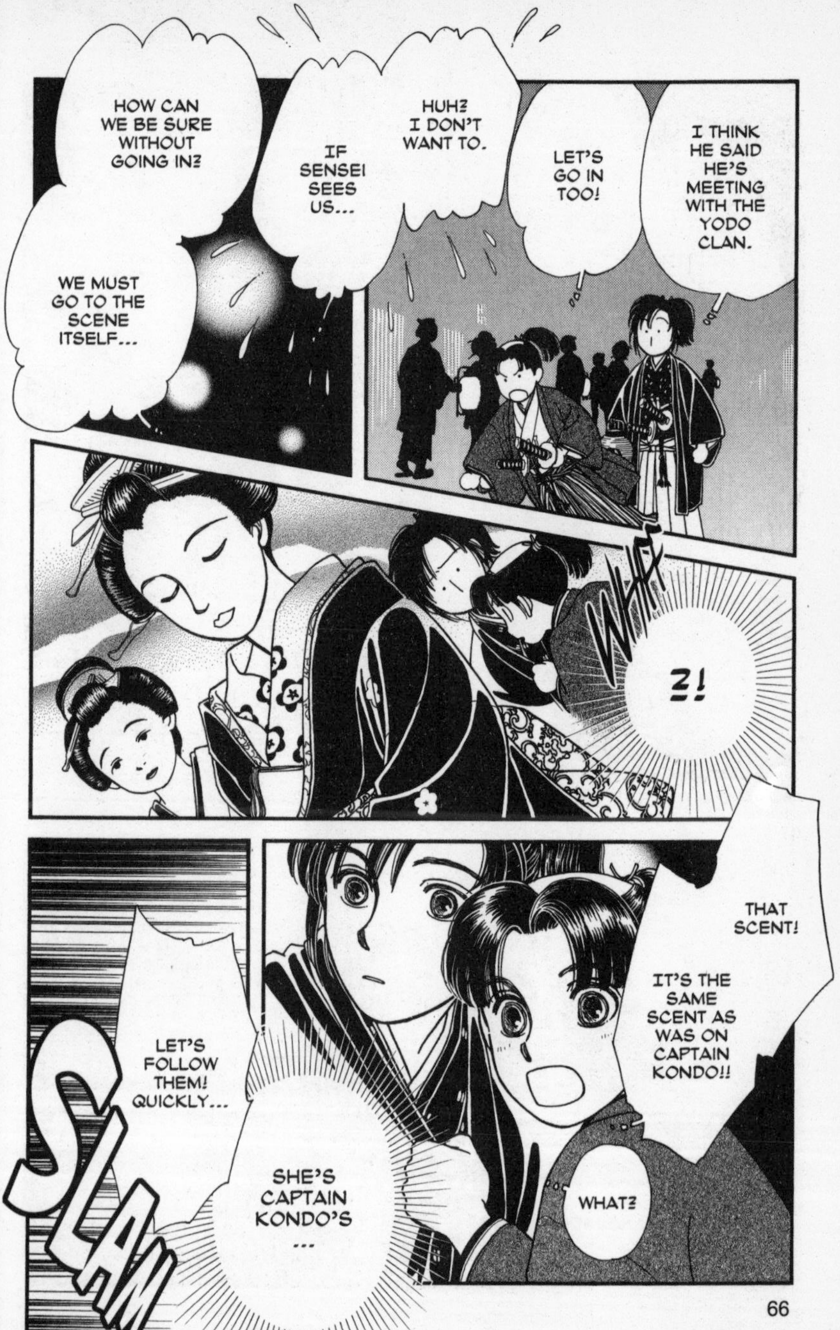
I THINK HE SAID HE'S MEETING WITH THE YODO CLAN.
LET'S GO IN TOO!
HUH? I DON'T WANT TO.
IF SENSEI SEES US...
HOW CAN WE BE SURE WITHOUT GOING IN?
WE MUST GO TO THE SCENE ITSELF...
WHIFF
?!
THAT SCENT!
IT'S THE SAME SCENT AS WAS ON CAPTAIN KONDO!!
WHAT?
SHE'S CAPTAIN KONDO'S ...
LET'S FOLLOW THEM! QUICKLY...
SLAM

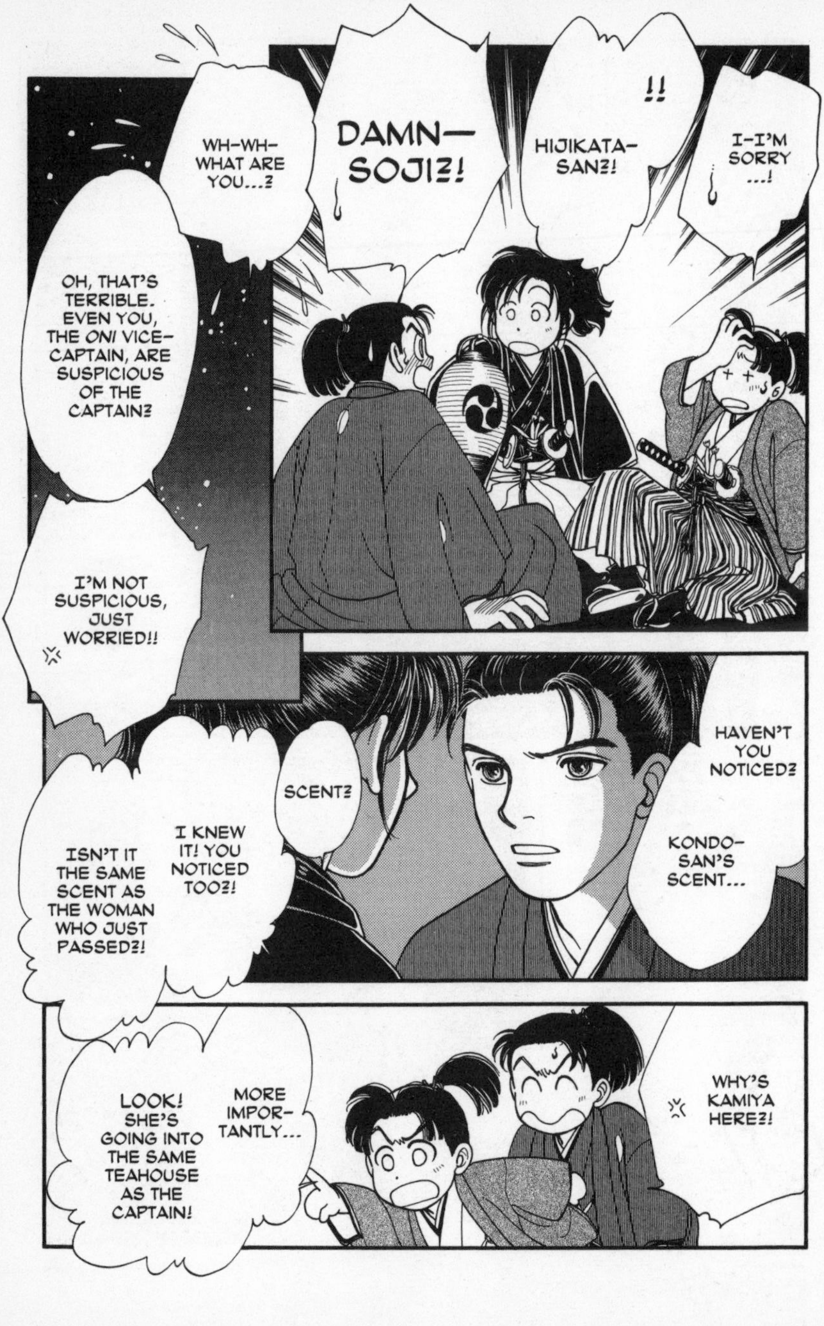
I-I'M SORRY ...!
!!
HIJIKATA-SAN?!
DAMN— SOJI?!
WH-WH-WHAT ARE YOU...?
OH, THAT'S TERRIBLE. EVEN YOU, THE *ONI* VICE-CAPTAIN, ARE SUSPICIOUS OF THE CAPTAIN?
I'M NOT SUSPICIOUS, JUST WORRIED!!
HAVEN'T YOU NOTICED?
KONDO-SAN'S SCENT...
SCENT?
I KNEW IT! YOU NOTICED TOO?!
ISN'T IT THE SAME SCENT AS THE WOMAN WHO JUST PASSED?!
WHY'S KAMIYA HERE?!
MORE IMPORTANTLY...
LOOK! SHE'S GOING INTO THE SAME TEAHOUSE AS THE CAPTAIN!

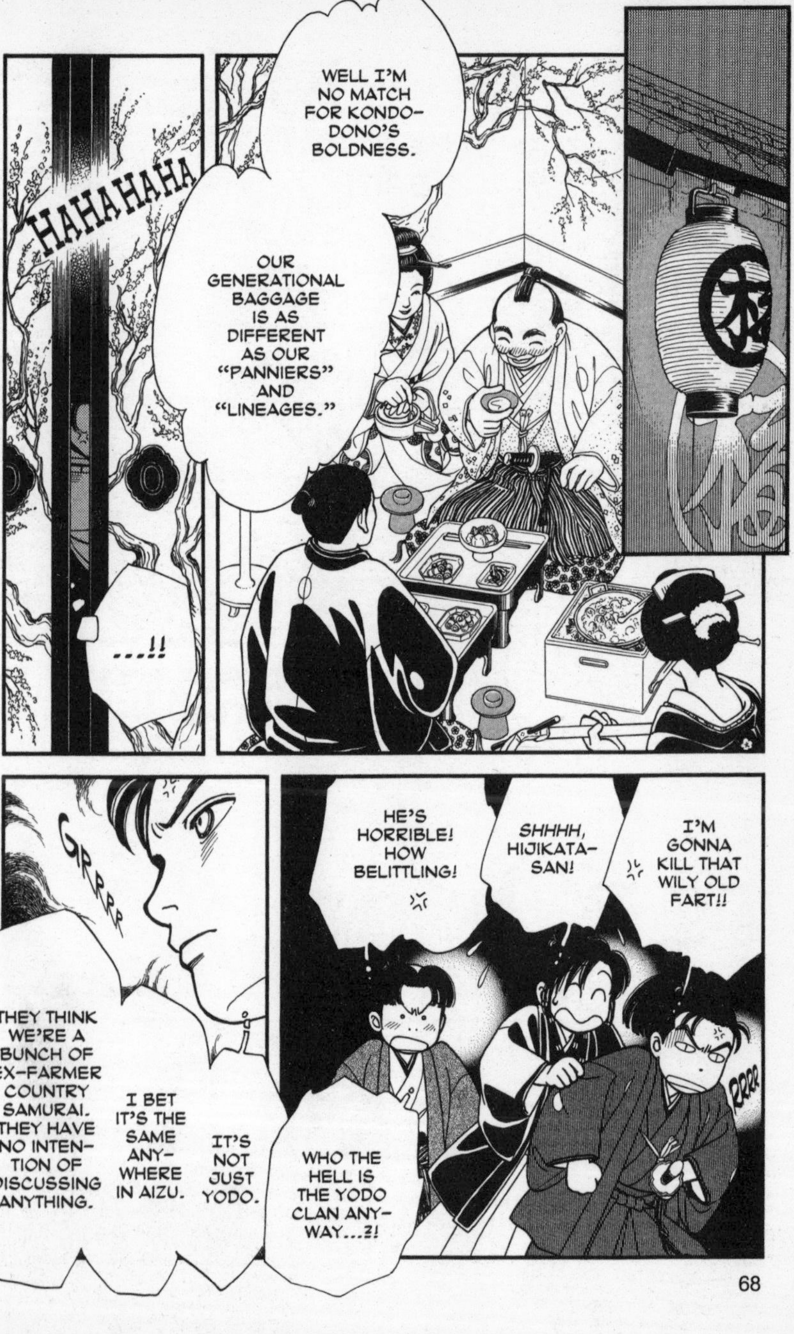
WELL I'M NO MATCH FOR KONDO-DONO'S BOLDNESS.
HAHAHAHA
OUR GENERATIONAL BAGGAGE IS AS DIFFERENT AS OUR "PANNIERS" AND "LINEAGES."
...!!
I'M GONNA KILL THAT WILY OLD FART!!
SHHHH, HIJIKATA-SAN!
HE'S HORRIBLE! HOW BELITTLING!
RRRR
WHO THE HELL IS THE YODO CLAN ANYWAY...?!
GRRRR
IT'S NOT JUST YODO.
I BET IT'S THE SAME ANYWHERE IN AIZU.
THEY THINK WE'RE A BUNCH OF EX-FARMER COUNTRY SAMURAI. THEY HAVE NO INTENTION OF DISCUSSING ANYTHING.

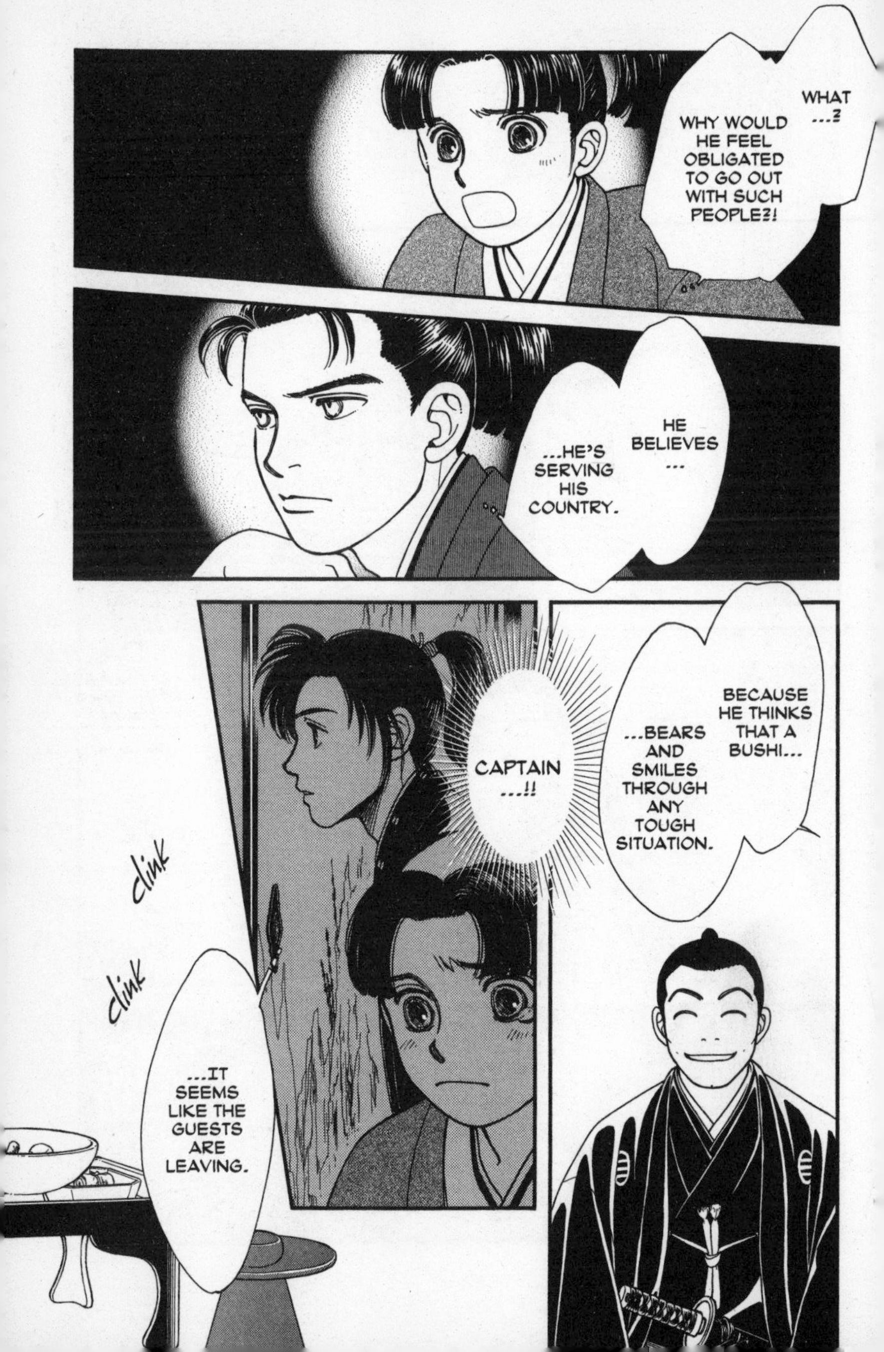
WHAT ...?
WHY WOULD HE FEEL OBLIGATED TO GO OUT WITH SUCH PEOPLE?!
HE BELIEVES ...
...HE'S SERVING HIS COUNTRY.
BECAUSE HE THINKS THAT A BUSHI...
...BEARS AND SMILES THROUGH ANY TOUGH SITUATION.
CAPTAIN ...!!
clink
clink
...IT SEEMS LIKE THE GUESTS ARE LEAVING.

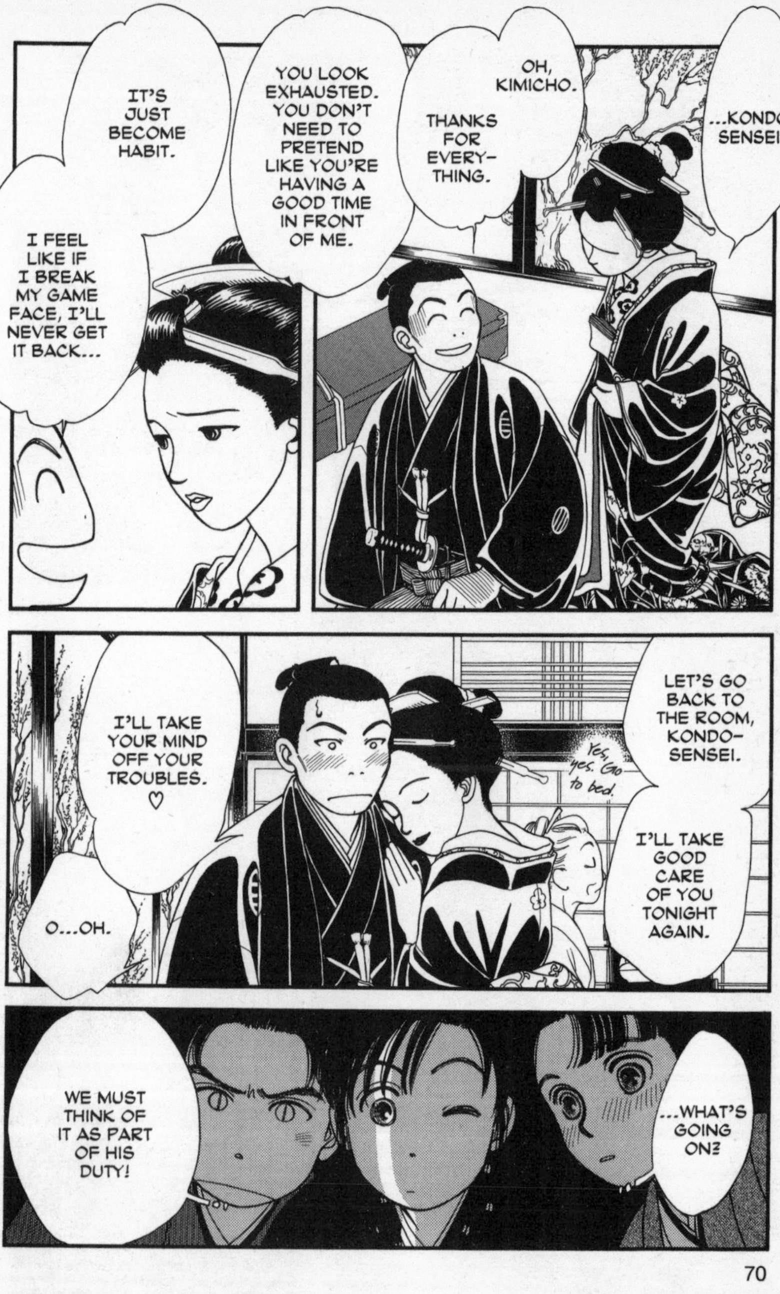
...KONDO-SENSEI?
OH, KIMICHO.
THANKS FOR EVERY-THING.
YOU LOOK EXHAUSTED. YOU DON'T NEED TO PRETEND LIKE YOU'RE HAVING A GOOD TIME IN FRONT OF ME.
IT'S JUST BECOME HABIT.
I FEEL LIKE IF I BREAK MY GAME FACE, I'LL NEVER GET IT BACK...
LET'S GO BACK TO THE ROOM, KONDO-SENSEI.
I'LL TAKE GOOD CARE OF YOU TONIGHT AGAIN.
Yes, yes. Go to bed.
I'LL TAKE YOUR MIND OFF YOUR TROUBLES. ♡
O...OH.
...WHAT'S GOING ON?
WE MUST THINK OF IT AS PART OF HIS DUTY!

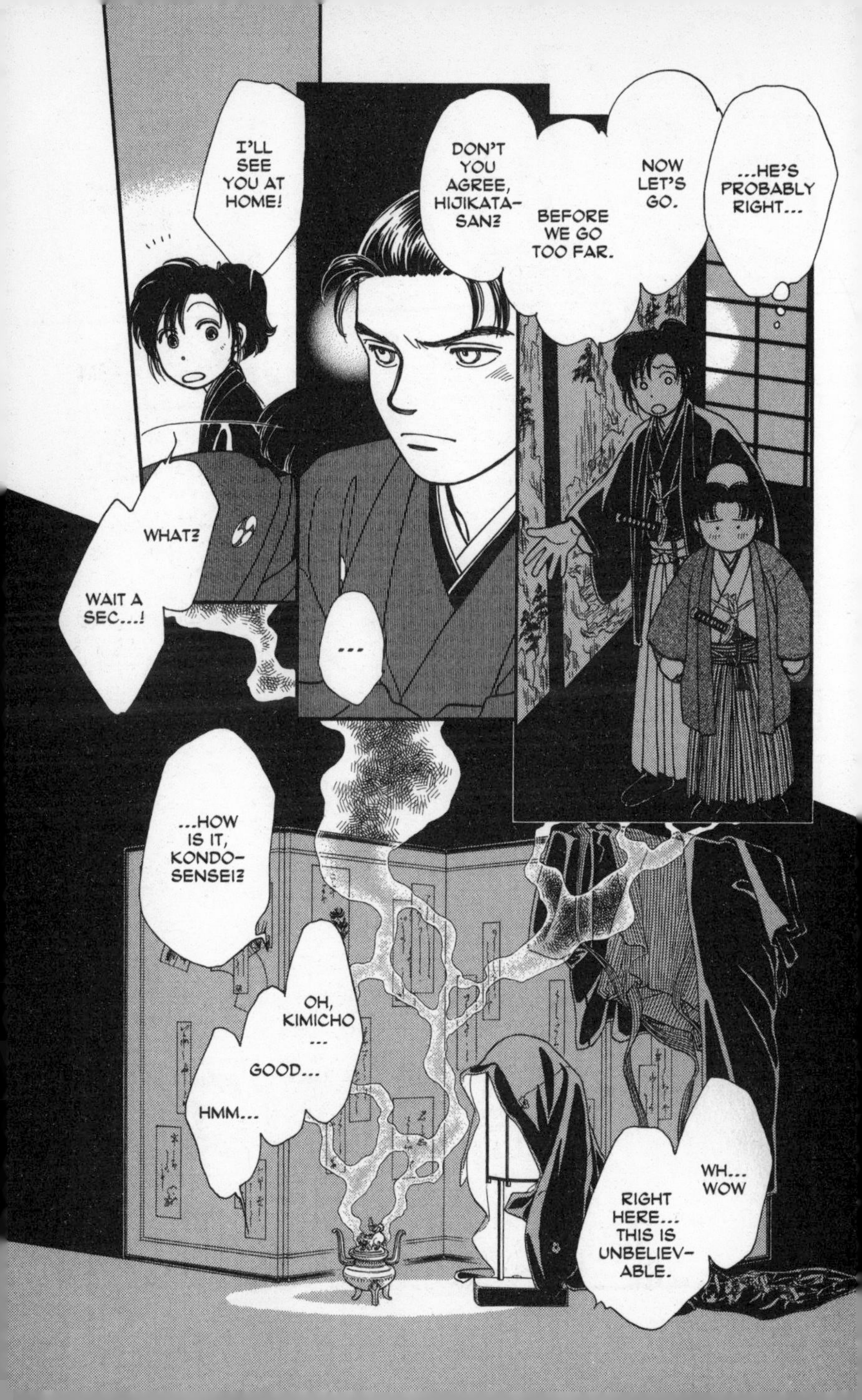
...HE'S PROBABLY RIGHT...
NOW LET'S GO.
BEFORE WE GO TOO FAR.
DON'T YOU AGREE, HIJIKATA-SAN?
...
I'LL SEE YOU AT HOME!
WHAT?
WAIT A SEC...!
...HOW IS IT, KONDO-SENSEI?
OH, KIMICHO... GOOD... HMM...
WH... WOW
RIGHT HERE... THIS IS UNBELIEV-ABLE.

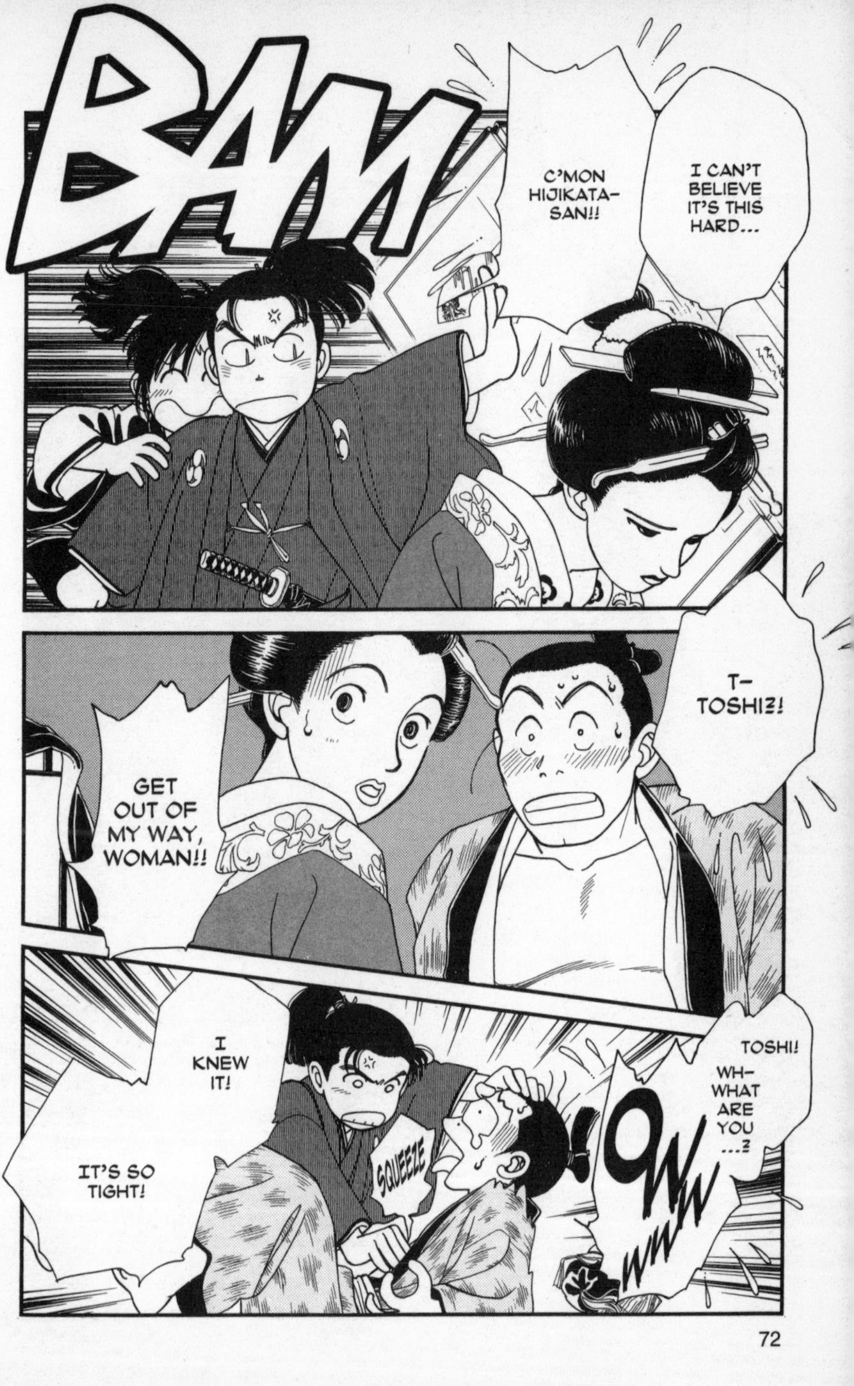
I CAN'T BELIEVE IT'S THIS HARD...
C'MON HIJIKATA-SAN!!
BAM
T-TOSHI?!
GET OUT OF MY WAY, WOMAN!!
TOSHI!
WH-WHAT ARE YOU...?
OWWW
SQUEEZE
I KNEW IT!
IT'S SO TIGHT!

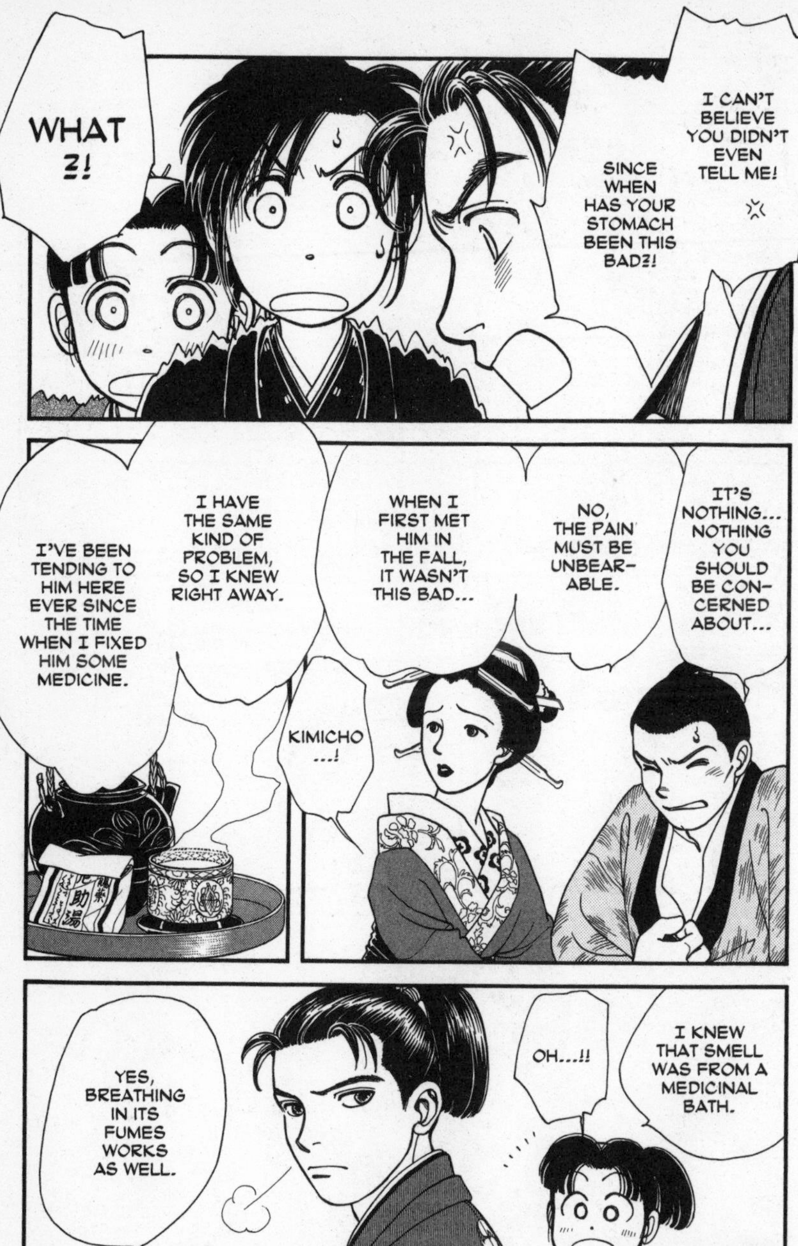
I CAN'T BELIEVE YOU DIDN'T EVEN TELL ME!
SINCE WHEN HAS YOUR STOMACH BEEN THIS BAD?!
WHAT ?!
IT'S NOTHING... NOTHING YOU SHOULD BE CONCERNED ABOUT...
NO, THE PAIN MUST BE UNBEARABLE.
WHEN I FIRST MET HIM IN THE FALL, IT WASN'T THIS BAD...
KIMICHO ...!
I HAVE THE SAME KIND OF PROBLEM, SO I KNEW RIGHT AWAY.
I'VE BEEN TENDING TO HIM HERE EVER SINCE THE TIME WHEN I FIXED HIM SOME MEDICINE.
I KNEW THAT SMELL WAS FROM A MEDICINAL BATH.
OH...!!
YES, BREATHING IN ITS FUMES WORKS AS WELL.

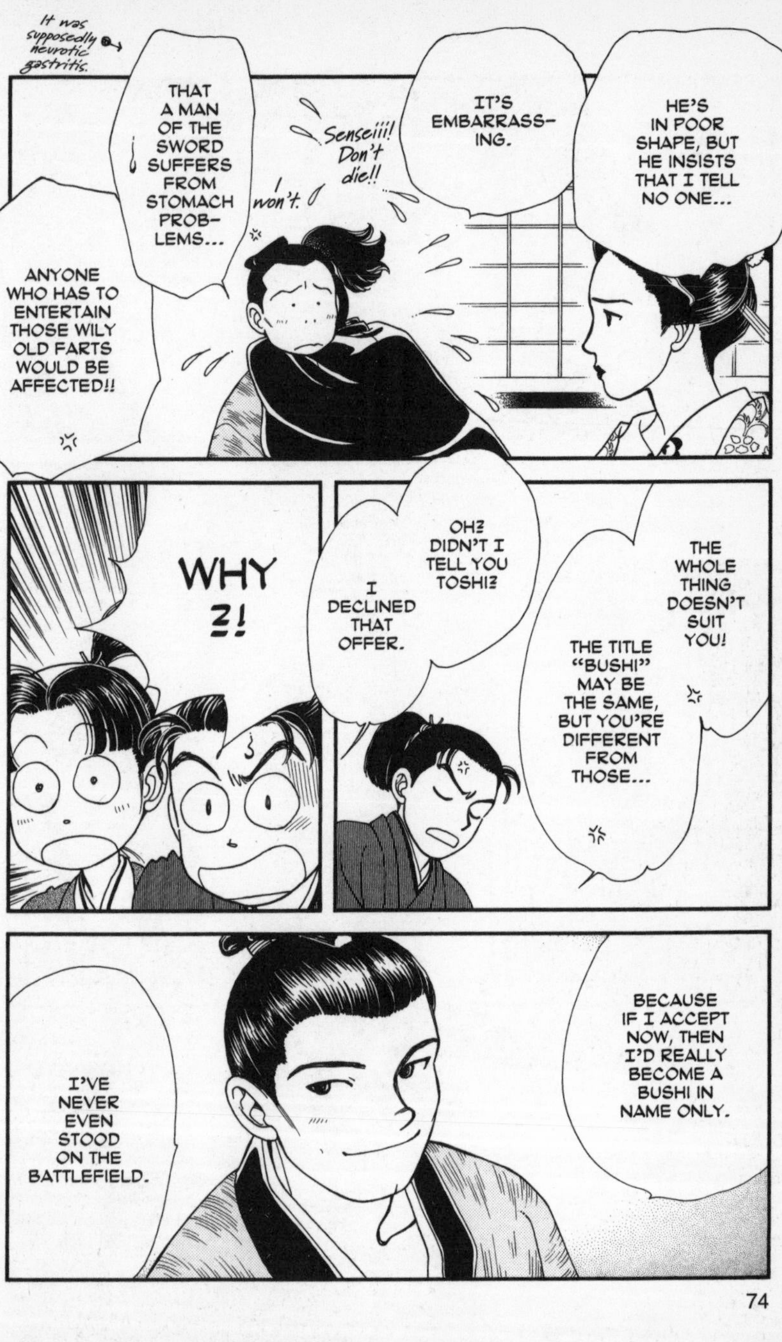
HE'S IN POOR SHAPE, BUT HE INSISTS THAT I TELL NO ONE...
IT'S EMBARRASS-ING.
Senseiii! Don't die!!
I won't.
THAT A MAN OF THE SWORD SUFFERS FROM STOMACH PROB-LEMS...
ANYONE WHO HAS TO ENTERTAIN THOSE WILY OLD FARTS WOULD BE AFFECTED!!
It was supposedly neurotic gastritis.
THE WHOLE THING DOESN'T SUIT YOU!
THE TITLE "BUSHI" MAY BE THE SAME, BUT YOU'RE DIFFERENT FROM THOSE...
OH? DIDN'T I TELL YOU TOSHI?
I DECLINED THAT OFFER.
WHY ?!
BECAUSE IF I ACCEPT NOW, THEN I'D REALLY BECOME A BUSHI IN NAME ONLY.
I'VE NEVER EVEN STOOD ON THE BATTLEFIELD.

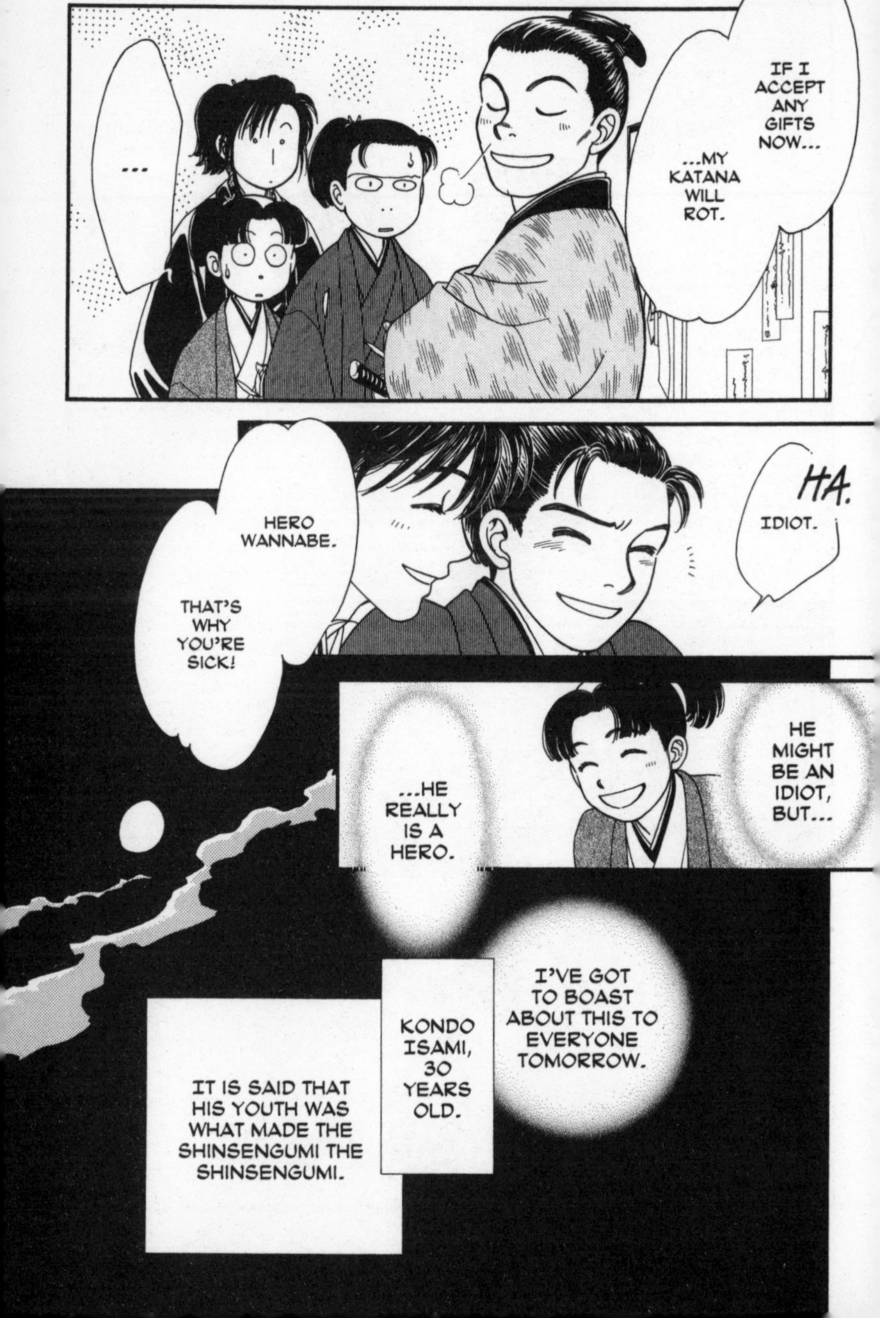
IF I ACCEPT ANY GIFTS NOW...
...MY KATANA WILL ROT.
...
HA.
IDIOT.
HERO WANNABE.
THAT'S WHY YOU'RE SICK!
HE MIGHT BE AN IDIOT, BUT...
...HE REALLY IS A HERO.
I'VE GOT TO BOAST ABOUT THIS TO EVERYONE TOMORROW.
KONDO ISAMI, 30 YEARS OLD.
IT IS SAID THAT HIS YOUTH WAS WHAT MADE THE SHINSENGUMI THE SHINSENGUMI.

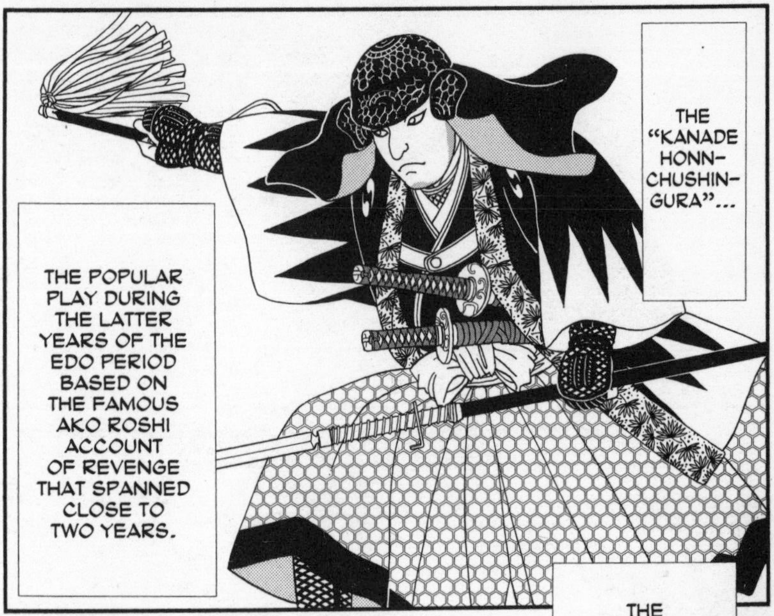

THE "KANADE HONN-CHUSHIN-GURA"...
THE POPULAR PLAY DURING THE LATTER YEARS OF THE EDO PERIOD BASED ON THE FAMOUS AKO ROSHI ACCOUNT OF REVENGE THAT SPANNED CLOSE TO TWO YEARS.

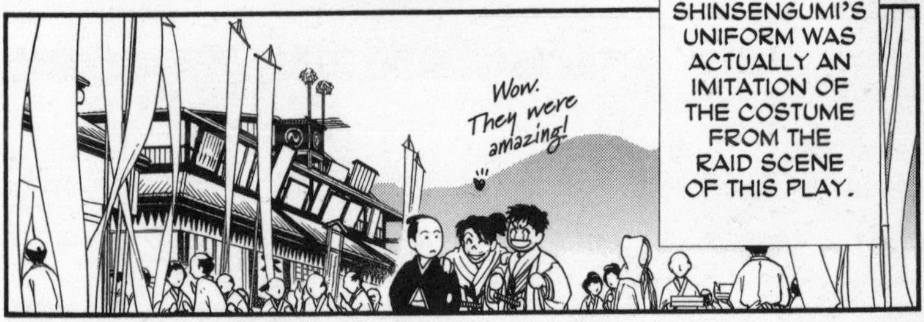

THE SHINSENGUMI'S UNIFORM WAS ACTUALLY AN IMITATION OF THE COSTUME FROM THE RAID SCENE OF THIS PLAY.
Wow. They were amazing!

KYOTO "IROHA" KARUTA GAME

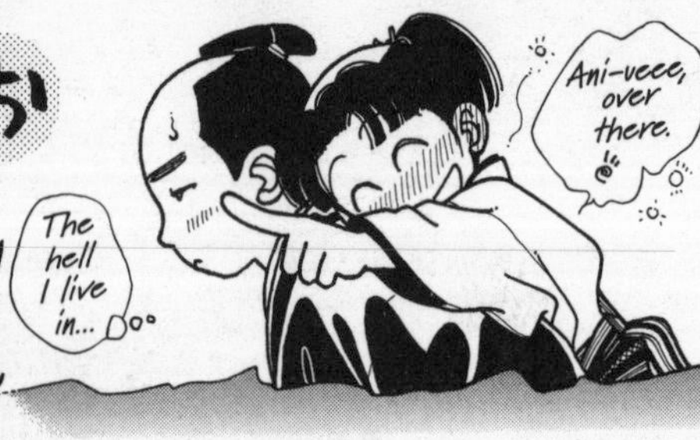

Ani-veee, over there.
The hell I live in...

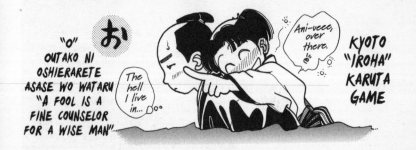

お

"O"
OUTAKO NI OSHIERARETE ASASE WO WATARU
"A FOOL IS A FINE COUNSELOR FOR A WISE MAN"

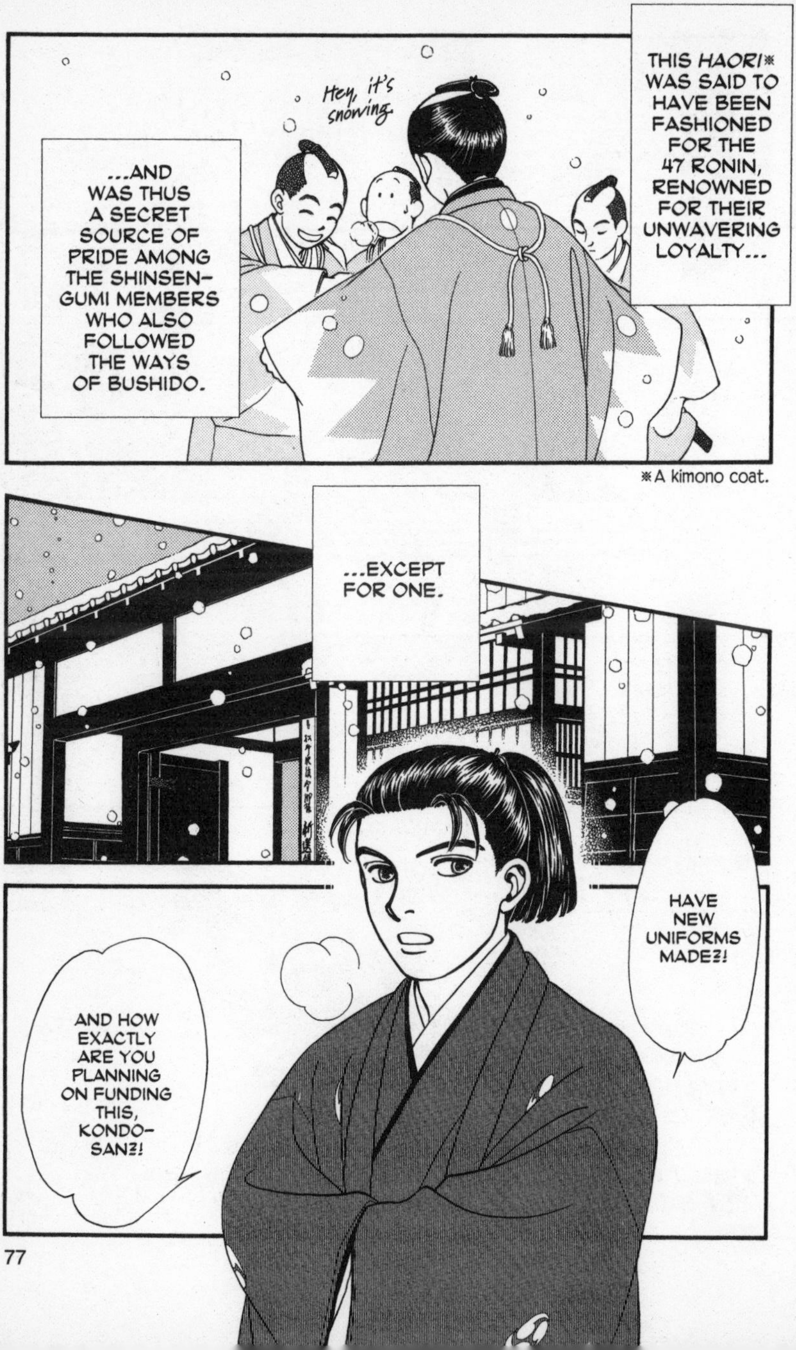
THIS HAORI※ WAS SAID TO HAVE BEEN FASHIONED FOR THE 47 RONIN, RENOWNED FOR THEIR UNWAVERING LOYALTY...
Hey, it's snowing.
...AND WAS THUS A SECRET SOURCE OF PRIDE AMONG THE SHINSEN-GUMI MEMBERS WHO ALSO FOLLOWED THE WAYS OF BUSHIDO.
...EXCEPT FOR ONE.
HAVE NEW UNIFORMS MADE?!
AND HOW EXACTLY ARE YOU PLANNING ON FUNDING THIS, KONDO-SAN?!

※A kimono coat.

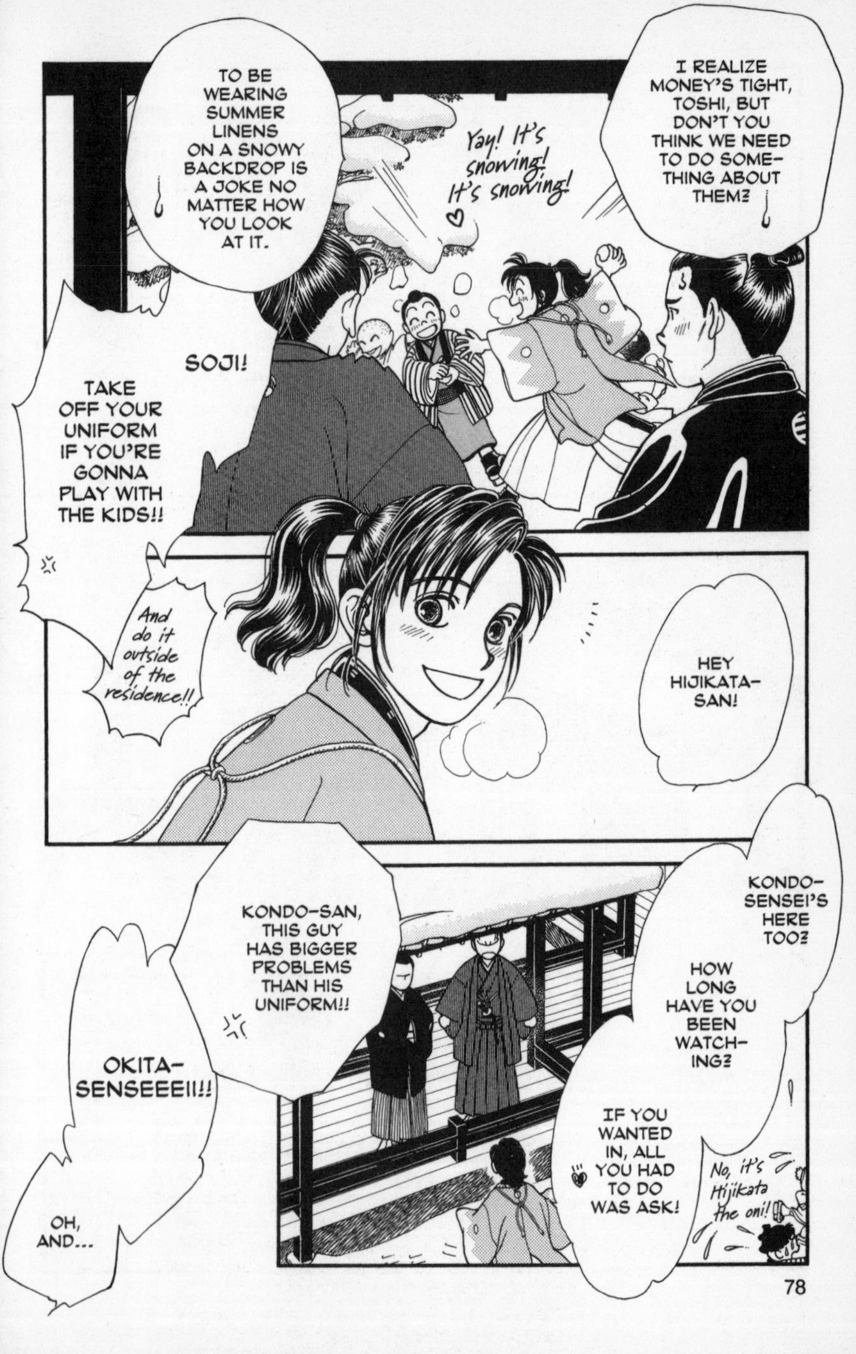
I REALIZE MONEY'S TIGHT, TOSHI, BUT DON'T YOU THINK WE NEED TO DO SOME-THING ABOUT THEM?
Yay! It's snowing! It's snowing!
TO BE WEARING SUMMER LINENS ON A SNOWY BACKDROP IS A JOKE NO MATTER HOW YOU LOOK AT IT.
SOJI!
TAKE OFF YOUR UNIFORM IF YOU'RE GONNA PLAY WITH THE KIDS!!
And do it outside of the residence!!
HEY HIJIKATA-SAN!
KONDO-SENSEI'S HERE TOO?
HOW LONG HAVE YOU BEEN WATCH-ING?
IF YOU WANTED IN, ALL YOU HAD TO DO WAS ASK!
No, it's Hijikata the oni!
KONDO-SAN, THIS GUY HAS BIGGER PROBLEMS THAN HIS UNIFORM!!
OKITA-SENSEEE!!!
OH, AND...

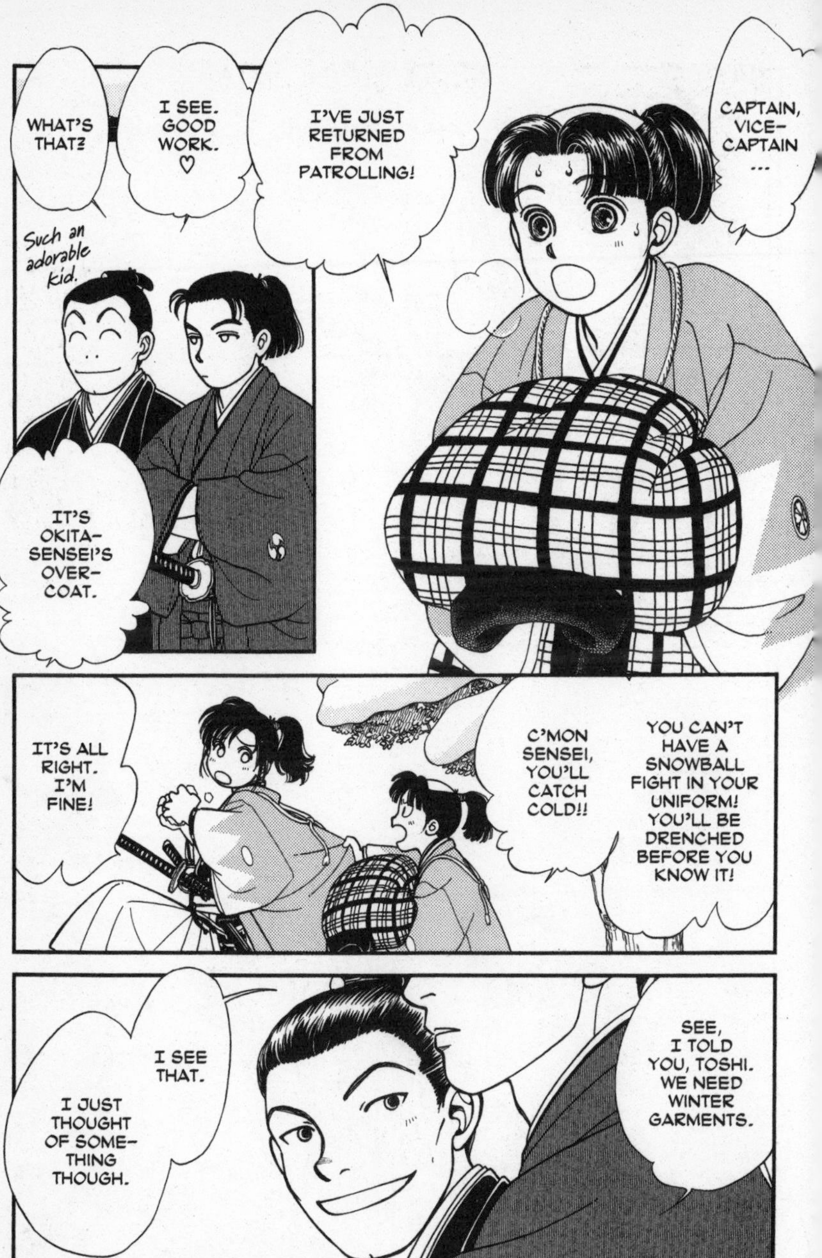
CAPTAIN, VICE-CAPTAIN ...
I'VE JUST RETURNED FROM PATROLLING!
I SEE. GOOD WORK. ♡
WHAT'S THAT?
Such an adorable kid.
IT'S OKITA-SENSEI'S OVERCOAT.
YOU CAN'T HAVE A SNOWBALL FIGHT IN YOUR UNIFORM! YOU'LL BE DRENCHED BEFORE YOU KNOW IT!
C'MON SENSEI, YOU'LL CATCH COLD!!
IT'S ALL RIGHT. I'M FINE!
SEE, I TOLD YOU, TOSHI. WE NEED WINTER GARMENTS.
I SEE THAT.
I JUST THOUGHT OF SOMETHING THOUGH.

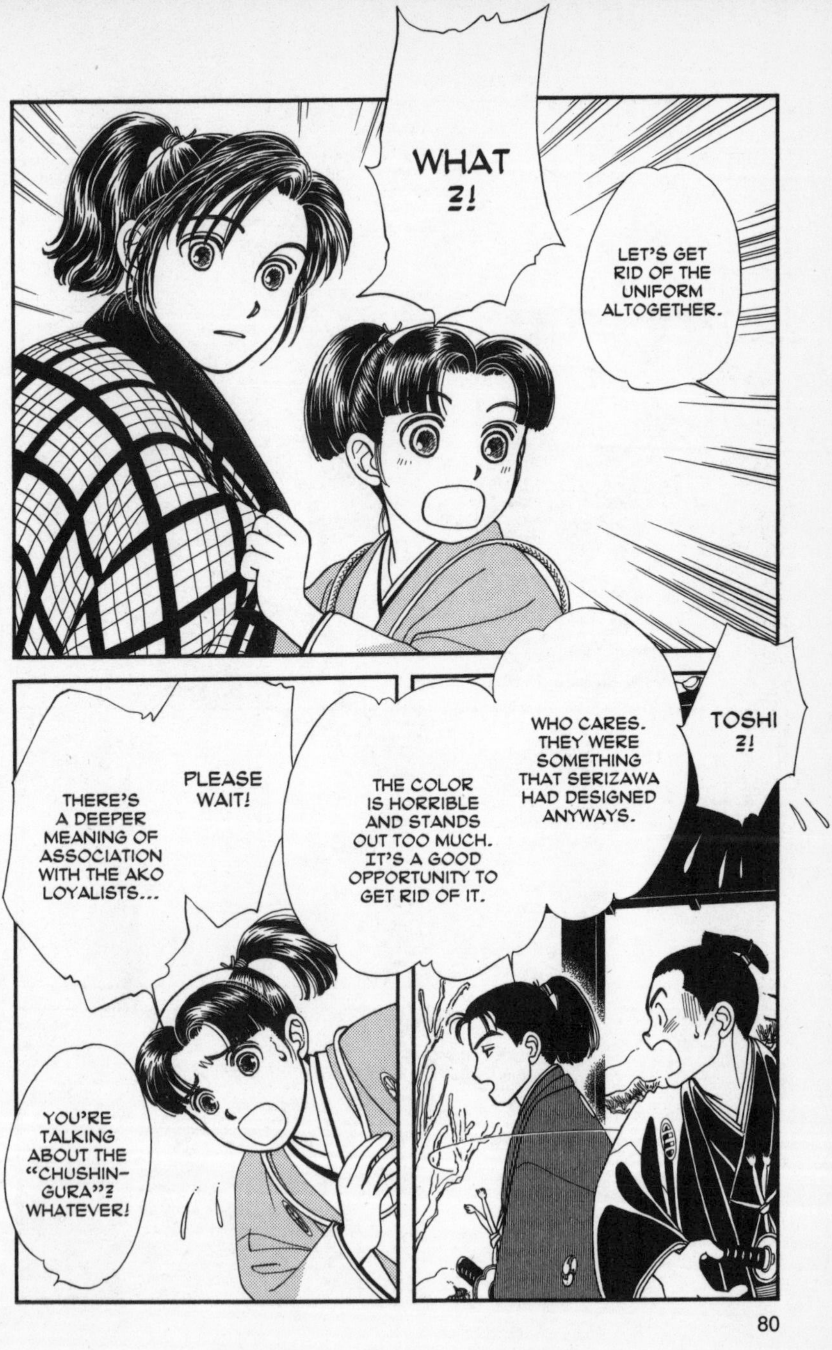
LET'S GET RID OF THE UNIFORM ALTOGETHER.
WHAT?!
TOSHI?!
WHO CARES. THEY WERE SOMETHING THAT SERIZAWA HAD DESIGNED ANYWAYS.
THE COLOR IS HORRIBLE AND STANDS OUT TOO MUCH. IT'S A GOOD OPPORTUNITY TO GET RID OF IT.
PLEASE WAIT!
THERE'S A DEEPER MEANING OF ASSOCIATION WITH THE AKO LOYALISTS...
YOU'RE TALKING ABOUT THE "CHUSHIN-GURA"? WHATEVER!

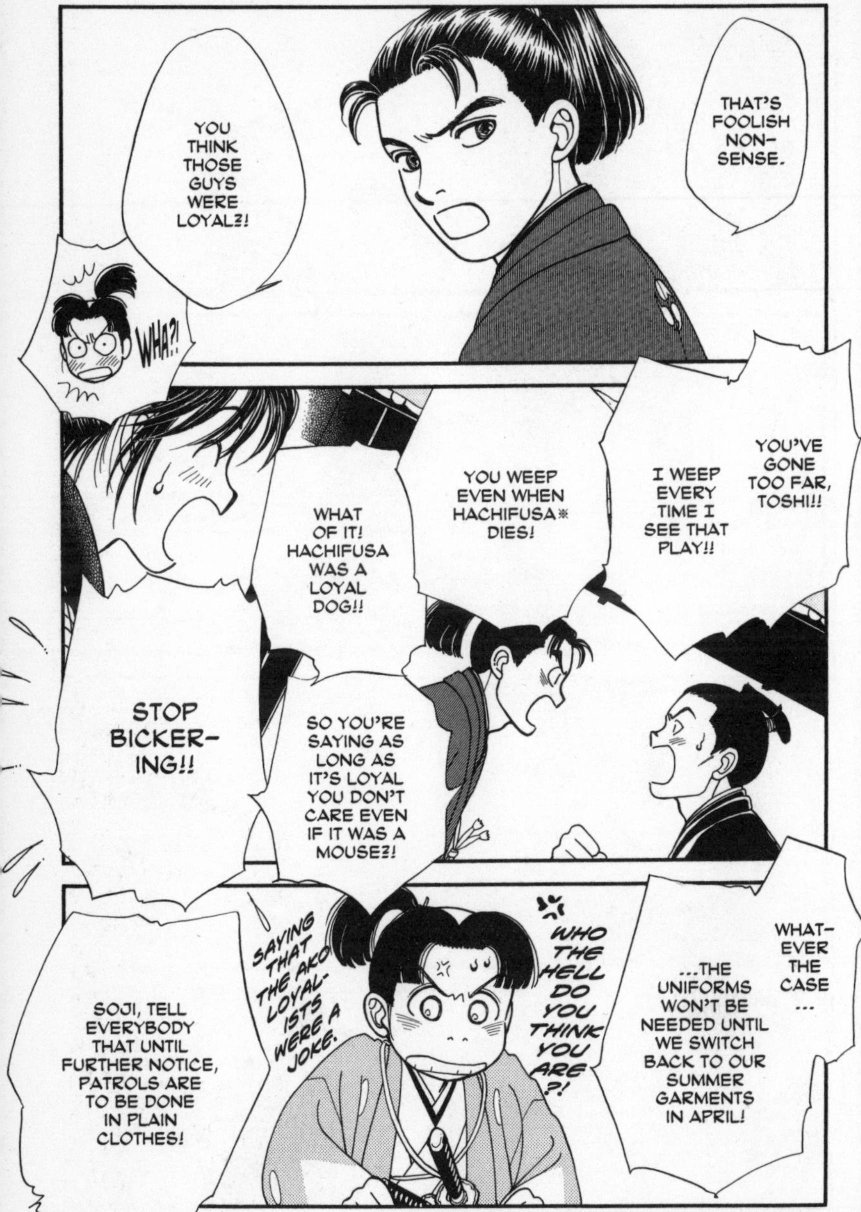
THAT'S FOOLISH NON-SENSE.
YOU THINK THOSE GUYS WERE LOYAL?!
WHA?!
YOU'VE GONE TOO FAR, TOSHI!!
I WEEP EVERY TIME I SEE THAT PLAY!!
YOU WEEP EVEN WHEN HACHIFUSA※ DIES!
WHAT OF IT! HACHIFUSA WAS A LOYAL DOG!!
SO YOU'RE SAYING AS LONG AS IT'S LOYAL YOU DON'T CARE EVEN IF IT WAS A MOUSE?!
STOP BICKER-ING!!
WHAT-EVER THE CASE ...
...THE UNIFORMS WON'T BE NEEDED UNTIL WE SWITCH BACK TO OUR SUMMER GARMENTS IN APRIL!
WHO THE HELL DO YOU THINK YOU ARE?!
SAYING THAT THE AKO LOYAL-ISTS WERE A JOKE.
SOJI, TELL EVERYBODY THAT UNTIL FURTHER NOTICE, PATROLS ARE TO BE DONE IN PLAIN CLOTHES!

※A dog that appears in Kyokutei Bakin's book, *Nansosatomi Hakenden*.

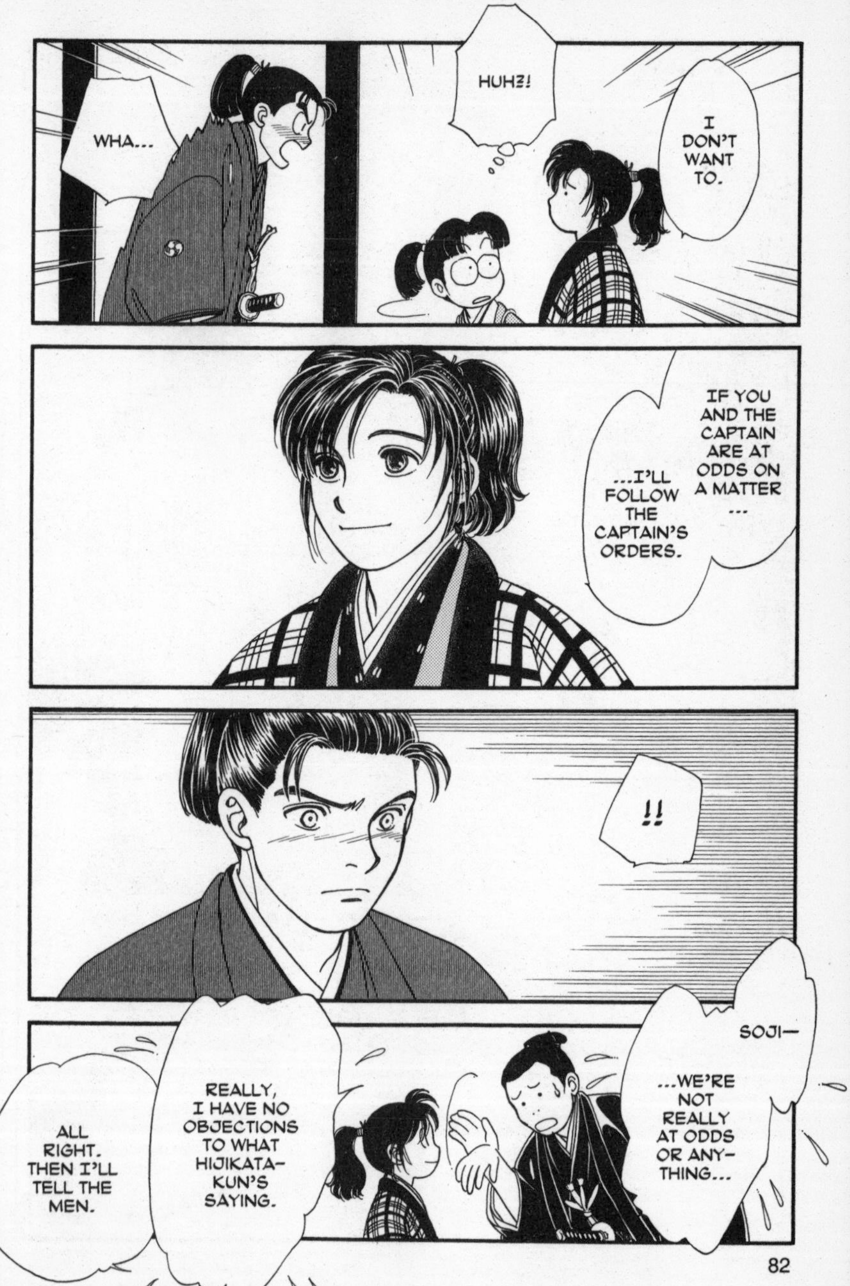
I DON'T WANT TO.
HUH?!
WHA...
IF YOU AND THE CAPTAIN ARE AT ODDS ON A MATTER...
...I'LL FOLLOW THE CAPTAIN'S ORDERS.
!!
SOJI—
...WE'RE NOT REALLY AT ODDS OR ANYTHING...
REALLY, I HAVE NO OBJECTIONS TO WHAT HIJIKATA-KUN'S SAYING.
ALL RIGHT. THEN I'LL TELL THE MEN.

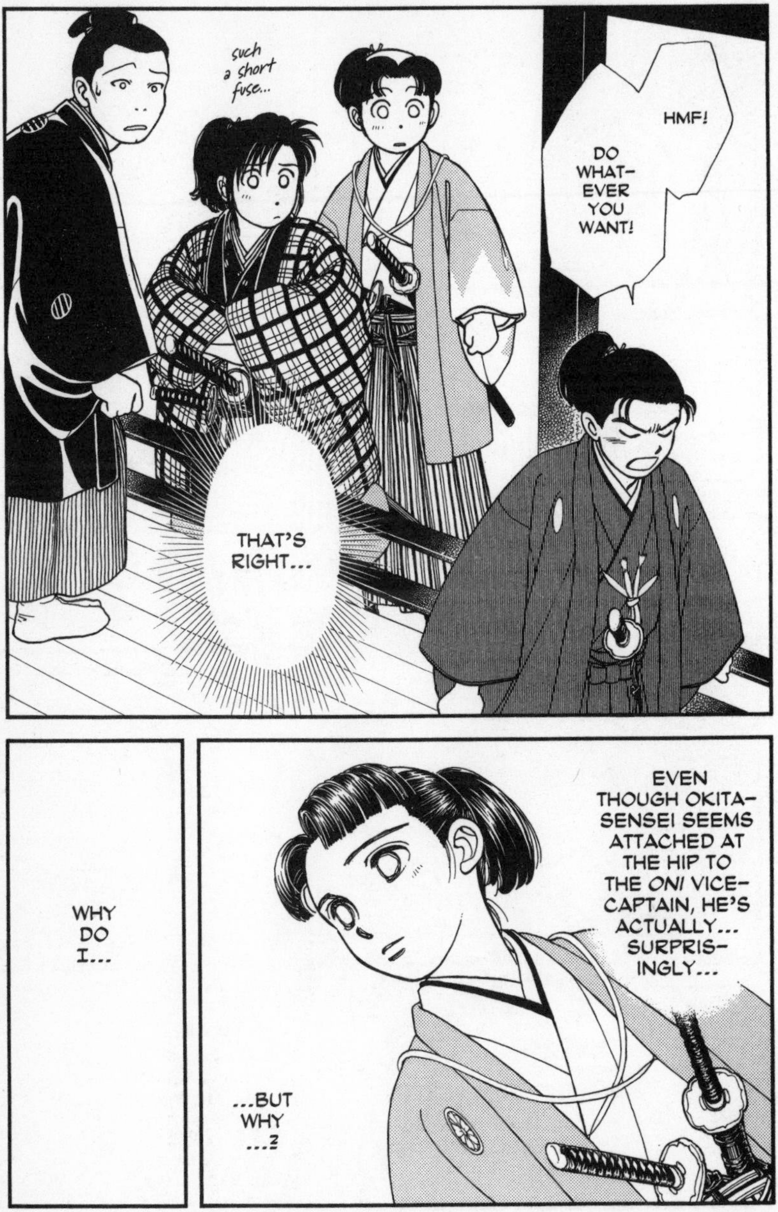
HMF!
DO WHATEVER YOU WANT!
such a short fuse...
THAT'S RIGHT...
EVEN THOUGH OKITA-SENSEI SEEMS ATTACHED AT THE HIP TO THE *ONI* VICE-CAPTAIN, HE'S ACTUALLY... SURPRISINGLY...
...BUT WHY ...?
WHY DO I...

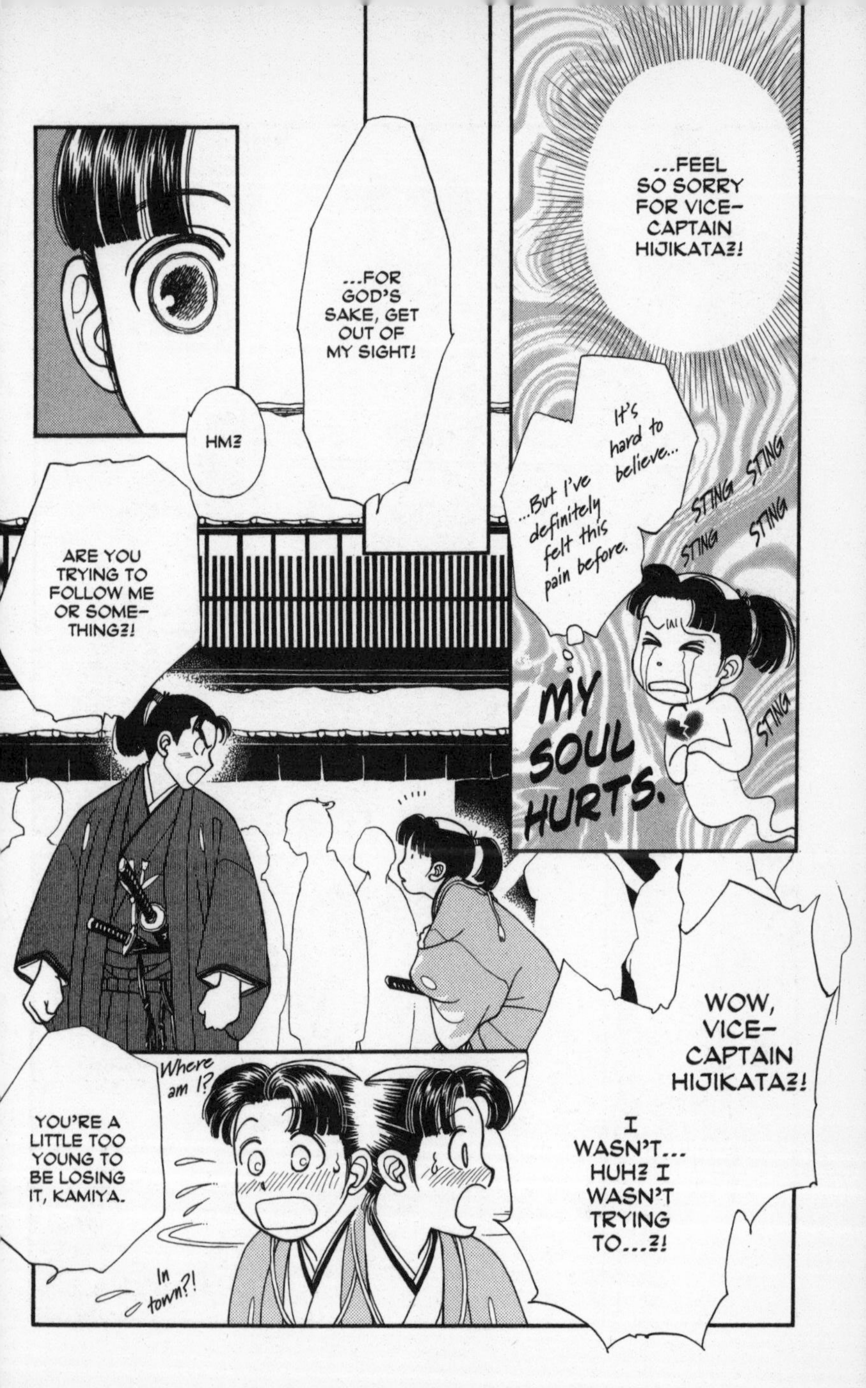
...FEEL SO SORRY FOR VICE-CAPTAIN HIJIKATA?!
It's hard to believe...
...But I've definitely felt this pain before.
STING STING STING STING STING
MY SOUL HURTS.
...FOR GOD'S SAKE, GET OUT OF MY SIGHT!
HM?
ARE YOU TRYING TO FOLLOW ME OR SOME-THING?!
WOW, VICE-CAPTAIN HIJIKATA?!
I WASN'T... HUH? I WASN'T TRYING TO...?!
Where am I?
In town?!
YOU'RE A LITTLE TOO YOUNG TO BE LOSING IT, KAMIYA.

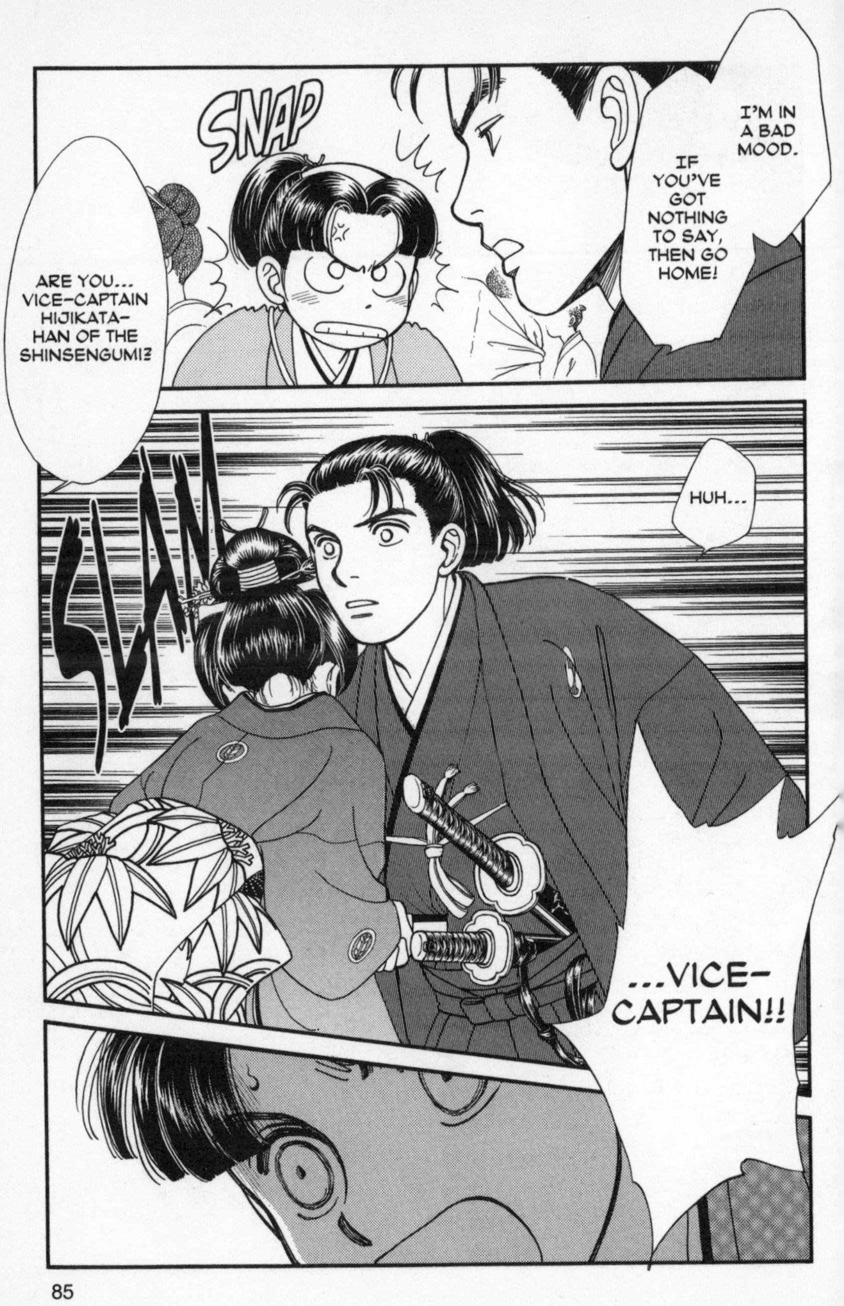
I'M IN A BAD MOOD.
IF YOU'VE GOT NOTHING TO SAY, THEN GO HOME!
SNAP
ARE YOU... VICE-CAPTAIN HIJIKATA-HAN OF THE SHINSENGUMI!?
HUH...
SLAM
...VICE-CAPTAIN!!

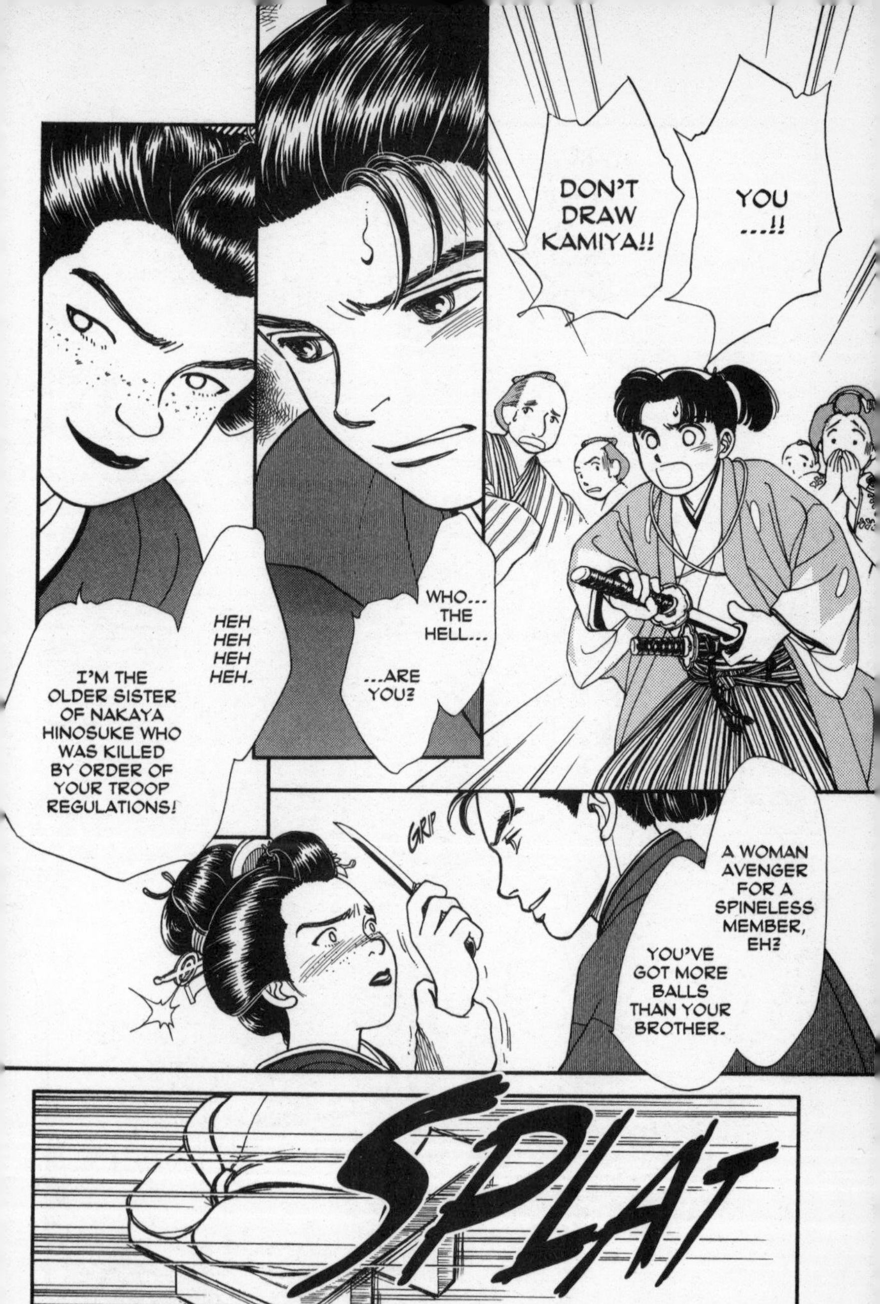
YOU ...!!
DON'T DRAW KAMIYA!!
WHO... THE HELL...
...ARE YOU?
HEH HEH HEH HEH.
I'M THE OLDER SISTER OF NAKAYA HINOSUKE WHO WAS KILLED BY ORDER OF YOUR TROOP REGULATIONS!
A WOMAN AVENGER FOR A SPINELESS MEMBER, EH?
YOU'VE GOT MORE BALLS THAN YOUR BROTHER.
GRIP
SPLAT

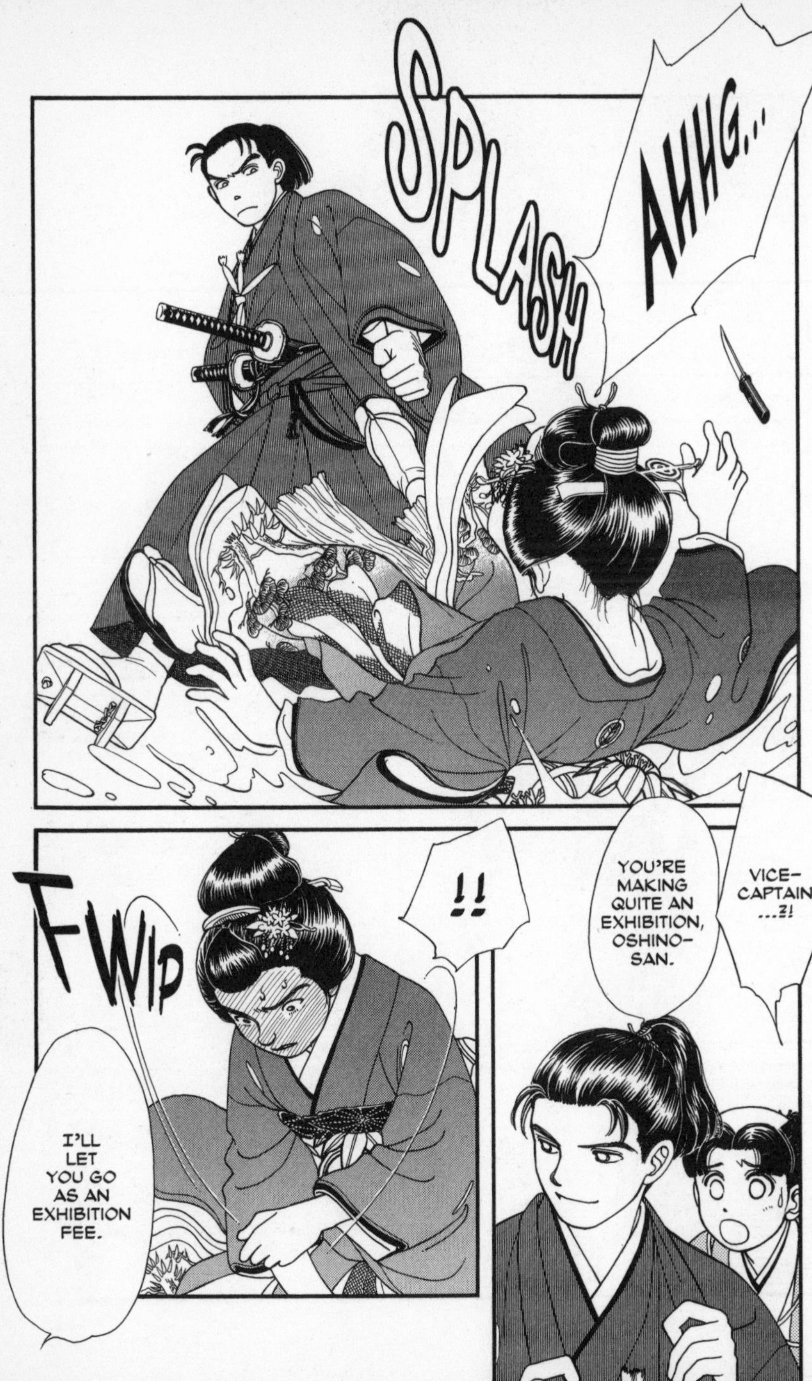
AHHG...
SPLASH
VICE-CAPTAIN ...?!
YOU'RE MAKING QUITE AN EXHIBITION, OSHINO-SAN.
!!
FWIP
I'LL LET YOU GO AS AN EXHIBITION FEE.

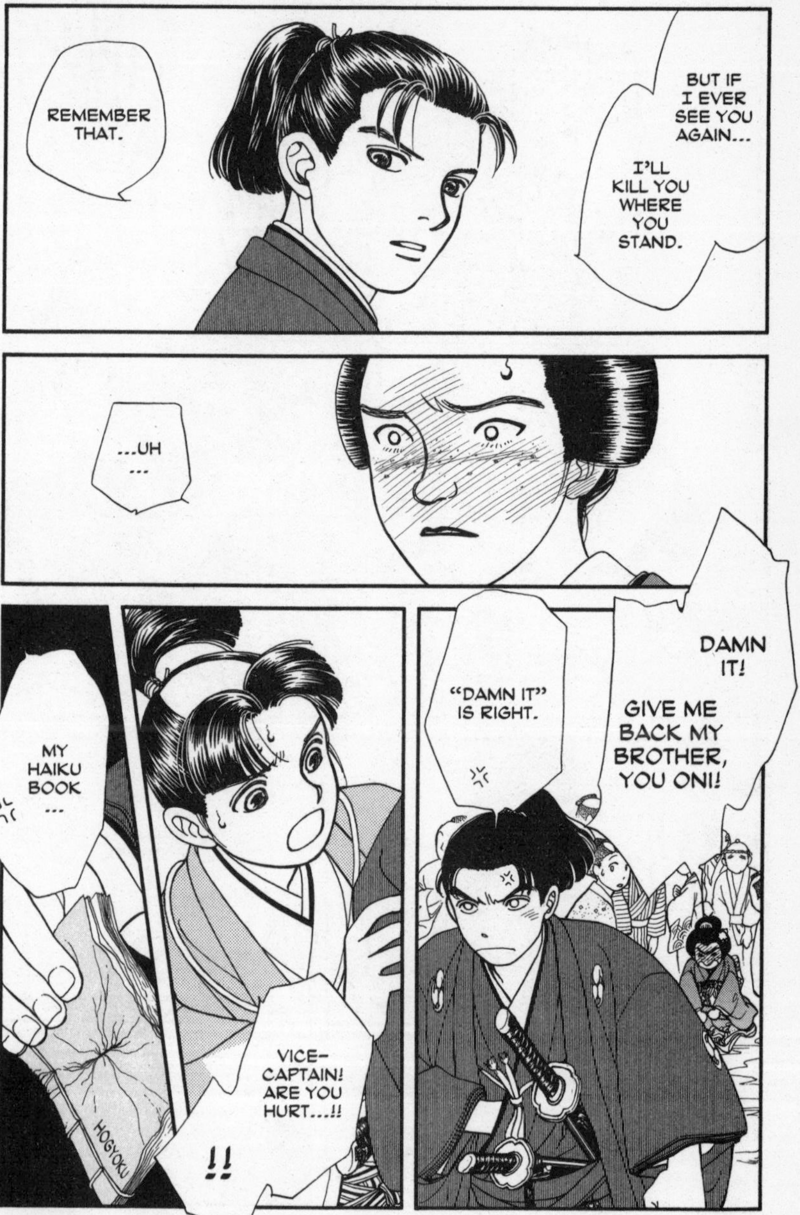
BUT IF I EVER SEE YOU AGAIN...
I'LL KILL YOU WHERE YOU STAND.
REMEMBER THAT.
...UH ...
DAMN IT!
GIVE ME BACK MY BROTHER, YOU ONI!
"DAMN IT" IS RIGHT.
VICE-CAPTAIN! ARE YOU HURT...!!
!!
MY HAIKU BOOK ...
HOGYOKU

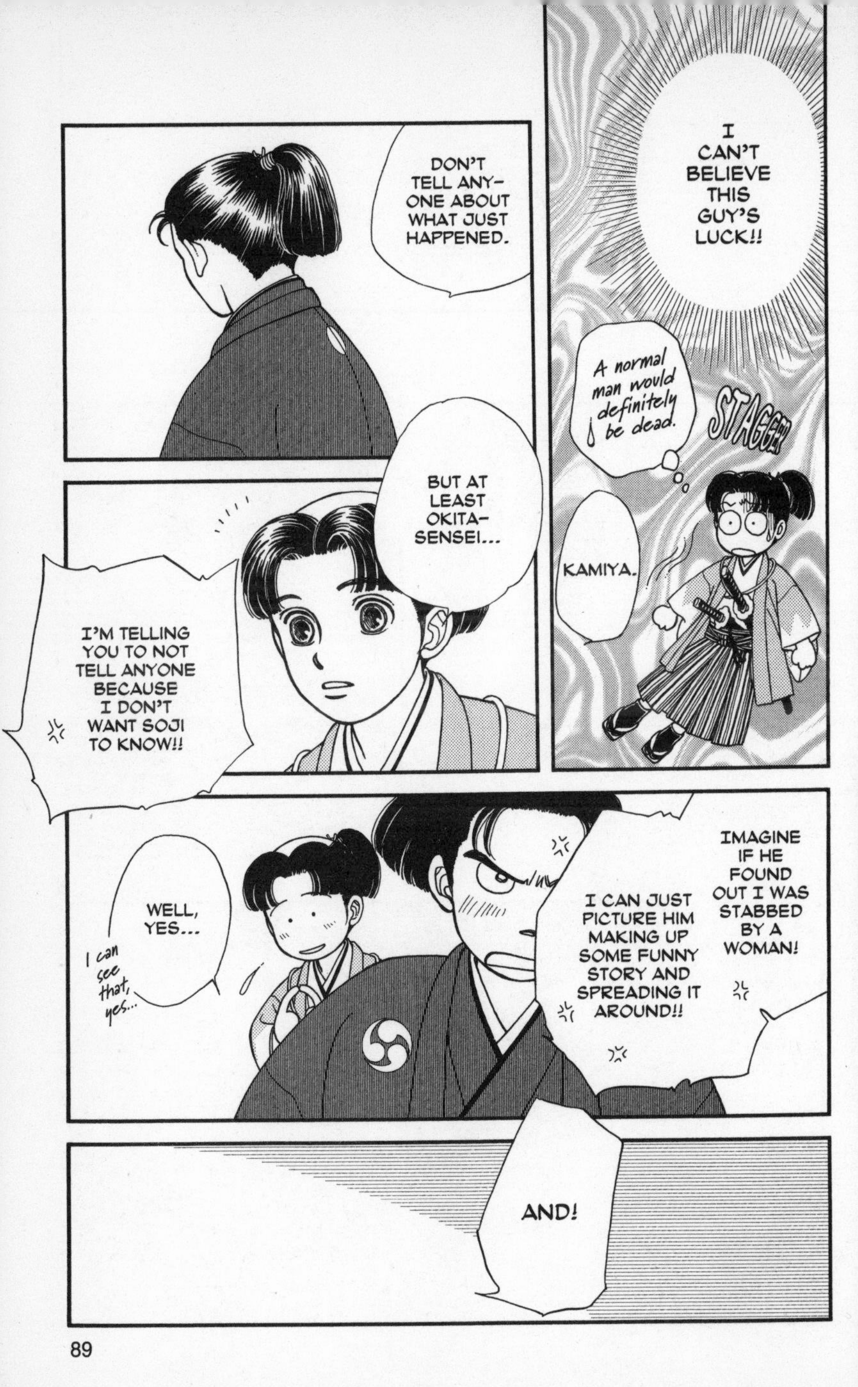
I CAN'T BELIEVE THIS GUY'S LUCK!!
A normal man would definitely be dead.
STAGGER
KAMIYA.
DON'T TELL ANYONE ABOUT WHAT JUST HAPPENED.
BUT AT LEAST OKITA-SENSEI...
I'M TELLING YOU TO NOT TELL ANYONE BECAUSE I DON'T WANT SOJI TO KNOW!!
IMAGINE IF HE FOUND OUT I WAS STABBED BY A WOMAN!
I CAN JUST PICTURE HIM MAKING UP SOME FUNNY STORY AND SPREADING IT AROUND!!
WELL, YES...
I can see that, yes...
AND!

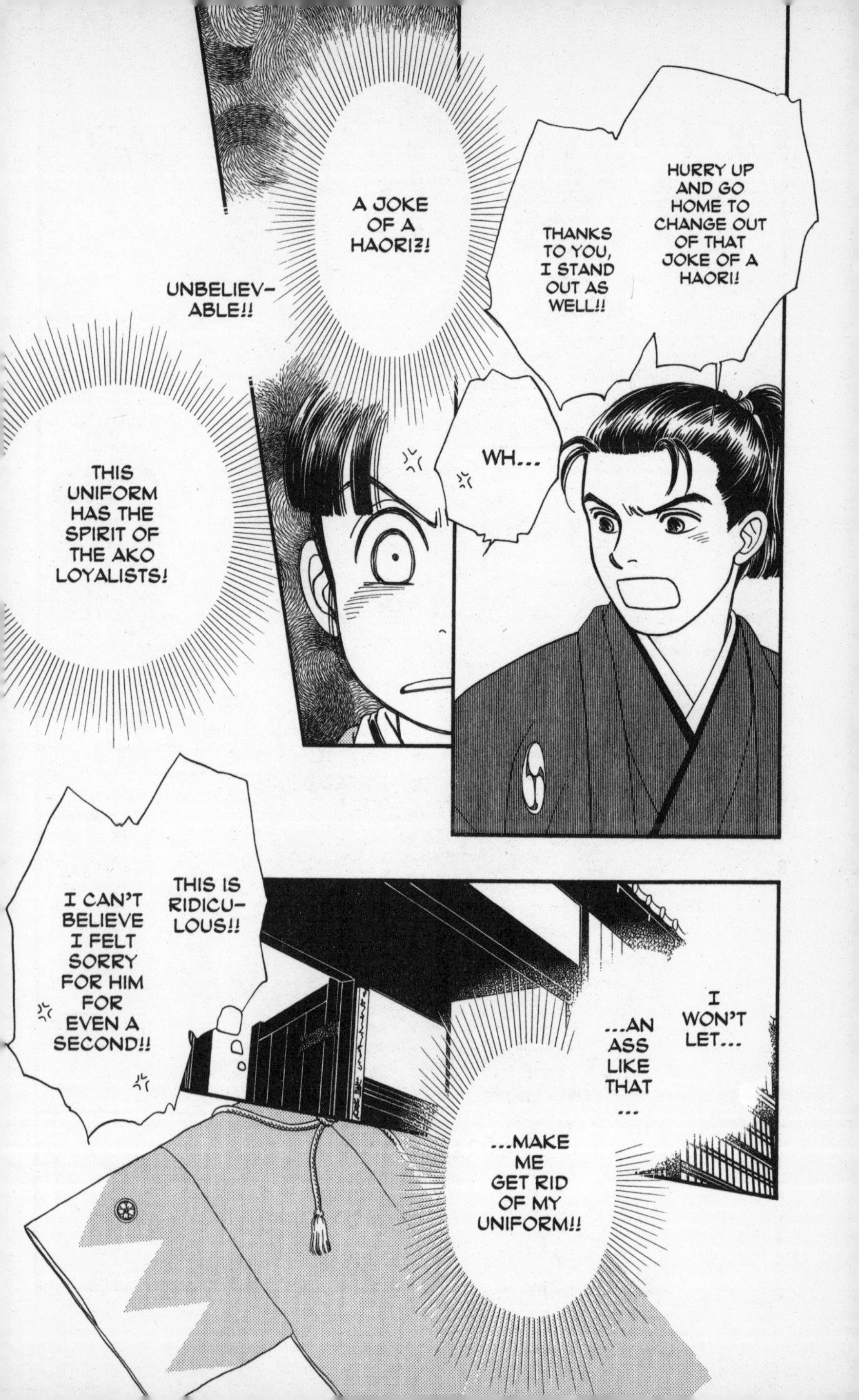
HURRY UP AND GO HOME TO CHANGE OUT OF THAT JOKE OF A HAORI!
THANKS TO YOU, I STAND OUT AS WELL!!
A JOKE OF A HAORI?!
UNBELIEV-ABLE!!
WH...
THIS UNIFORM HAS THE SPIRIT OF THE AKO LOYALISTS!
I WON'T LET...
...AN ASS LIKE THAT...
...MAKE ME GET RID OF MY UNIFORM!!
THIS IS RIDICULOUS!!
I CAN'T BELIEVE I FELT SORRY FOR HIM FOR EVEN A SECOND!!

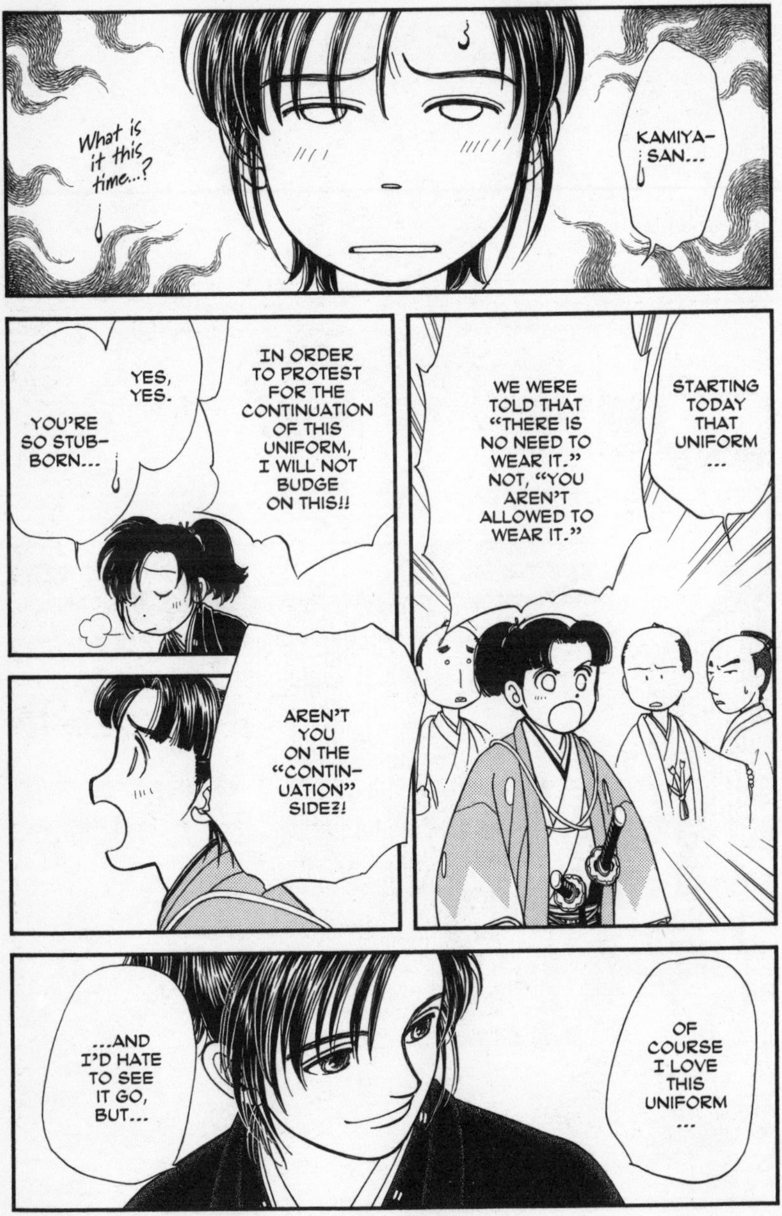
KAMIYA-SAN...
What is it this time...?
STARTING TODAY THAT UNIFORM...
WE WERE TOLD THAT "THERE IS NO NEED TO WEAR IT." NOT, "YOU AREN'T ALLOWED TO WEAR IT."
IN ORDER TO PROTEST FOR THE CONTINUATION OF THIS UNIFORM, I WILL NOT BUDGE ON THIS!!
YES, YES.
YOU'RE SO STUBBORN...
AREN'T YOU ON THE "CONTINUATION" SIDE?!
OF COURSE I LOVE THIS UNIFORM...
...AND I'D HATE TO SEE IT GO, BUT...

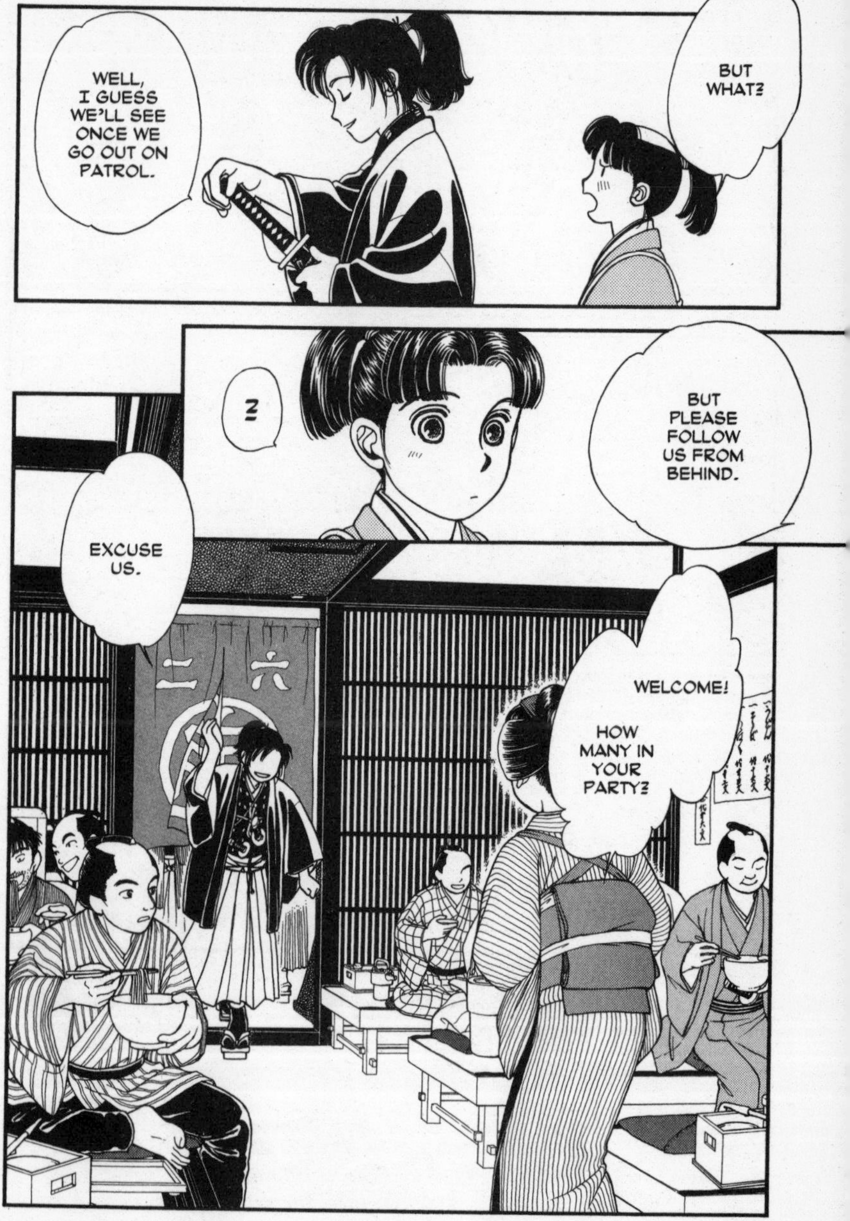
BUT WHAT?
WELL, I GUESS WE'LL SEE ONCE WE GO OUT ON PATROL.
BUT PLEASE FOLLOW US FROM BEHIND.
?!
EXCUSE US.
WELCOME!
HOW MANY IN YOUR PARTY?

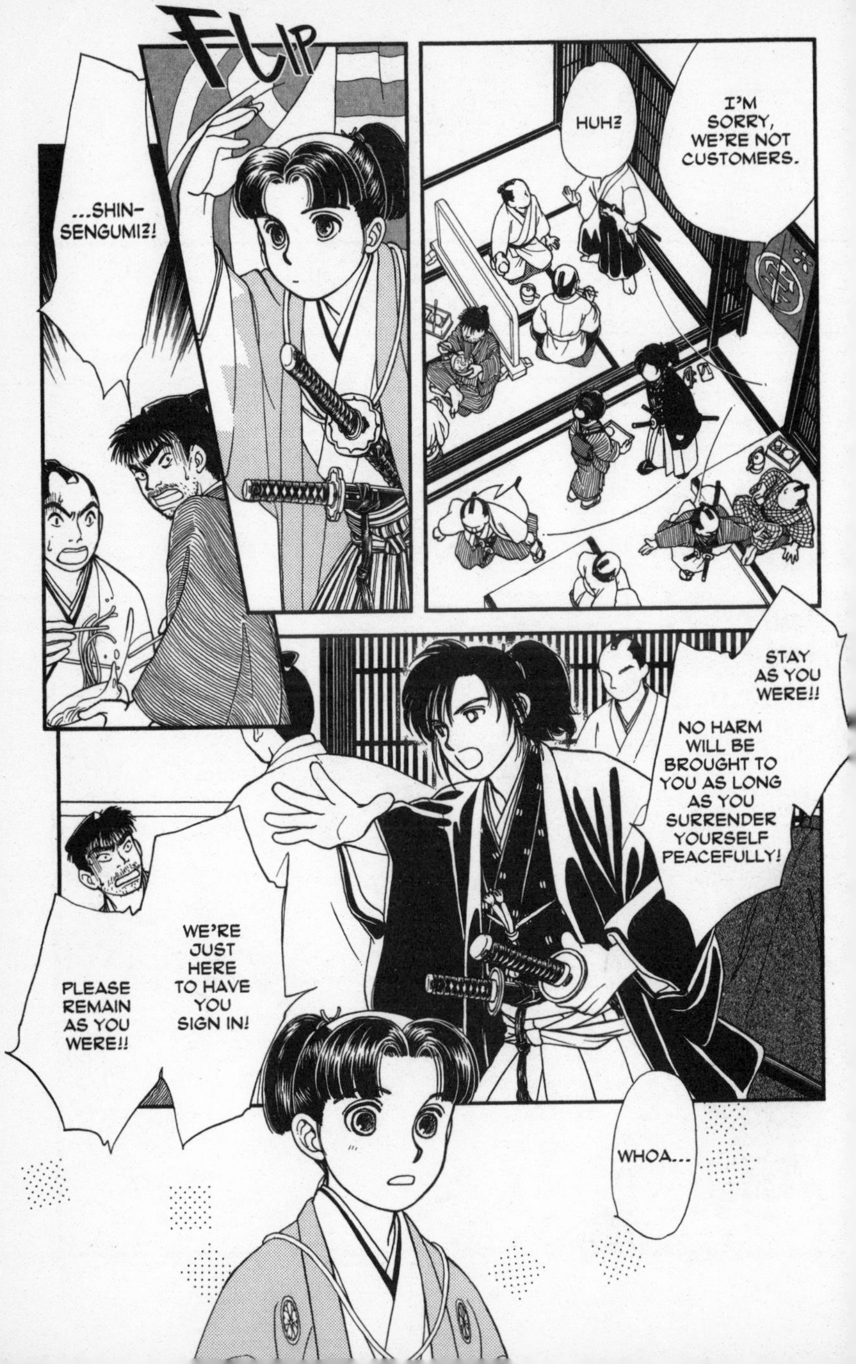
I'M SORRY, WE'RE NOT CUSTOMERS.
HUH?
FLIP
...SHIN-SENGUMI?!
STAY AS YOU WERE!!
NO HARM WILL BE BROUGHT TO YOU AS LONG AS YOU SURRENDER YOURSELF PEACEFULLY!
WE'RE JUST HERE TO HAVE YOU SIGN IN!
PLEASE REMAIN AS YOU WERE!!
WHOA...

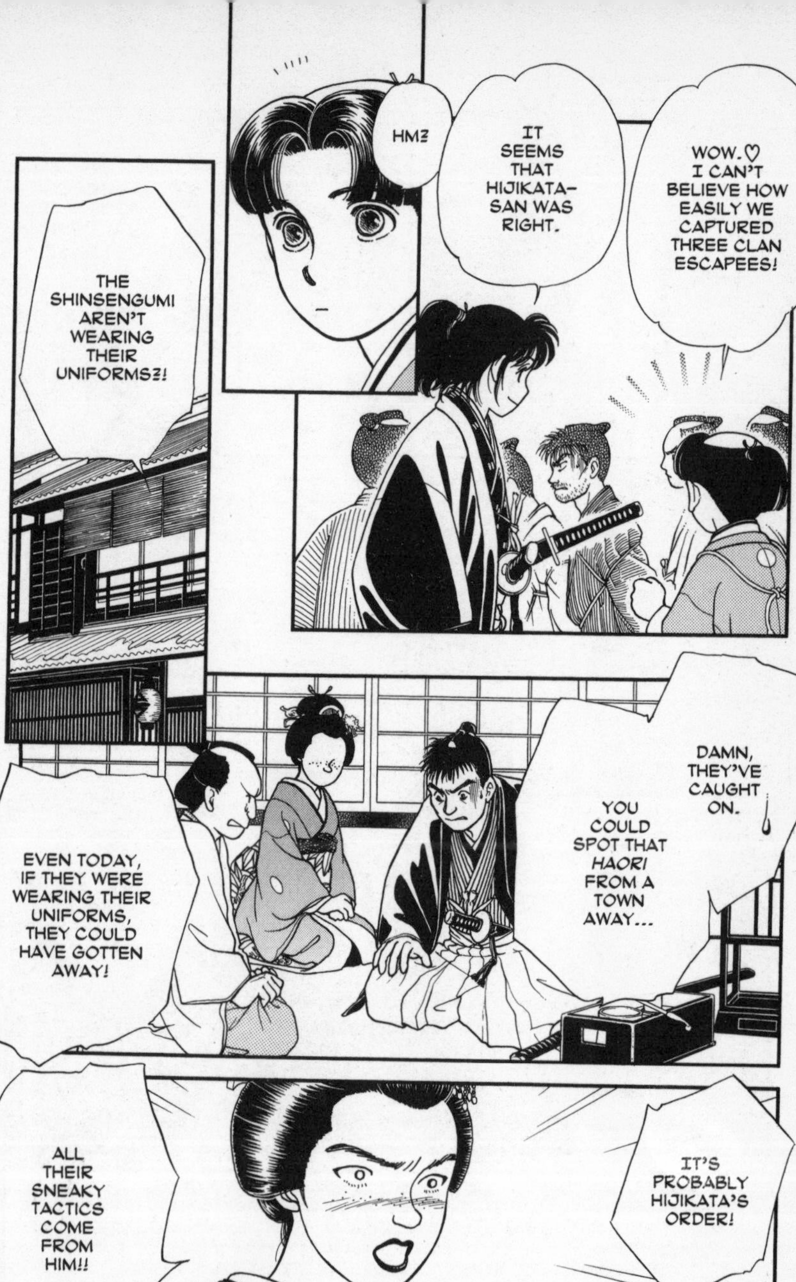
WOW. ♡ I CAN'T BELIEVE HOW EASILY WE CAPTURED THREE CLAN ESCAPEES!
IT SEEMS THAT HIJIKATA-SAN WAS RIGHT.
HM?
THE SHINSENGUMI AREN'T WEARING THEIR UNIFORMS?!
DAMN, THEY'VE CAUGHT ON.
YOU COULD SPOT THAT *HAORI* FROM A TOWN AWAY...
EVEN TODAY, IF THEY WERE WEARING THEIR UNIFORMS, THEY COULD HAVE GOTTEN AWAY!
IT'S PROBABLY HIJIKATA'S ORDER!
ALL THEIR SNEAKY TACTICS COME FROM HIM!!

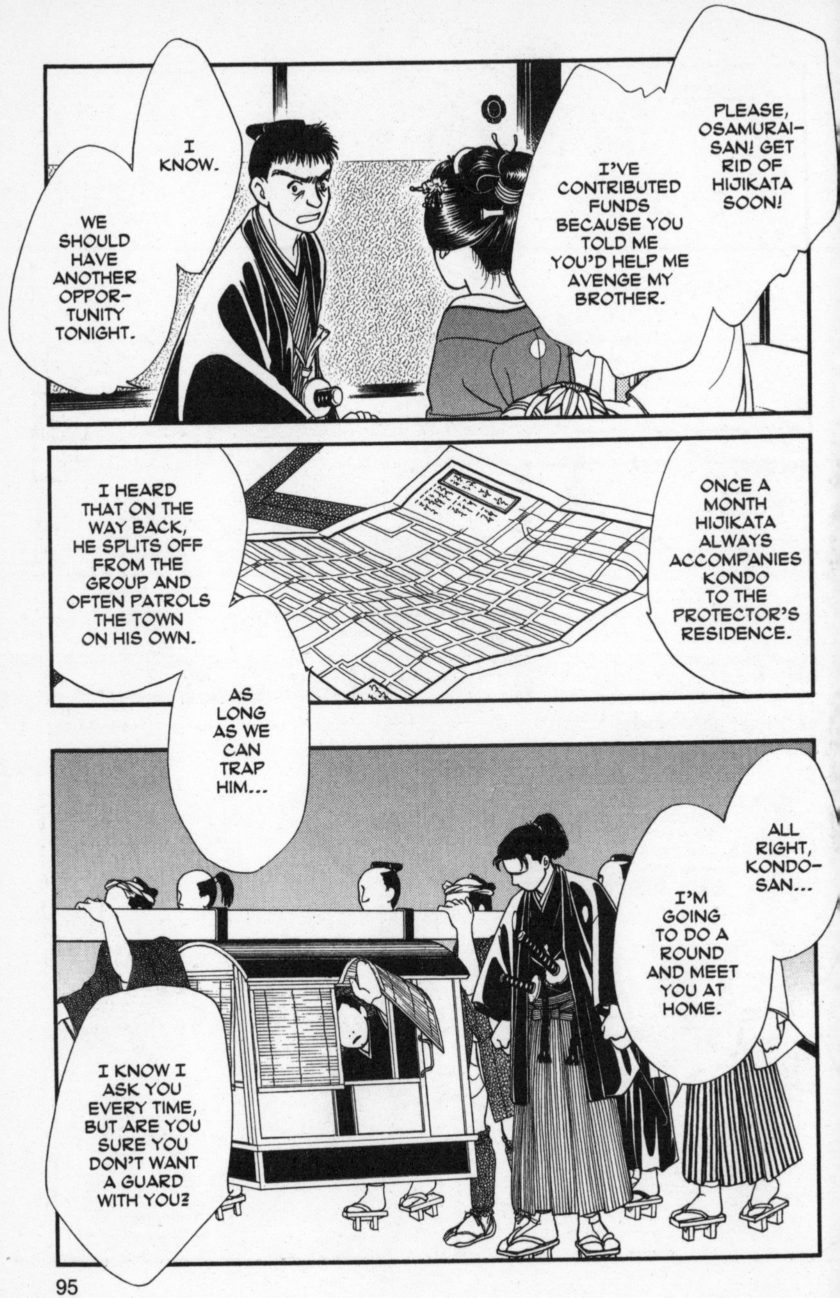
PLEASE, OSAMURAI-SAN! GET RID OF HIJIKATA SOON!
I'VE CONTRIBUTED FUNDS BECAUSE YOU TOLD ME YOU'D HELP ME AVENGE MY BROTHER.
I KNOW.
WE SHOULD HAVE ANOTHER OPPOR-TUNITY TONIGHT.
ONCE A MONTH HIJIKATA ALWAYS ACCOMPANIES KONDO TO THE PROTECTOR'S RESIDENCE.
I HEARD THAT ON THE WAY BACK, HE SPLITS OFF FROM THE GROUP AND OFTEN PATROLS THE TOWN ON HIS OWN.
AS LONG AS WE CAN TRAP HIM...
ALL RIGHT, KONDO-SAN...
I'M GOING TO DO A ROUND AND MEET YOU AT HOME.
I KNOW I ASK YOU EVERY TIME, BUT ARE YOU SURE YOU DON'T WANT A GUARD WITH YOU?

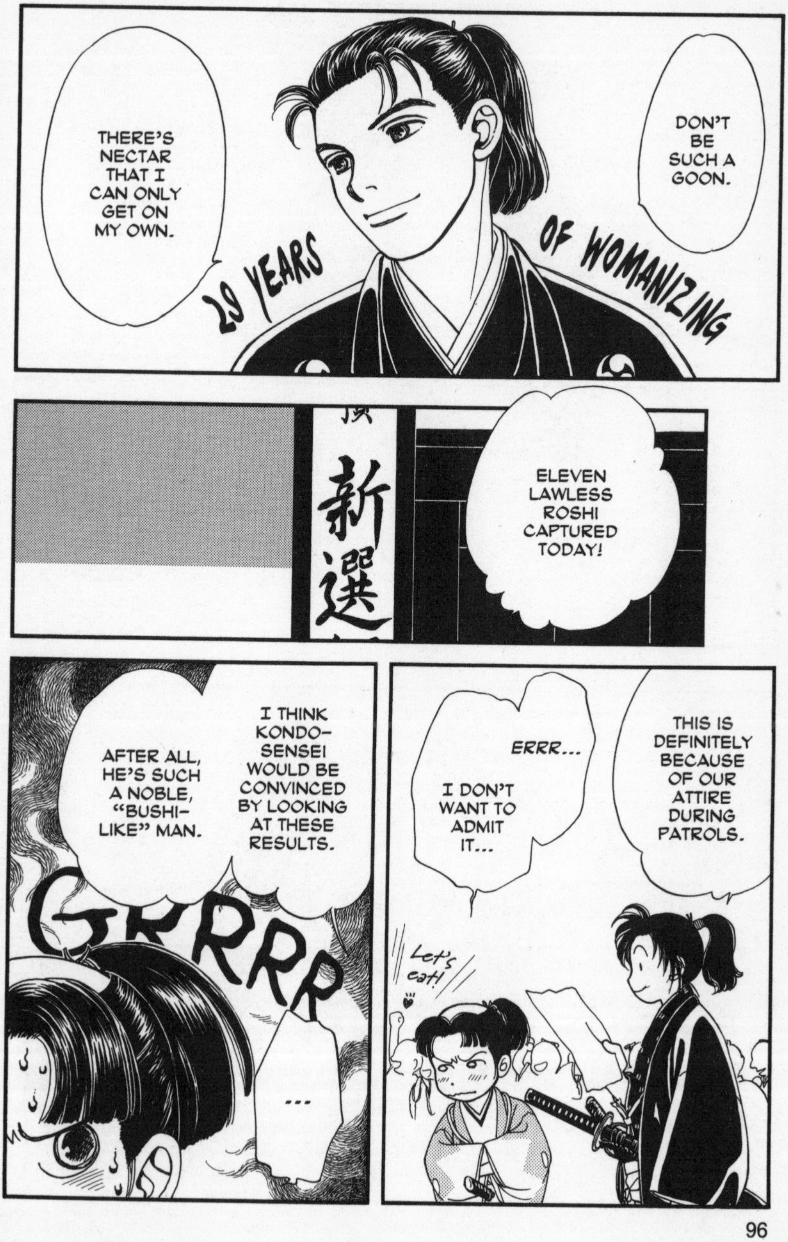
DON'T BE SUCH A GOON.
THERE'S NECTAR THAT I CAN ONLY GET ON MY OWN.
29 YEARS OF WOMANIZING
新選
ELEVEN LAWLESS ROSHI CAPTURED TODAY!
THIS IS DEFINITELY BECAUSE OF OUR ATTIRE DURING PATROLS.
ERRR...
I DON'T WANT TO ADMIT IT...
Let's eat!
I THINK KONDO-SENSEI WOULD BE CONVINCED BY LOOKING AT THESE RESULTS.
AFTER ALL, HE'S SUCH A NOBLE, "BUSHI-LIKE" MAN.
GRRRR
...

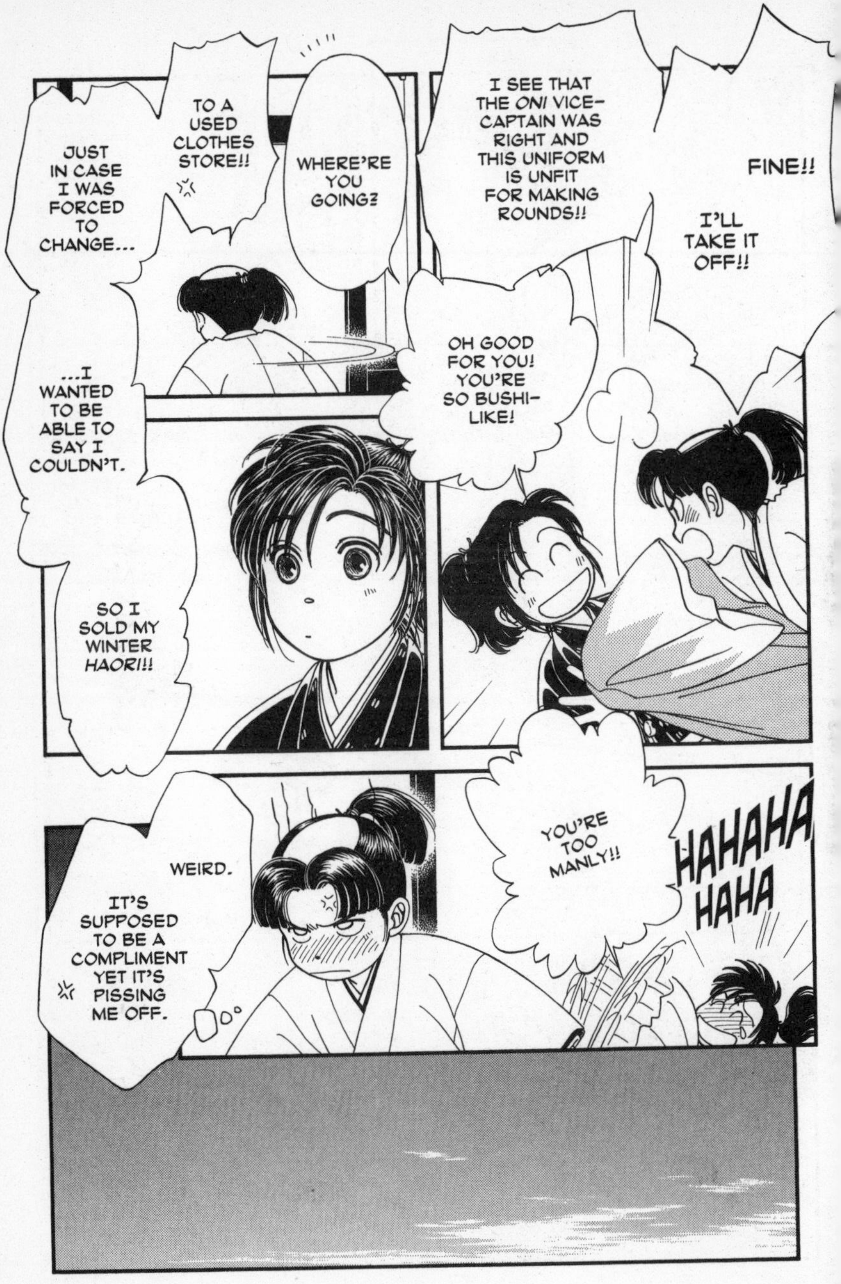
I SEE THAT THE *ONI* VICE-CAPTAIN WAS RIGHT AND THIS UNIFORM IS UNFIT FOR MAKING ROUNDS!!
FINE!! I'LL TAKE IT OFF!!
WHERE'RE YOU GOING?
TO A USED CLOTHES STORE!!
JUST IN CASE I WAS FORCED TO CHANGE...
...I WANTED TO BE ABLE TO SAY I COULDN'T.
SO I SOLD MY WINTER *HAORI*!!
OH GOOD FOR YOU! YOU'RE SO BUSHI-LIKE!
YOU'RE TOO MANLY!!
HAHAHA HAHA
WEIRD.
IT'S SUPPOSED TO BE A COMPLIMENT YET IT'S PISSING ME OFF.

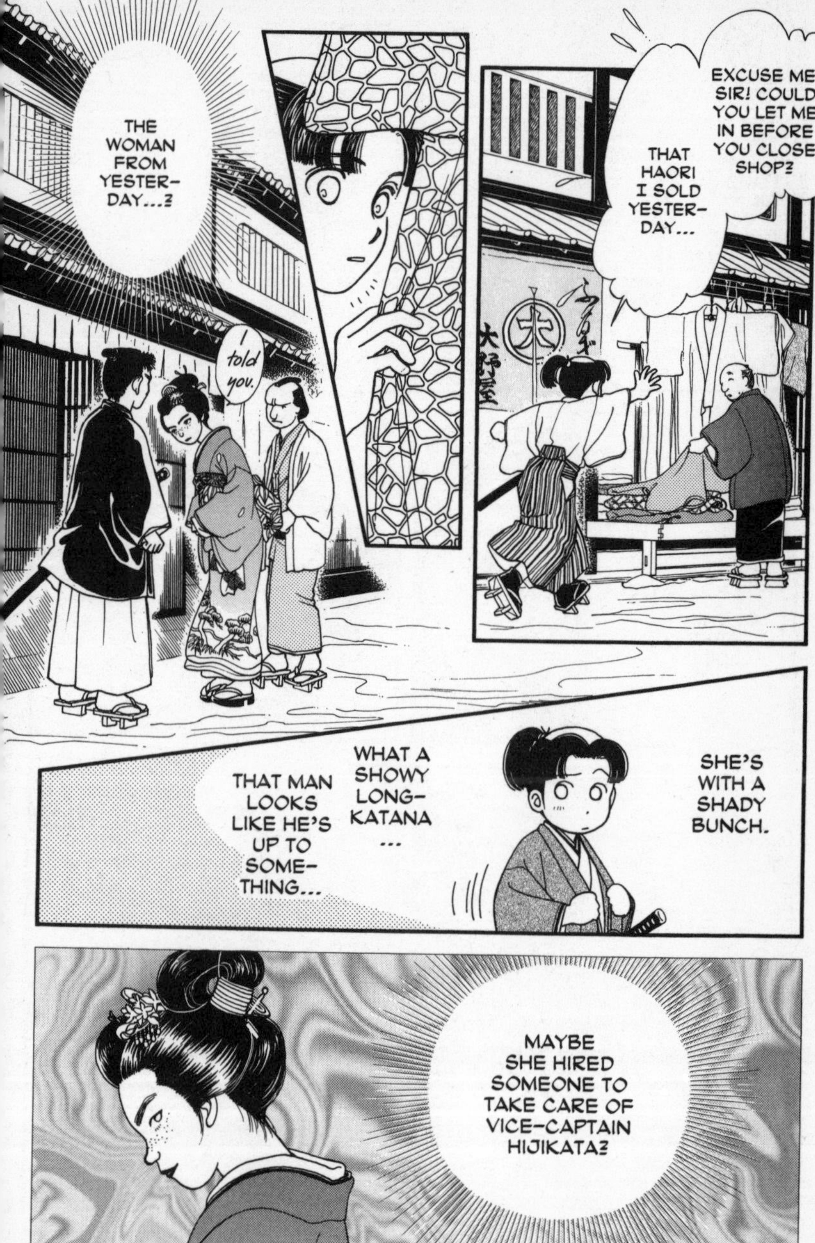

EXCUSE ME, SIR! COULD YOU LET ME IN BEFORE YOU CLOSE SHOP?
THAT HAORI I SOLD YESTERDAY...
大野屋
THE WOMAN FROM YESTERDAY...?
I told you.
SHE'S WITH A SHADY BUNCH.
WHAT A SHOWY LONG-KATANA...
THAT MAN LOOKS LIKE HE'S UP TO SOMETHING...
MAYBE SHE HIRED SOMEONE TO TAKE CARE OF VICE-CAPTAIN HIJIKATA?

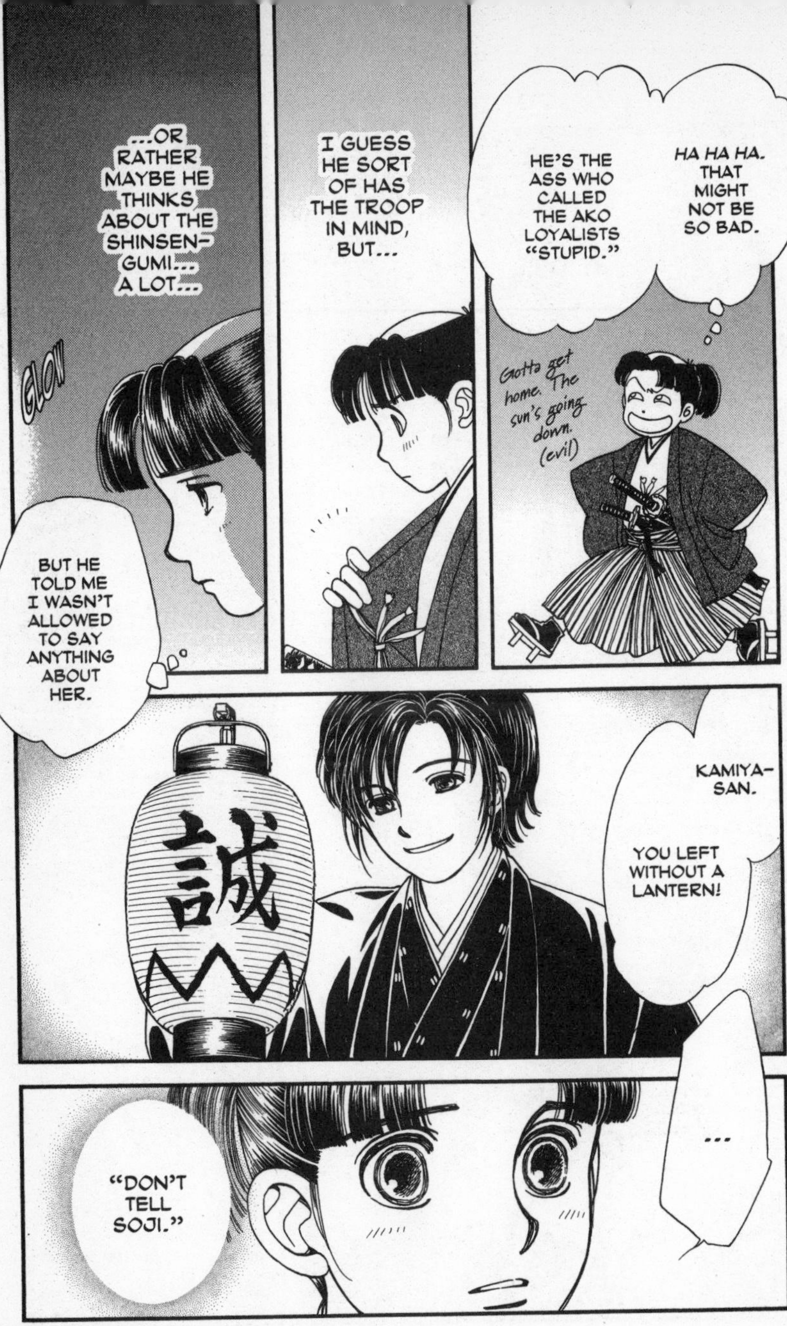
HA HA HA. THAT MIGHT NOT BE SO BAD.
HE'S THE ASS WHO CALLED THE AKO LOYALISTS "STUPID."
Gotta get home. The sun's going down. (evil)
I GUESS HE SORT OF HAS THE TROOP IN MIND, BUT...
...OR RATHER MAYBE HE THINKS ABOUT THE SHINSEN-GUMI... A LOT...
GLOW
BUT HE TOLD ME I WASN'T ALLOWED TO SAY ANYTHING ABOUT HER.
KAMIYA-SAN.
YOU LEFT WITHOUT A LANTERN!
...
"DON'T TELL SOJI."

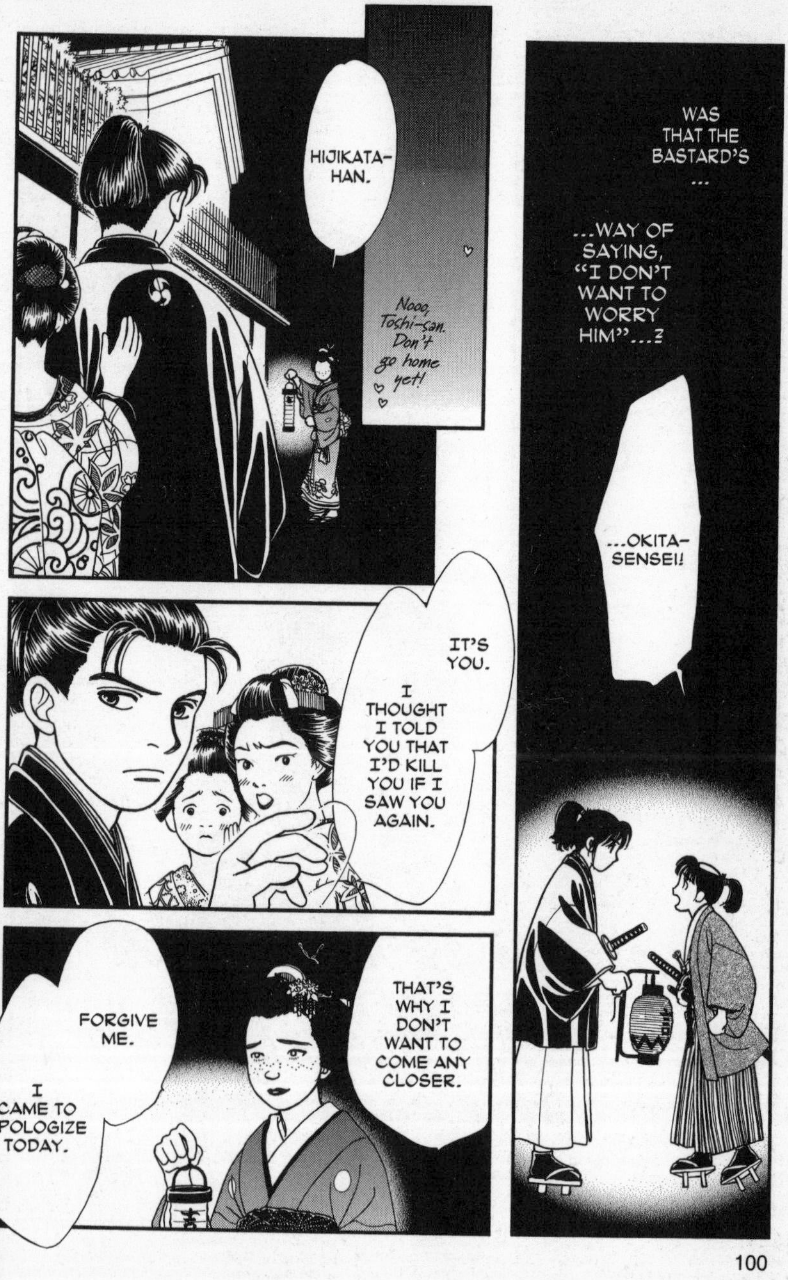
WAS THAT THE BASTARD'S ...
...WAY OF SAYING, "I DON'T WANT TO WORRY HIM"...?
...OKITA-SENSEI!
Nooo, Toshi-san. Don't go home yet!
HIJIKATA-HAN.
IT'S YOU.
I THOUGHT I TOLD YOU THAT I'D KILL YOU IF I SAW YOU AGAIN.
THAT'S WHY I DON'T WANT TO COME ANY CLOSER.
FORGIVE ME.
I CAME TO APOLOGIZE TODAY.

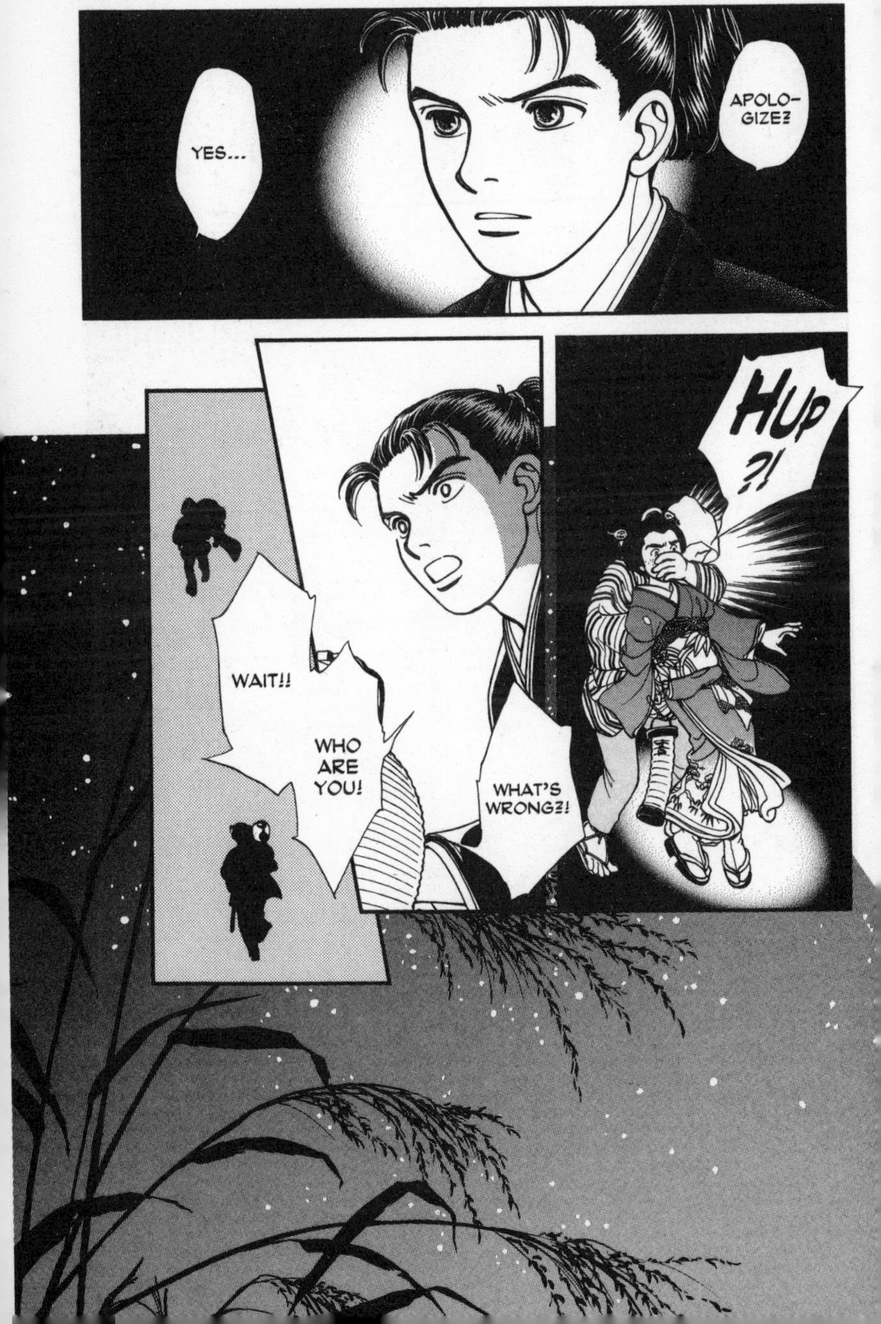
APOLO-
GIZE?!
YES...
HUP
?!
WHAT'S
WRONG?!
WAIT!!
WHO
ARE
YOU!

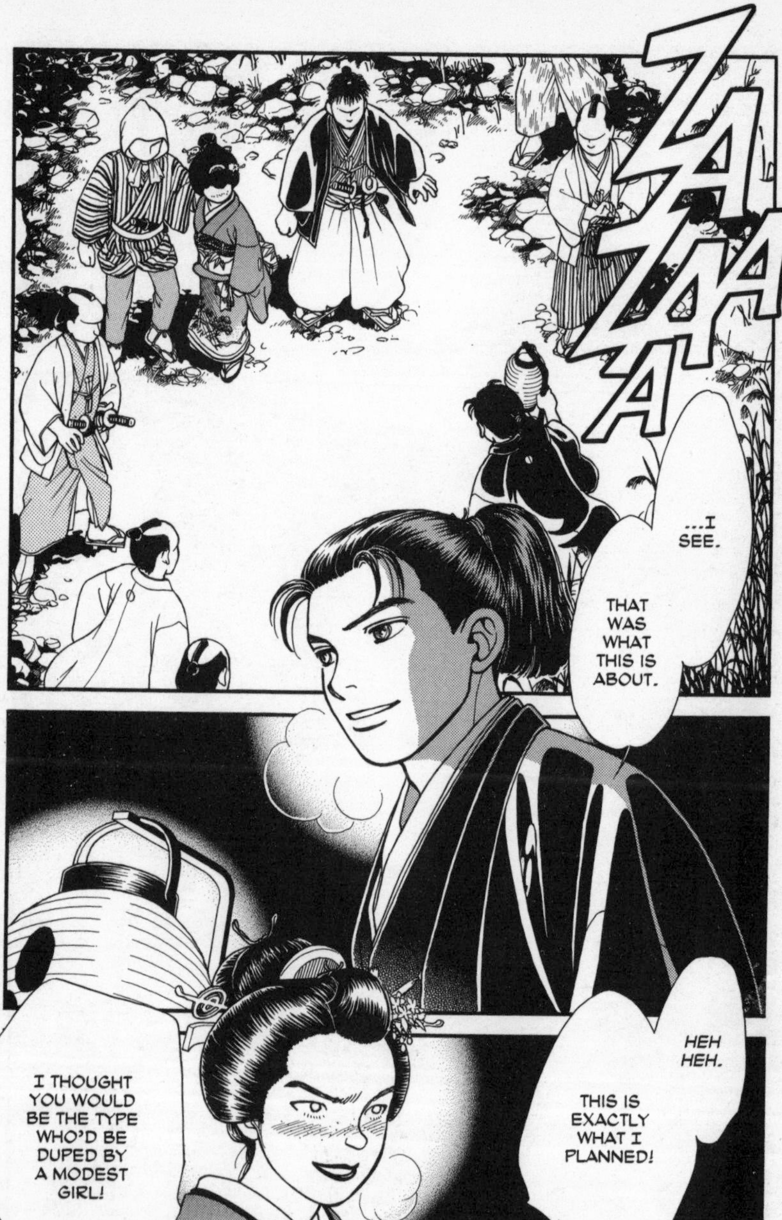
ZAZAAA
...I SEE.
THAT WAS WHAT THIS IS ABOUT.
HEH HEH.
THIS IS EXACTLY WHAT I PLANNED!
I THOUGHT YOU WOULD BE THE TYPE WHO'D BE DUPED BY A MODEST GIRL!

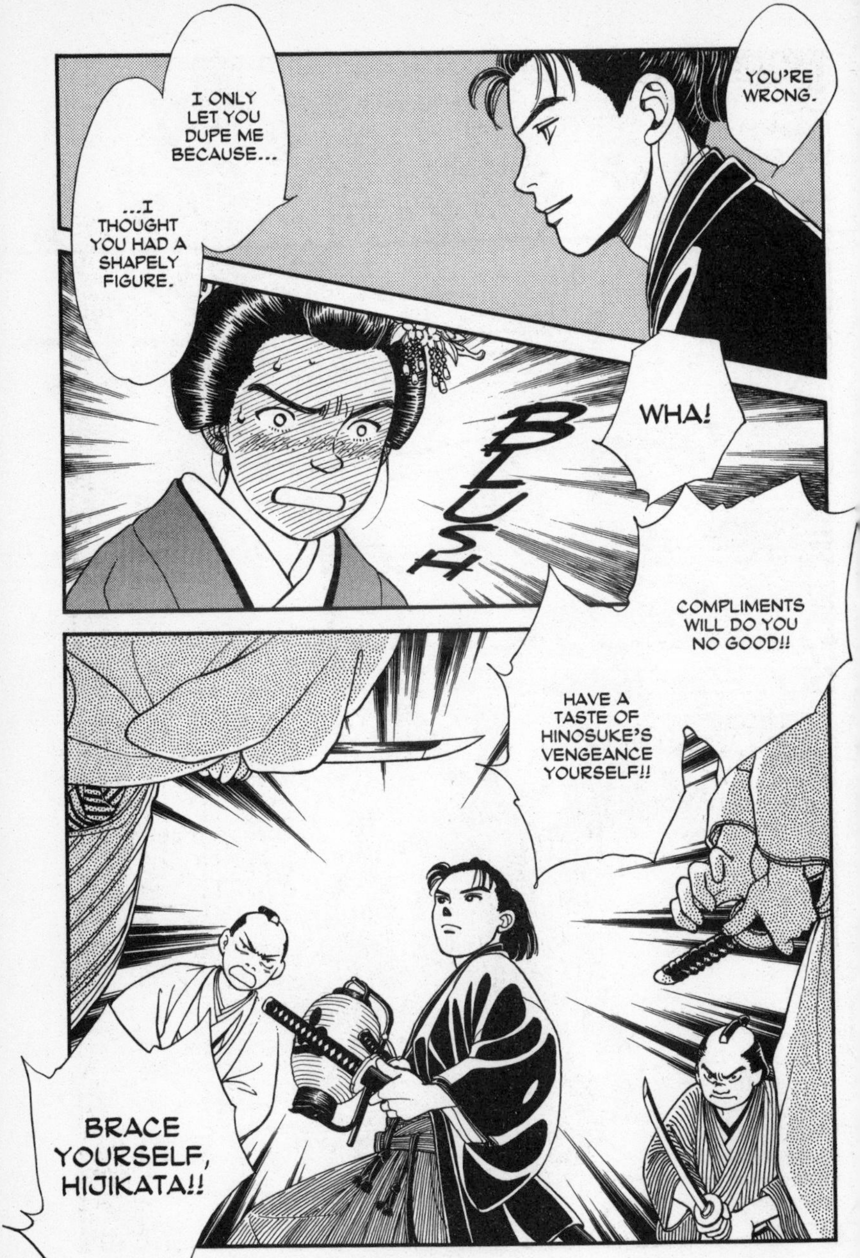
YOU'RE WRONG.
I ONLY LET YOU DUPE ME BECAUSE...
...I THOUGHT YOU HAD A SHAPELY FIGURE.
WHA!
BLUSH
COMPLIMENTS WILL DO YOU NO GOOD!!
HAVE A TASTE OF HINOSUKE'S VENGEANCE YOURSELF!!
BRACE YOURSELF, HIJIKATA!!

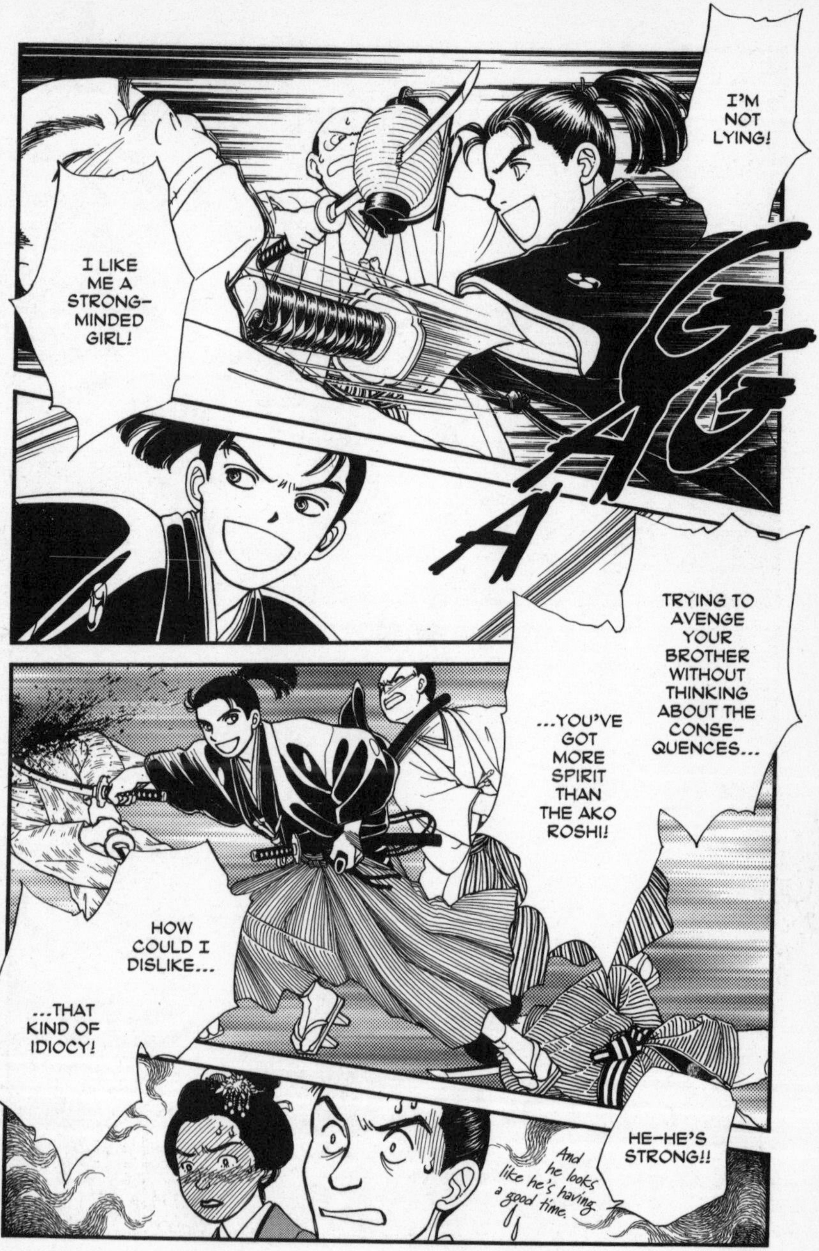
I'M NOT LYING!
I LIKE ME A STRONG-MINDED GIRL!
TRYING TO AVENGE YOUR BROTHER WITHOUT THINKING ABOUT THE CONSE-QUENCES...
...YOU'VE GOT MORE SPIRIT THAN THE AKO ROSHI!
HOW COULD I DISLIKE...
...THAT KIND OF IDIOCY!
HE-HE'S STRONG!!
And he looks like he's having a good time.

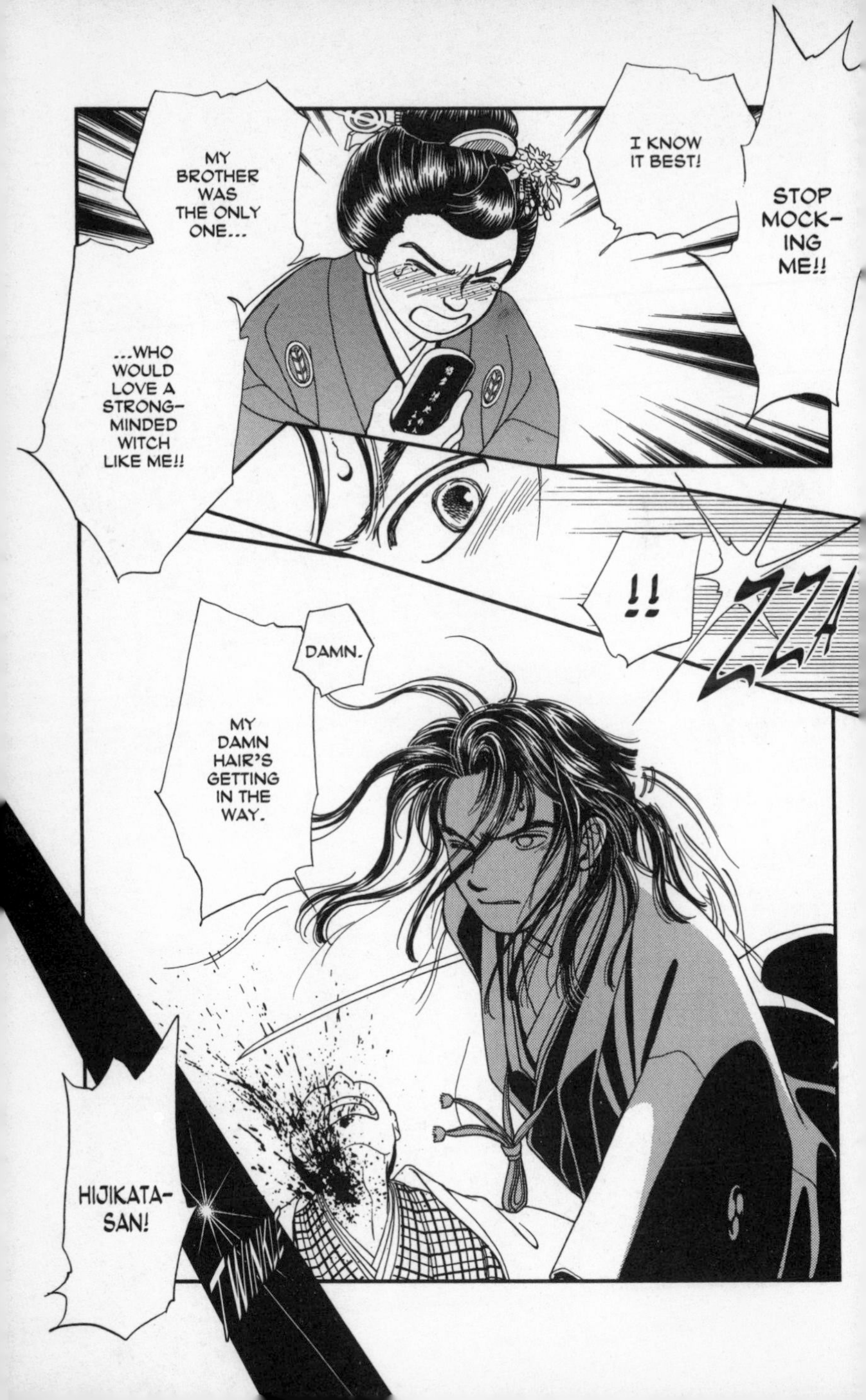

I KNOW IT BEST!
STOP MOCKING ME!!
MY BROTHER WAS THE ONLY ONE...
...WHO WOULD LOVE A STRONG-MINDED WITCH LIKE ME!!
!!
ZZA
DAMN.
MY DAMN HAIR'S GETTING IN THE WAY.
HIJIKATA-SAN!

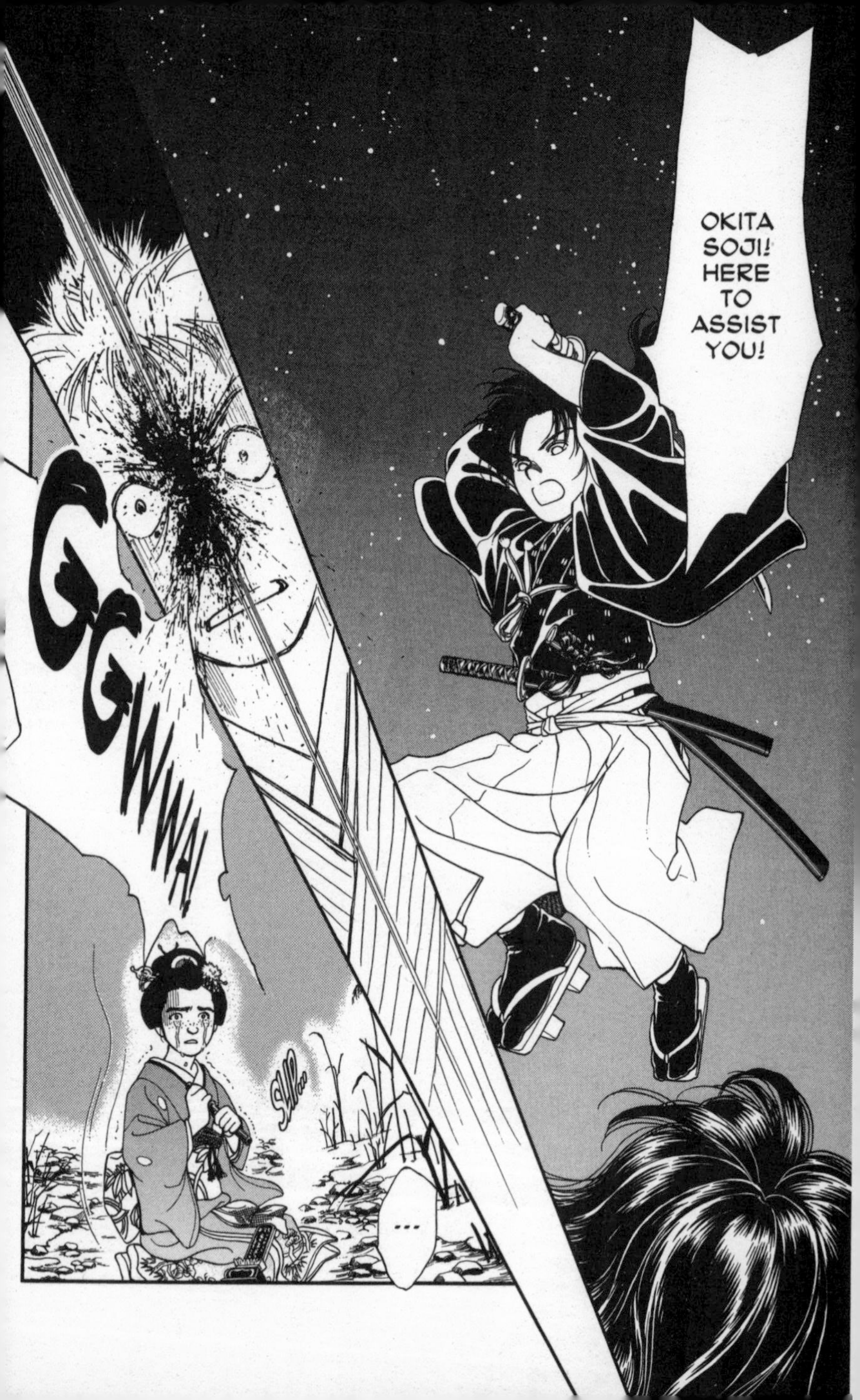
OKITA SOJI! HERE TO ASSIST YOU!
GGWWA!
SLIP...
...

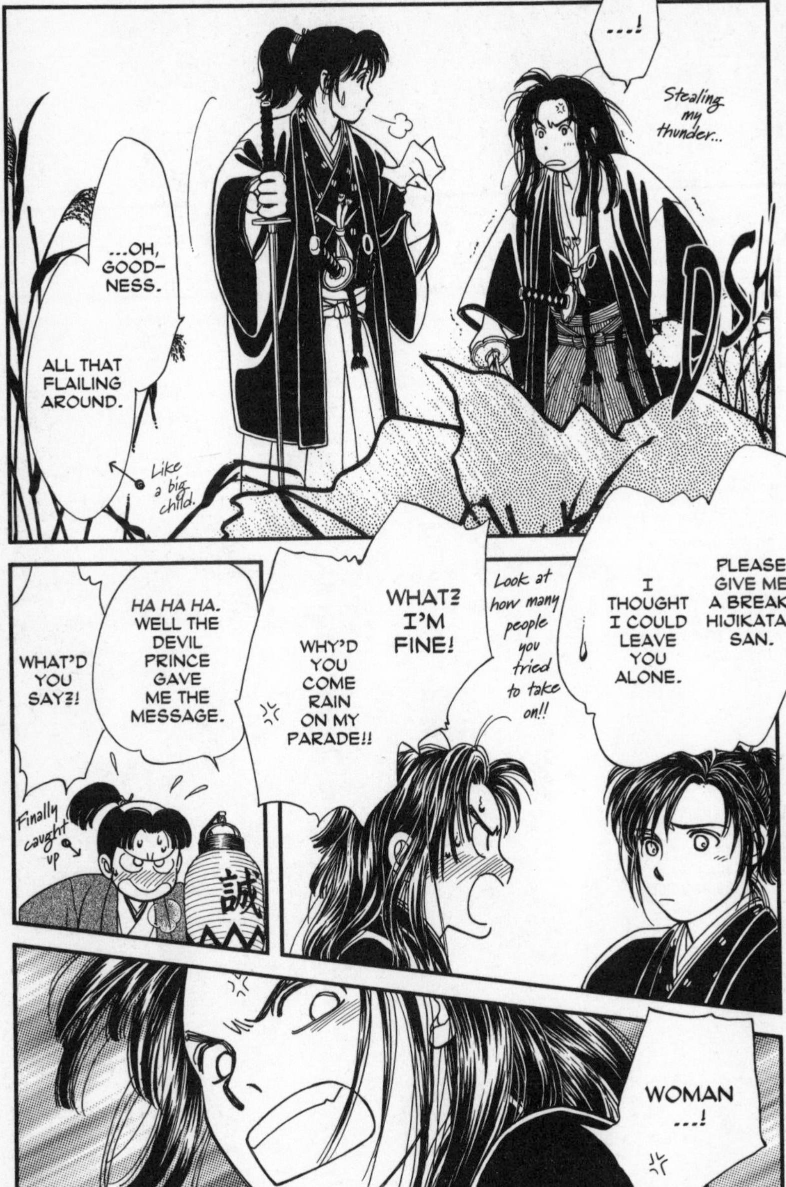
...!
Stealing my thunder...
DSH
...OH, GOODNESS.
ALL THAT FLAILING AROUND.
Like a big child.
PLEASE GIVE ME A BREAK, HIJIKATA-SAN.
I THOUGHT I COULD LEAVE YOU ALONE.
Look at how many people you tried to take on!!
WHAT?! I'M FINE!
WHY'D YOU COME RAIN ON MY PARADE!!
HA HA HA. WELL THE DEVIL PRINCE GAVE ME THE MESSAGE.
WHAT'D YOU SAY?!
Finally caught up
WOMAN ...!

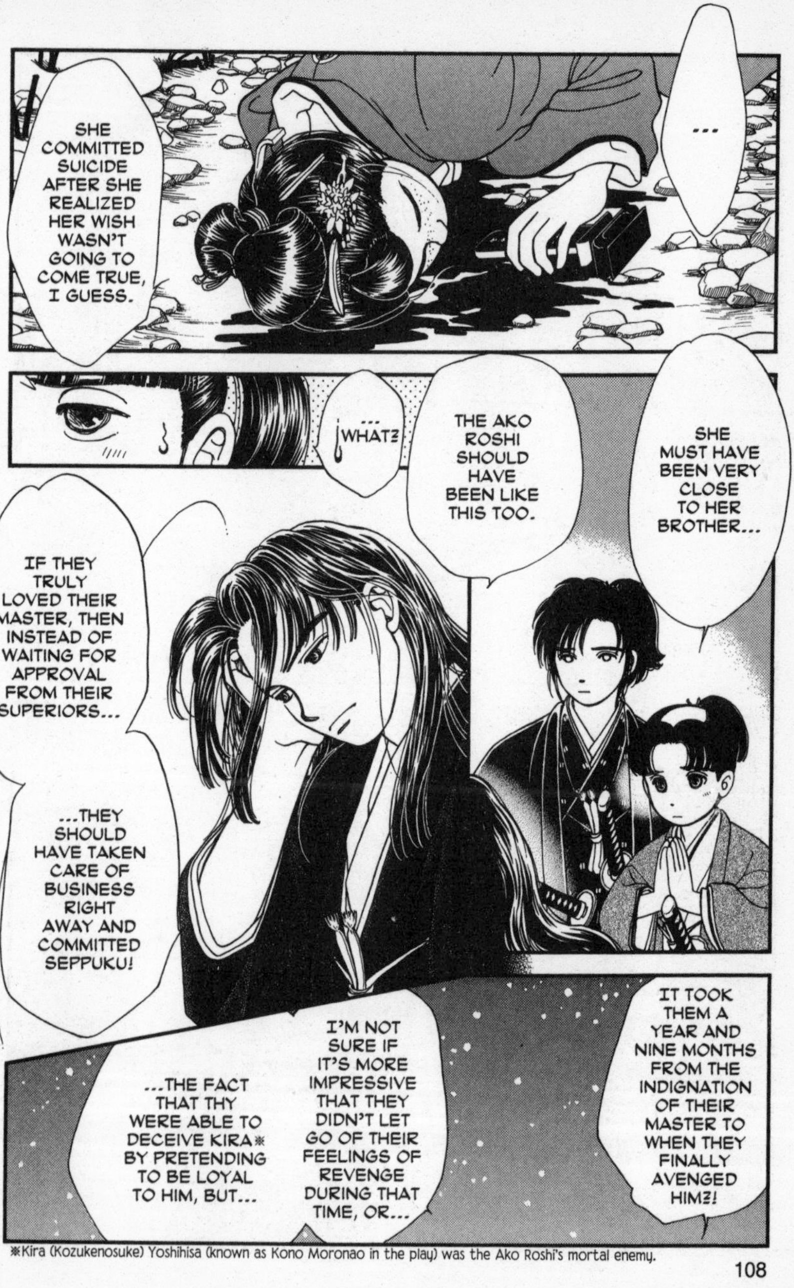
...
SHE COMMITTED SUICIDE AFTER SHE REALIZED HER WISH WASN'T GOING TO COME TRUE, I GUESS.
SHE MUST HAVE BEEN VERY CLOSE TO HER BROTHER...
THE AKO ROSHI SHOULD HAVE BEEN LIKE THIS TOO.
...WHAT?
IF THEY TRULY LOVED THEIR MASTER, THEN INSTEAD OF WAITING FOR APPROVAL FROM THEIR SUPERIORS...
...THEY SHOULD HAVE TAKEN CARE OF BUSINESS RIGHT AWAY AND COMMITTED SEPPUKU!
IT TOOK THEM A YEAR AND NINE MONTHS FROM THE INDIGNATION OF THEIR MASTER TO WHEN THEY FINALLY AVENGED HIM?!
I'M NOT SURE IF IT'S MORE IMPRESSIVE THAT THEY DIDN'T LET GO OF THEIR FEELINGS OF REVENGE DURING THAT TIME, OR...
...THE FACT THAT THY WERE ABLE TO DECEIVE KIRA※ BY PRETENDING TO BE LOYAL TO HIM, BUT...

※Kira (Kozukenosuke) Yoshihisa (known as Kono Moronao in the play) was the Ako Roshi's mortal enemy.

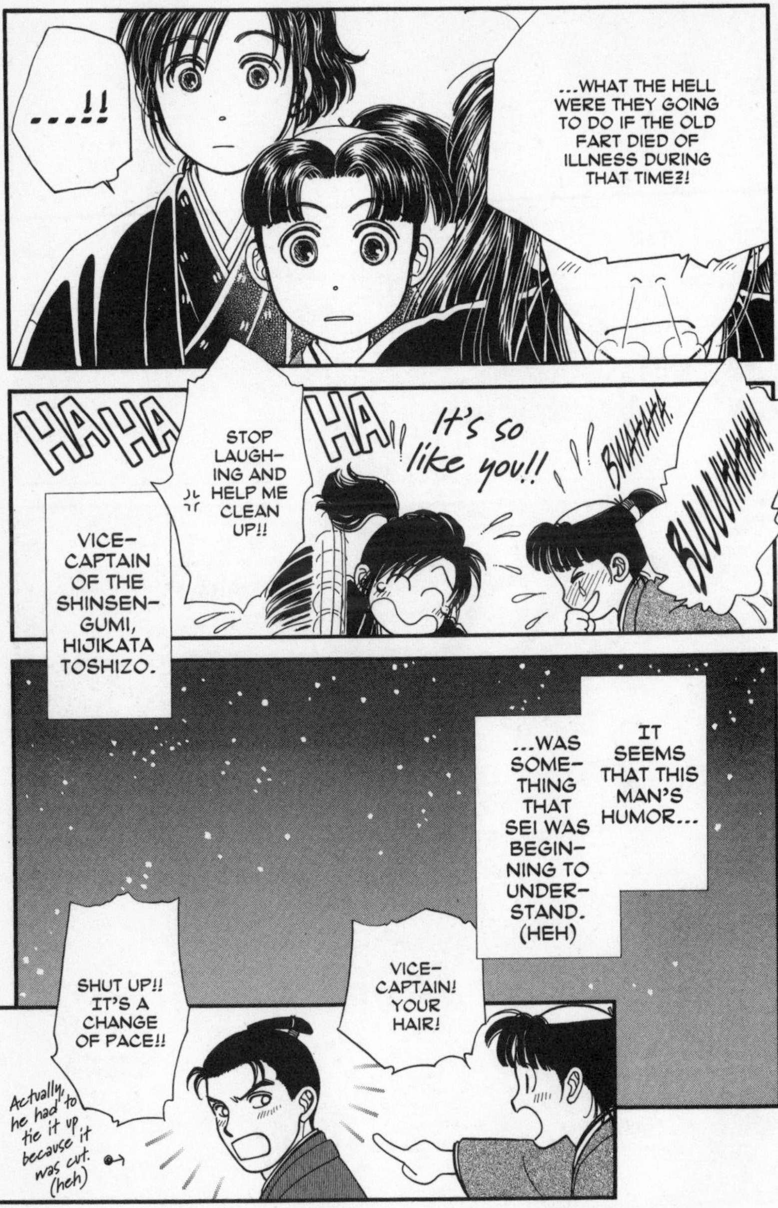
...WHAT THE HELL WERE THEY GOING TO DO IF THE OLD FART DIED OF ILLNESS DURING THAT TIME?!
...!!
BUUUWAHAHA.
BWAHAHA.
It's so like you!!
HA
STOP LAUGHING AND HELP ME CLEAN UP!!
HAHA
VICE-CAPTAIN OF THE SHINSEN-GUMI, HIJIKATA TOSHIZO.
IT SEEMS THAT THIS MAN'S HUMOR...
...WAS SOMETHING THAT SEI WAS BEGINNING TO UNDERSTAND. (HEH)
VICE-CAPTAIN! YOUR HAIR!
SHUT UP!! IT'S A CHANGE OF PACE!!
Actually, he had to tie it up because it was cut. (heh)

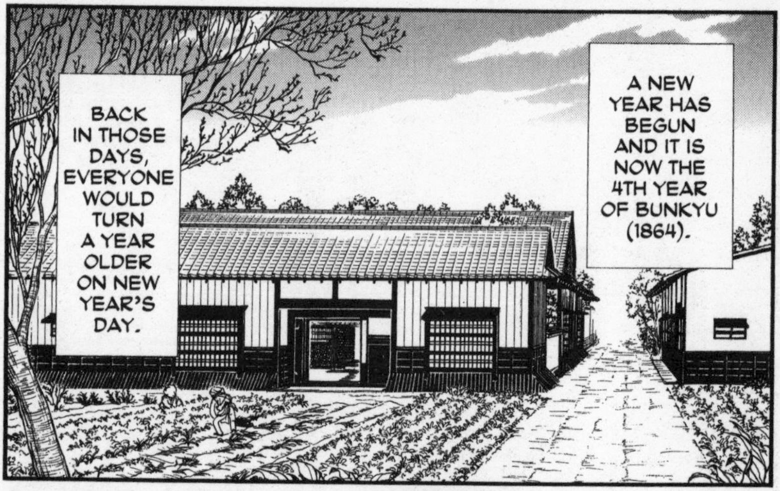
A NEW YEAR HAS BEGUN AND IT IS NOW THE 4TH YEAR OF BUNKYU (1864).
BACK IN THOSE DAYS, EVERYONE WOULD TURN A YEAR OLDER ON NEW YEAR'S DAY.

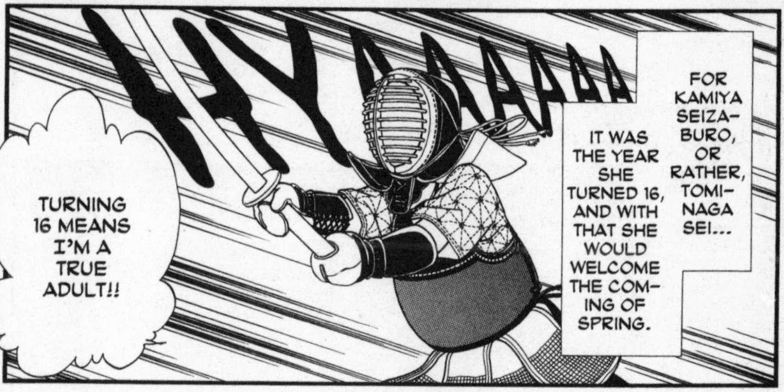
FOR KAMIYA SEIZABURO, OR RATHER, TOMINAGA SEI...
IT WAS THE YEAR SHE TURNED 16, AND WITH THAT SHE WOULD WELCOME THE COMING OF SPRING.
HYAAAAAA
TURNING 16 MEANS I'M A TRUE ADULT!!

KYOTO "IROHA" KARUTA GAME

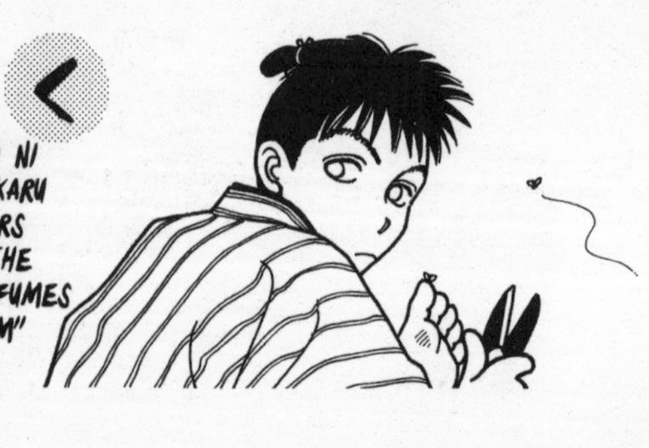
く

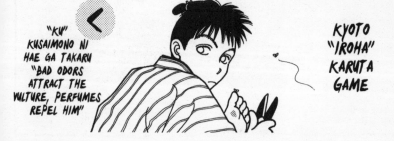

"KU"
KUSAIMONO NI HAE GA TAKARU
"BAD ODORS ATTRACT THE VULTURE, PERFUMES REPEL HIM"

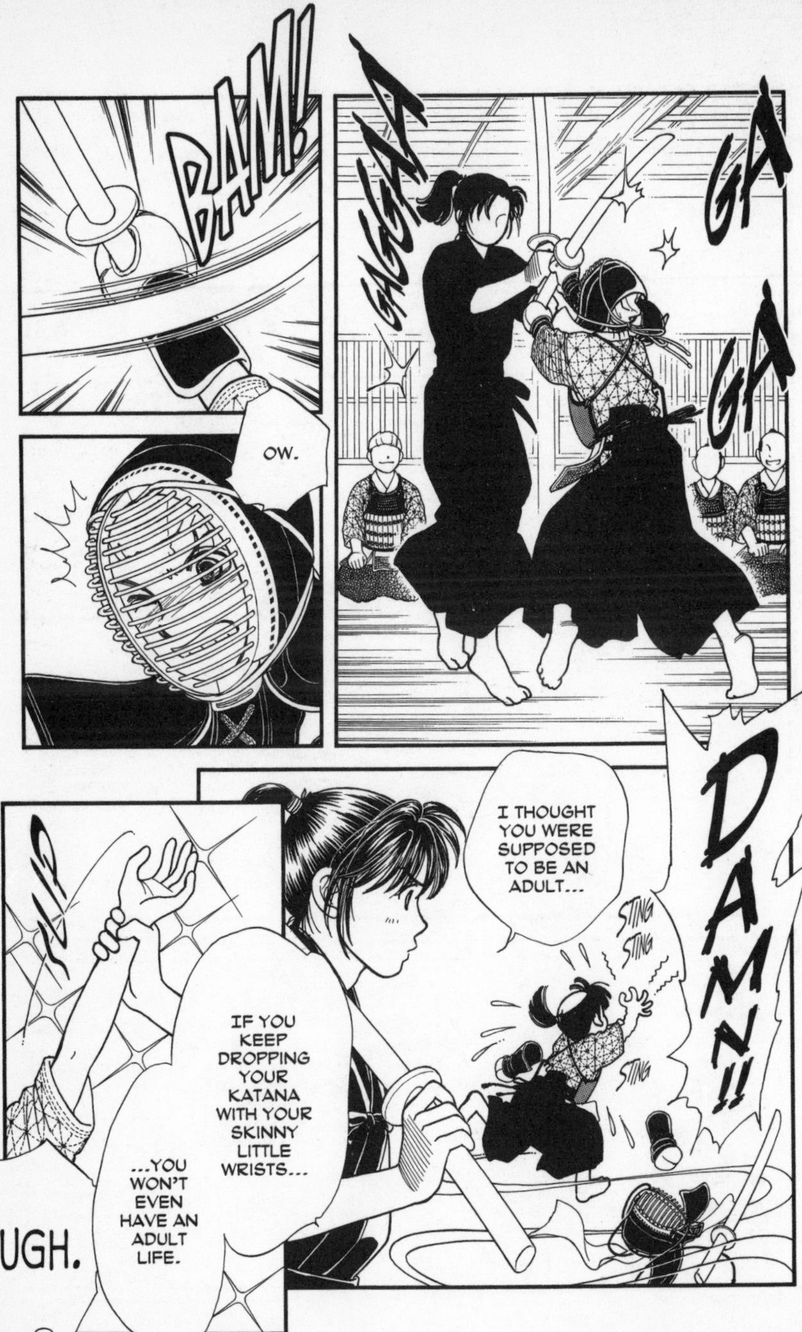
GA
GA
BAM!
OW.
DAMN!!
I THOUGHT YOU WERE SUPPOSED TO BE AN ADULT...
STING
STING
STING
SLIP
IF YOU KEEP DROPPING YOUR KATANA WITH YOUR SKINNY LITTLE WRISTS...
...YOU WON'T EVEN HAVE AN ADULT LIFE.
UGH.

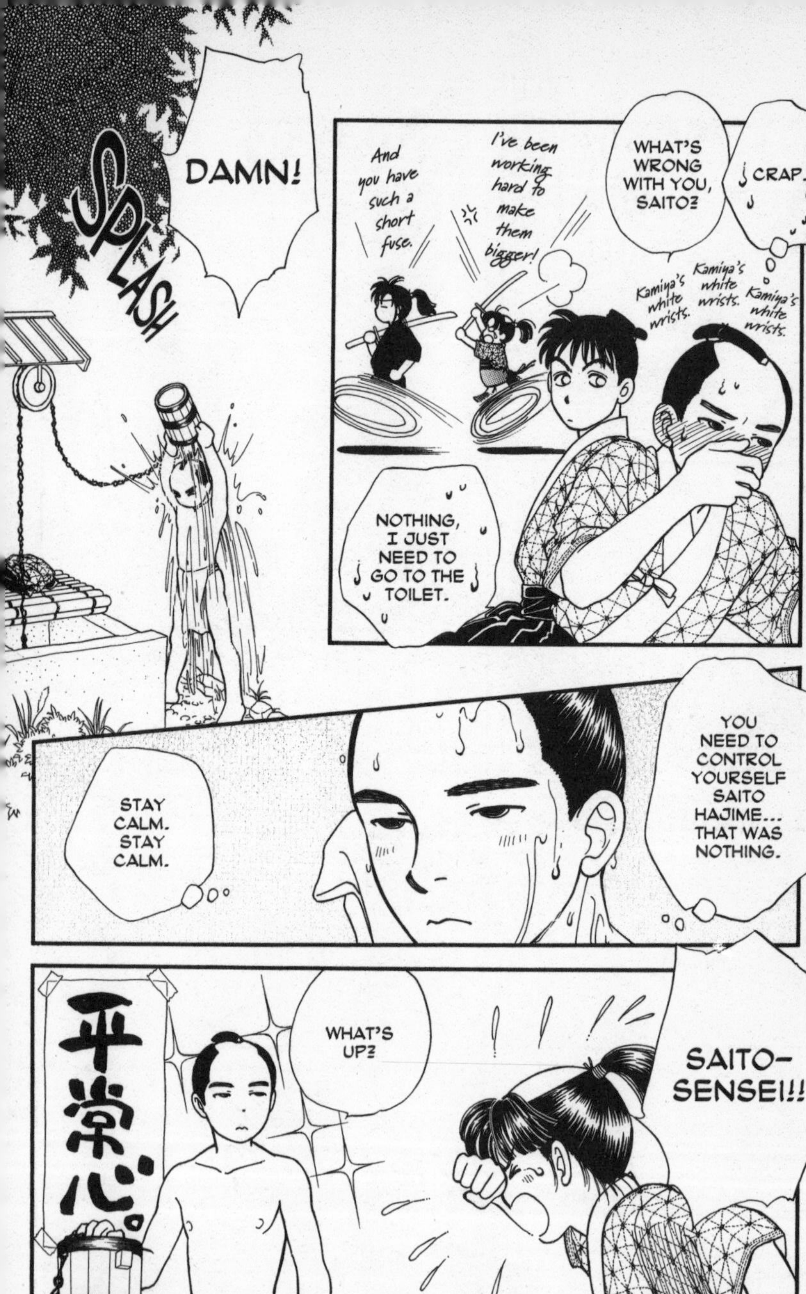
CRAP.
Kamiya's white wrists. Kamiya's white wrists. Kamiya's white wrists.
WHAT'S WRONG WITH YOU, SAITO?
I've been working hard to make them bigger!
And you have such a short fuse.
NOTHING, I JUST NEED TO GO TO THE TOILET.
DAMN!
SPLASH
YOU NEED TO CONTROL YOURSELF SAITO HAJIME... THAT WAS NOTHING.
STAY CALM. STAY CALM.
SAITO-SENSEI!!!
WHAT'S UP?
平常心。
Sign: Staying calm.

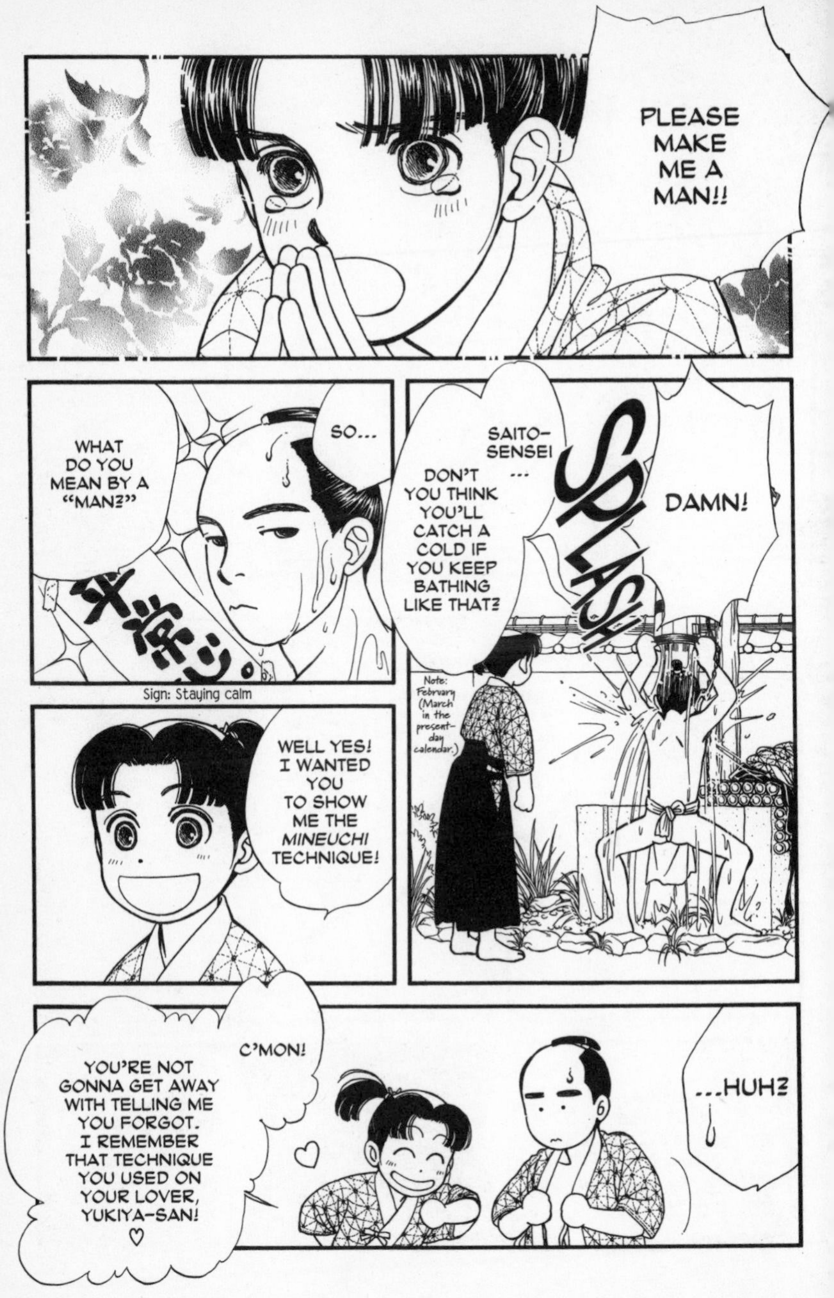
PLEASE MAKE ME A MAN!!
DAMN!
SPLASH
SAITO-SENSEI ...
DON'T YOU THINK YOU'LL CATCH A COLD IF YOU KEEP BATHING LIKE THAT?
Note: February (March in the present-day calendar.)
SO...
WHAT DO YOU MEAN BY A "MAN?"
Sign: Staying calm
WELL YES! I WANTED YOU TO SHOW ME THE *MINEUCHI* TECHNIQUE!
...HUH?
C'MON!
YOU'RE NOT GONNA GET AWAY WITH TELLING ME YOU FORGOT. I REMEMBER THAT TECHNIQUE YOU USED ON YOUR LOVER, YUKIYA-SAN! ♡

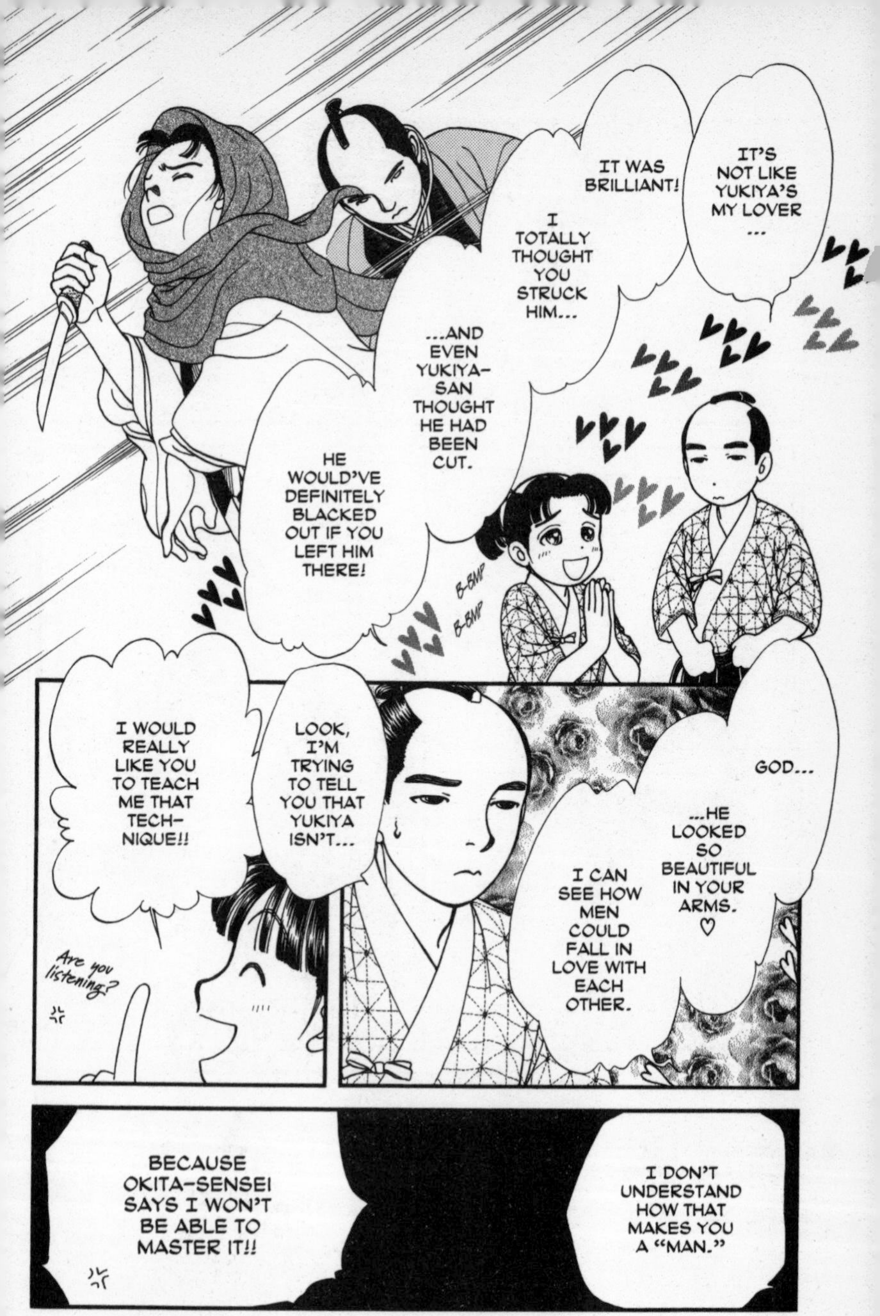
IT'S NOT LIKE YUKIYA'S MY LOVER...
IT WAS BRILLIANT!
I TOTALLY THOUGHT YOU STRUCK HIM...
...AND EVEN YUKIYA-SAN THOUGHT HE HAD BEEN CUT.
HE WOULD'VE DEFINITELY BLACKED OUT IF YOU LEFT HIM THERE!
B-BMP
B-BMP
GOD...
...HE LOOKED SO BEAUTIFUL IN YOUR ARMS. ♡
I CAN SEE HOW MEN COULD FALL IN LOVE WITH EACH OTHER.
LOOK, I'M TRYING TO TELL YOU THAT YUKIYA ISN'T...
I WOULD REALLY LIKE YOU TO TEACH ME THAT TECH-NIQUE!!
Are you listening?
I DON'T UNDERSTAND HOW THAT MAKES YOU A "MAN."
BECAUSE OKITA-SENSEI SAYS I WON'T BE ABLE TO MASTER IT!!

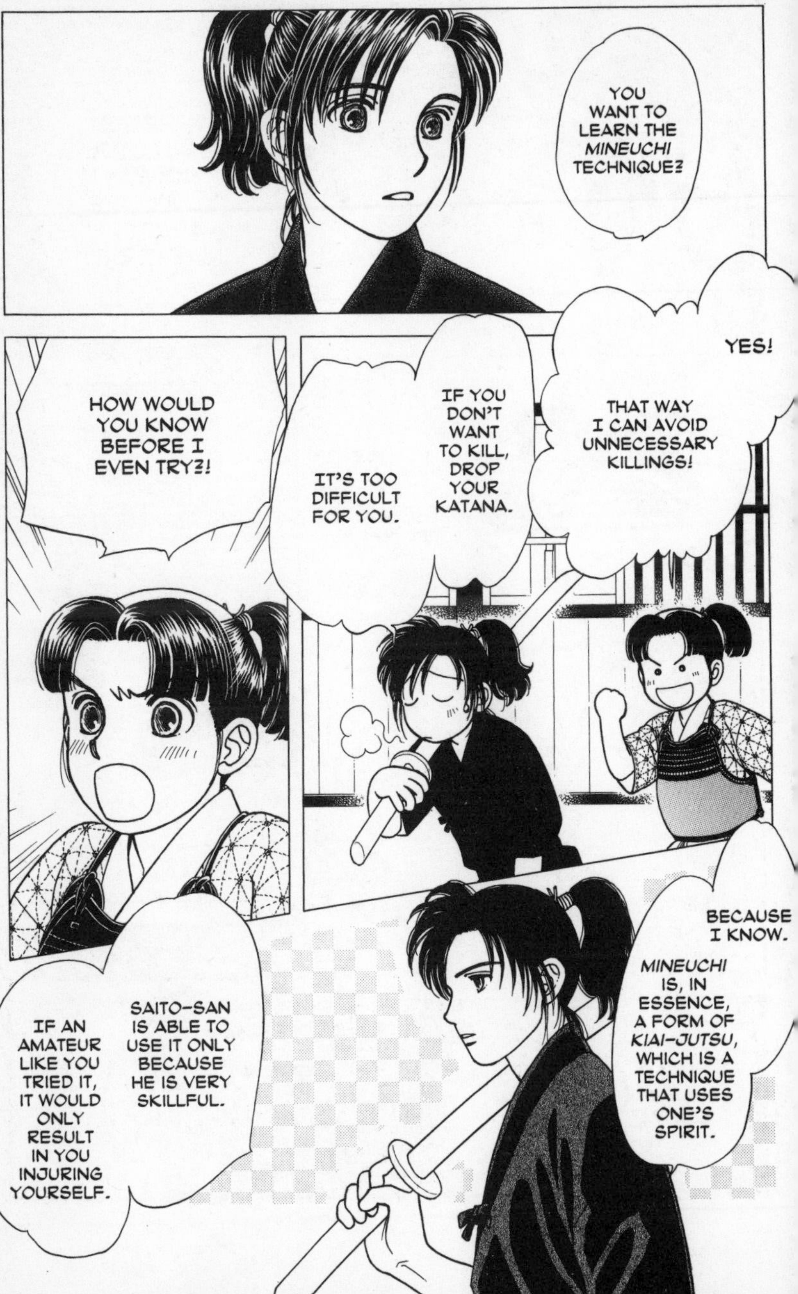
YOU WANT TO LEARN THE *MINEUCHI* TECHNIQUE?
YES!
THAT WAY I CAN AVOID UNNECESSARY KILLINGS!
IF YOU DON'T WANT TO KILL, DROP YOUR KATANA.
IT'S TOO DIFFICULT FOR YOU.
HOW WOULD YOU KNOW BEFORE I EVEN TRY?!
BECAUSE I KNOW.
MINEUCHI IS, IN ESSENCE, A FORM OF *KIAI-JUTSU*, WHICH IS A TECHNIQUE THAT USES ONE'S SPIRIT.
SAITO-SAN IS ABLE TO USE IT ONLY BECAUSE HE IS VERY SKILLFUL.
IF AN AMATEUR LIKE YOU TRIED IT, IT WOULD ONLY RESULT IN YOU INJURING YOURSELF.

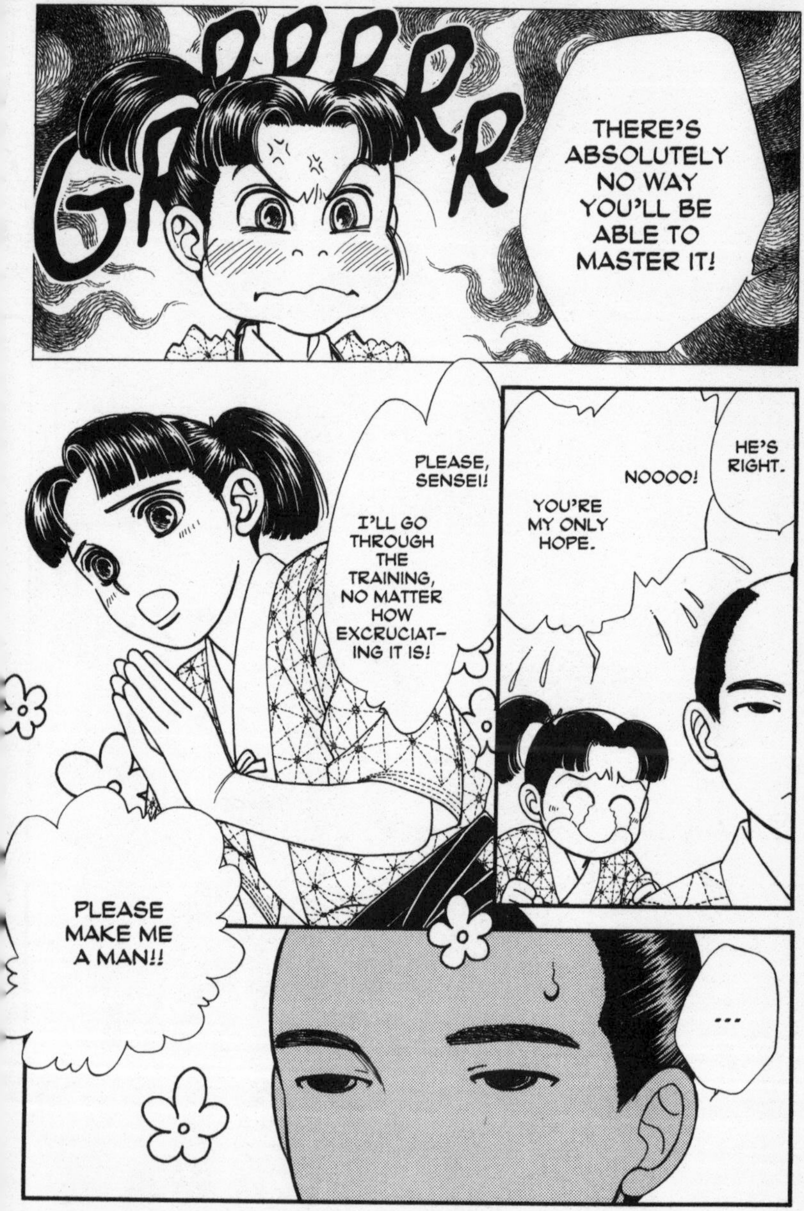
THERE'S ABSOLUTELY NO WAY YOU'LL BE ABLE TO MASTER IT!
GRRRRRR
HE'S RIGHT.
NOOOO!
YOU'RE MY ONLY HOPE.
PLEASE, SENSEI!
I'LL GO THROUGH THE TRAINING, NO MATTER HOW EXCRUCIAT-ING IT IS!
PLEASE MAKE ME A MAN!!
...

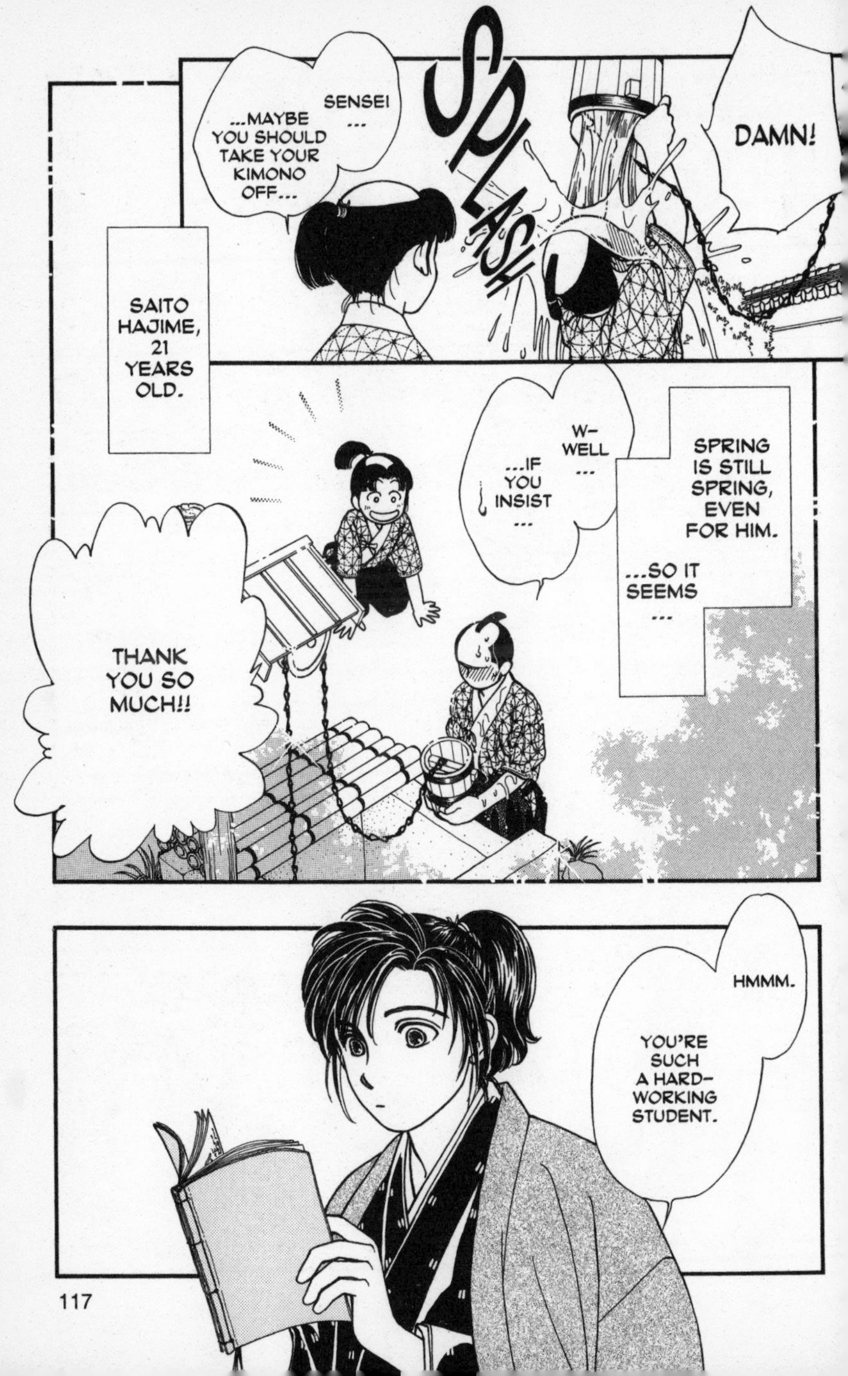
DAMN!
SPLASH
SENSEI...
...MAYBE YOU SHOULD TAKE YOUR KIMONO OFF...
SAITO HAJIME, 21 YEARS OLD.
SPRING IS STILL SPRING, EVEN FOR HIM.
...SO IT SEEMS...
W-WELL...
...IF YOU INSIST...
THANK YOU SO MUCH!!
HMMM.
YOU'RE SUCH A HARD-WORKING STUDENT.

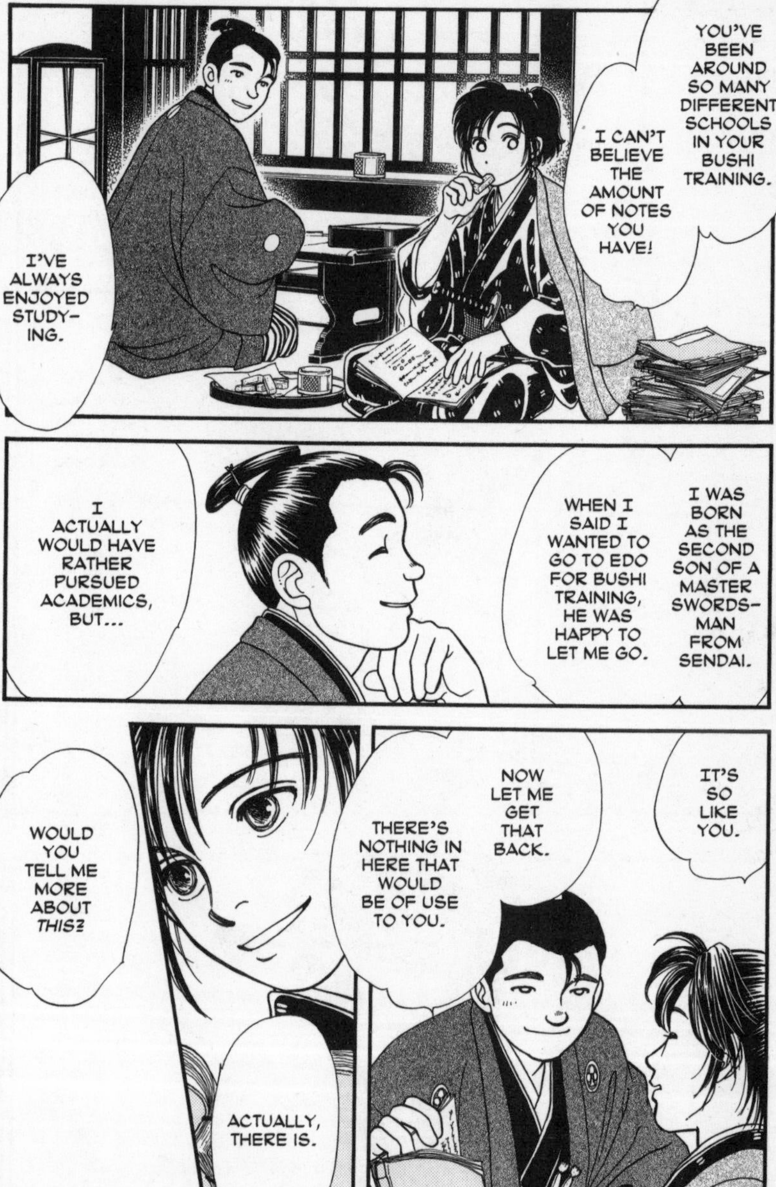
YOU'VE BEEN AROUND SO MANY DIFFERENT SCHOOLS IN YOUR BUSHI TRAINING.
I CAN'T BELIEVE THE AMOUNT OF NOTES YOU HAVE!
I'VE ALWAYS ENJOYED STUDYING.
I WAS BORN AS THE SECOND SON OF A MASTER SWORDSMAN FROM SENDAI.
WHEN I SAID I WANTED TO GO TO EDO FOR BUSHI TRAINING, HE WAS HAPPY TO LET ME GO.
I ACTUALLY WOULD HAVE RATHER PURSUED ACADEMICS, BUT...
IT'S SO LIKE YOU.
NOW LET ME GET THAT BACK.
THERE'S NOTHING IN HERE THAT WOULD BE OF USE TO YOU.
ACTUALLY, THERE IS.
WOULD YOU TELL ME MORE ABOUT *THIS?*

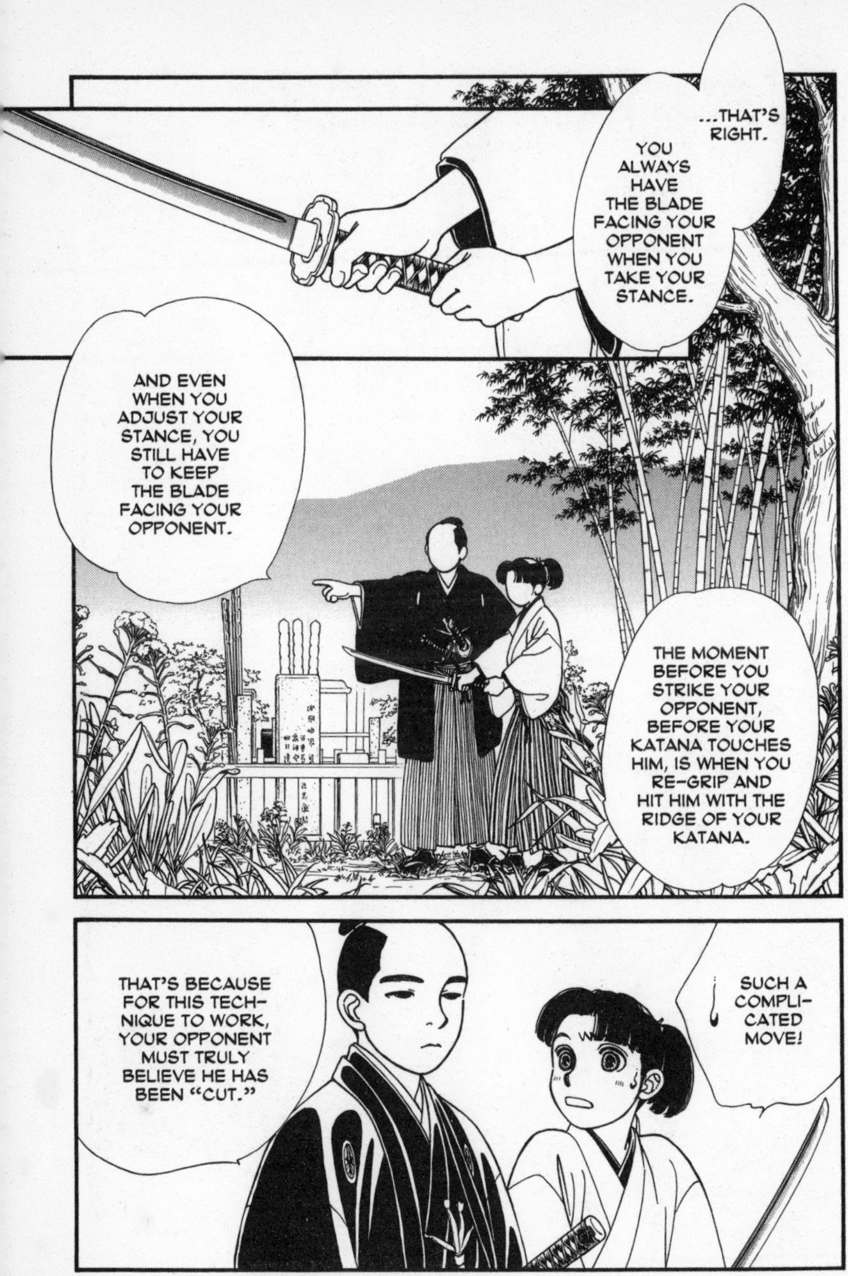
...THAT'S RIGHT. YOU ALWAYS HAVE THE BLADE FACING YOUR OPPONENT WHEN YOU TAKE YOUR STANCE.
AND EVEN WHEN YOU ADJUST YOUR STANCE, YOU STILL HAVE TO KEEP THE BLADE FACING YOUR OPPONENT.
THE MOMENT BEFORE YOU STRIKE YOUR OPPONENT, BEFORE YOUR KATANA TOUCHES HIM, IS WHEN YOU RE-GRIP AND HIT HIM WITH THE RIDGE OF YOUR KATANA.
SUCH A COMPLI-CATED MOVE!
THAT'S BECAUSE FOR THIS TECH-NIQUE TO WORK, YOUR OPPONENT MUST TRULY BELIEVE HE HAS BEEN "CUT."

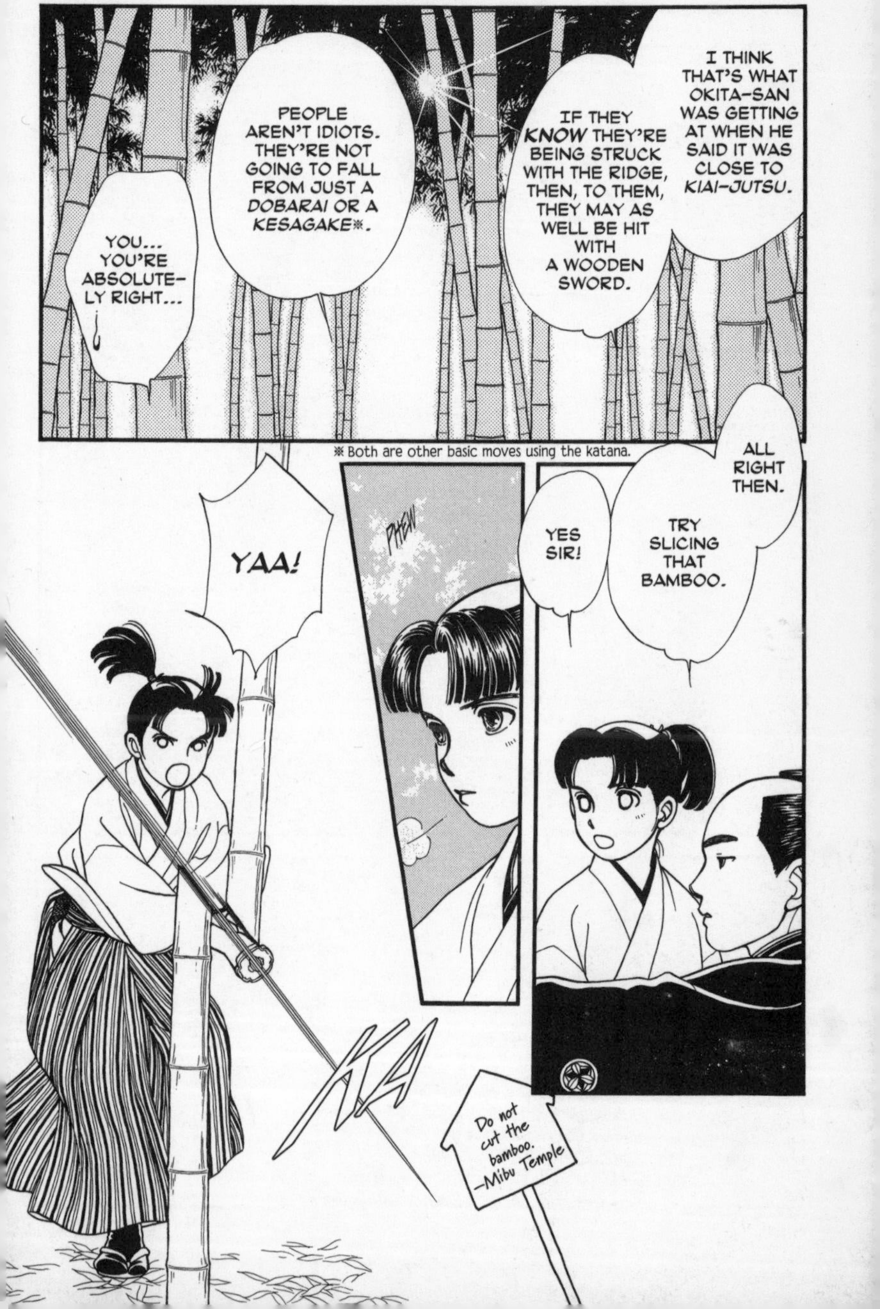
I THINK THAT'S WHAT OKITA-SAN WAS GETTING AT WHEN HE SAID IT WAS CLOSE TO *KIAI-JUTSU*.
IF THEY *KNOW* THEY'RE BEING STRUCK WITH THE RIDGE, THEN, TO THEM, THEY MAY AS WELL BE HIT WITH A WOODEN SWORD.
PEOPLE AREN'T IDIOTS. THEY'RE NOT GOING TO FALL FROM JUST A *DOBARAI* OR A *KESAGAKE*※.
YOU... YOU'RE ABSOLUTE-LY RIGHT...
ALL RIGHT THEN.
TRY SLICING THAT BAMBOO.
YES SIR!
PHEW
YAA!
KA
Do not cut the bamboo. —Mibu Temple
※ Both are other basic moves using the katana.

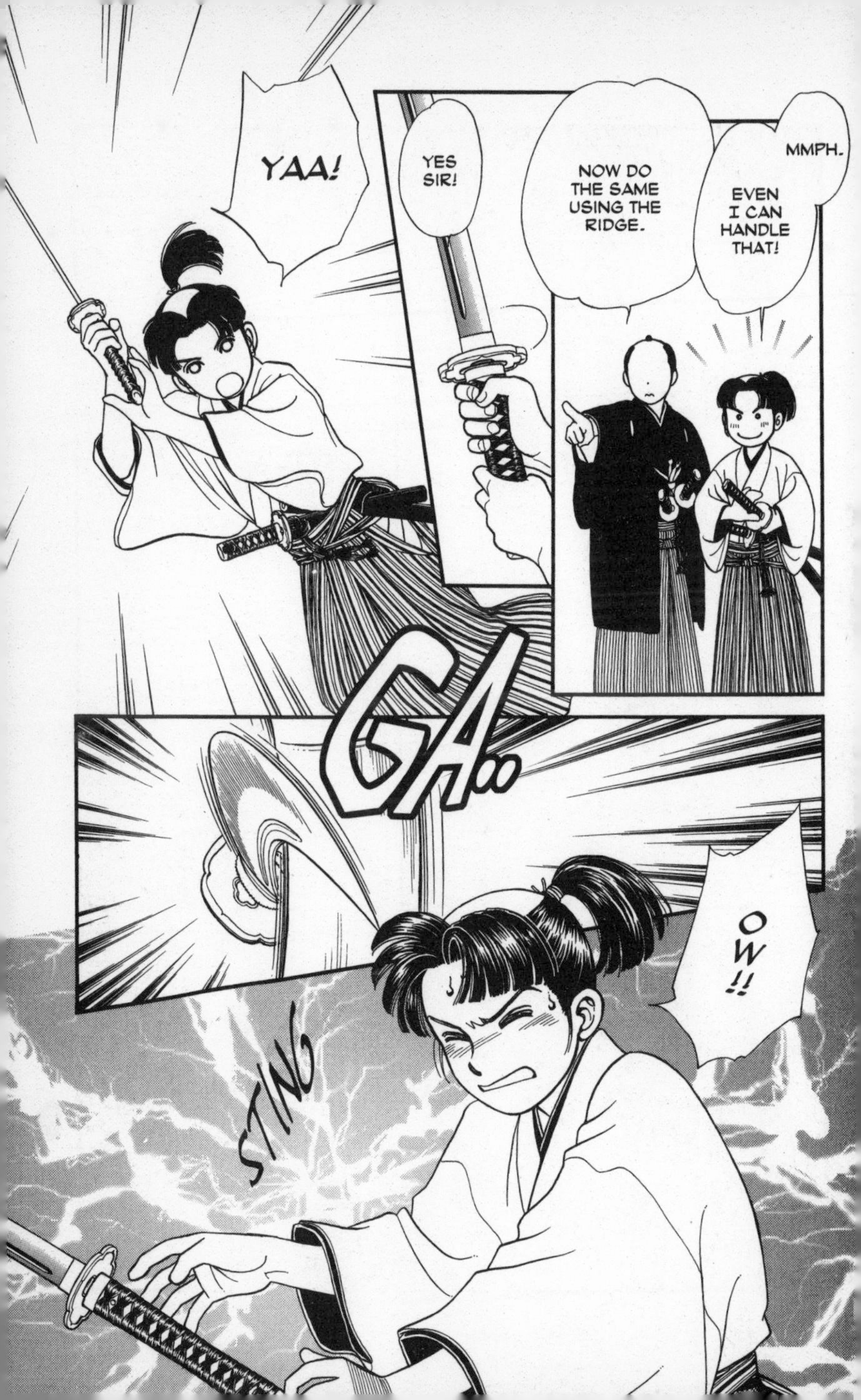
NOW DO THE SAME USING THE RIDGE.
MMPH. EVEN I CAN HANDLE THAT!
YES SIR!
YAA!
GA..
OW!!
STING

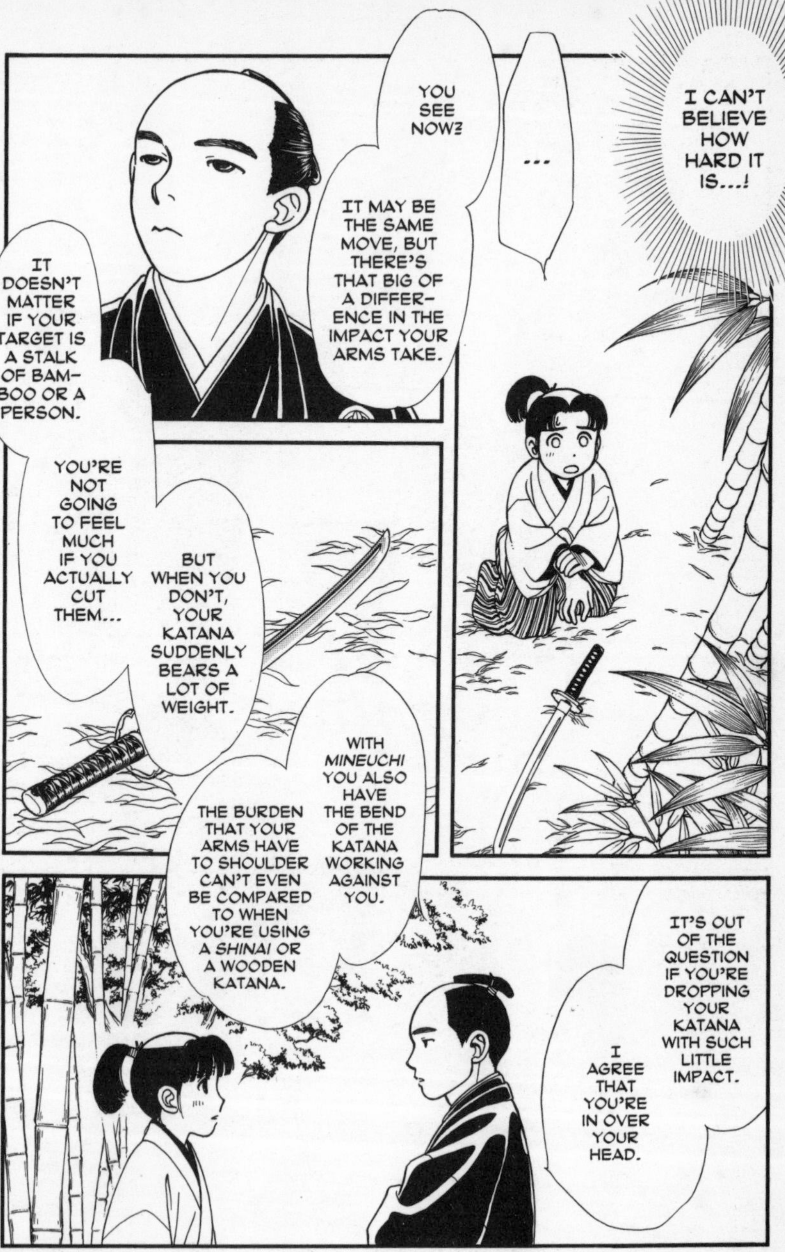
I CAN'T BELIEVE HOW HARD IT IS...!
...
YOU SEE NOW?
IT MAY BE THE SAME MOVE, BUT THERE'S THAT BIG OF A DIFFERENCE IN THE IMPACT YOUR ARMS TAKE.
IT DOESN'T MATTER IF YOUR TARGET IS A STALK OF BAMBOO OR A PERSON.
YOU'RE NOT GOING TO FEEL MUCH IF YOU ACTUALLY CUT THEM...
BUT WHEN YOU DON'T, YOUR KATANA SUDDENLY BEARS A LOT OF WEIGHT.
WITH *MINEUCHI* YOU ALSO HAVE THE BEND OF THE KATANA WORKING AGAINST YOU.
THE BURDEN THAT YOUR ARMS HAVE TO SHOULDER CAN'T EVEN BE COMPARED TO WHEN YOU'RE USING A *SHINAI* OR A WOODEN KATANA.
IT'S OUT OF THE QUESTION IF YOU'RE DROPPING YOUR KATANA WITH SUCH LITTLE IMPACT.
I AGREE THAT YOU'RE IN OVER YOUR HEAD.

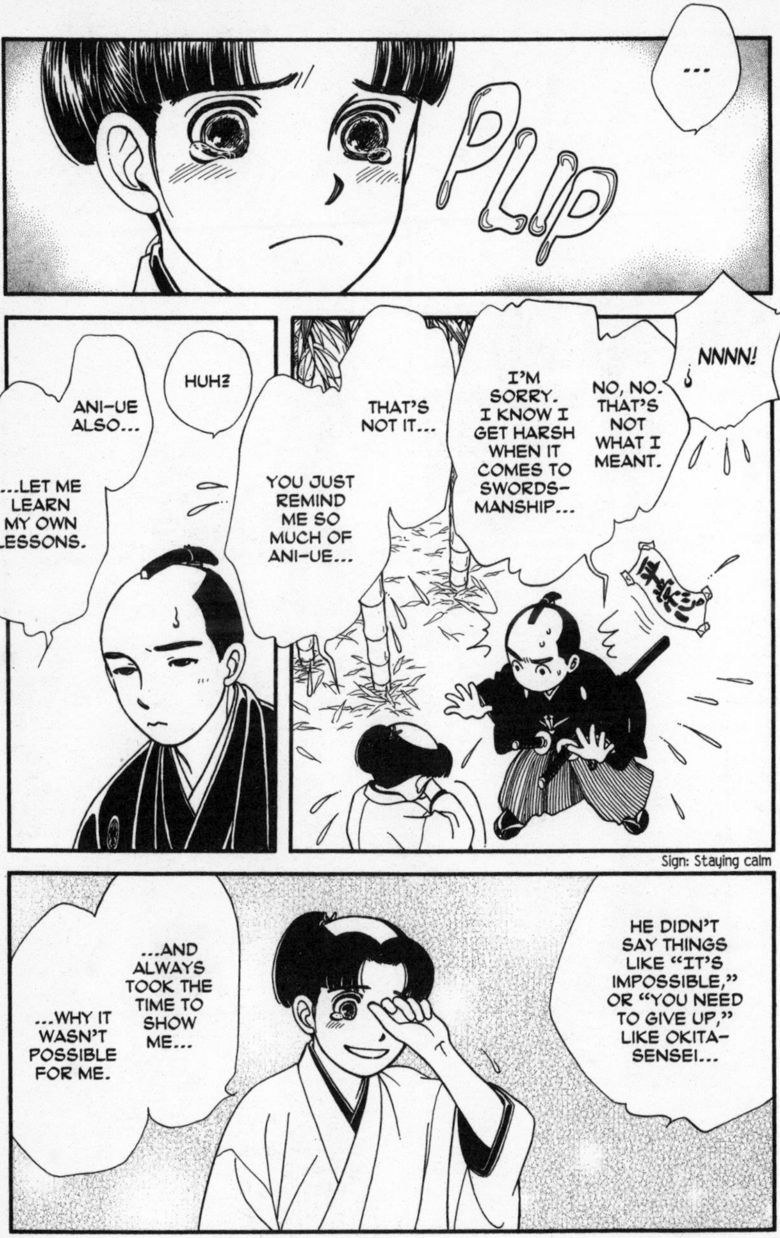
...
PLIP
NNNN!
NO, NO. THAT'S NOT WHAT I MEANT.
I'M SORRY. I KNOW I GET HARSH WHEN IT COMES TO SWORDSMANSHIP...
THAT'S NOT IT...
YOU JUST REMIND ME SO MUCH OF ANI-UE...
HUH?
ANI-UE ALSO...
...LET ME LEARN MY OWN LESSONS.
HE DIDN'T SAY THINGS LIKE "IT'S IMPOSSIBLE," OR "YOU NEED TO GIVE UP," LIKE OKITA-SENSEI...
...AND ALWAYS TOOK THE TIME TO SHOW ME...
...WHY IT WASN'T POSSIBLE FOR ME.

Sign: Staying calm

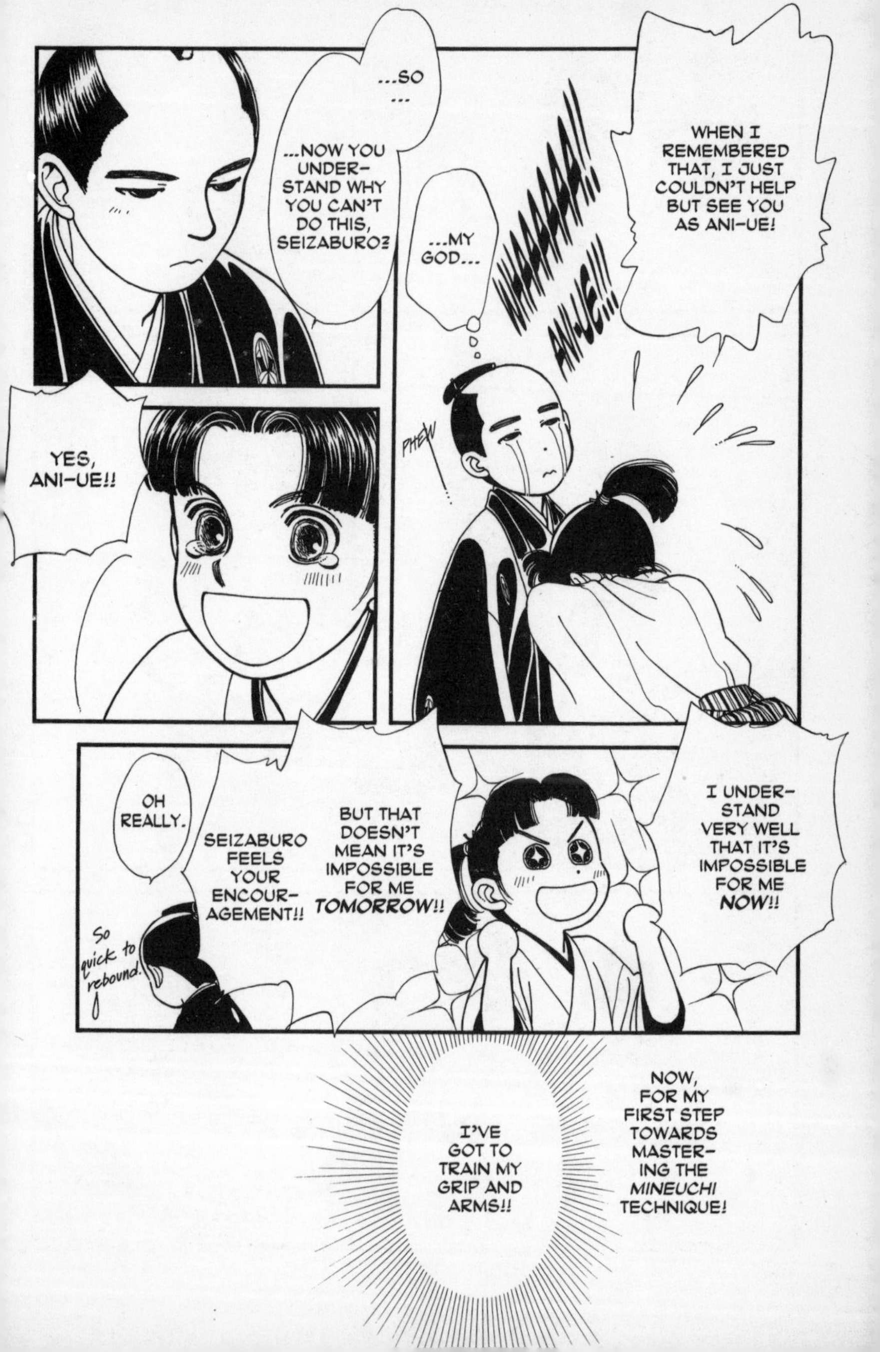
WHEN I REMEMBERED THAT, I JUST COULDN'T HELP BUT SEE YOU AS ANI-UE!
WAAAAH!! ANI-UE!!
...MY GOD...
PHEW
...SO ...
...NOW YOU UNDER-STAND WHY YOU CAN'T DO THIS, SEIZABURO?
YES, ANI-UE!!
I UNDER-STAND VERY WELL THAT IT'S IMPOSSIBLE FOR ME *NOW*!!
BUT THAT DOESN'T MEAN IT'S IMPOSSIBLE FOR ME *TOMORROW*!!
SEIZABURO FEELS YOUR ENCOUR-AGEMENT!!
OH REALLY.
So quick to rebound.
NOW, FOR MY FIRST STEP TOWARDS MASTER-ING THE *MINEUCHI* TECHNIQUE!
I'VE GOT TO TRAIN MY GRIP AND ARMS!!

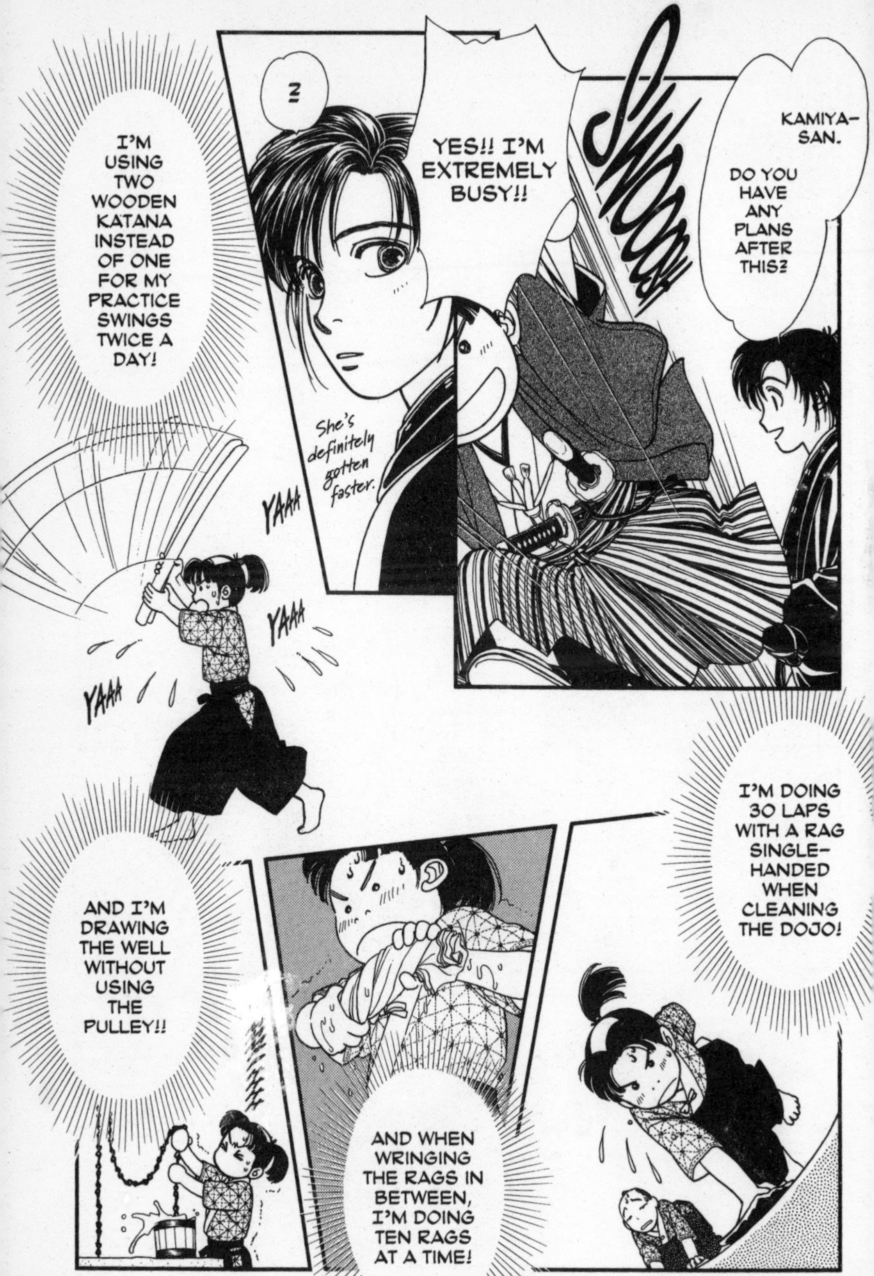
KAMIYA-SAN.
DO YOU HAVE ANY PLANS AFTER THIS?
SWOOOSH!
YES!! I'M EXTREMELY BUSY!!
?
She's definitely gotten faster.
I'M USING TWO WOODEN KATANA INSTEAD OF ONE FOR MY PRACTICE SWINGS TWICE A DAY!
YAAA
YAAA
YAAA
I'M DOING 30 LAPS WITH A RAG SINGLE-HANDED WHEN CLEANING THE DOJO!
AND WHEN WRINGING THE RAGS IN BETWEEN, I'M DOING TEN RAGS AT A TIME!
AND I'M DRAWING THE WELL WITHOUT USING THE PULLEY!!

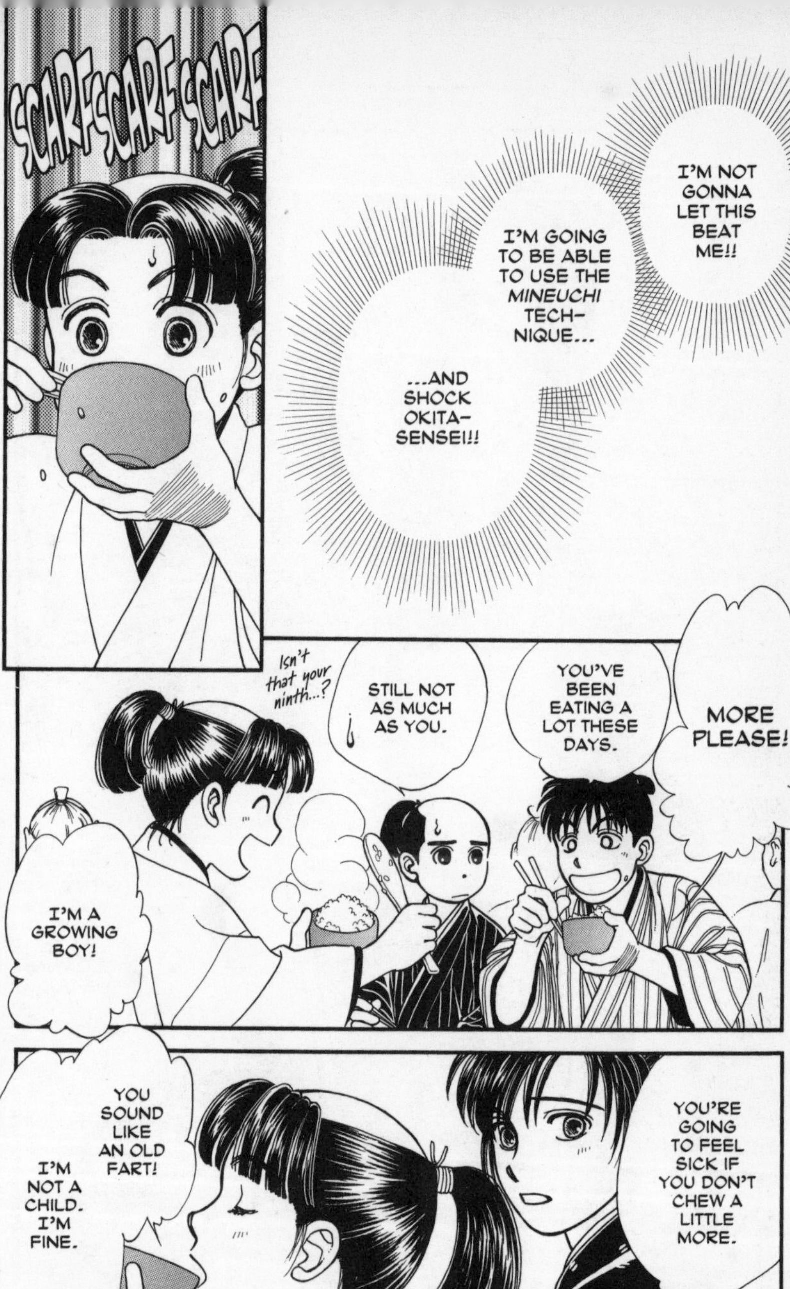

I'M NOT GONNA LET THIS BEAT ME!!
I'M GOING TO BE ABLE TO USE THE *MINEUCHI* TECHNIQUE...
...AND SHOCK OKITA-SENSEI!!!
SCARF SCARF SCARF
MORE PLEASE!
YOU'VE BEEN EATING A LOT THESE DAYS.
STILL NOT AS MUCH AS YOU.
Isn't that your ninth...?
I'M A GROWING BOY!
YOU'RE GOING TO FEEL SICK IF YOU DON'T CHEW A LITTLE MORE.
YOU SOUND LIKE AN OLD FART!
I'M NOT A CHILD. I'M FINE.

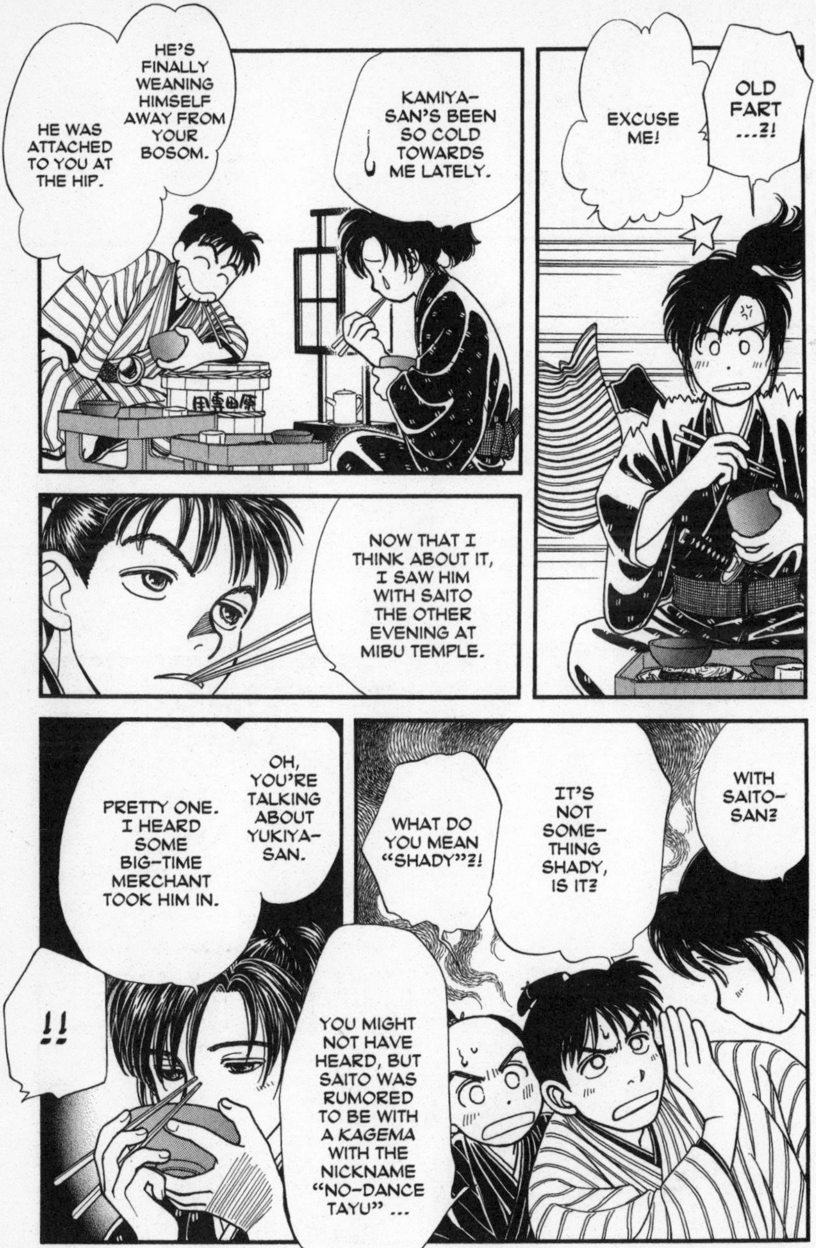

OLD FART ...?!
EXCUSE ME!
KAMIYA-SAN'S BEEN SO COLD TOWARDS ME LATELY.
HE'S FINALLY WEANING HIMSELF AWAY FROM YOUR BOSOM.
HE WAS ATTACHED TO YOU AT THE HIP.
NOW THAT I THINK ABOUT IT, I SAW HIM WITH SAITO THE OTHER EVENING AT MIBU TEMPLE.
WITH SAITO-SAN?
IT'S NOT SOMETHING SHADY, IS IT?
WHAT DO YOU MEAN "SHADY"?!
YOU MIGHT NOT HAVE HEARD, BUT SAITO WAS RUMORED TO BE WITH A *KAGEMA* WITH THE NICKNAME "NO-DANCE TAYU" ...
OH, YOU'RE TALKING ABOUT YUKIYA-SAN.
PRETTY ONE. I HEARD SOME BIG-TIME MERCHANT TOOK HIM IN.
!!

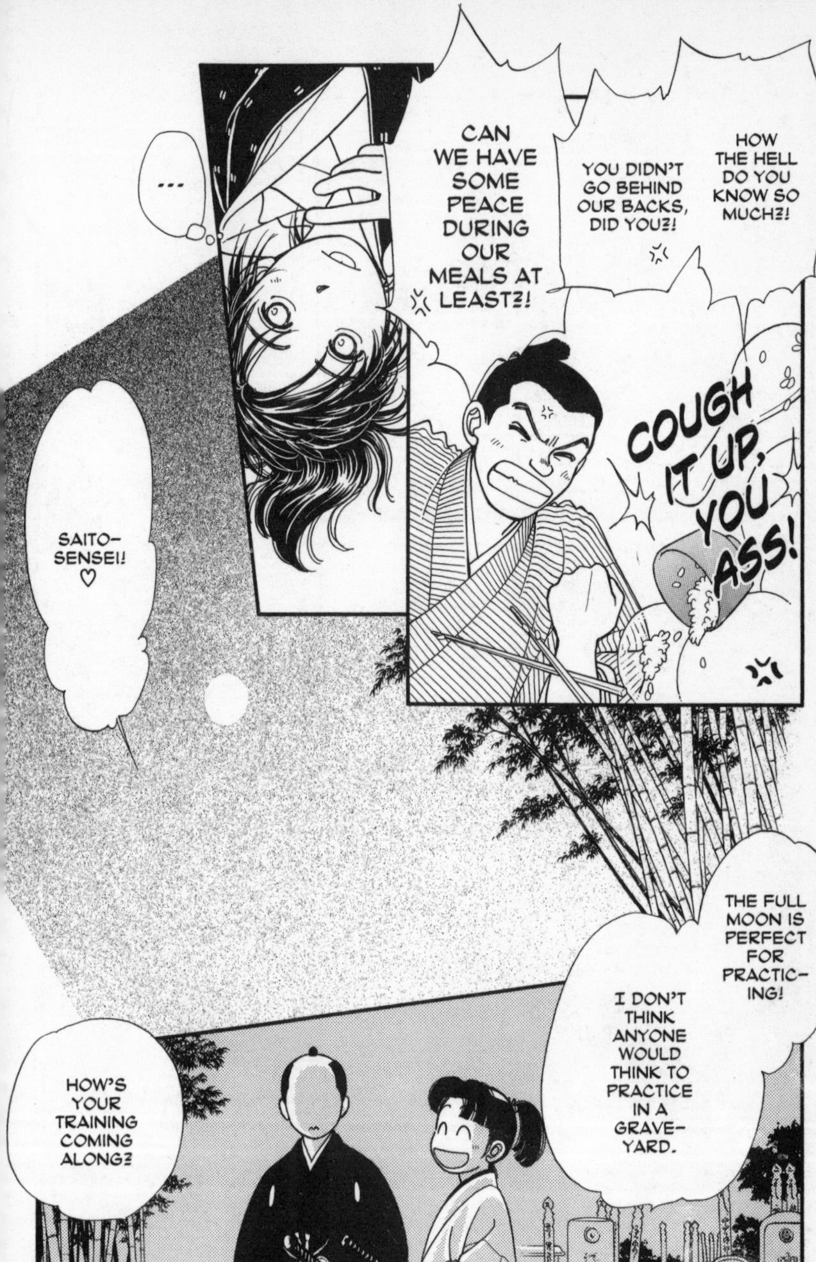
HOW THE HELL DO YOU KNOW SO MUCH?!
YOU DIDN'T GO BEHIND OUR BACKS, DID YOU?!
CAN WE HAVE SOME PEACE DURING OUR MEALS AT LEAST?!
COUGH IT UP, YOU ASS!
...
SAITO-SENSEI! ♡
THE FULL MOON IS PERFECT FOR PRACTICING!
I DON'T THINK ANYONE WOULD THINK TO PRACTICE IN A GRAVEYARD.
HOW'S YOUR TRAINING COMING ALONG?

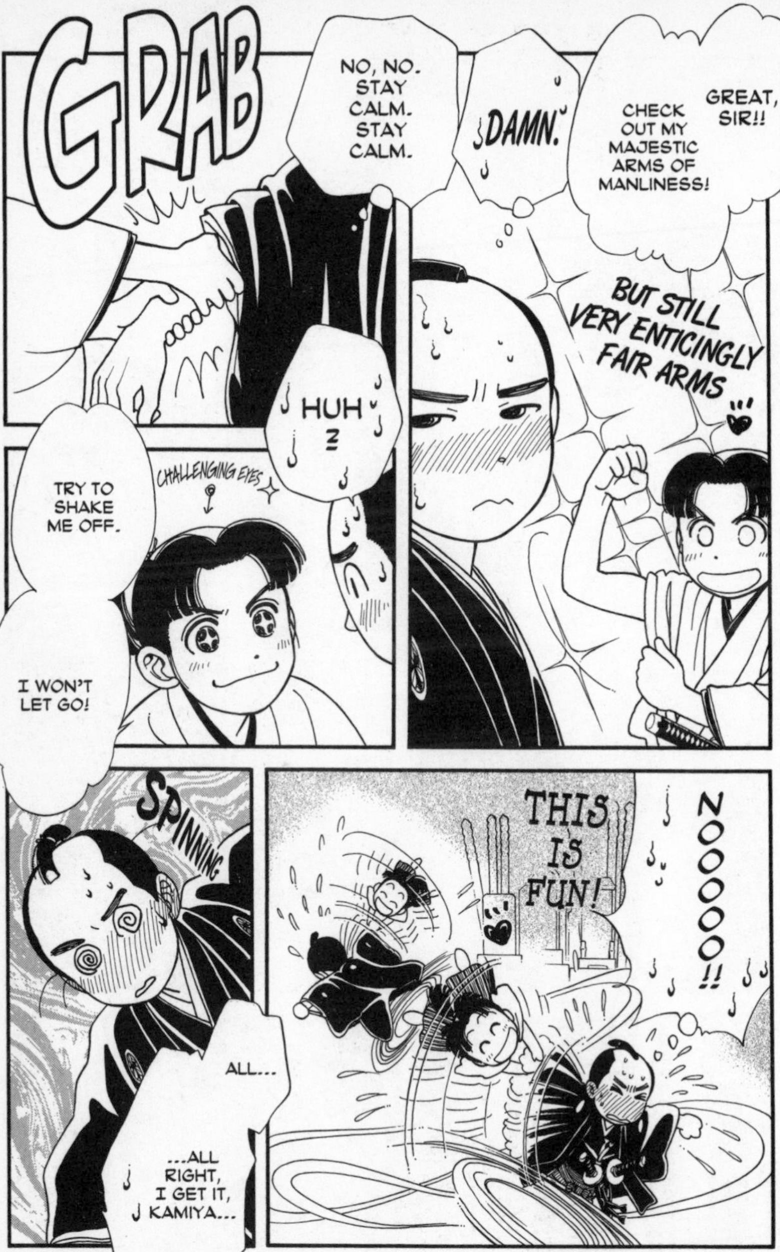
GREAT, SIR!!
CHECK OUT MY MAJESTIC ARMS OF MANLINESS!
DAMN.
BUT STILL VERY ENTICINGLY FAIR ARMS
GRAB
NO, NO. STAY CALM. STAY CALM.
HUH?
TRY TO SHAKE ME OFF.
CHALLENGING EYES
I WON'T LET GO!
NOOOOOO!!
THIS IS FUN!
SPINNING
ALL...
...ALL RIGHT, I GET IT, KAMIYA...

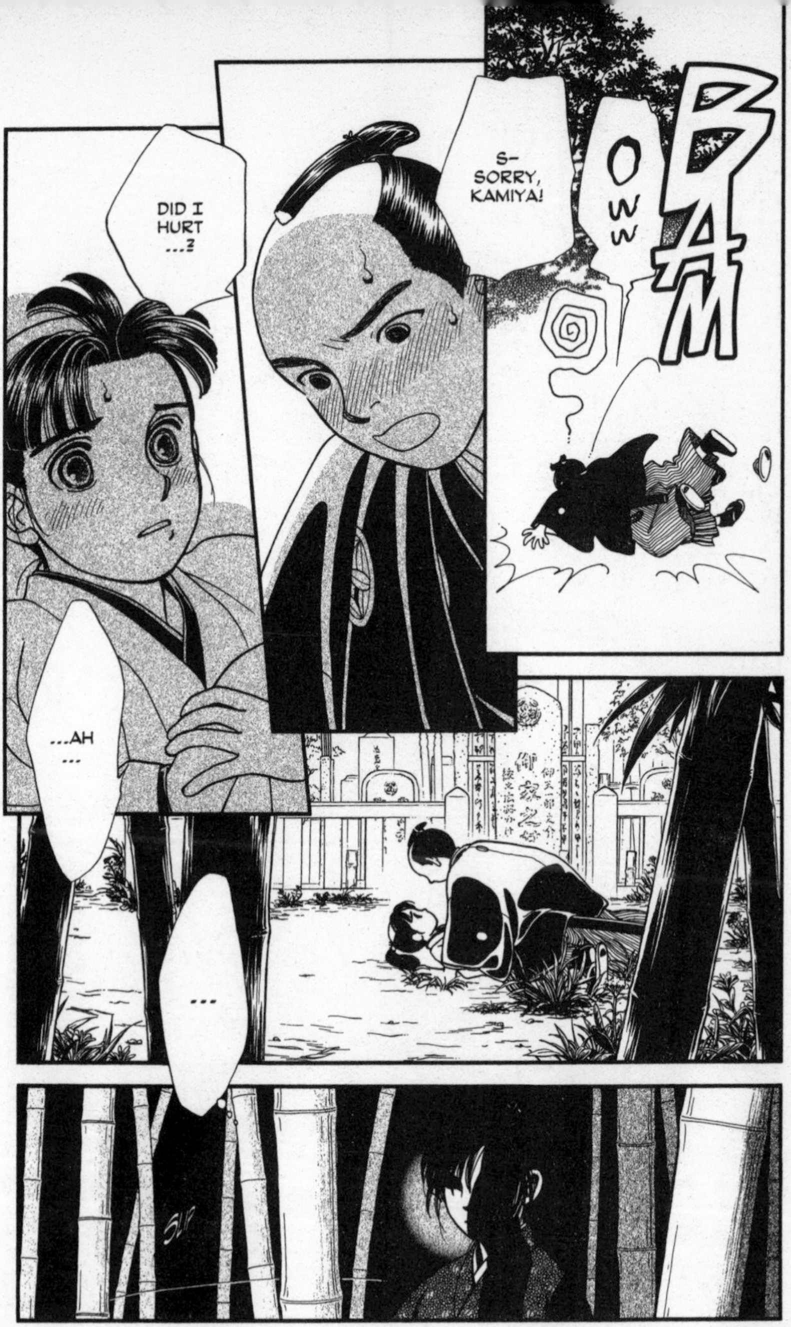
BAM
OWW
S-SORRY, KAMIYA!
DID I HURT ...?
...AH ...
...
SLIP

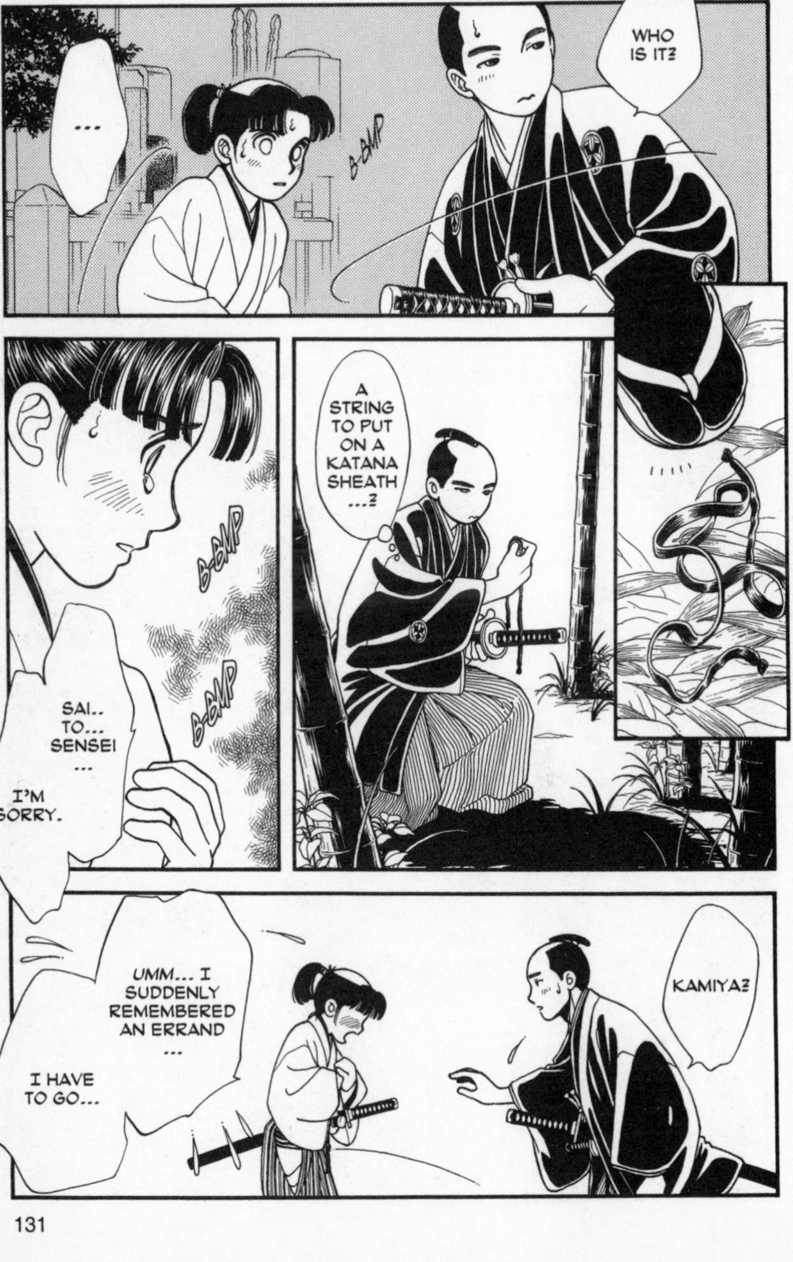

WHO IS IT?
B-BMP
...
A STRING TO PUT ON A KATANA SHEATH ...?
B-BMP
B-BMP
SAI.. TO... SENSEI ...
I'M SORRY.
KAMIYA?
UMM... I SUDDENLY REMEMBERED AN ERRAND ...
I HAVE TO GO...

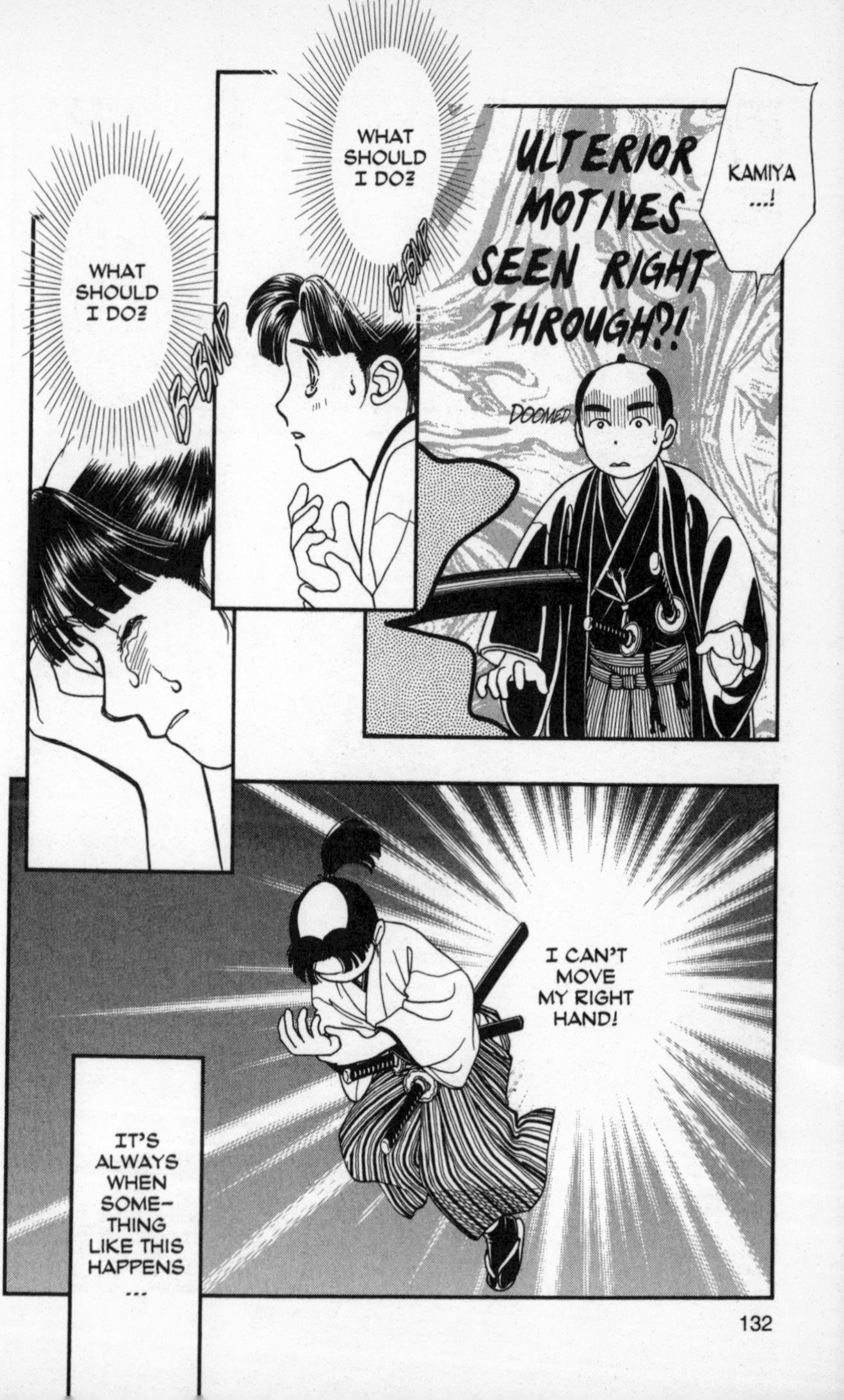
KAMIYA ...!
ULTERIOR MOTIVES SEEN RIGHT THROUGH?!
DOOMED
WHAT SHOULD I DO?
B-BMP
WHAT SHOULD I DO?
B-BMP
I CAN'T MOVE MY RIGHT HAND!
IT'S ALWAYS WHEN SOME-THING LIKE THIS HAPPENS ...

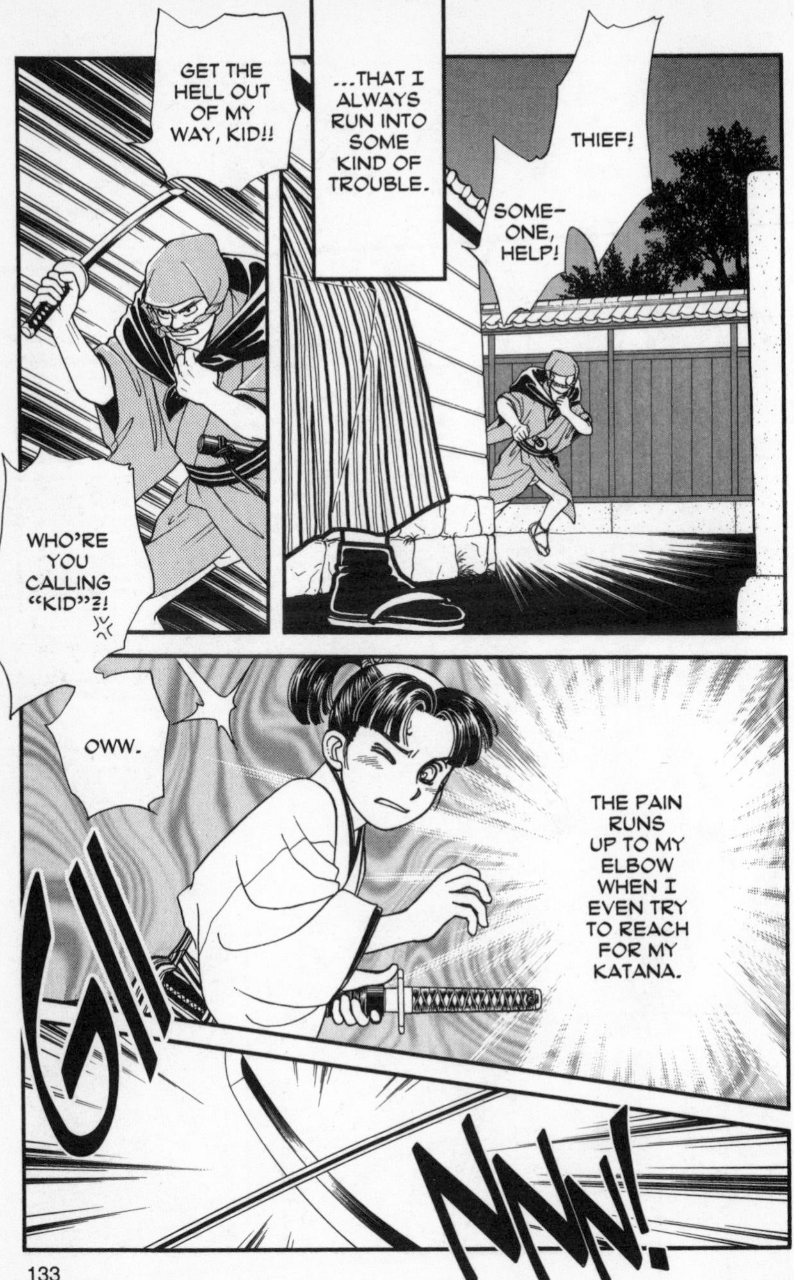
THIEF!
SOME-ONE, HELP!
...THAT I ALWAYS RUN INTO SOME KIND OF TROUBLE.
GET THE HELL OUT OF MY WAY, KID!!
WHO'RE YOU CALLING "KID"?!
THE PAIN RUNS UP TO MY ELBOW WHEN I EVEN TRY TO REACH FOR MY KATANA.
OWW.
GIINNN!

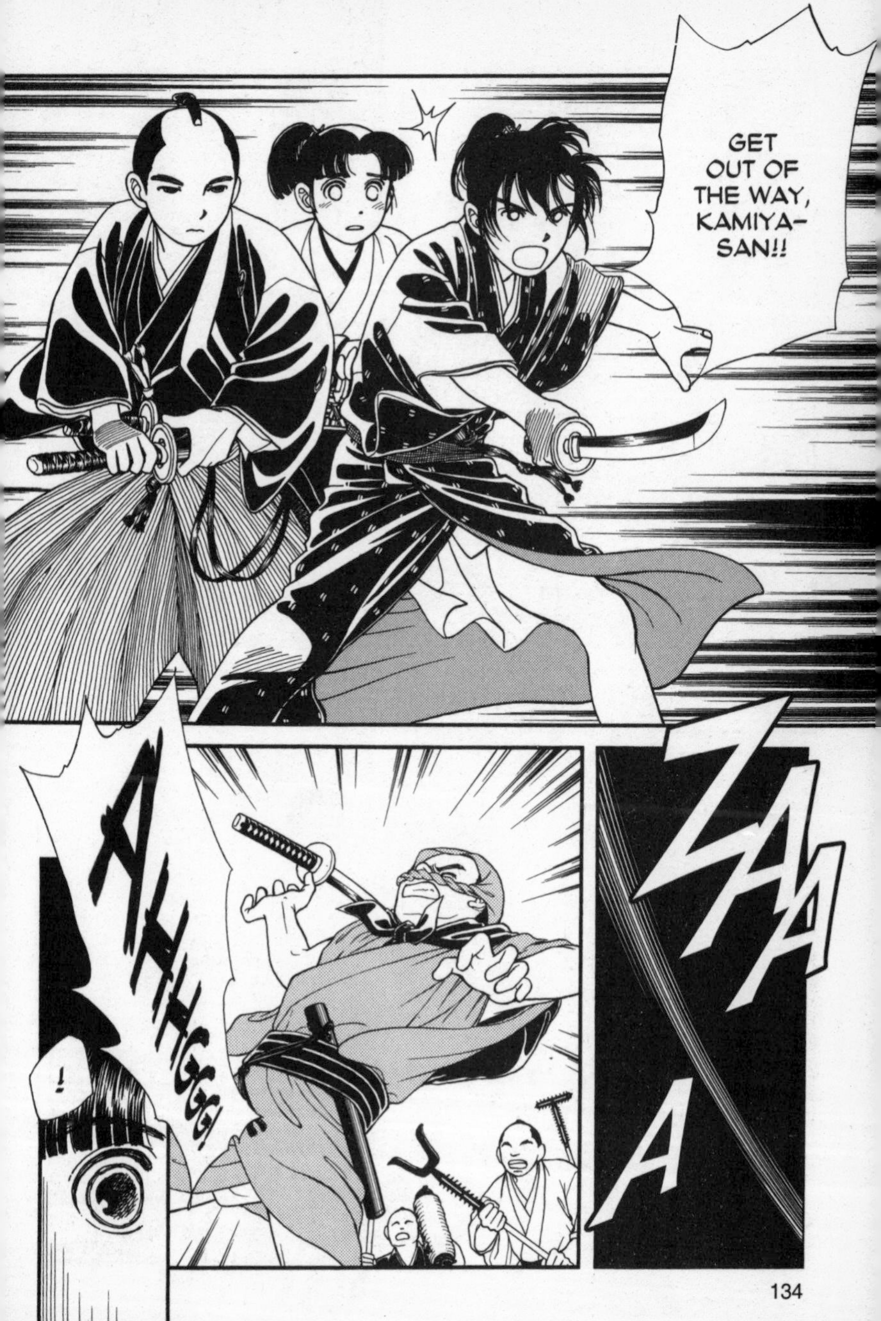
GET OUT OF THE WAY, KAMIYA-SAN!!
ZAAAA
AHHGGG!
!

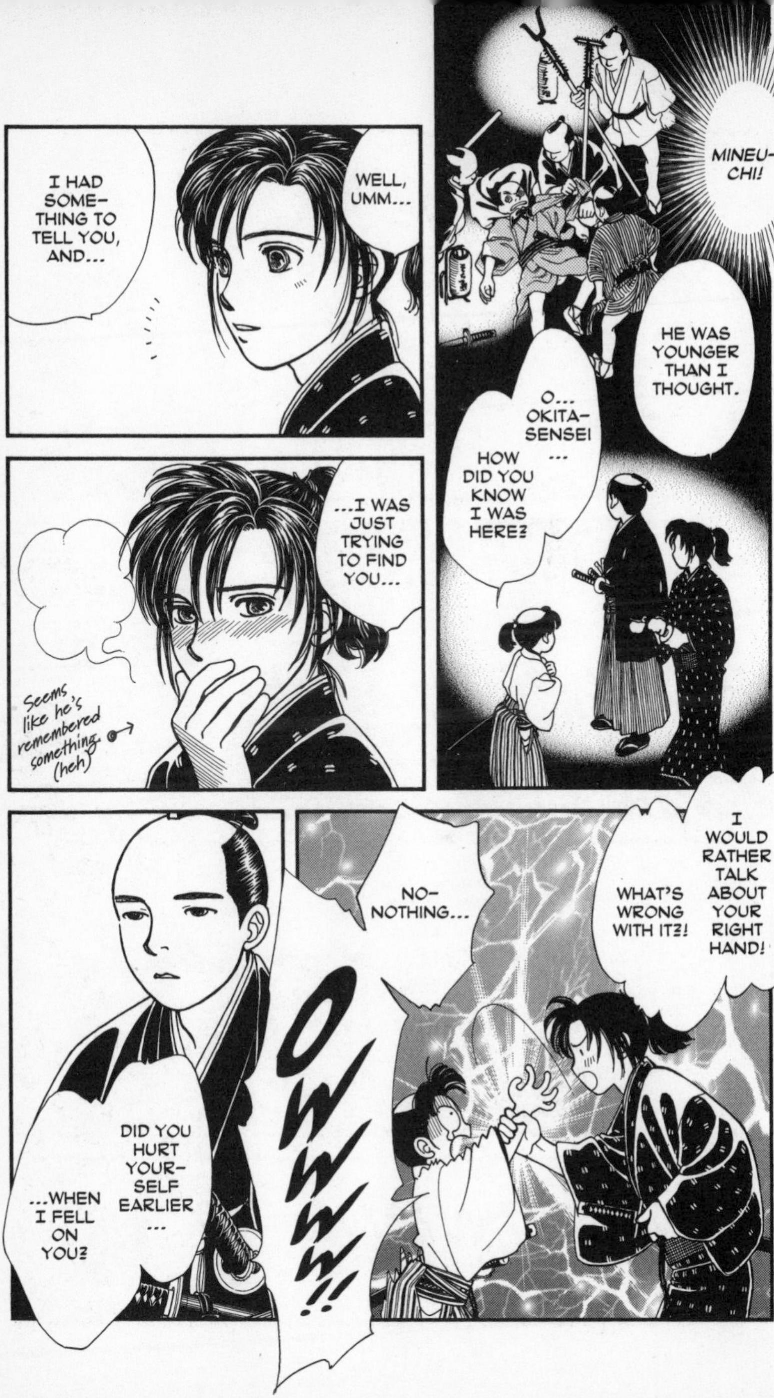
MINEU-CHI!
HE WAS YOUNGER THAN I THOUGHT.
O... OKITA-SENSEI...
HOW DID YOU KNOW I WAS HERE?
WELL, UMM...
I HAD SOME-THING TO TELL YOU, AND...
...I WAS JUST TRYING TO FIND YOU...
Seems like he's remembered something. (heh)
I WOULD RATHER TALK ABOUT YOUR RIGHT HAND!
WHAT'S WRONG WITH IT?!
NO-NOTHING...
OWWW!!
DID YOU HURT YOUR-SELF EARLIER...
...WHEN I FELL ON YOU?

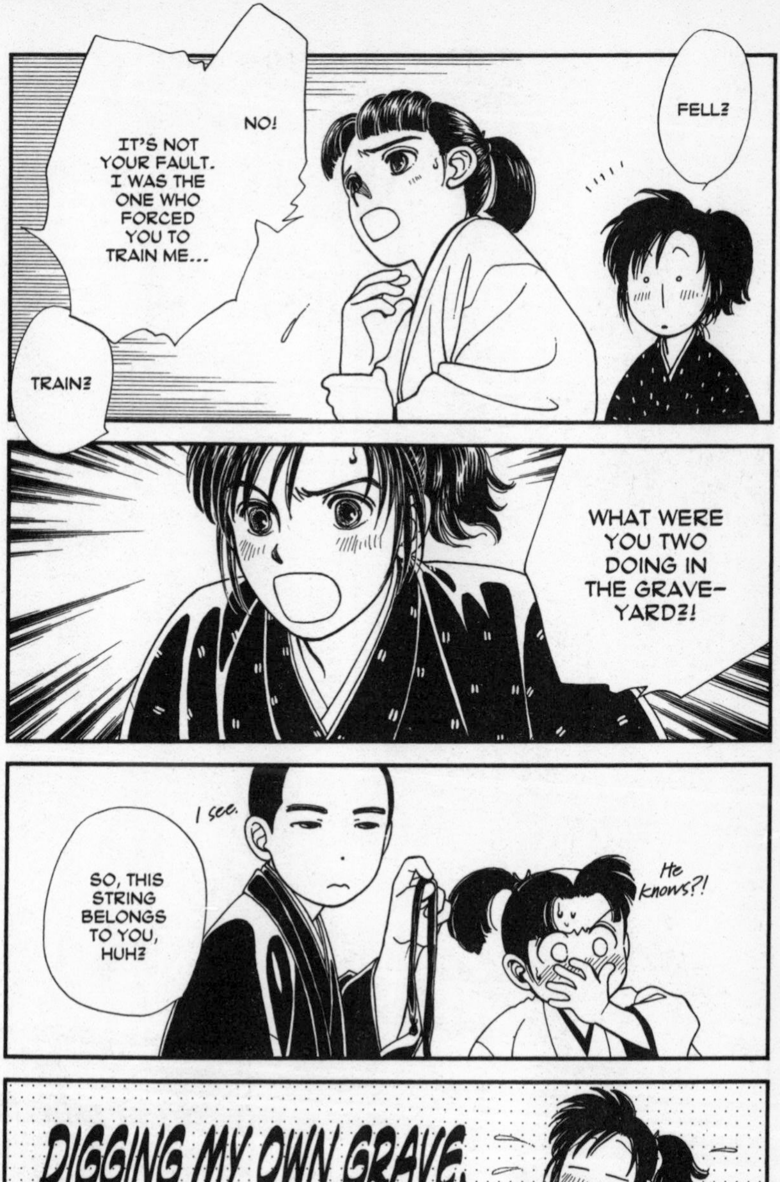
FELL?
NO!
IT'S NOT YOUR FAULT. I WAS THE ONE WHO FORCED YOU TO TRAIN ME...
TRAIN?
WHAT WERE YOU TWO DOING IN THE GRAVE-YARD?!
I see.
SO, THIS STRING BELONGS TO YOU, HUH?
He knows?!
DIGGING MY OWN GRAVE.

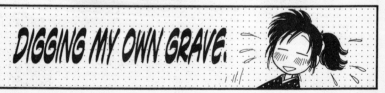

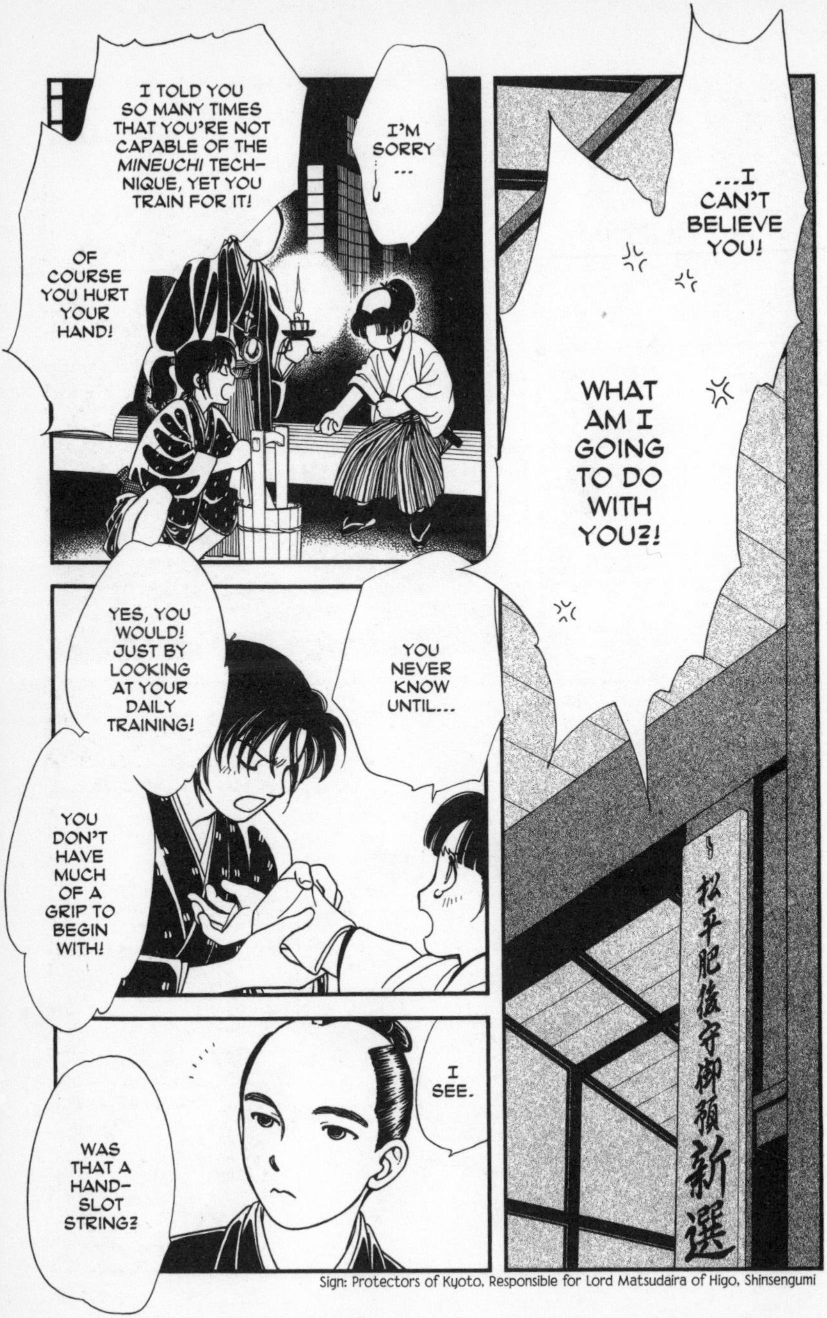
...I CAN'T BELIEVE YOU!
WHAT AM I GOING TO DO WITH YOU?!
松平肥後守御預新選
I TOLD YOU SO MANY TIMES THAT YOU'RE NOT CAPABLE OF THE *MINEUCHI* TECH-NIQUE, YET YOU TRAIN FOR IT!
I'M SORRY...
OF COURSE YOU HURT YOUR HAND!
YOU NEVER KNOW UNTIL...
YES, YOU WOULD! JUST BY LOOKING AT YOUR DAILY TRAINING!
YOU DON'T HAVE MUCH OF A GRIP TO BEGIN WITH!
I SEE.
WAS THAT A HAND-SLOT STRING?
Sign: Protectors of Kyoto, Responsible for Lord Matsudaira of Higo, Shinsengumi

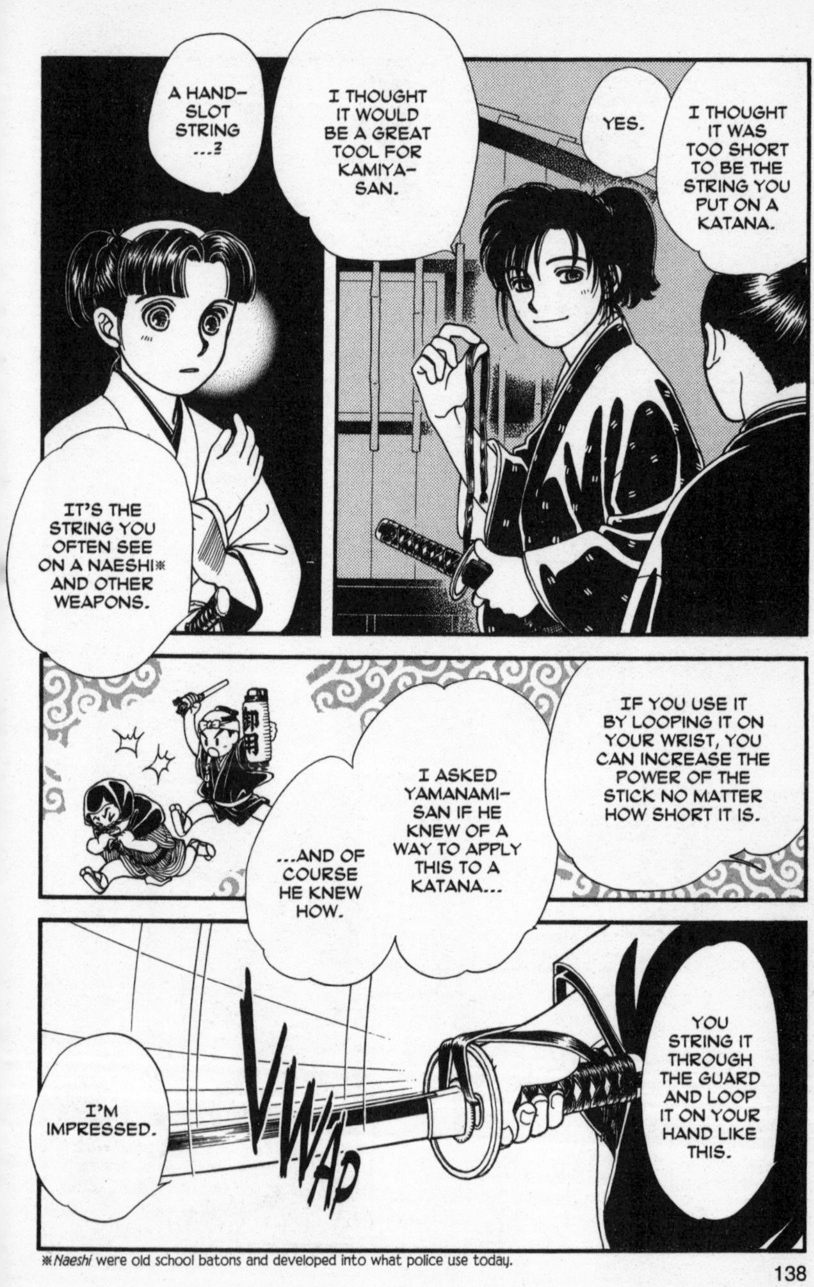
I THOUGHT IT WAS TOO SHORT TO BE THE STRING YOU PUT ON A KATANA.
YES.
I THOUGHT IT WOULD BE A GREAT TOOL FOR KAMIYA-SAN.
A HAND-SLOT STRING ...?
IT'S THE STRING YOU OFTEN SEE ON A NAESHI※ AND OTHER WEAPONS.
IF YOU USE IT BY LOOPING IT ON YOUR WRIST, YOU CAN INCREASE THE POWER OF THE STICK NO MATTER HOW SHORT IT IS.
I ASKED YAMANAMI-SAN IF HE KNEW OF A WAY TO APPLY THIS TO A KATANA...
...AND OF COURSE HE KNEW HOW.
YOU STRING IT THROUGH THE GUARD AND LOOP IT ON YOUR HAND LIKE THIS.
VWAP
I'M IMPRESSED.

※*Naeshi* were old school batons and developed into what police use today.

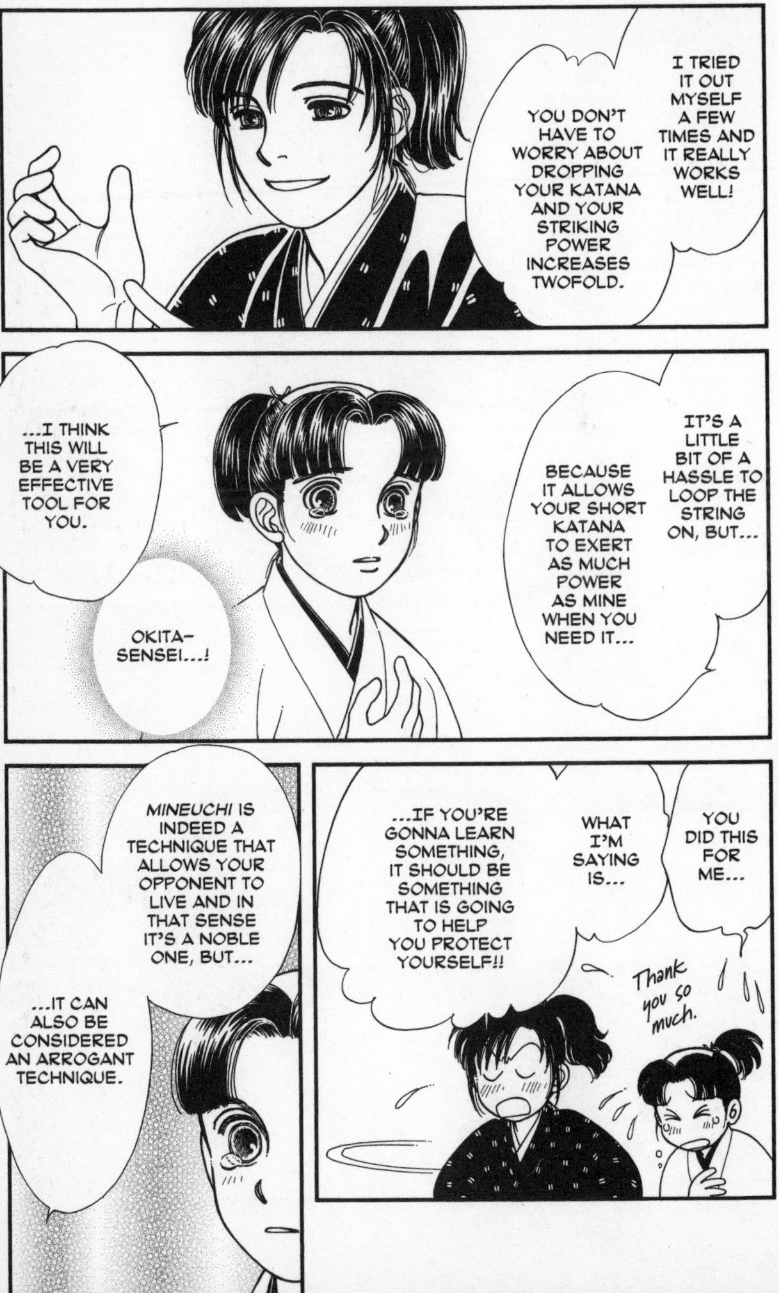
I TRIED IT OUT MYSELF A FEW TIMES AND IT REALLY WORKS WELL!
YOU DON'T HAVE TO WORRY ABOUT DROPPING YOUR KATANA AND YOUR STRIKING POWER INCREASES TWOFOLD.
IT'S A LITTLE BIT OF A HASSLE TO LOOP THE STRING ON, BUT...
BECAUSE IT ALLOWS YOUR SHORT KATANA TO EXERT AS MUCH POWER AS MINE WHEN YOU NEED IT...
...I THINK THIS WILL BE A VERY EFFECTIVE TOOL FOR YOU.
OKITA-SENSEI...!
YOU DID THIS FOR ME...
WHAT I'M SAYING IS...
...IF YOU'RE GONNA LEARN SOMETHING, IT SHOULD BE SOMETHING THAT IS GOING TO HELP YOU PROTECT YOURSELF!!
Thank you so much.
MINEUCHI IS INDEED A TECHNIQUE THAT ALLOWS YOUR OPPONENT TO LIVE AND IN THAT SENSE IT'S A NOBLE ONE, BUT...
...IT CAN ALSO BE CONSIDERED AN ARROGANT TECHNIQUE.

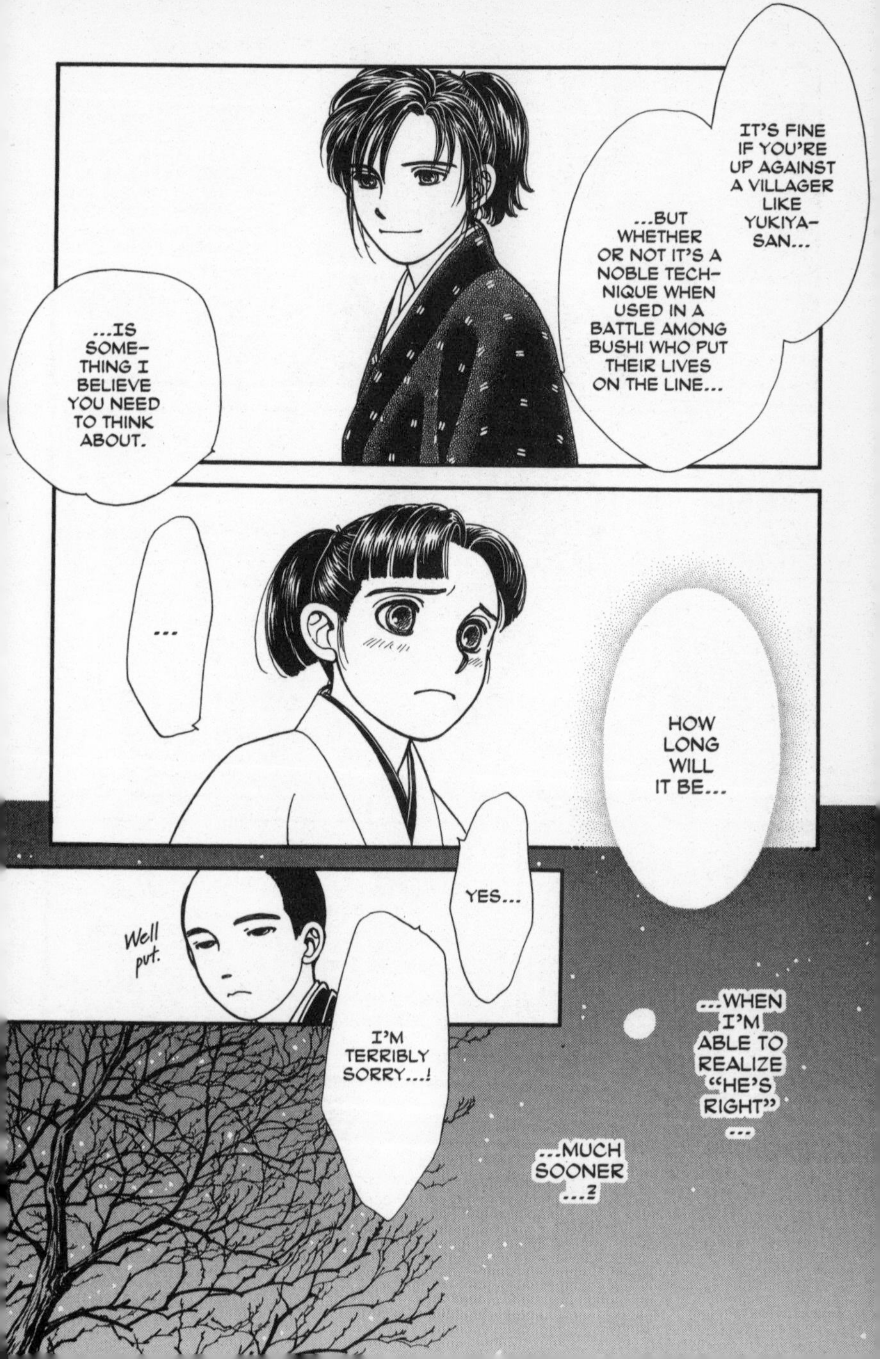
IT'S FINE IF YOU'RE UP AGAINST A VILLAGER LIKE YUKIYA-SAN...
...BUT WHETHER OR NOT IT'S A NOBLE TECHNIQUE WHEN USED IN A BATTLE AMONG BUSHI WHO PUT THEIR LIVES ON THE LINE...
...IS SOMETHING I BELIEVE YOU NEED TO THINK ABOUT.
...
HOW LONG WILL IT BE...
YES...
Well put.
I'M TERRIBLY SORRY...!
...WHEN I'M ABLE TO REALIZE "HE'S RIGHT" ...
...MUCH SOONER ...?

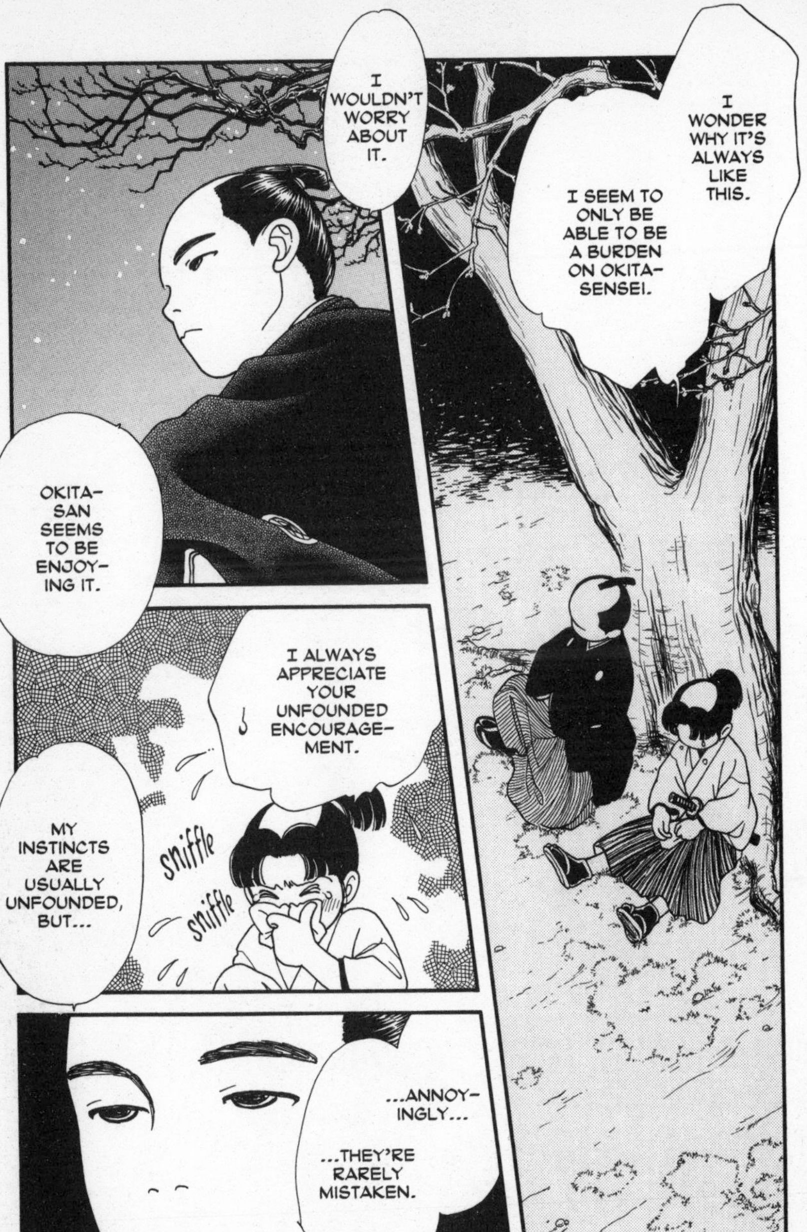
I WONDER WHY IT'S ALWAYS LIKE THIS.
I SEEM TO ONLY BE ABLE TO BE A BURDEN ON OKITA-SENSEI.
I WOULDN'T WORRY ABOUT IT.
OKITA-SAN SEEMS TO BE ENJOYING IT.
I ALWAYS APPRECIATE YOUR UNFOUNDED ENCOURAGEMENT.
sniffle
sniffle
MY INSTINCTS ARE USUALLY UNFOUNDED, BUT...
...ANNOYINGLY...
...THEY'RE RARELY MISTAKEN.

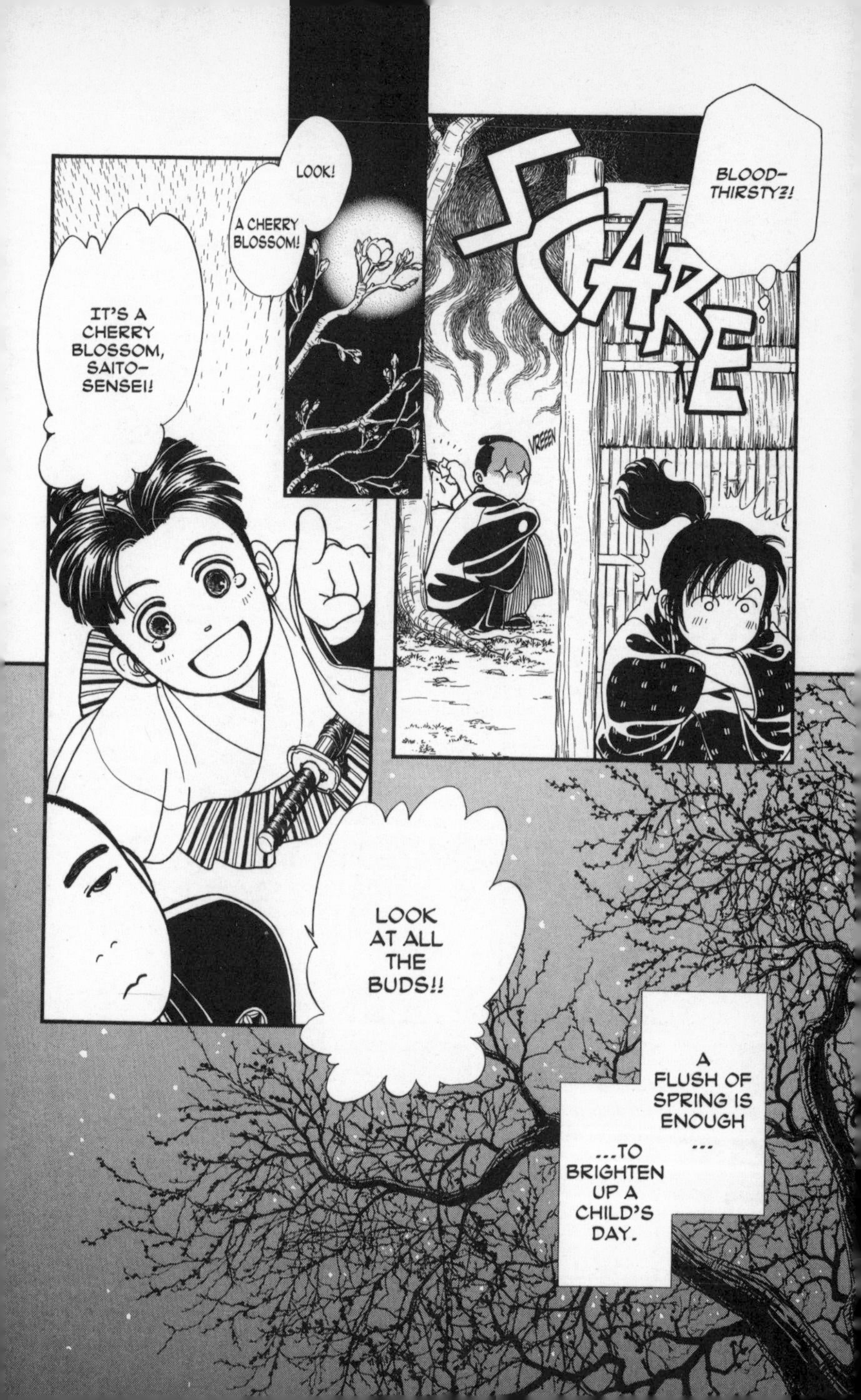
BLOOD-THIRSTY?!
SCARE
VREEEN
LOOK!
A CHERRY BLOSSOM!
IT'S A CHERRY BLOSSOM, SAITO-SENSEI!
LOOK AT ALL THE BUDS!!
A FLUSH OF SPRING IS ENOUGH ...
...TO BRIGHTEN UP A CHILD'S DAY.

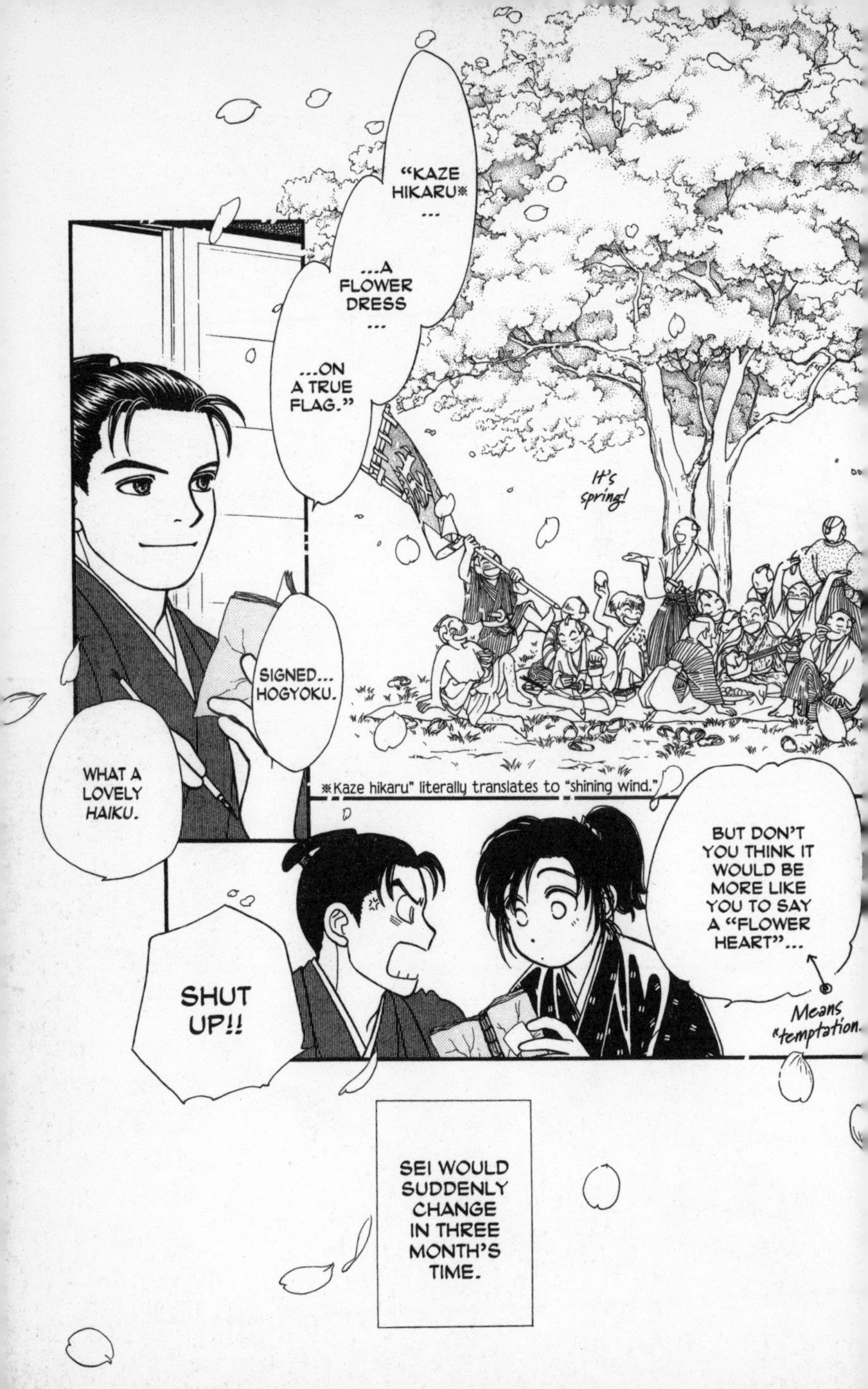
"KAZE HIKARU※...
...A FLOWER DRESS...
...ON A TRUE FLAG."
It's spring!
※Kaze hikaru" literally translates to "shining wind."
SIGNED... HOGYOKU.
WHAT A LOVELY HAIKU.
BUT DON'T YOU THINK IT WOULD BE MORE LIKE YOU TO SAY A "FLOWER HEART"...
Means "temptation.
SHUT UP!!
SEI WOULD SUDDENLY CHANGE IN THREE MONTH'S TIME.

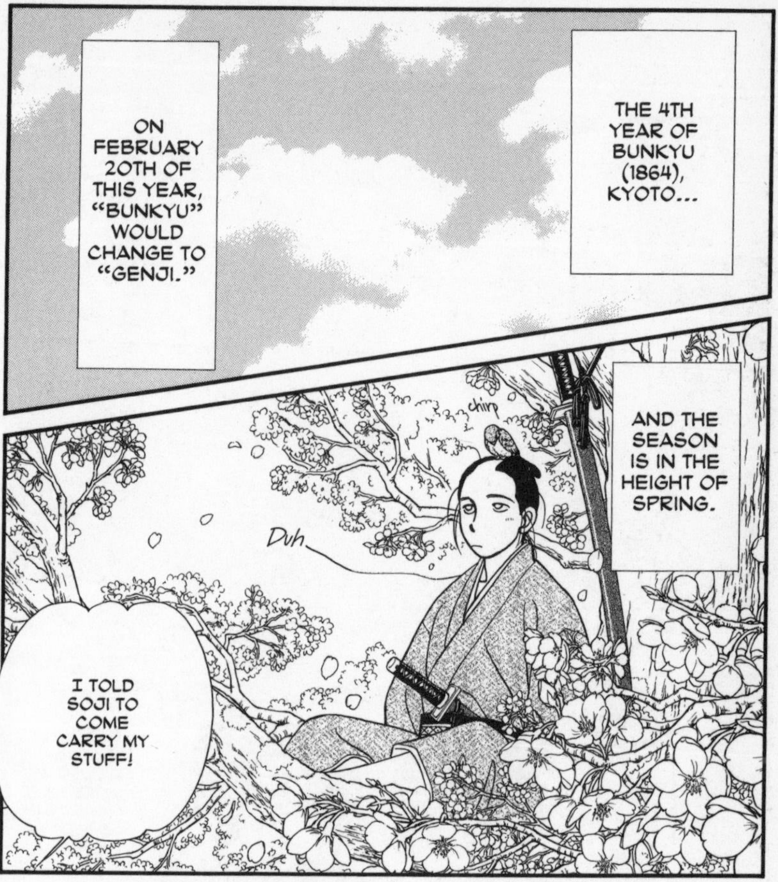
THE 4TH YEAR OF BUNKYU (1864), KYOTO...
ON FEBRUARY 20TH OF THIS YEAR, "BUNKYU" WOULD CHANGE TO "GENJI."
AND THE SEASON IS IN THE HEIGHT OF SPRING.
chirp
Duh
I TOLD SOJI TO COME CARRY MY STUFF!

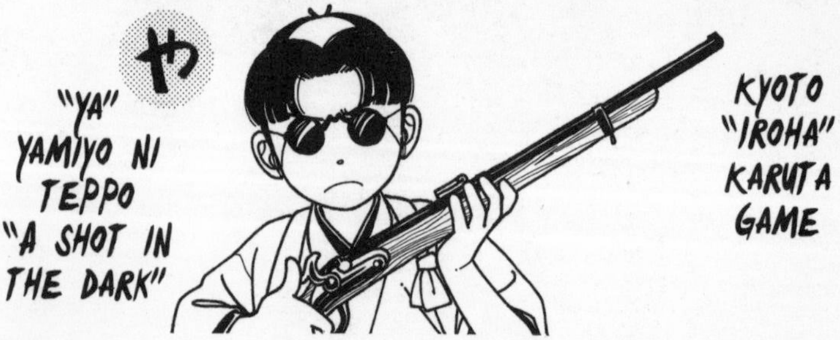
KYOTO "IROHA" KARUTA GAME
や
"YA" YAMIYO NI TEPPO "A SHOT IN THE DARK"

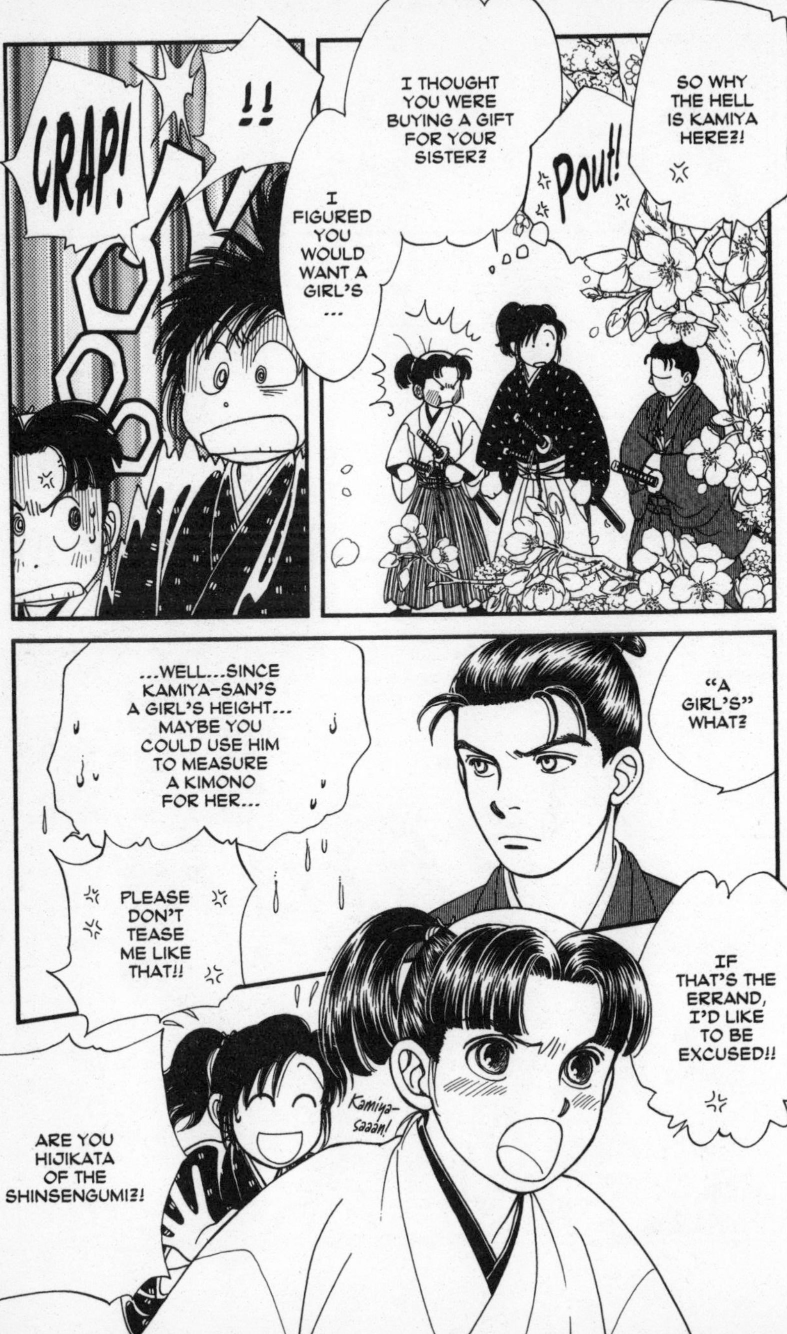
SO WHY THE HELL IS KAMIYA HERE?!
Pout!
I THOUGHT YOU WERE BUYING A GIFT FOR YOUR SISTER?
I FIGURED YOU WOULD WANT A GIRL'S ...
!!
CRAP!
"A GIRL'S" WHAT?
...WELL...SINCE KAMIYA-SAN'S A GIRL'S HEIGHT... MAYBE YOU COULD USE HIM TO MEASURE A KIMONO FOR HER...
PLEASE DON'T TEASE ME LIKE THAT!!
IF THAT'S THE ERRAND, I'D LIKE TO BE EXCUSED!!
Kamiya-saaan!
ARE YOU HIJIKATA OF THE SHINSENGUMI?!

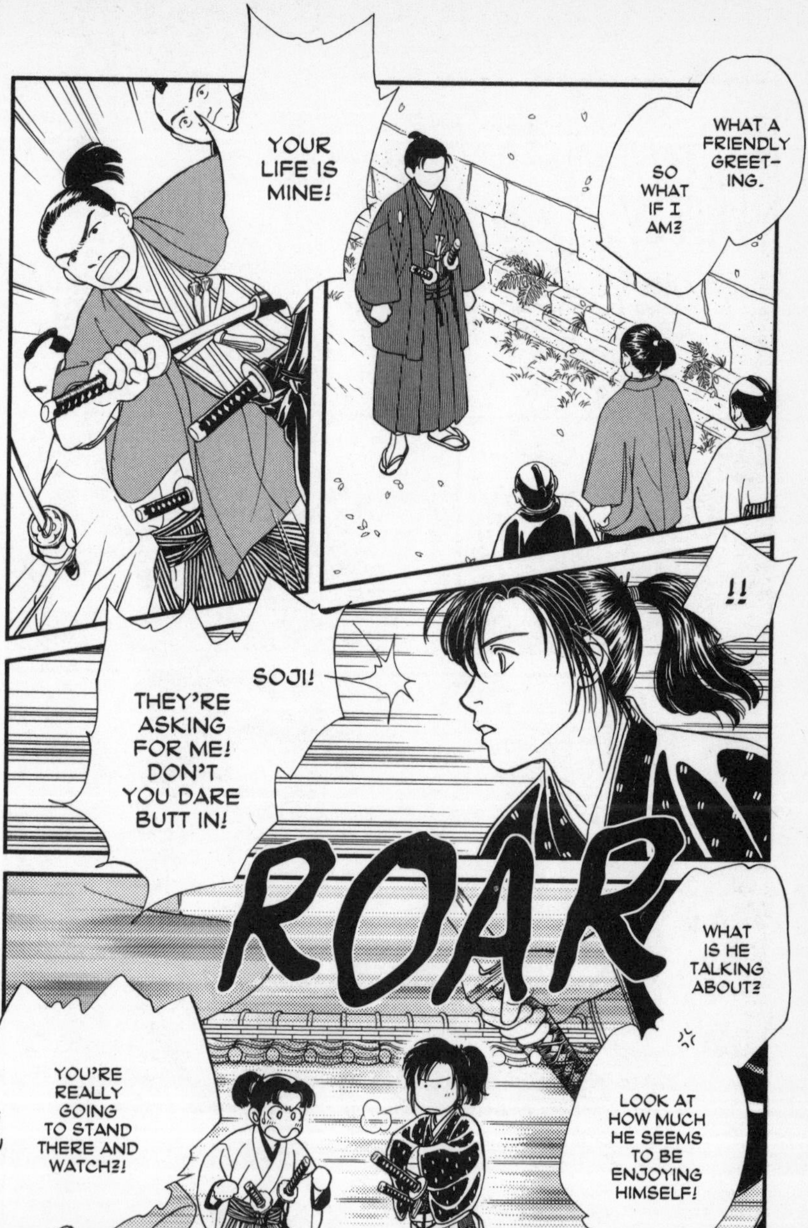
WHAT A FRIENDLY GREET-ING.
SO WHAT IF I AM?
YOUR LIFE IS MINE!
!!
SOJI!
THEY'RE ASKING FOR ME! DON'T YOU DARE BUTT IN!
ROAR
WHAT IS HE TALKING ABOUT?
LOOK AT HOW MUCH HE SEEMS TO BE ENJOYING HIMSELF!
YOU'RE REALLY GOING TO STAND THERE AND WATCH?!

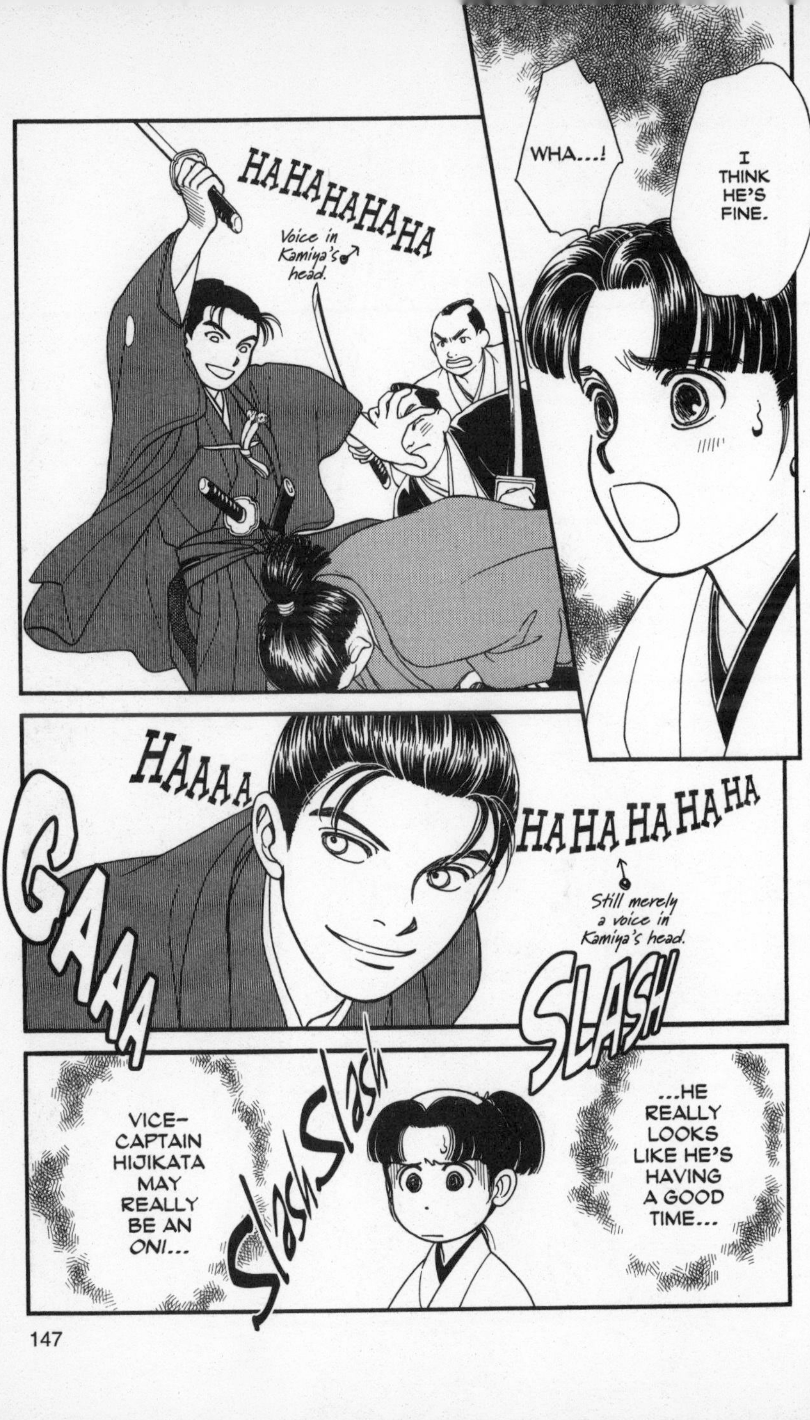
I THINK HE'S FINE.
WHA...!
HAHAHAHAHA
Voice in Kamiya's head.
HAHAHAHAHA
Still merely a voice in Kamiya's head.
SLASH
HAAAA
GAAAA
...HE REALLY LOOKS LIKE HE'S HAVING A GOOD TIME...
Slash Slash
VICE-CAPTAIN HIJIKATA MAY REALLY BE AN ONI...

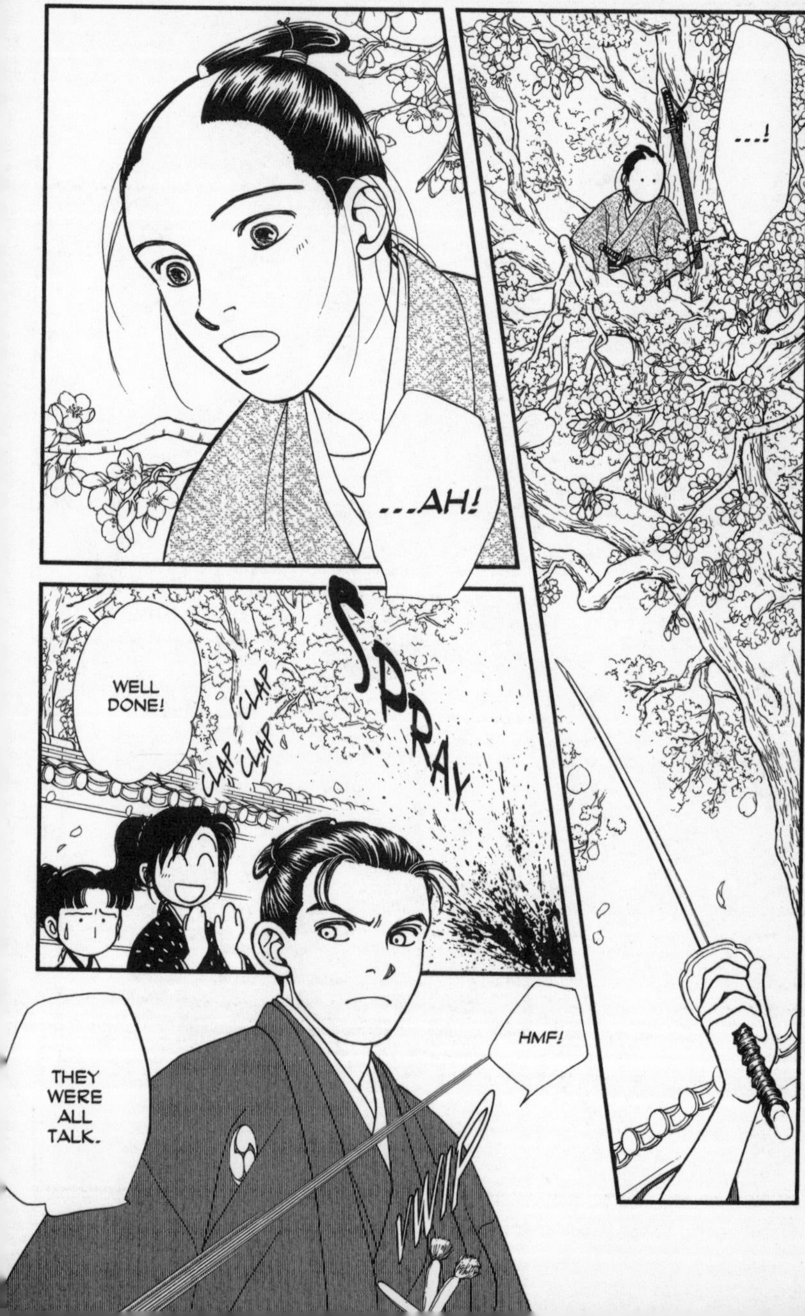
...!
...AH!
SPRAY
WELL DONE!
CLAP CLAP
CLAP
HMF!
THEY WERE ALL TALK.

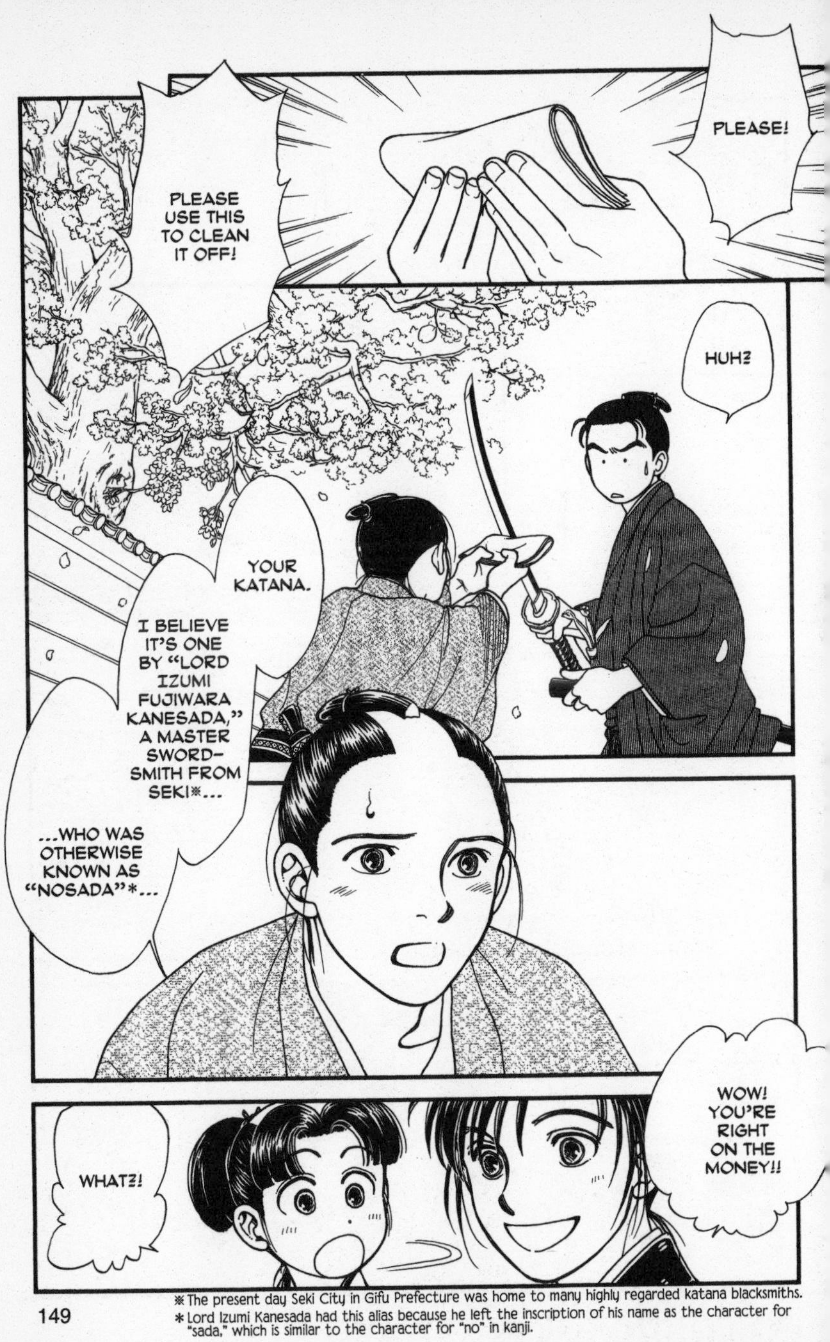
PLEASE!
PLEASE USE THIS TO CLEAN IT OFF!
HUH?
YOUR KATANA.
I BELIEVE IT'S ONE BY "LORD IZUMI FUJIWARA KANESADA," A MASTER SWORD-SMITH FROM SEKI※...
...WHO WAS OTHERWISE KNOWN AS "NOSADA"*...
WOW! YOU'RE RIGHT ON THE MONEY!!
WHAT?!

※ The present day Seki City in Gifu Prefecture was home to many highly regarded katana blacksmiths.

* Lord Izumi Kanesada had this alias because he left the inscription of his name as the character for "sada," which is similar to the character for "no" in kanji.

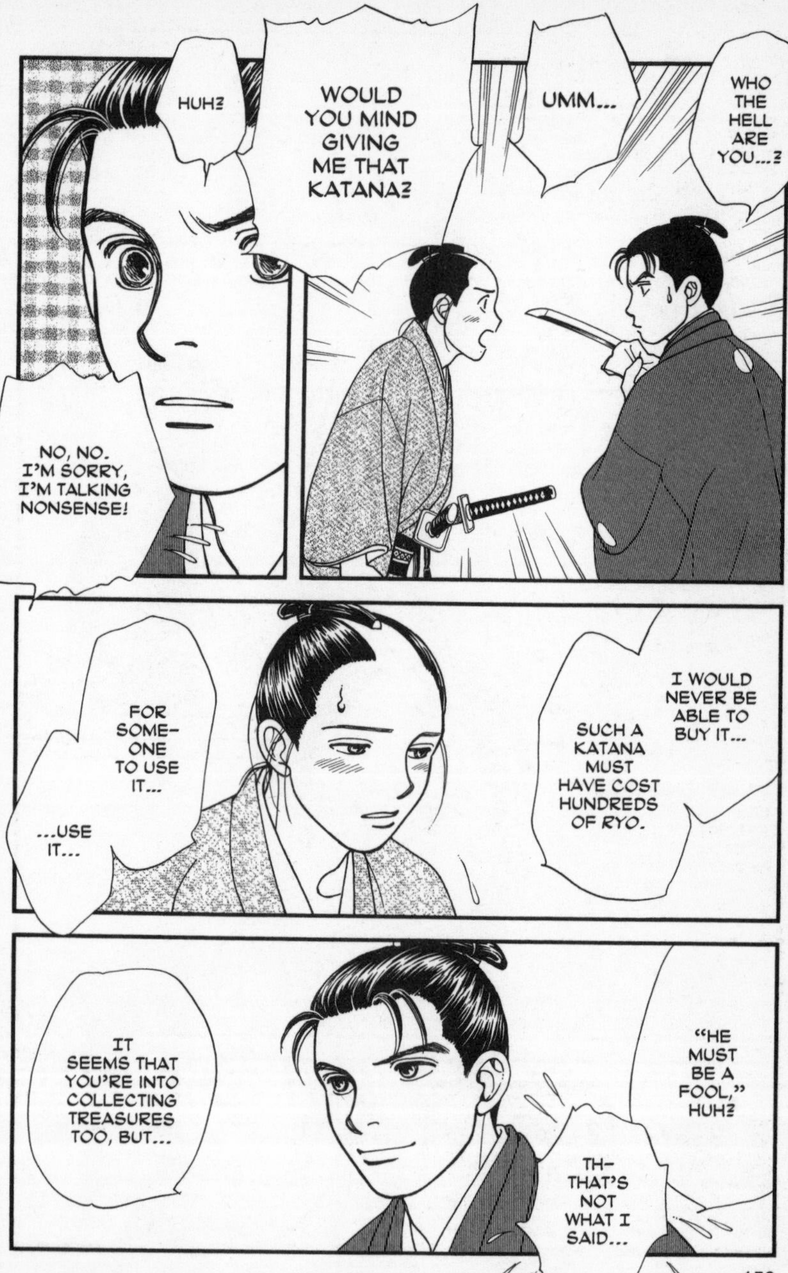
WHO THE HELL ARE YOU...?
UMM...
WOULD YOU MIND GIVING ME THAT KATANA?
HUH?
NO, NO. I'M SORRY, I'M TALKING NONSENSE!
I WOULD NEVER BE ABLE TO BUY IT...
SUCH A KATANA MUST HAVE COST HUNDREDS OF *RYO*.
FOR SOME-ONE TO USE IT...
...USE IT...
"HE MUST BE A FOOL," HUH?
TH-THAT'S NOT WHAT I SAID...
IT SEEMS THAT YOU'RE INTO COLLECTING TREASURES TOO, BUT...

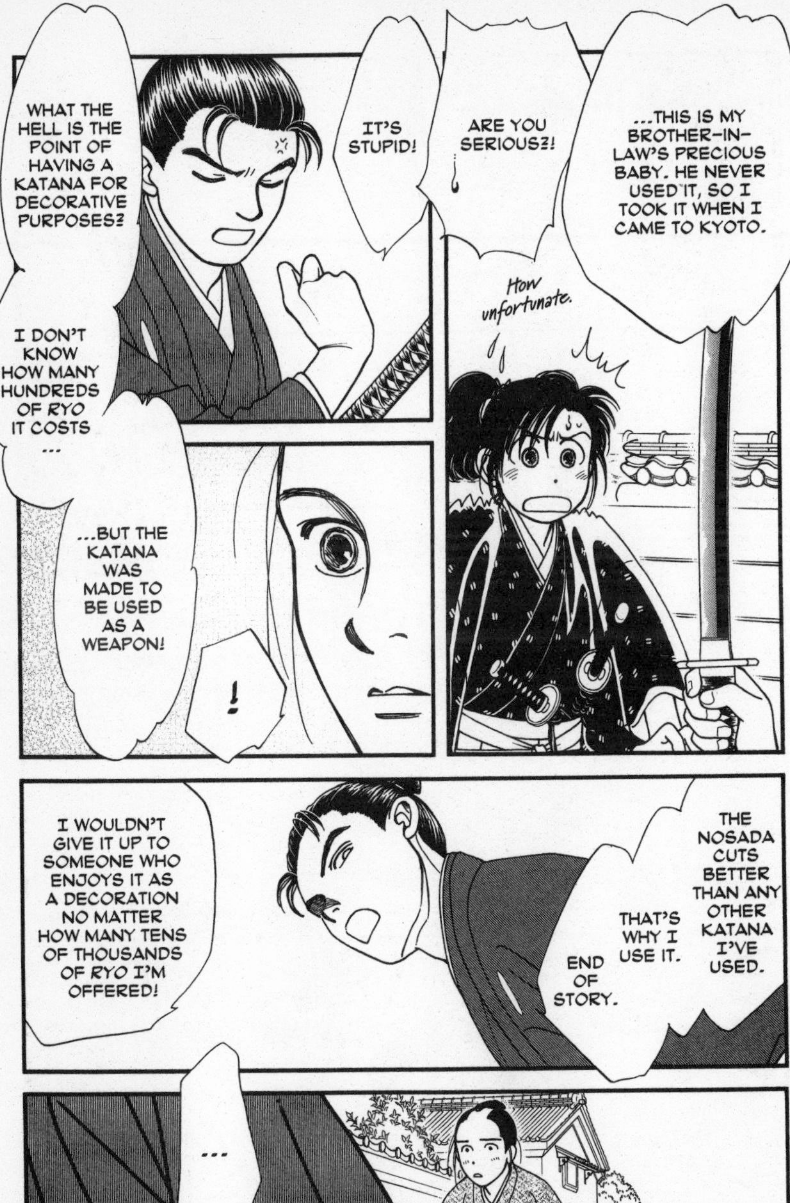
...THIS IS MY BROTHER-IN-LAW'S PRECIOUS BABY. HE NEVER USED IT, SO I TOOK IT WHEN I CAME TO KYOTO.
ARE YOU SERIOUS?!
How unfortunate.
IT'S STUPID!
WHAT THE HELL IS THE POINT OF HAVING A KATANA FOR DECORATIVE PURPOSES?
I DON'T KNOW HOW MANY HUNDREDS OF *RYO* IT COSTS ...
...BUT THE KATANA WAS MADE TO BE USED AS A WEAPON!
!
THE NOSADA CUTS BETTER THAN ANY OTHER KATANA I'VE USED.
THAT'S WHY I USE IT.
END OF STORY.
I WOULDN'T GIVE IT UP TO SOMEONE WHO ENJOYS IT AS A DECORATION NO MATTER HOW MANY TENS OF THOUSANDS OF *RYO* I'M OFFERED!
...

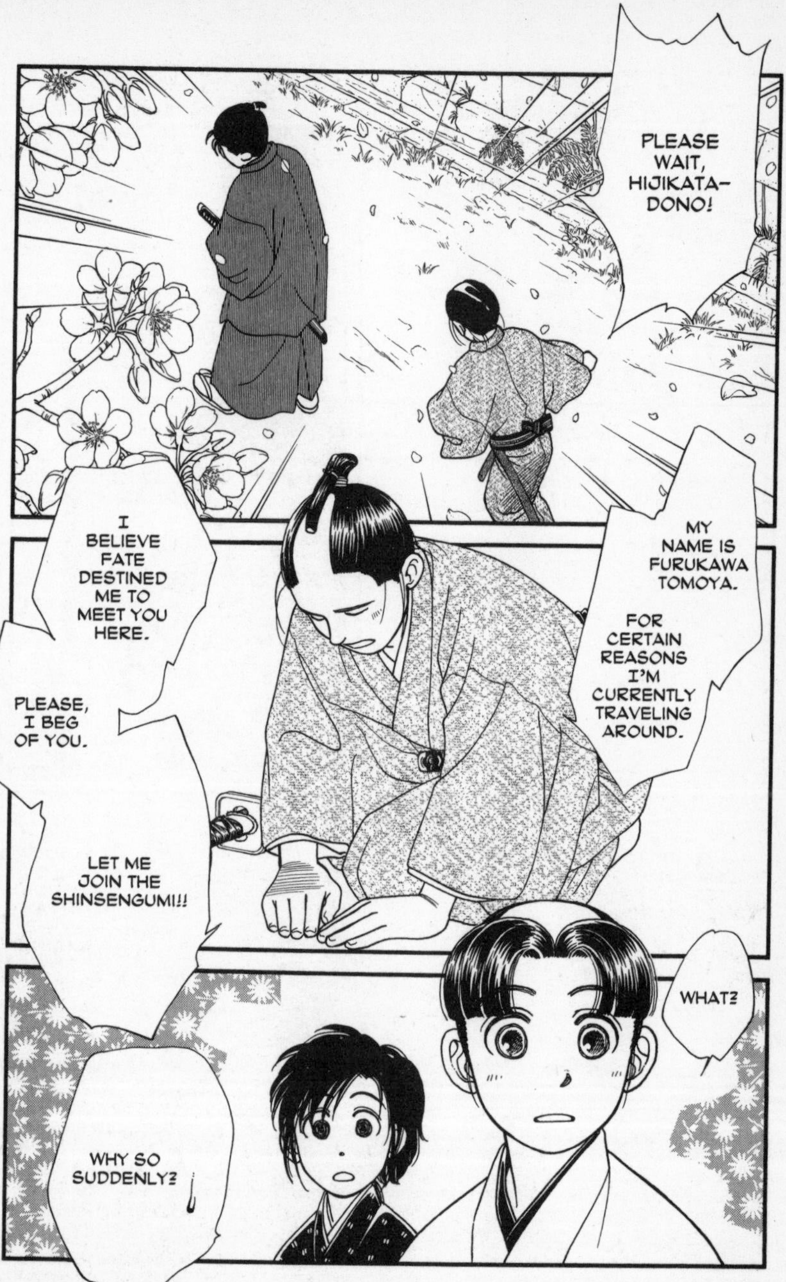
PLEASE WAIT, HIJIKATA-DONO!
MY NAME IS FURUKAWA TOMOYA.
FOR CERTAIN REASONS I'M CURRENTLY TRAVELING AROUND.
I BELIEVE FATE DESTINED ME TO MEET YOU HERE.
PLEASE, I BEG OF YOU.
LET ME JOIN THE SHINSENGUMI!!
WHAT?
WHY SO SUDDENLY?

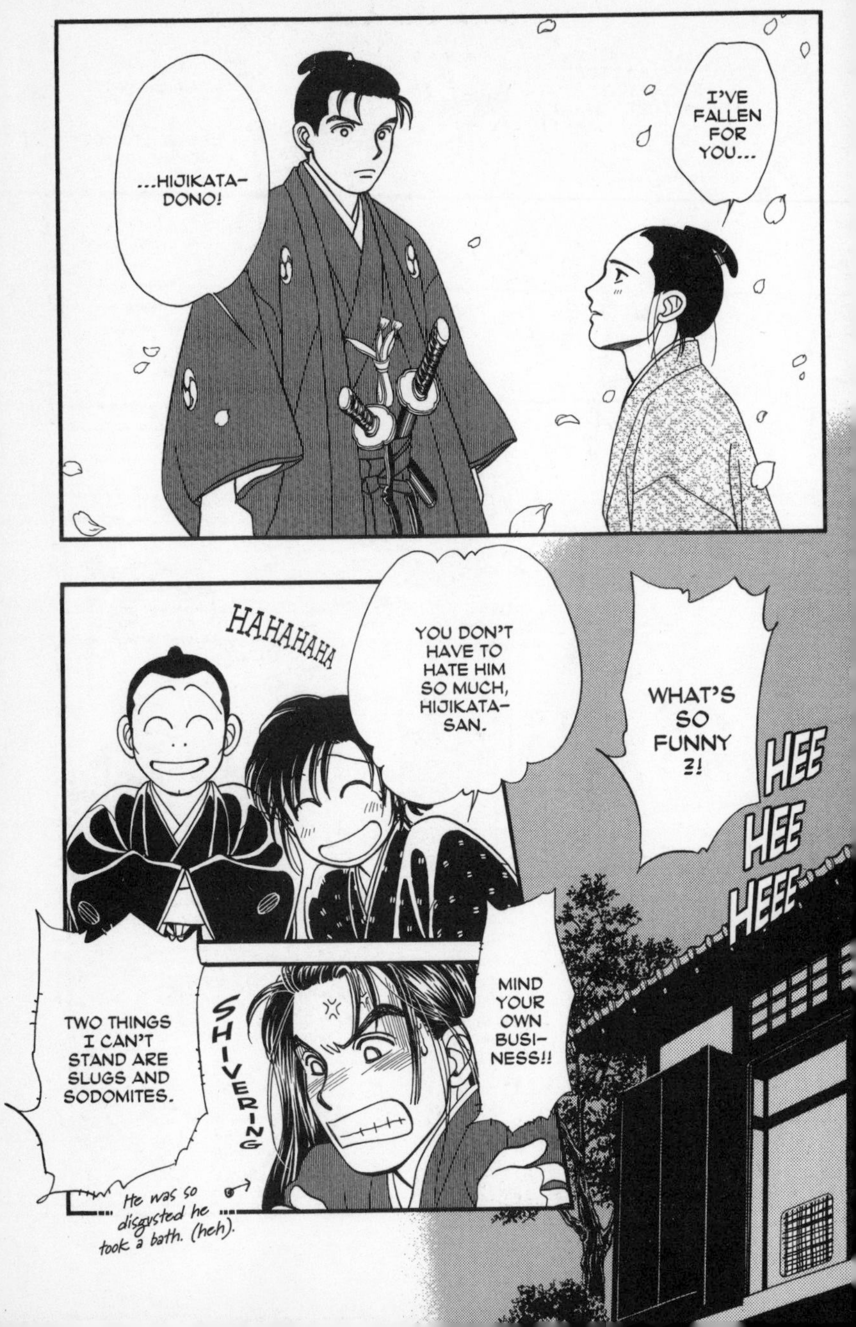
I'VE FALLEN FOR YOU...
...HIJIKATA-DONO!
WHAT'S SO FUNNY?!
HEE HEE HEEE
YOU DON'T HAVE TO HATE HIM SO MUCH, HIJIKATA-SAN.
HAHAHAHA
MIND YOUR OWN BUSI-NESS!!
SHIVERING
TWO THINGS I CAN'T STAND ARE SLUGS AND SODOMITES.
He was so disgusted he took a bath. (heh).

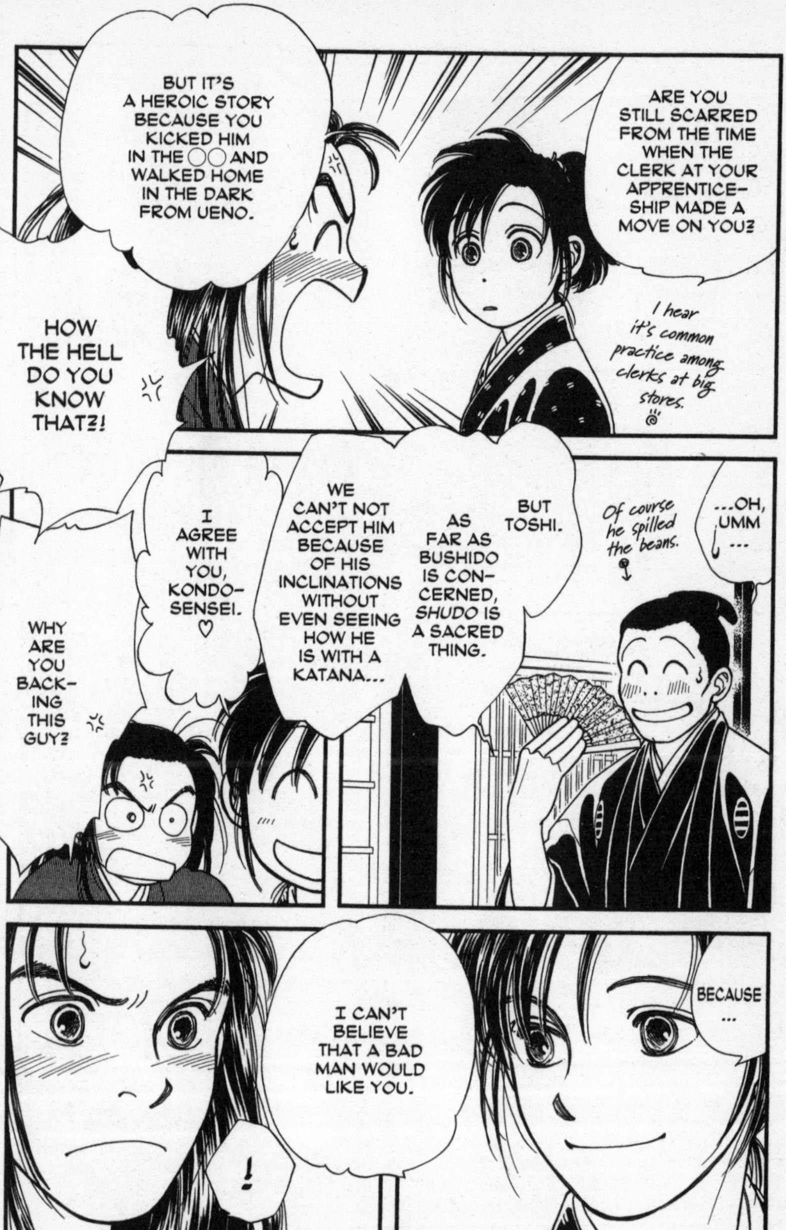
ARE YOU STILL SCARRED FROM THE TIME WHEN THE CLERK AT YOUR APPRENTICESHIP MADE A MOVE ON YOU?!
I hear it's common practice among clerks at big stores.
BUT IT'S A HEROIC STORY BECAUSE YOU KICKED HIM IN THE ○○ AND WALKED HOME IN THE DARK FROM UENO.
HOW THE HELL DO YOU KNOW THAT?!!
...OH, UMM...
Of course he spilled the beans.
BUT TOSHI.
AS FAR AS BUSHIDO IS CONCERNED, SHUDO IS A SACRED THING.
WE CAN'T NOT ACCEPT HIM BECAUSE OF HIS INCLINATIONS WITHOUT EVEN SEEING HOW HE IS WITH A KATANA...
I AGREE WITH YOU, KONDO-SENSEI. ♡
WHY ARE YOU BACKING THIS GUY?!
BECAUSE...
I CAN'T BELIEVE THAT A BAD MAN WOULD LIKE YOU.
!

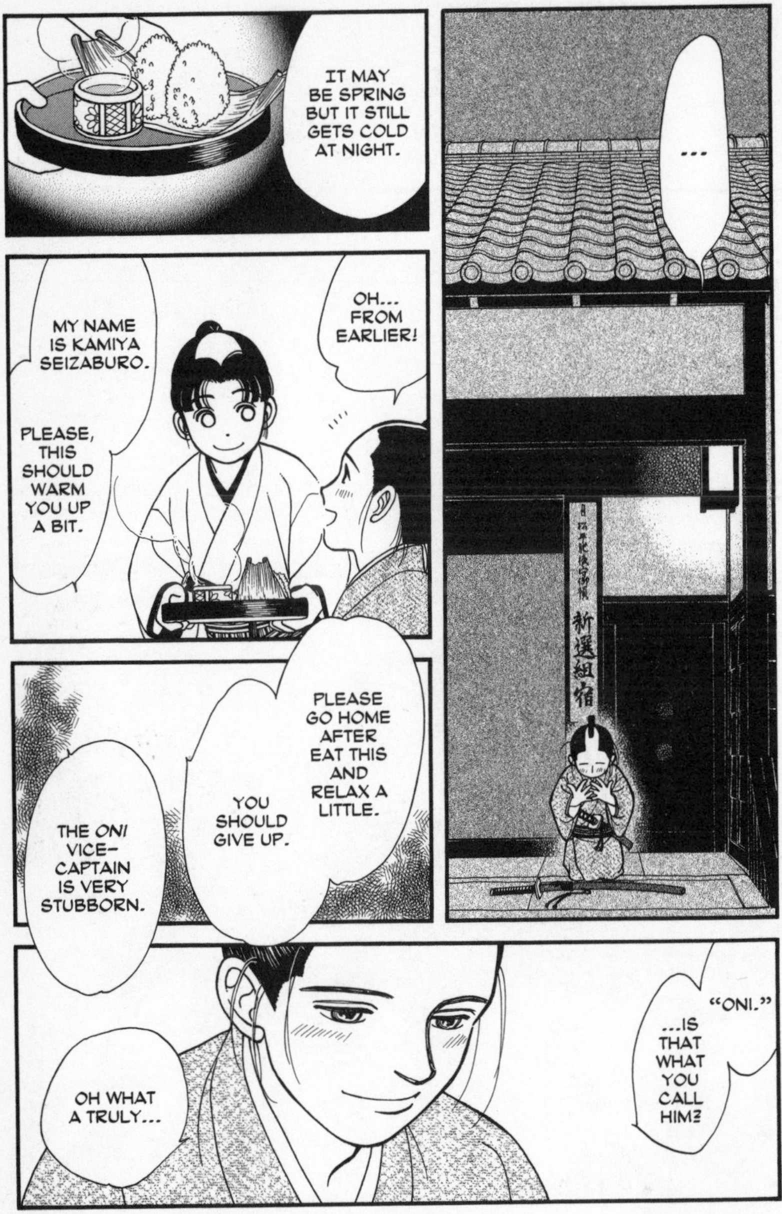
...
新選組宿
IT MAY BE SPRING BUT IT STILL GETS COLD AT NIGHT.
OH... FROM EARLIER!
MY NAME IS KAMIYA SEIZABURO.
PLEASE, THIS SHOULD WARM YOU UP A BIT.
PLEASE GO HOME AFTER EAT THIS AND RELAX A LITTLE.
YOU SHOULD GIVE UP.
THE *ONI* VICE-CAPTAIN IS VERY STUBBORN.
"ONI."
...IS THAT WHAT YOU CALL HIM?
OH WHAT A TRULY...

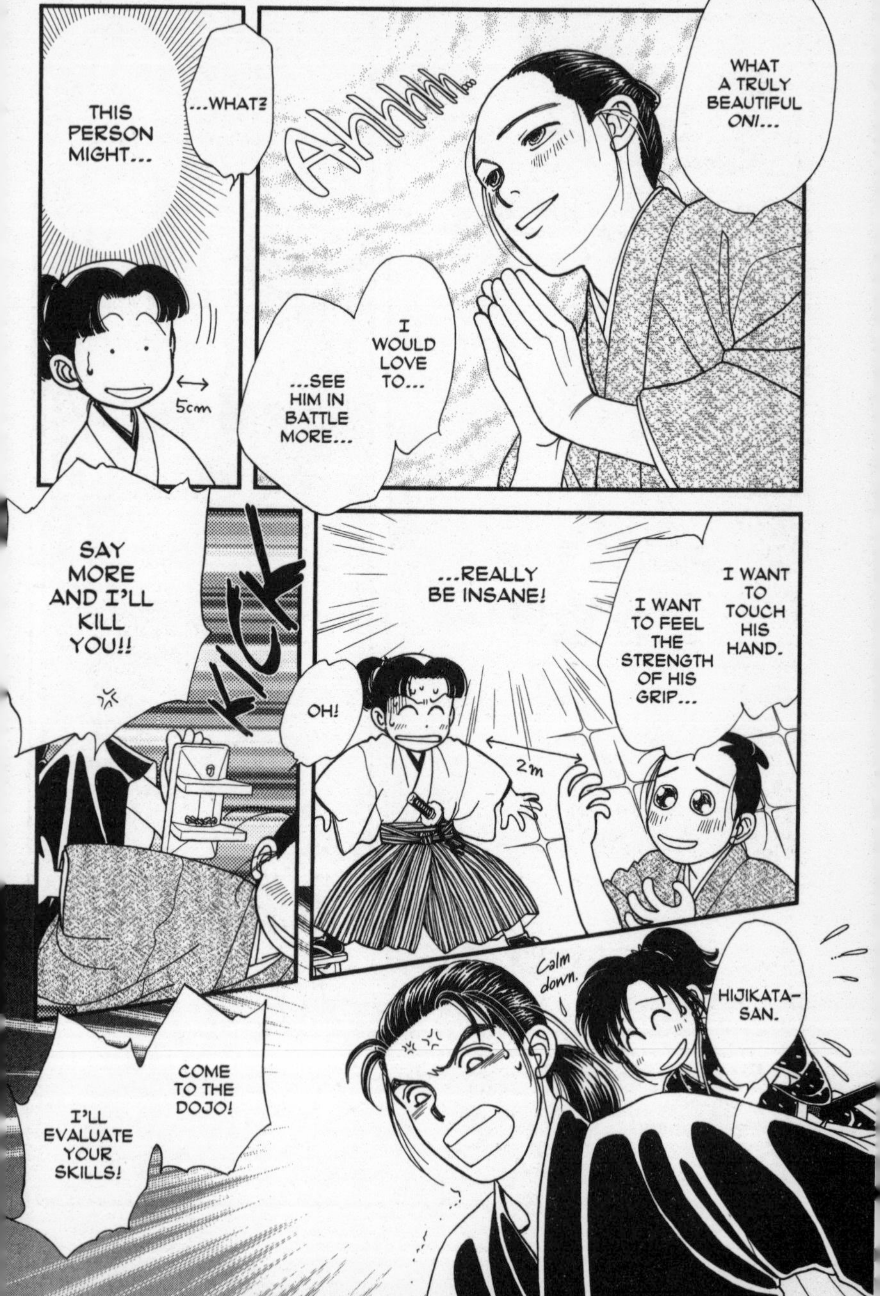
WHAT A TRULY BEAUTIFUL ONI...
Ahhhh...
I WOULD LOVE TO...
...SEE HIM IN BATTLE MORE...
THIS PERSON MIGHT...
...WHAT?
5cm
I WANT TO TOUCH HIS HAND.
I WANT TO FEEL THE STRENGTH OF HIS GRIP...
...REALLY BE INSANE!
OH!
2m
KICK
SAY MORE AND I'LL KILL YOU!!
HIJIKATA-SAN.
Calm down.
COME TO THE DOJO!
I'LL EVALUATE YOUR SKILLS!

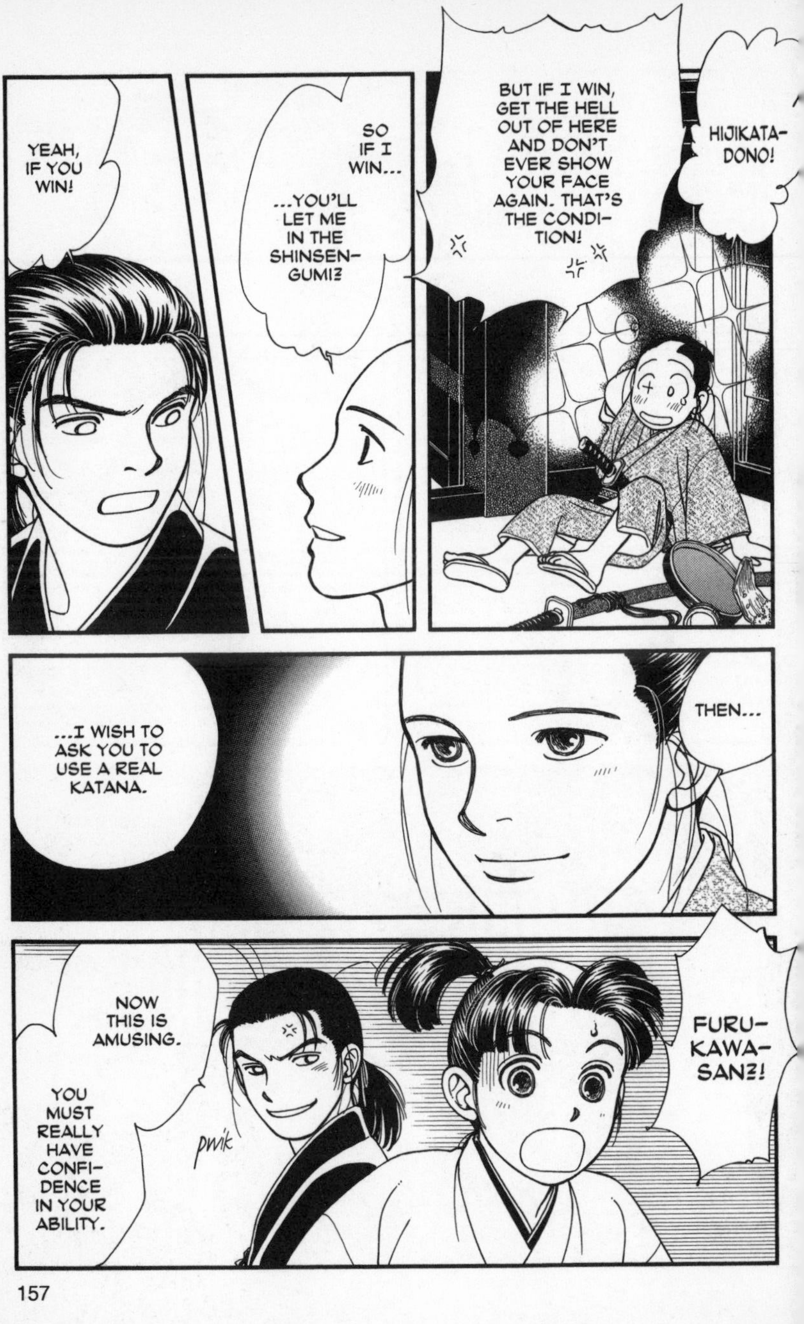
HIJIKATA-DONO!
BUT IF I WIN, GET THE HELL OUT OF HERE AND DON'T EVER SHOW YOUR FACE AGAIN. THAT'S THE CONDITION!
SO IF I WIN...
...YOU'LL LET ME IN THE SHINSENGUMI?
YEAH, IF YOU WIN!
THEN...
...I WISH TO ASK YOU TO USE A REAL KATANA.
FURUKAWA-SAN?!
NOW THIS IS AMUSING.
YOU MUST REALLY HAVE CONFIDENCE IN YOUR ABILITY.
pwik

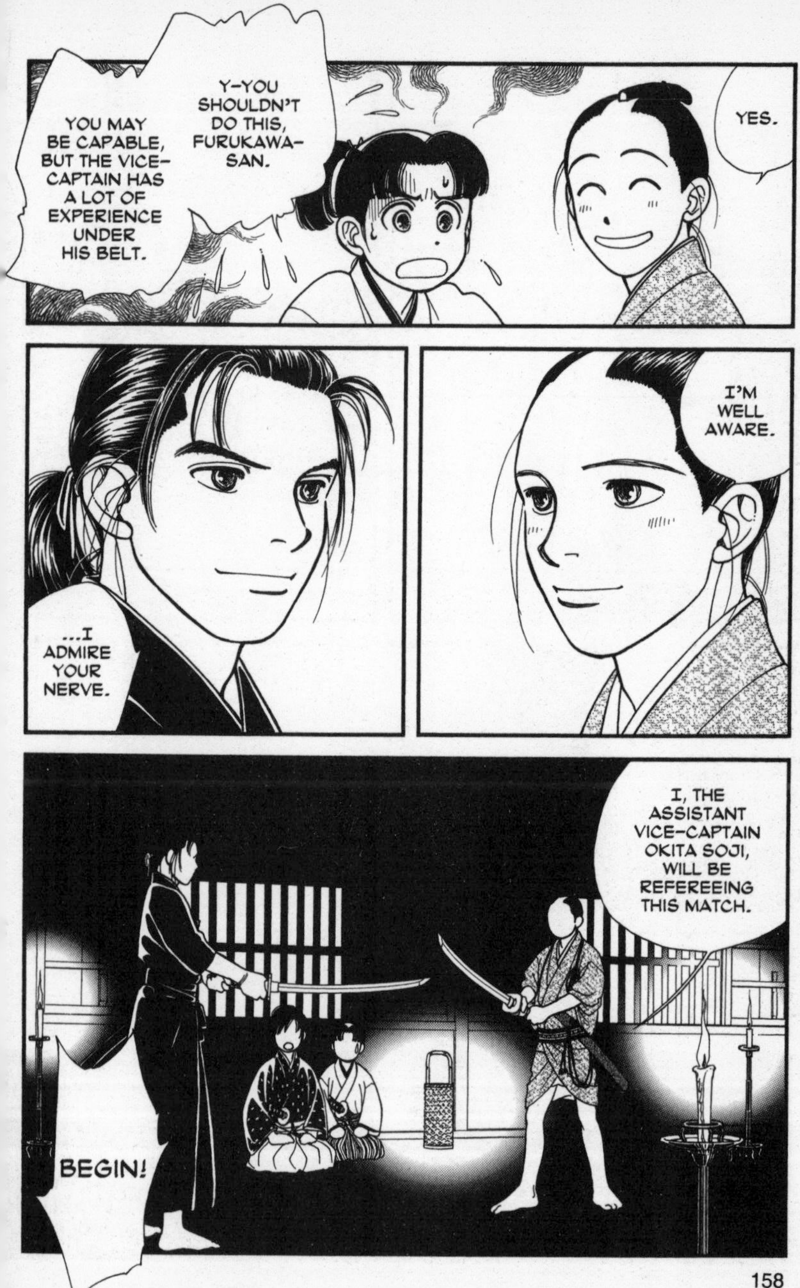
YES.
Y-YOU SHOULDN'T DO THIS, FURUKAWA-SAN.
YOU MAY BE CAPABLE, BUT THE VICE-CAPTAIN HAS A LOT OF EXPERIENCE UNDER HIS BELT.
I'M WELL AWARE.
...I ADMIRE YOUR NERVE.
I, THE ASSISTANT VICE-CAPTAIN OKITA SOJI, WILL BE REFEREEING THIS MATCH.
BEGIN!

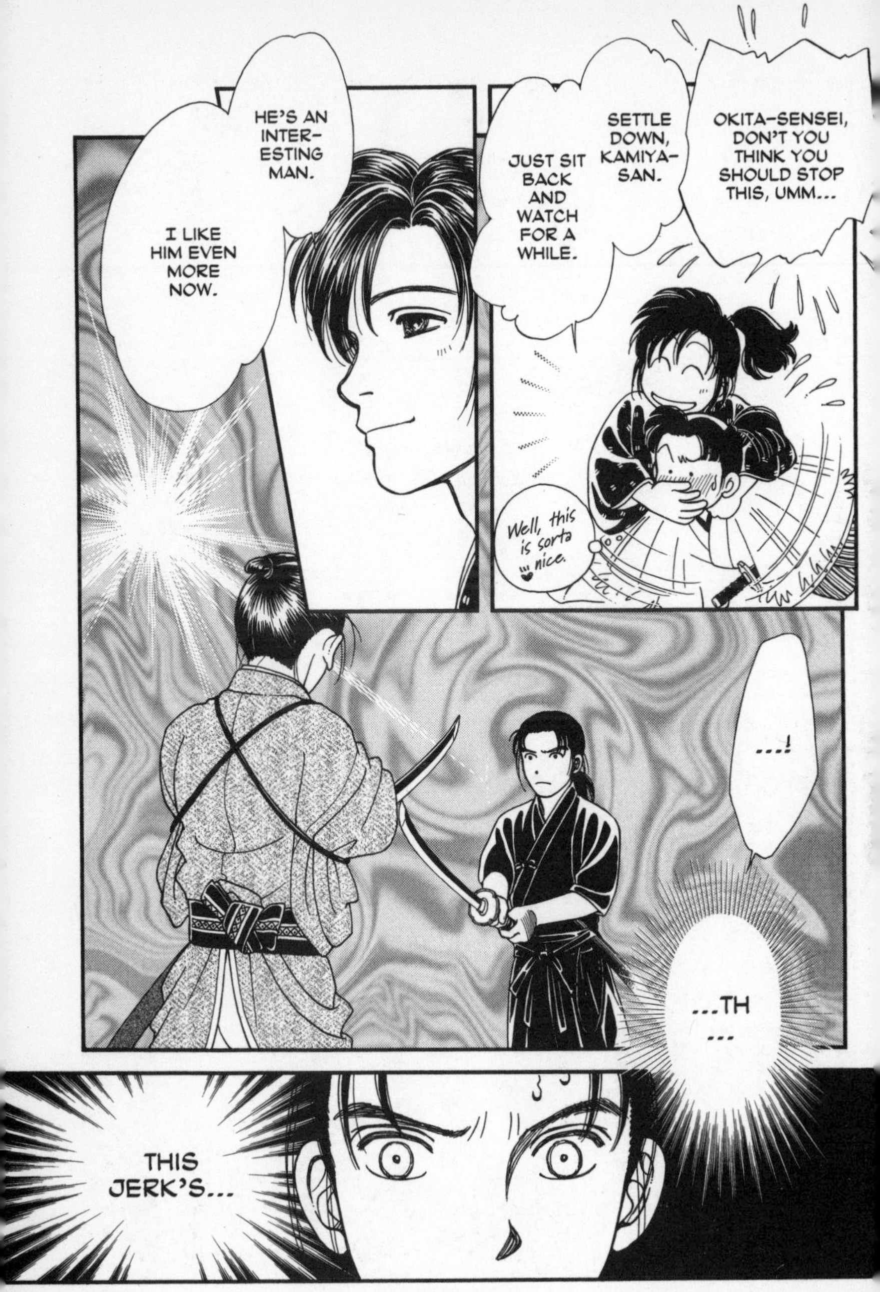
OKITA-SENSEI, DON'T YOU THINK YOU SHOULD STOP THIS, UMM...
SETTLE DOWN, KAMIYA-SAN.
JUST SIT BACK AND WATCH FOR A WHILE.
Well, this is sorta nice.
HE'S AN INTERESTING MAN.
I LIKE HIM EVEN MORE NOW.
...!
...TH ...
THIS JERK'S...

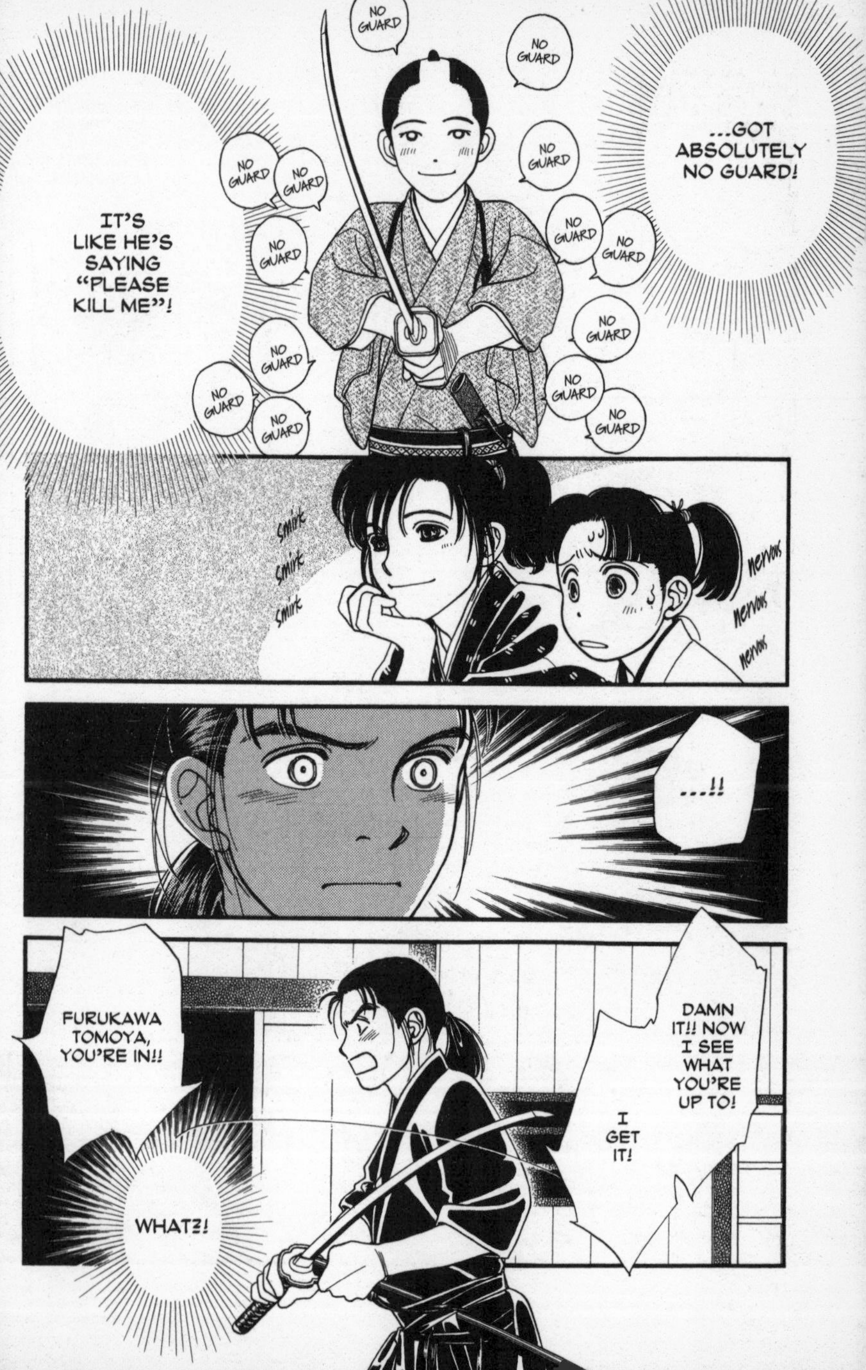
...GOT ABSOLUTELY NO GUARD!
NO GUARD
NO GUARD
NO GUARD
NO GUARD
NO GUARD
NO GUARD
NO GUARD
NO GUARD
NO GUARD
NO GUARD
NO GUARD
NO GUARD
NO GUARD
NO GUARD
IT'S LIKE HE'S SAYING "PLEASE KILL ME"!
nervous nervous nervous
smirk smirk smirk
...!!
DAMN IT!! NOW I SEE WHAT YOU'RE UP TO!
I GET IT!
FURUKAWA TOMOYA, YOU'RE IN!!
WHAT?!

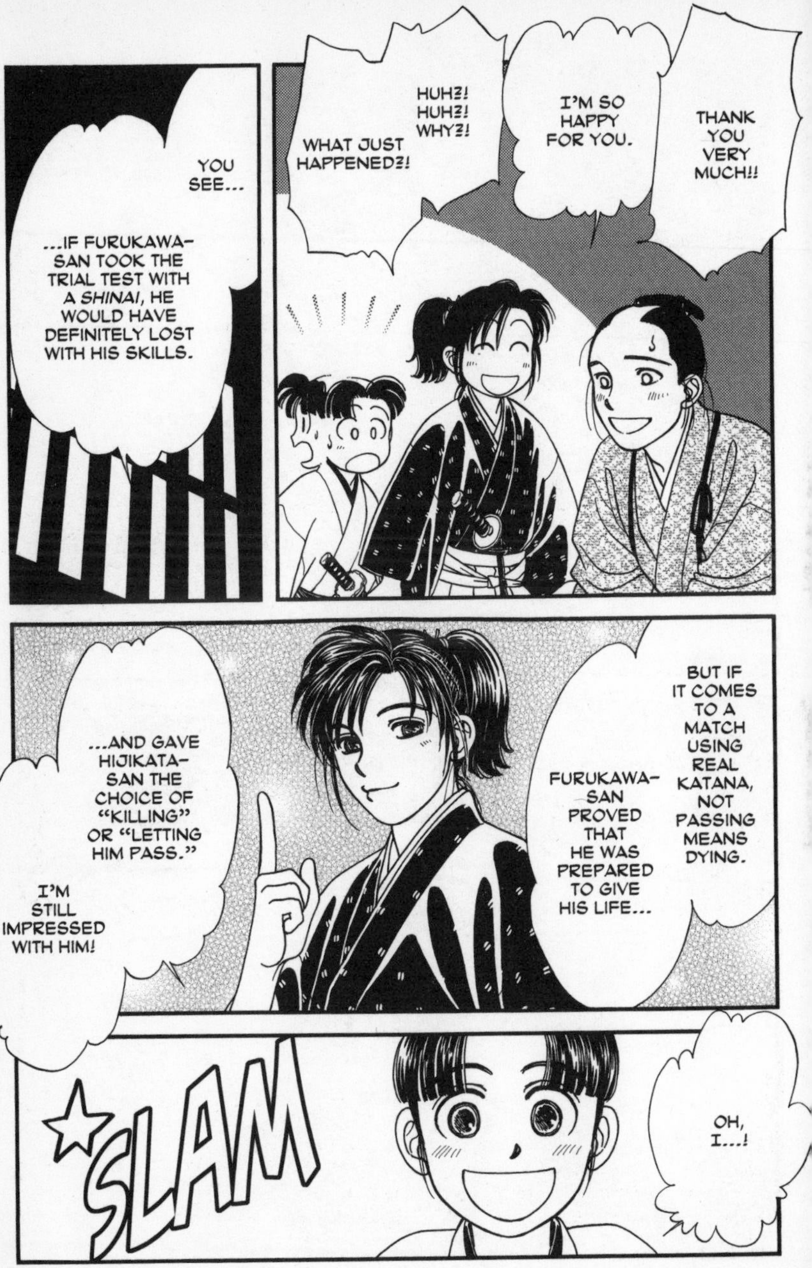
THANK YOU VERY MUCH!!
I'M SO HAPPY FOR YOU.
HUH?! HUH?! WHY?!
WHAT JUST HAPPENED?!
YOU SEE...
...IF FURUKAWA-SAN TOOK THE TRIAL TEST WITH A *SHINAI*, HE WOULD HAVE DEFINITELY LOST WITH HIS SKILLS.
BUT IF IT COMES TO A MATCH USING REAL KATANA, NOT PASSING MEANS DYING.
FURUKAWA-SAN PROVED THAT HE WAS PREPARED TO GIVE HIS LIFE...
...AND GAVE HIJIKATA-SAN THE CHOICE OF "KILLING" OR "LETTING HIM PASS."
I'M STILL IMPRESSED WITH HIM!
OH, I...!
SLAM

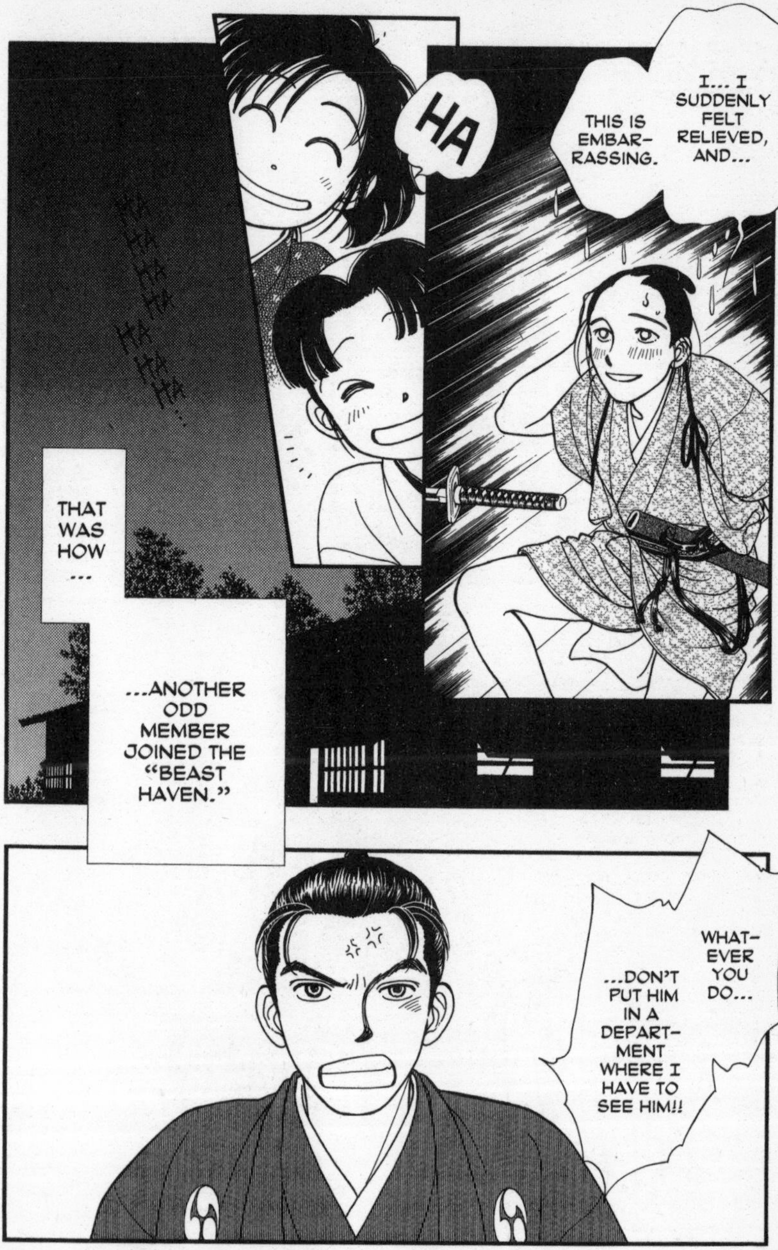
I... I SUDDENLY FELT RELIEVED, AND...
THIS IS EMBARRASSING.
HA
HA HA HA HA HA HA HA...
THAT WAS HOW...
...ANOTHER ODD MEMBER JOINED THE "BEAST HAVEN."
WHATEVER YOU DO...
...DON'T PUT HIM IN A DEPARTMENT WHERE I HAVE TO SEE HIM!!

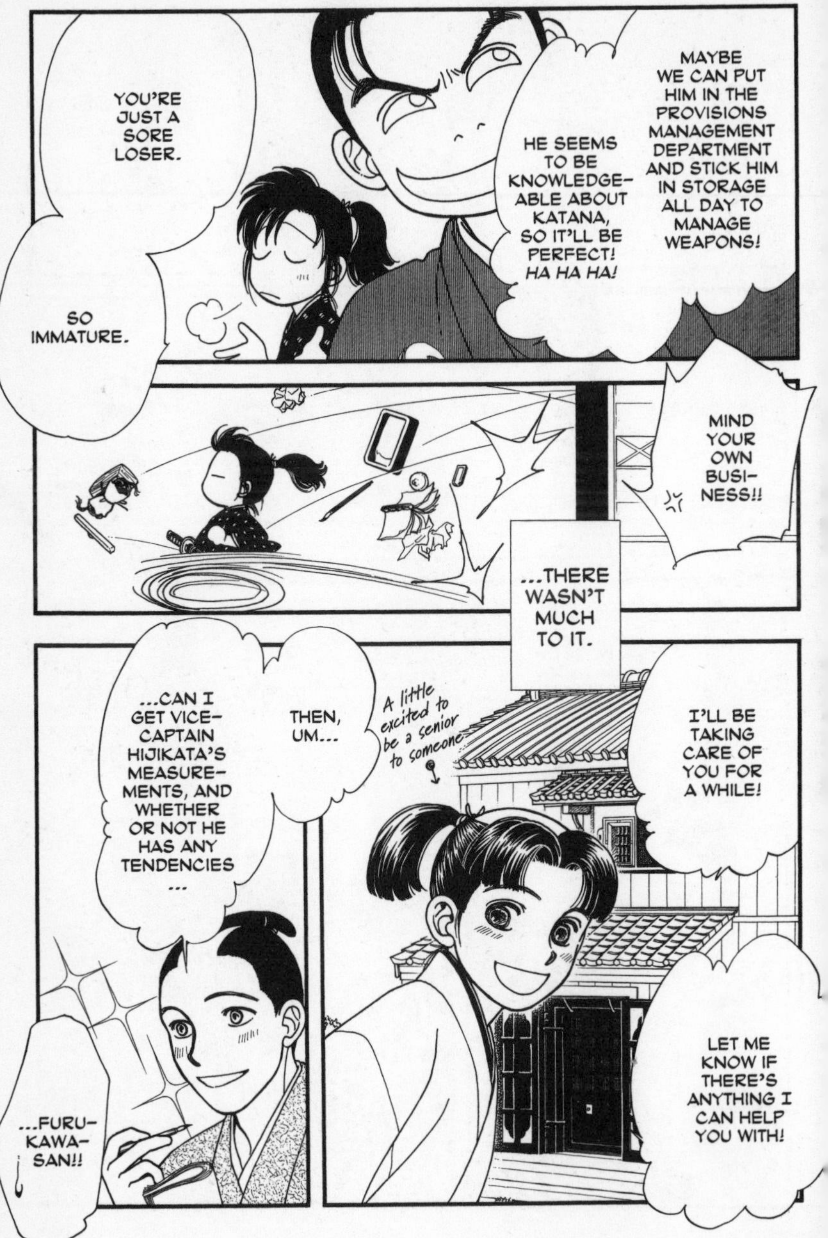
MAYBE WE CAN PUT HIM IN THE PROVISIONS MANAGEMENT DEPARTMENT AND STICK HIM IN STORAGE ALL DAY TO MANAGE WEAPONS!
HE SEEMS TO BE KNOWLEDGE-ABLE ABOUT KATANA, SO IT'LL BE PERFECT! *HA HA HA!*
YOU'RE JUST A SORE LOSER.
SO IMMATURE.
MIND YOUR OWN BUSI-NESS!!
...THERE WASN'T MUCH TO IT.
I'LL BE TAKING CARE OF YOU FOR A WHILE!
A little excited to be a senior to someone
LET ME KNOW IF THERE'S ANYTHING I CAN HELP YOU WITH!
THEN, UM...
...CAN I GET VICE-CAPTAIN HIJIKATA'S MEASURE-MENTS, AND WHETHER OR NOT HE HAS ANY TENDENCIES...
...FURU-KAWA-SAN!!

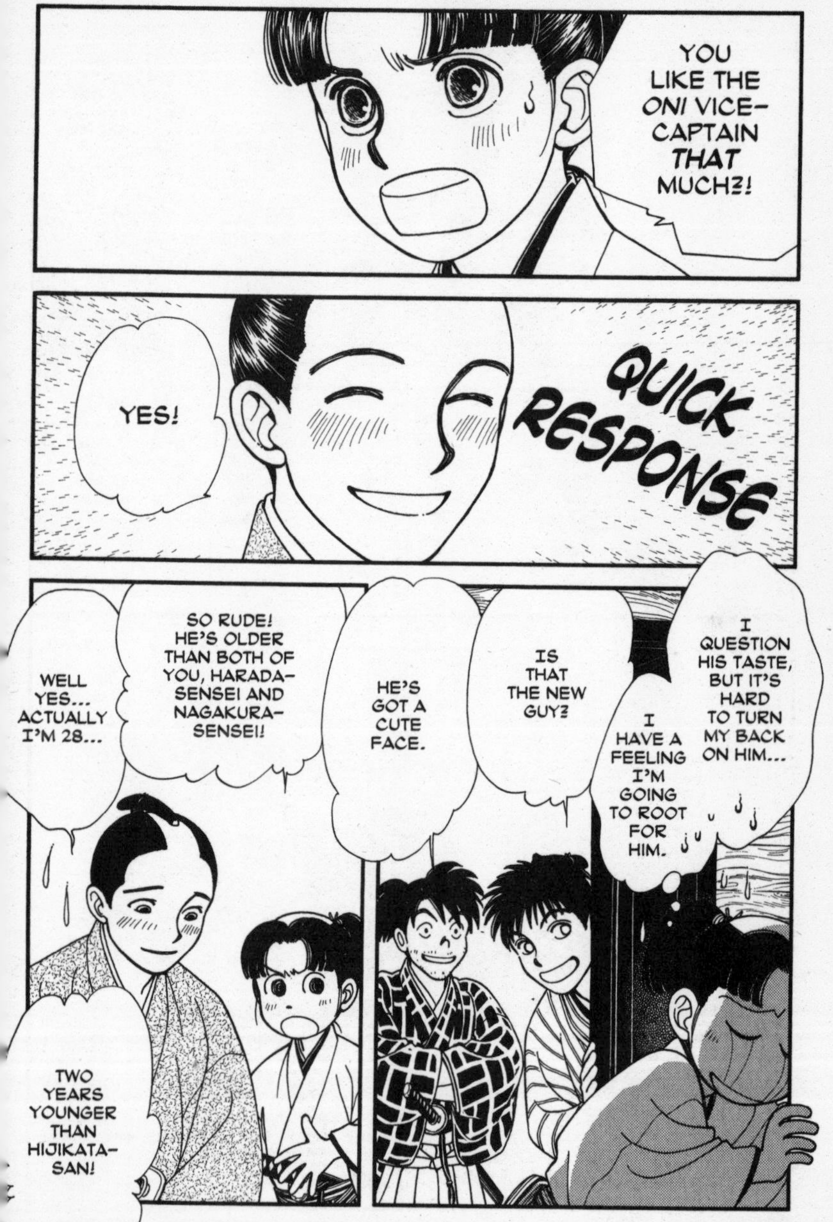
YOU LIKE THE *ONI* VICE-CAPTAIN *THAT* MUCH?!
YES!
QUICK RESPONSE
I QUESTION HIS TASTE, BUT IT'S HARD TO TURN MY BACK ON HIM...
I HAVE A FEELING I'M GOING TO ROOT FOR HIM.
IS THAT THE NEW GUY?
HE'S GOT A CUTE FACE.
SO RUDE! HE'S OLDER THAN BOTH OF YOU, HARADA-SENSEI AND NAGAKURA-SENSEI!
WELL YES... ACTUALLY I'M 28...
TWO YEARS YOUNGER THAN HIJIKATA-SAN!

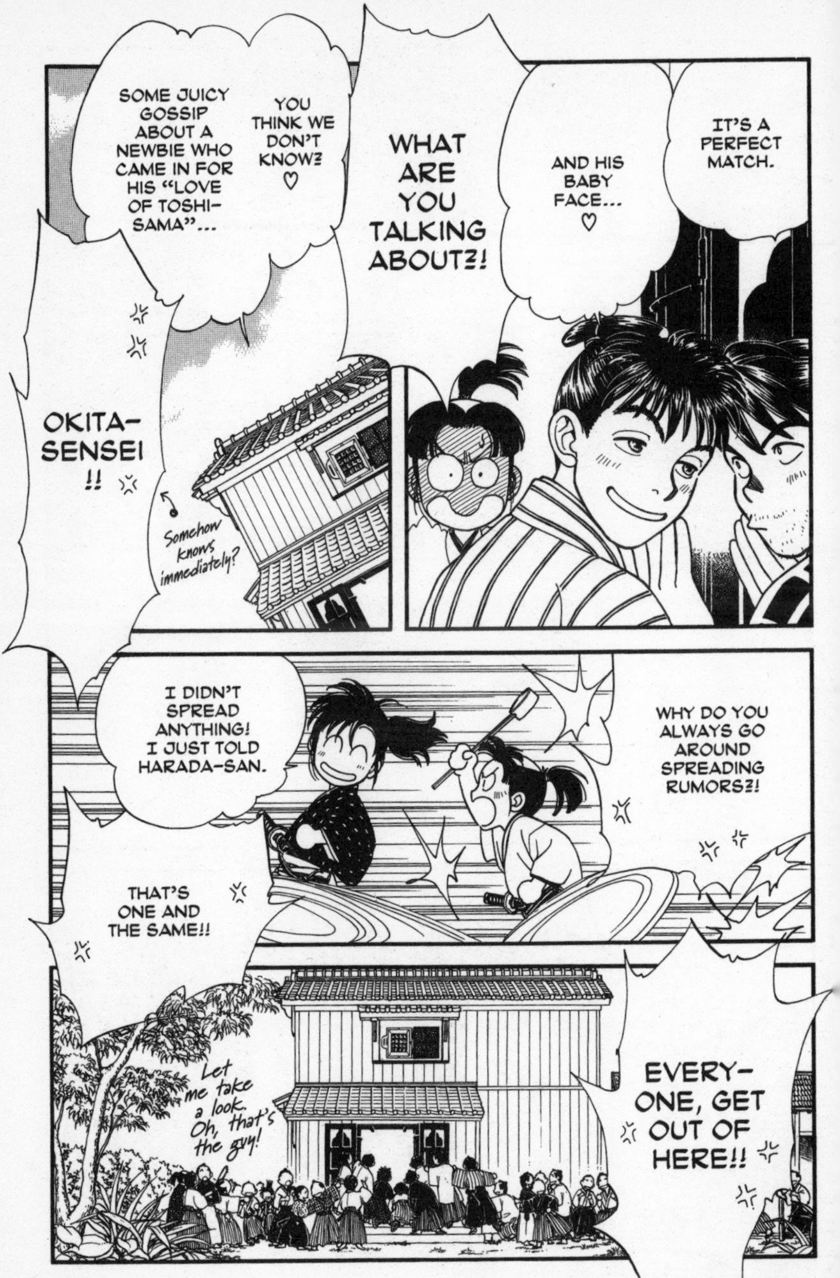
IT'S A PERFECT MATCH.
AND HIS BABY FACE... ♡
WHAT ARE YOU TALKING ABOUT?!
YOU THINK WE DON'T KNOW? ♡
SOME JUICY GOSSIP ABOUT A NEWBIE WHO CAME IN FOR HIS "LOVE OF TOSHI-SAMA"...
OKITA-SENSEI!!
Somehow knows immediately?
WHY DO YOU ALWAYS GO AROUND SPREADING RUMORS?!
I DIDN'T SPREAD ANYTHING! I JUST TOLD HARADA-SAN.
THAT'S ONE AND THE SAME!!
EVERY-ONE, GET OUT OF HERE!!
Let me take a look. Oh, that's the guy!

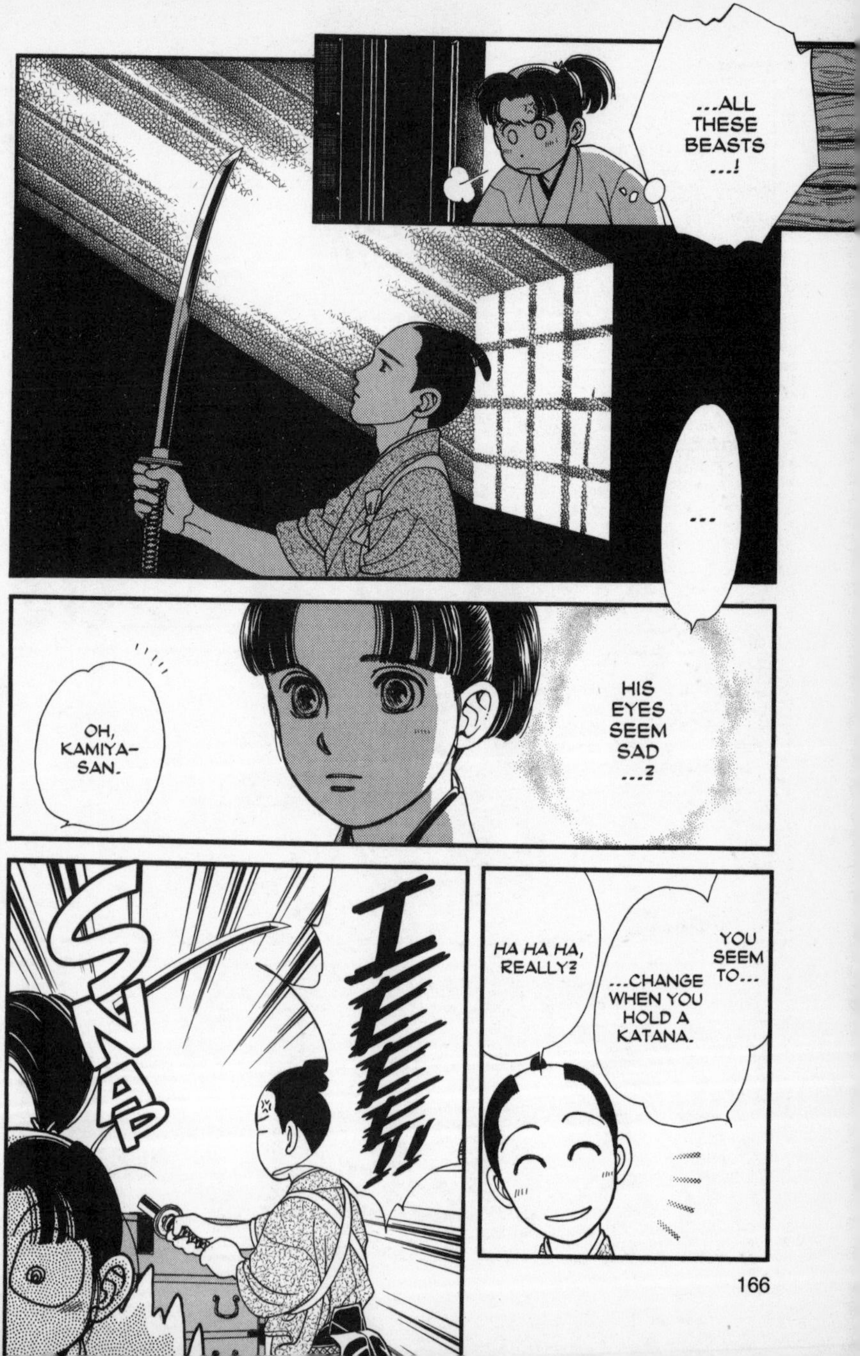

...ALL THESE BEASTS ...!
...
HIS EYES SEEM SAD ...?
OH, KAMIYA-SAN.
YOU SEEM TO...
...CHANGE WHEN YOU HOLD A KATANA.
HA HA HA, REALLY?
IEEEE!!
SNAP

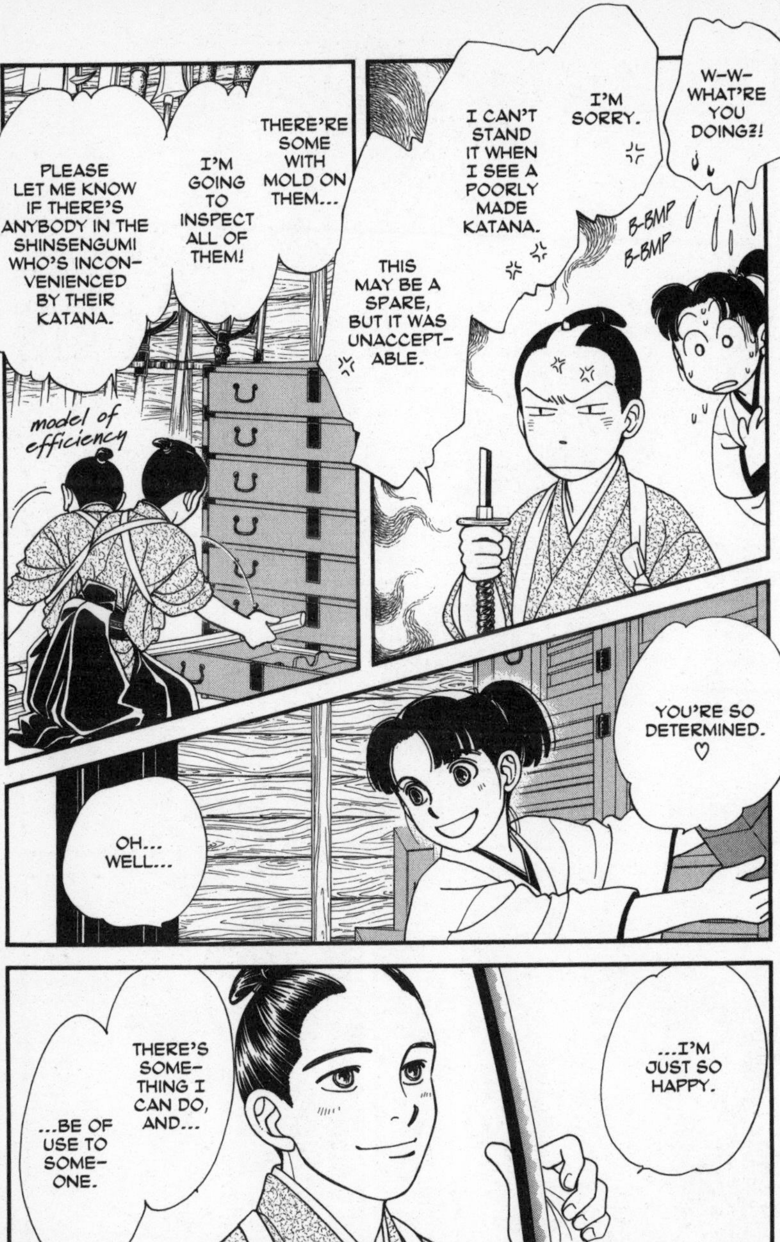
W-W-WHAT'RE YOU DOING?!
I'M SORRY.
I CAN'T STAND IT WHEN I SEE A POORLY MADE KATANA.
B-BMP B-BMP
THIS MAY BE A SPARE, BUT IT WAS UNACCEPTABLE.
THERE'RE SOME WITH MOLD ON THEM...
I'M GOING TO INSPECT ALL OF THEM!
PLEASE LET ME KNOW IF THERE'S ANYBODY IN THE SHINSENGUMI WHO'S INCONVENIENCED BY THEIR KATANA.
model of efficiency
YOU'RE SO DETERMINED. ♡
OH... WELL...
...I'M JUST SO HAPPY.
THERE'S SOMETHING I CAN DO, AND...
...BE OF USE TO SOMEONE.

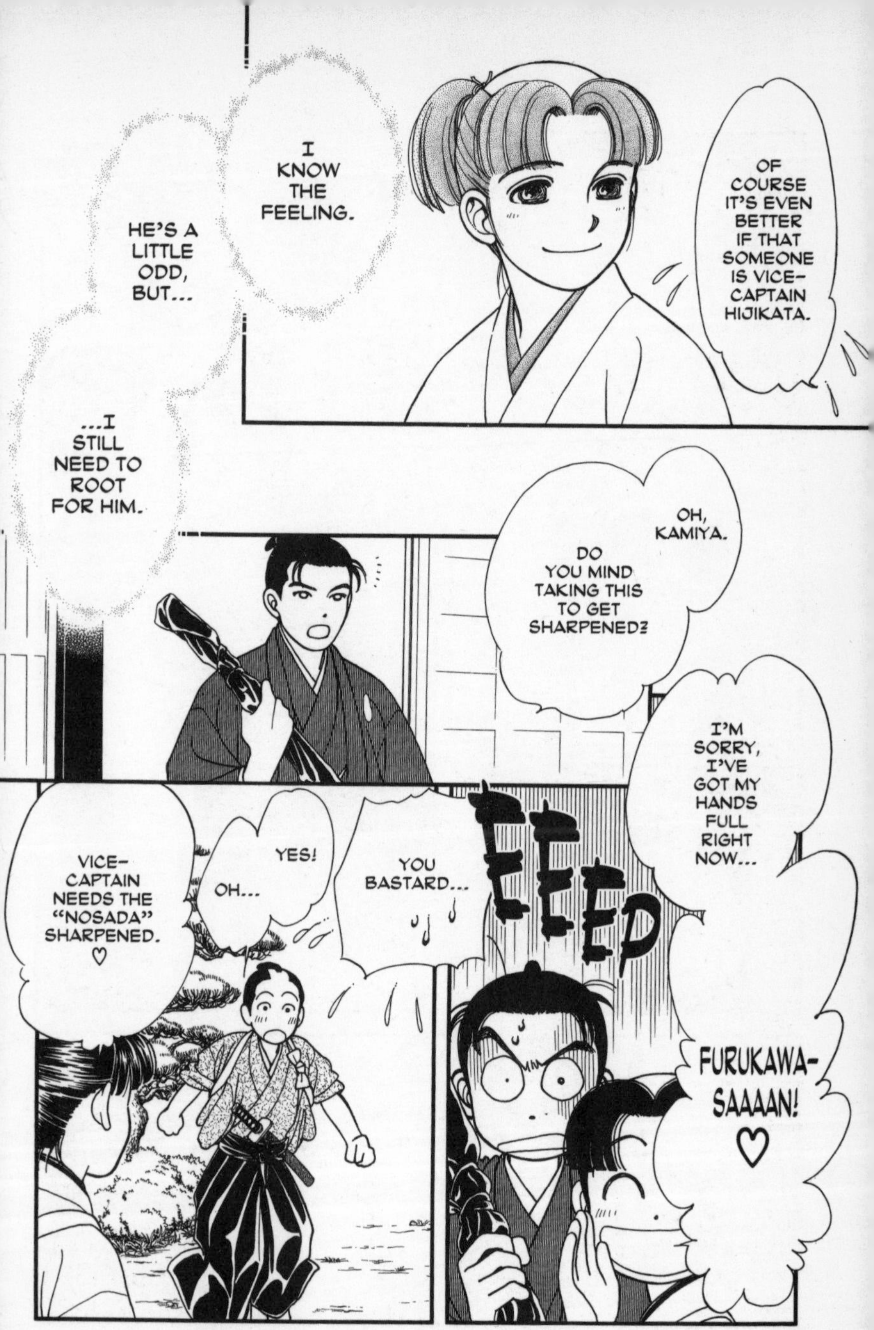
OF COURSE IT'S EVEN BETTER IF THAT SOMEONE IS VICE-CAPTAIN HIJIKATA.
I KNOW THE FEELING.
HE'S A LITTLE ODD, BUT...
...I STILL NEED TO ROOT FOR HIM.
OH, KAMIYA.
DO YOU MIND TAKING THIS TO GET SHARPENED?
I'M SORRY, I'VE GOT MY HANDS FULL RIGHT NOW...
EEEP
FURUKAWA-SAAAAN! ♡
YOU BASTARD...
YES!
OH...
VICE-CAPTAIN NEEDS THE "NOSADA" SHARPENED. ♡

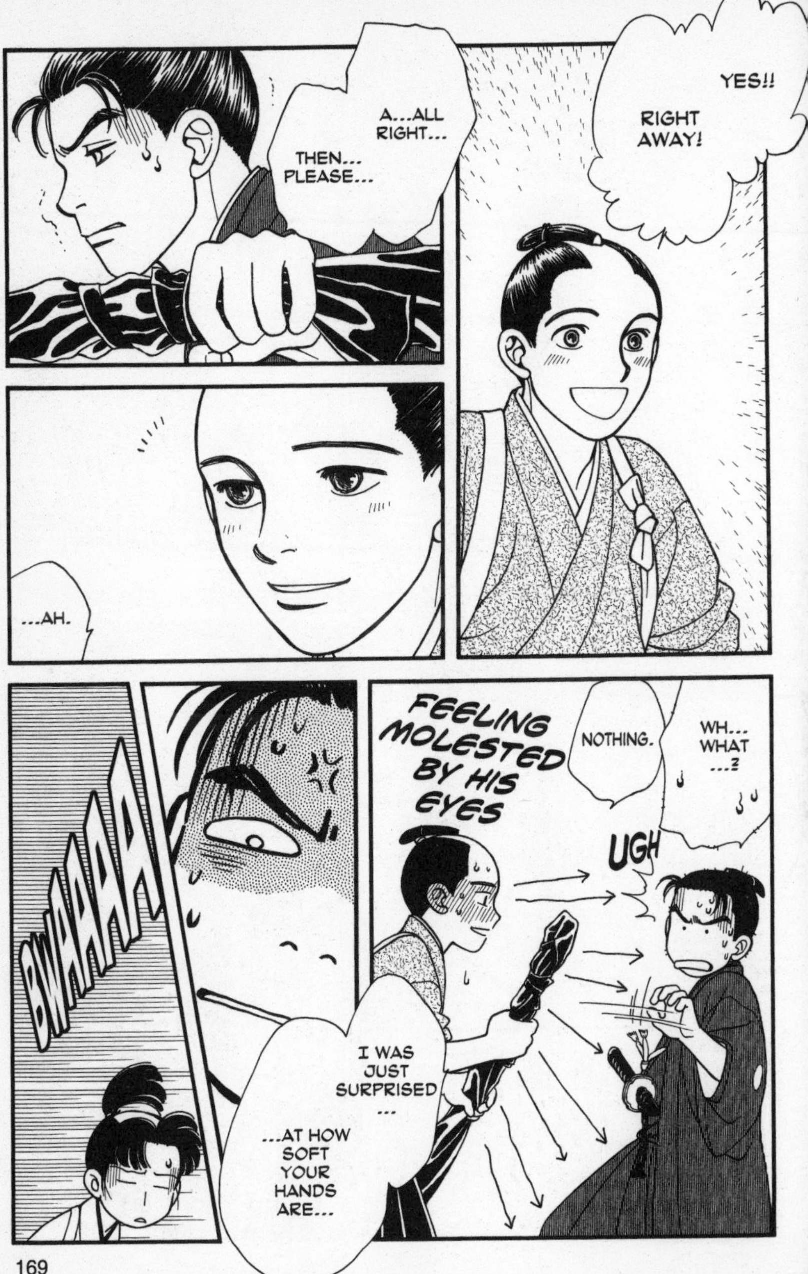
YES!!
RIGHT AWAY!
A...ALL RIGHT...
THEN... PLEASE...
...AH.
WH... WHAT ...?
NOTHING.
FEELING MOLESTED BY HIS EYES
UGH
I WAS JUST SURPRISED ...
...AT HOW SOFT YOUR HANDS ARE...
BWAAAA

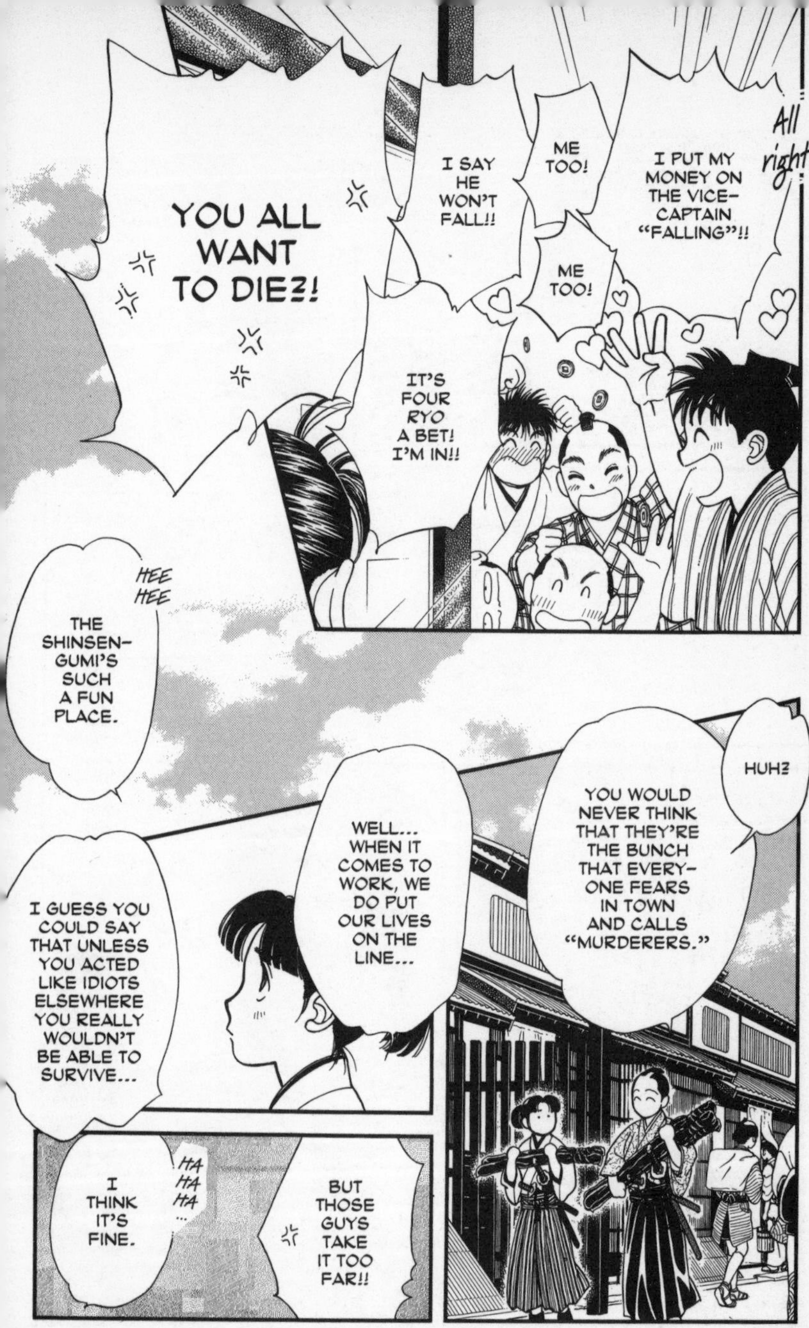
All right!
I PUT MY MONEY ON THE VICE-CAPTAIN "FALLING"!!
ME TOO!
ME TOO!
I SAY HE WON'T FALL!!
IT'S FOUR RYO A BET! I'M IN!!
YOU ALL WANT TO DIE?!
HEE HEE
THE SHINSEN-GUMI'S SUCH A FUN PLACE.
HUH?
YOU WOULD NEVER THINK THAT THEY'RE THE BUNCH THAT EVERY-ONE FEARS IN TOWN AND CALLS "MURDERERS."
WELL... WHEN IT COMES TO WORK, WE DO PUT OUR LIVES ON THE LINE...
I GUESS YOU COULD SAY THAT UNLESS YOU ACTED LIKE IDIOTS ELSEWHERE YOU REALLY WOULDN'T BE ABLE TO SURVIVE...
BUT THOSE GUYS TAKE IT TOO FAR!!
HA HA HA...
I THINK IT'S FINE.

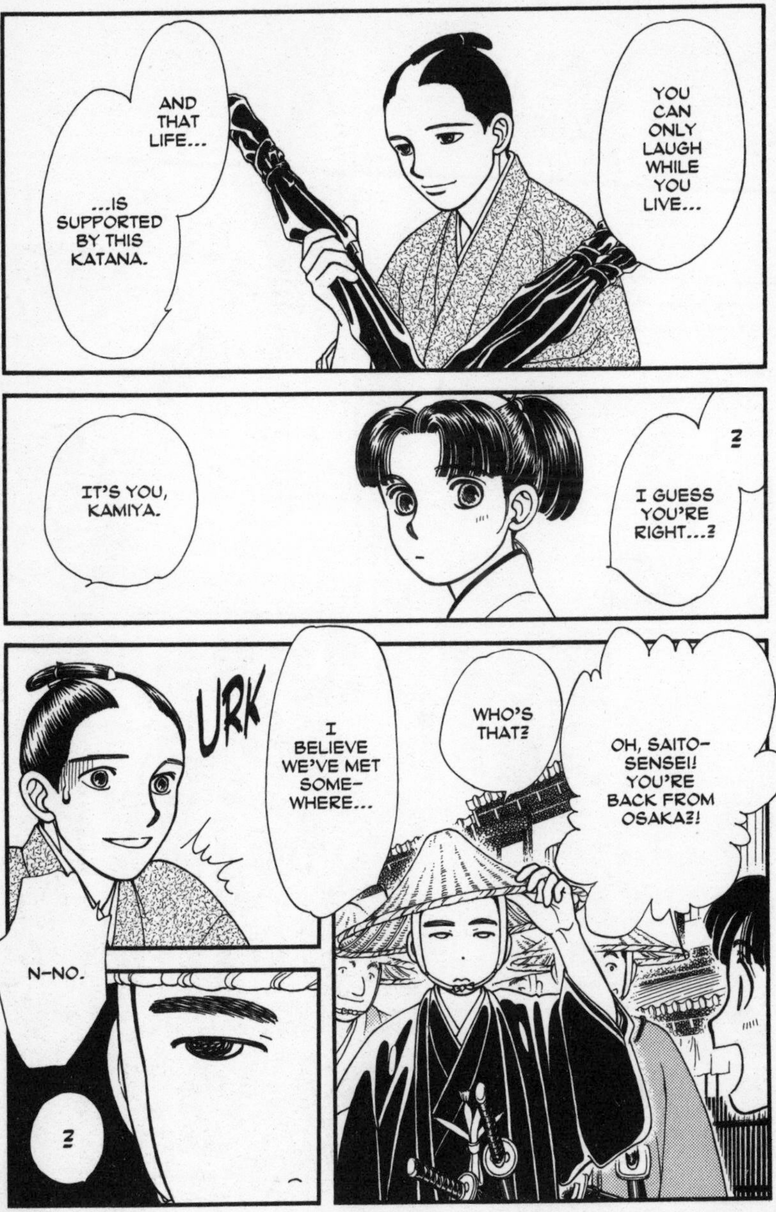
YOU CAN ONLY LAUGH WHILE YOU LIVE...
AND THAT LIFE...
...IS SUPPORTED BY THIS KATANA.
?
I GUESS YOU'RE RIGHT...?
IT'S YOU, KAMIYA.
OH, SAITO-SENSEI! YOU'RE BACK FROM OSAKA?!
WHO'S THAT?
I BELIEVE WE'VE MET SOME-WHERE...
URK
N-NO.
?

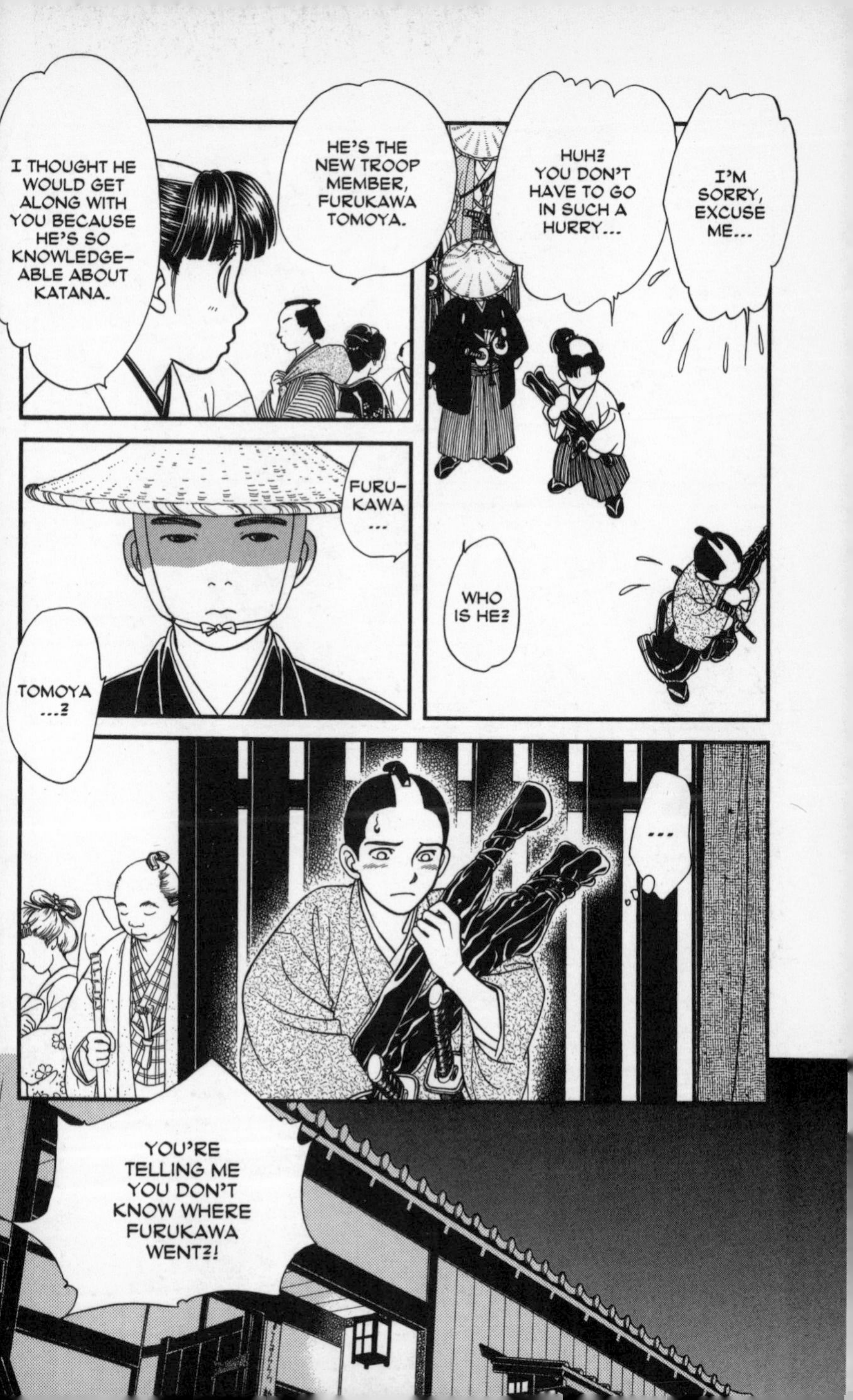
I'M SORRY, EXCUSE ME...
HUH? YOU DON'T HAVE TO GO IN SUCH A HURRY...
WHO IS HE?
HE'S THE NEW TROOP MEMBER, FURUKAWA TOMOYA.
I THOUGHT HE WOULD GET ALONG WITH YOU BECAUSE HE'S SO KNOWLEDGE-ABLE ABOUT KATANA.
FURU-KAWA ...
TOMOYA ...?
...
YOU'RE TELLING ME YOU DON'T KNOW WHERE FURUKAWA WENT?!

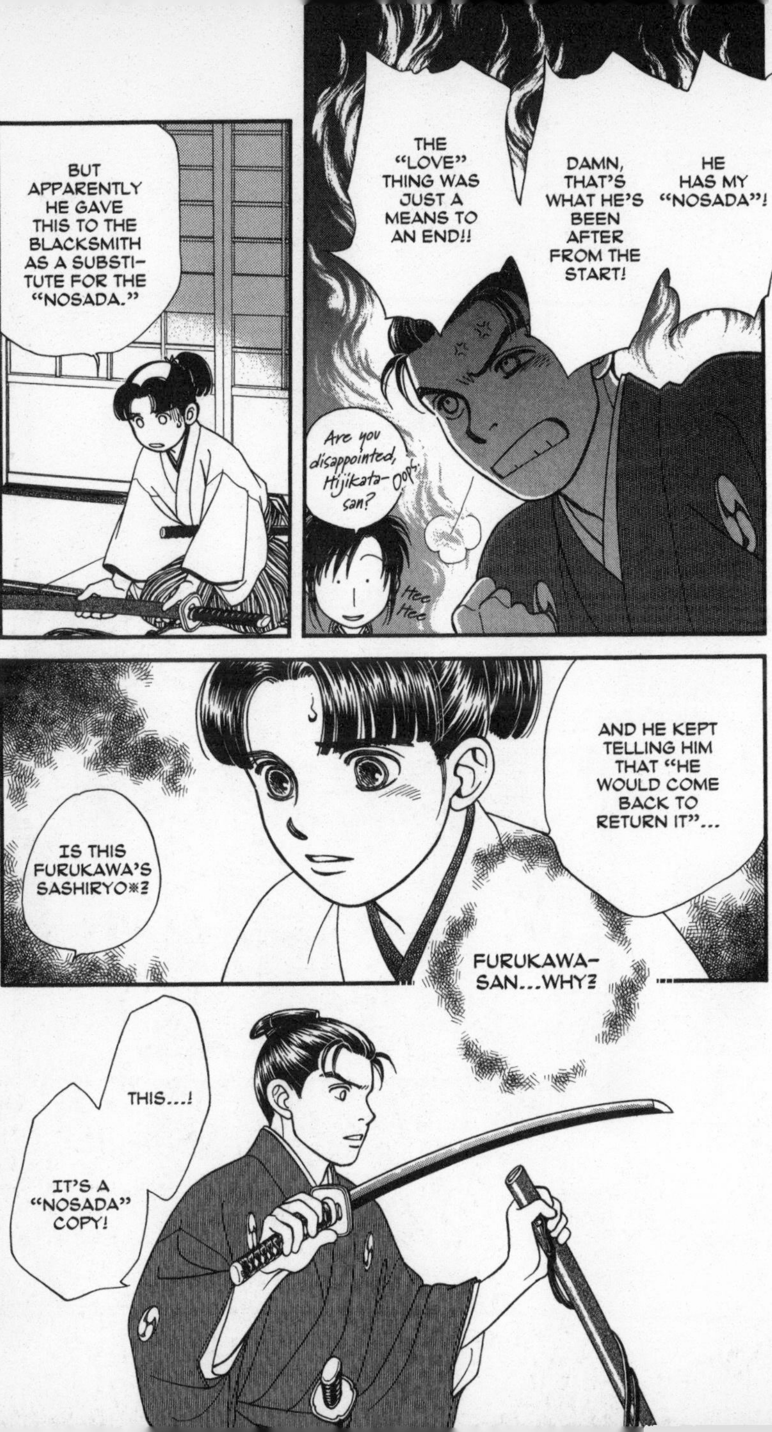
HE HAS MY "NOSADA"!
DAMN, THAT'S WHAT HE'S BEEN AFTER FROM THE START!
THE "LOVE" THING WAS JUST A MEANS TO AN END!!
Are you disappointed, Hijikata-san?
Oops!
Hee Hee
BUT APPARENTLY HE GAVE THIS TO THE BLACKSMITH AS A SUBSTITUTE FOR THE "NOSADA."
AND HE KEPT TELLING HIM THAT "HE WOULD COME BACK TO RETURN IT"...
IS THIS FURUKAWA'S SASHIRYO※?
FURUKAWA-SAN...WHY?
THIS...!
IT'S A "NOSADA" COPY!

※ A katana that hangs from one's waist.

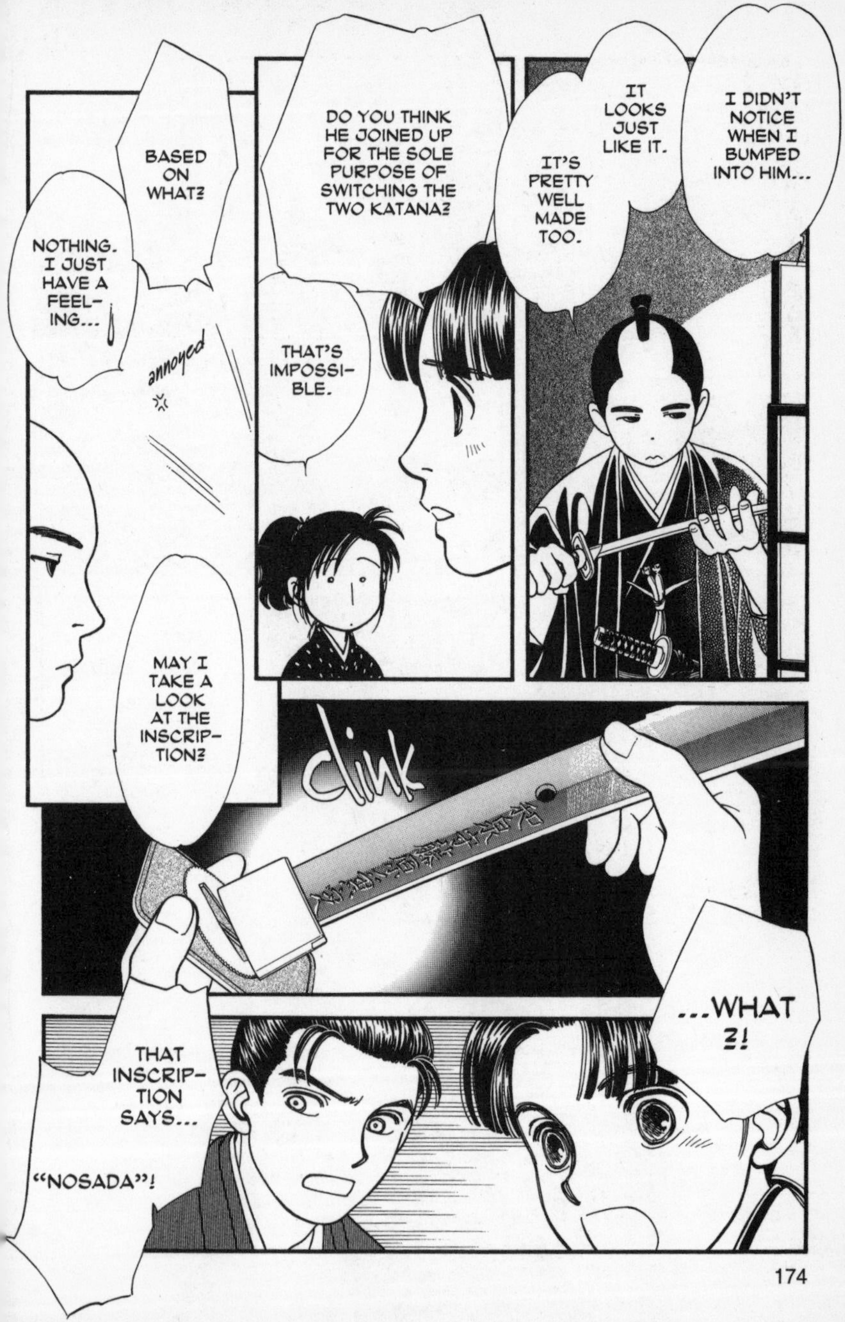
I DIDN'T NOTICE WHEN I BUMPED INTO HIM...
IT LOOKS JUST LIKE IT.
IT'S PRETTY WELL MADE TOO.
DO YOU THINK HE JOINED UP FOR THE SOLE PURPOSE OF SWITCHING THE TWO KATANA?
THAT'S IMPOSSI-BLE.
BASED ON WHAT?
NOTHING. I JUST HAVE A FEEL-ING...
annoyed
MAY I TAKE A LOOK AT THE INSCRIP-TION?
clink
...WHAT?!
THAT INSCRIP-TION SAYS...
"NOSADA"!

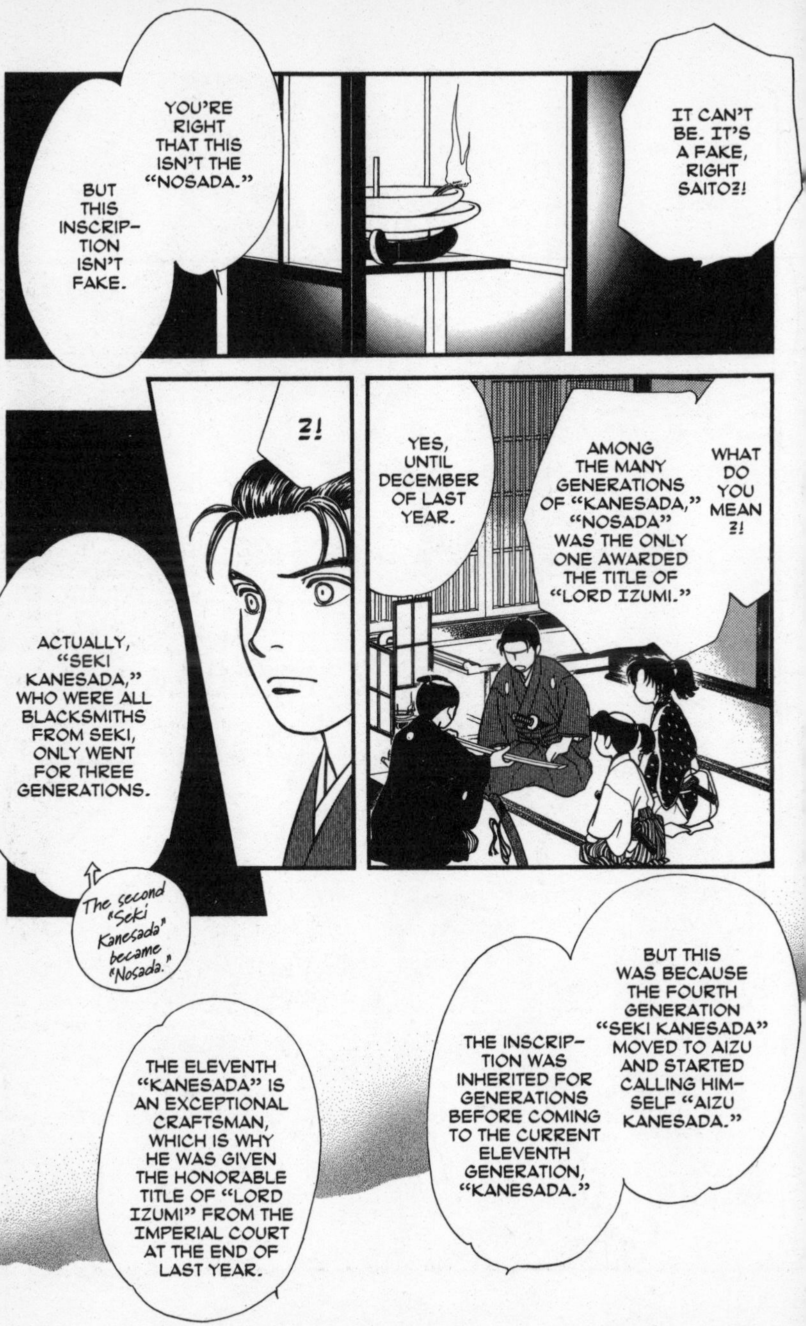

IT CAN'T BE. IT'S A FAKE, RIGHT SAITO?!
YOU'RE RIGHT THAT THIS ISN'T THE "NOSADA."
BUT THIS INSCRIPTION ISN'T FAKE.
WHAT DO YOU MEAN?!
AMONG THE MANY GENERATIONS OF "KANESADA," "NOSADA" WAS THE ONLY ONE AWARDED THE TITLE OF "LORD IZUMI."
YES, UNTIL DECEMBER OF LAST YEAR.
?!
ACTUALLY, "SEKI KANESADA," WHO WERE ALL BLACKSMITHS FROM SEKI, ONLY WENT FOR THREE GENERATIONS.
The second "Seki Kanesada" became "Nosada."
BUT THIS WAS BECAUSE THE FOURTH GENERATION "SEKI KANESADA" MOVED TO AIZU AND STARTED CALLING HIMSELF "AIZU KANESADA."
THE INSCRIPTION WAS INHERITED FOR GENERATIONS BEFORE COMING TO THE CURRENT ELEVENTH GENERATION, "KANESADA."
THE ELEVENTH "KANESADA" IS AN EXCEPTIONAL CRAFTSMAN, WHICH IS WHY HE WAS GIVEN THE HONORABLE TITLE OF "LORD IZUMI" FROM THE IMPERIAL COURT AT THE END OF LAST YEAR.

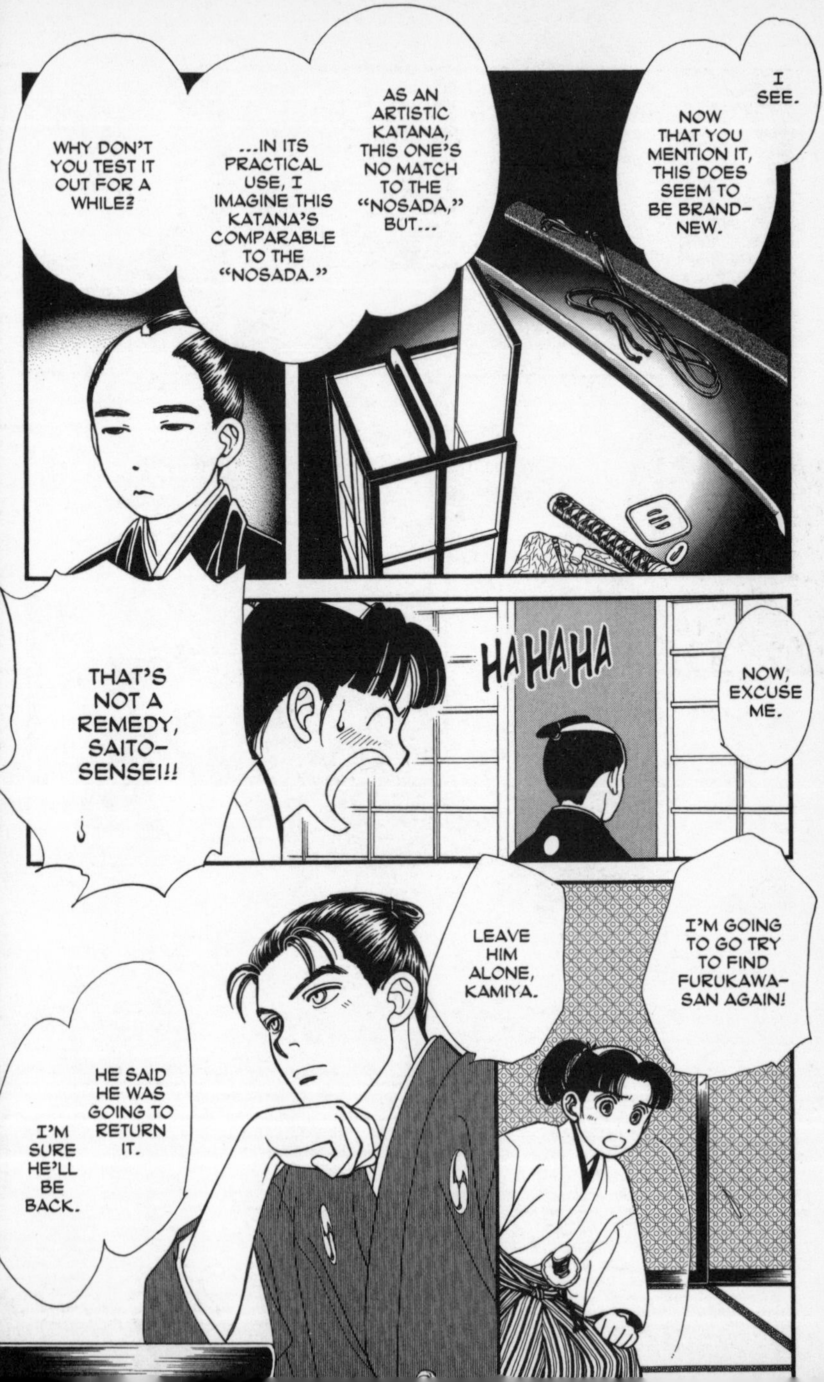
I SEE.
NOW THAT YOU MENTION IT, THIS DOES SEEM TO BE BRAND-NEW.
AS AN ARTISTIC KATANA, THIS ONE'S NO MATCH TO THE "NOSADA," BUT...
...IN ITS PRACTICAL USE, I IMAGINE THIS KATANA'S COMPARABLE TO THE "NOSADA."
WHY DON'T YOU TEST IT OUT FOR A WHILE?
NOW, EXCUSE ME.
HAHAHA
THAT'S NOT A REMEDY, SAITO-SENSEI!!!
I'M GOING TO GO TRY TO FIND FURUKAWA-SAN AGAIN!
LEAVE HIM ALONE, KAMIYA.
HE SAID HE WAS GOING TO RETURN IT.
I'M SURE HE'LL BE BACK.

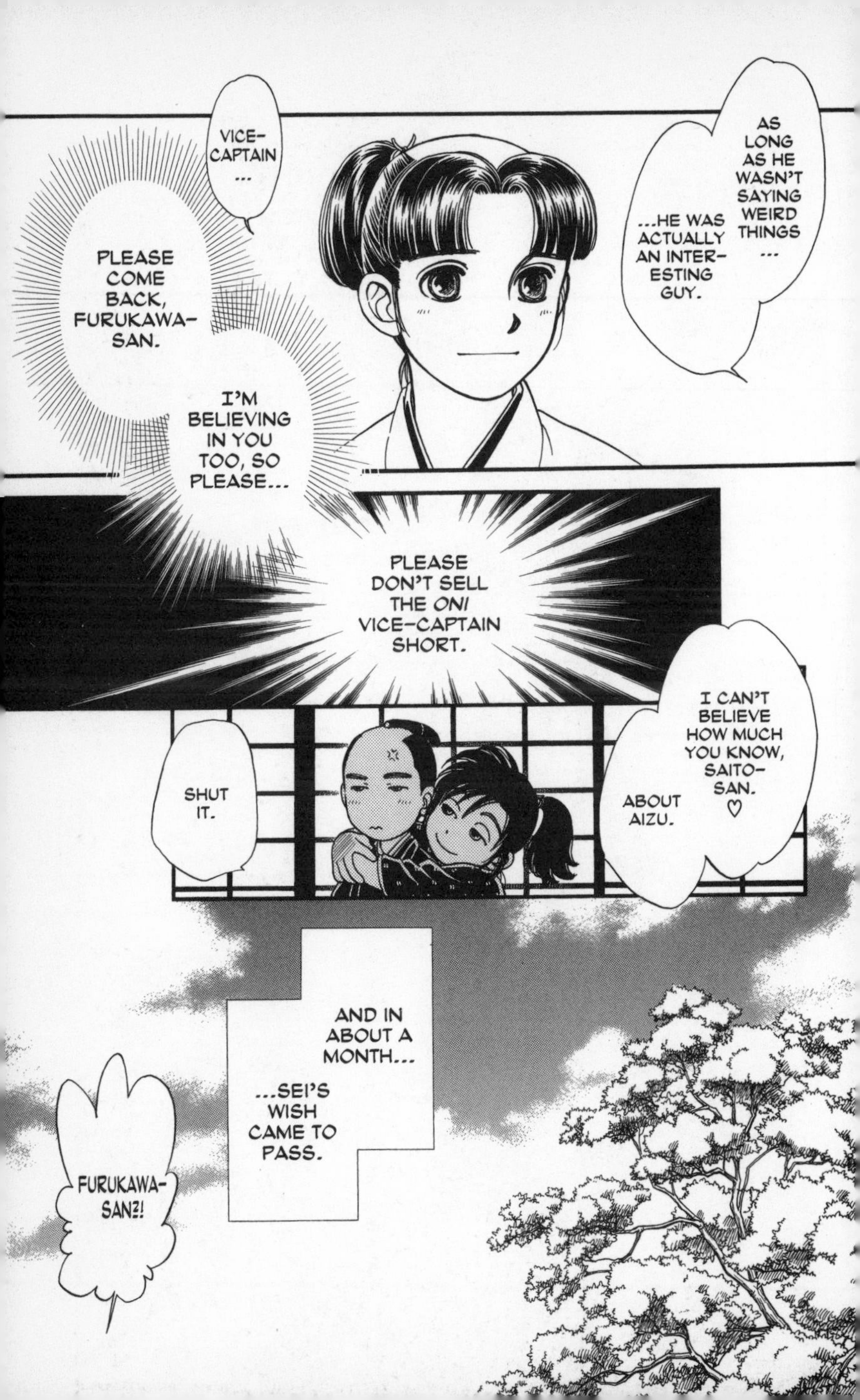
AS LONG AS HE WASN'T SAYING WEIRD THINGS...
...HE WAS ACTUALLY AN INTER-ESTING GUY.
VICE-CAPTAIN...
PLEASE COME BACK, FURUKAWA-SAN.
I'M BELIEVING IN YOU TOO, SO PLEASE...
PLEASE DON'T SELL THE *ONI* VICE-CAPTAIN SHORT.
I CAN'T BELIEVE HOW MUCH YOU KNOW, SAITO-SAN. ♡
ABOUT AIZU.
SHUT IT.
AND IN ABOUT A MONTH...
...SEI'S WISH CAME TO PASS.
FURUKAWA-SAN?!

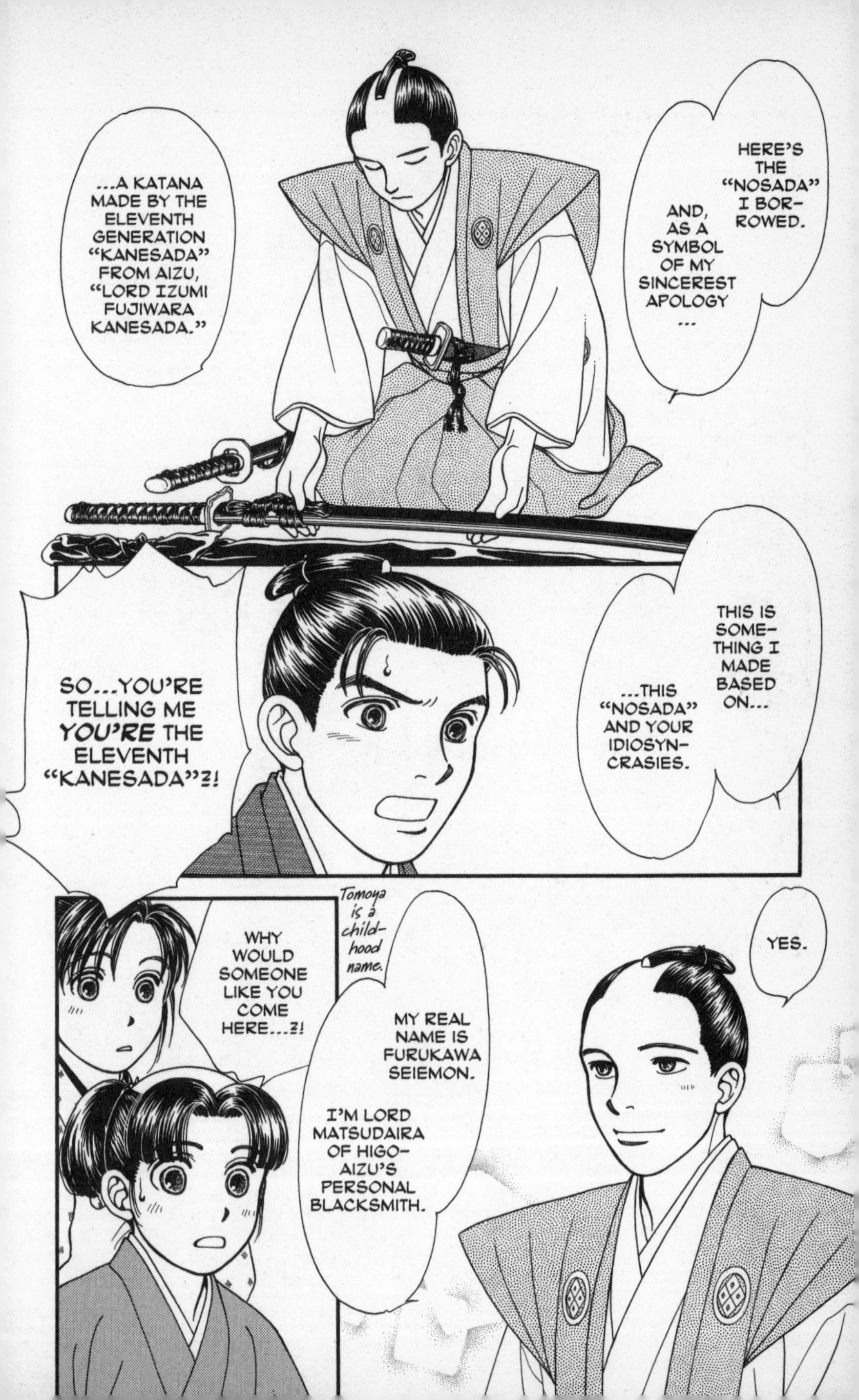
HERE'S THE "NOSADA" I BORROWED.
AND, AS A SYMBOL OF MY SINCEREST APOLOGY...
...A KATANA MADE BY THE ELEVENTH GENERATION "KANESADA" FROM AIZU, "LORD IZUMI FUJIWARA KANESADA."
THIS IS SOMETHING I MADE BASED ON...
...THIS "NOSADA" AND YOUR IDIOSYNCRASIES.
SO...YOU'RE TELLING ME *YOU'RE* THE ELEVENTH "KANESADA"?!
YES.
MY REAL NAME IS FURUKAWA SEIEMON.
I'M LORD MATSUDAIRA OF HIGO-AIZU'S PERSONAL BLACKSMITH.
Tomoya is a childhood name.
WHY WOULD SOMEONE LIKE YOU COME HERE...?!

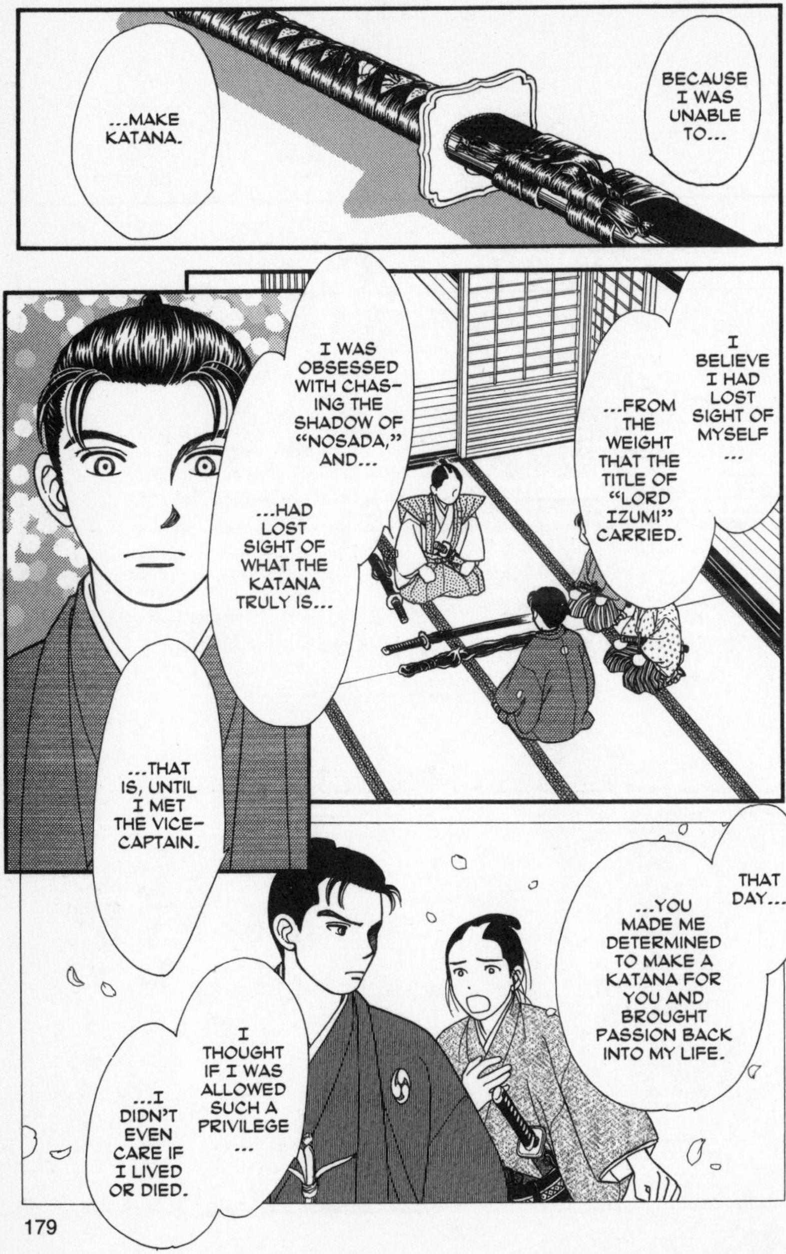
BECAUSE I WAS UNABLE TO...
...MAKE KATANA.
I BELIEVE I HAD LOST SIGHT OF MYSELF ...
...FROM THE WEIGHT THAT THE TITLE OF "LORD IZUMI" CARRIED.
I WAS OBSESSED WITH CHASING THE SHADOW OF "NOSADA," AND...
...HAD LOST SIGHT OF WHAT THE KATANA TRULY IS...
...THAT IS, UNTIL I MET THE VICE-CAPTAIN.
THAT DAY...
...YOU MADE ME DETERMINED TO MAKE A KATANA FOR YOU AND BROUGHT PASSION BACK INTO MY LIFE.
I THOUGHT IF I WAS ALLOWED SUCH A PRIVILEGE ...
...I DIDN'T EVEN CARE IF I LIVED OR DIED.

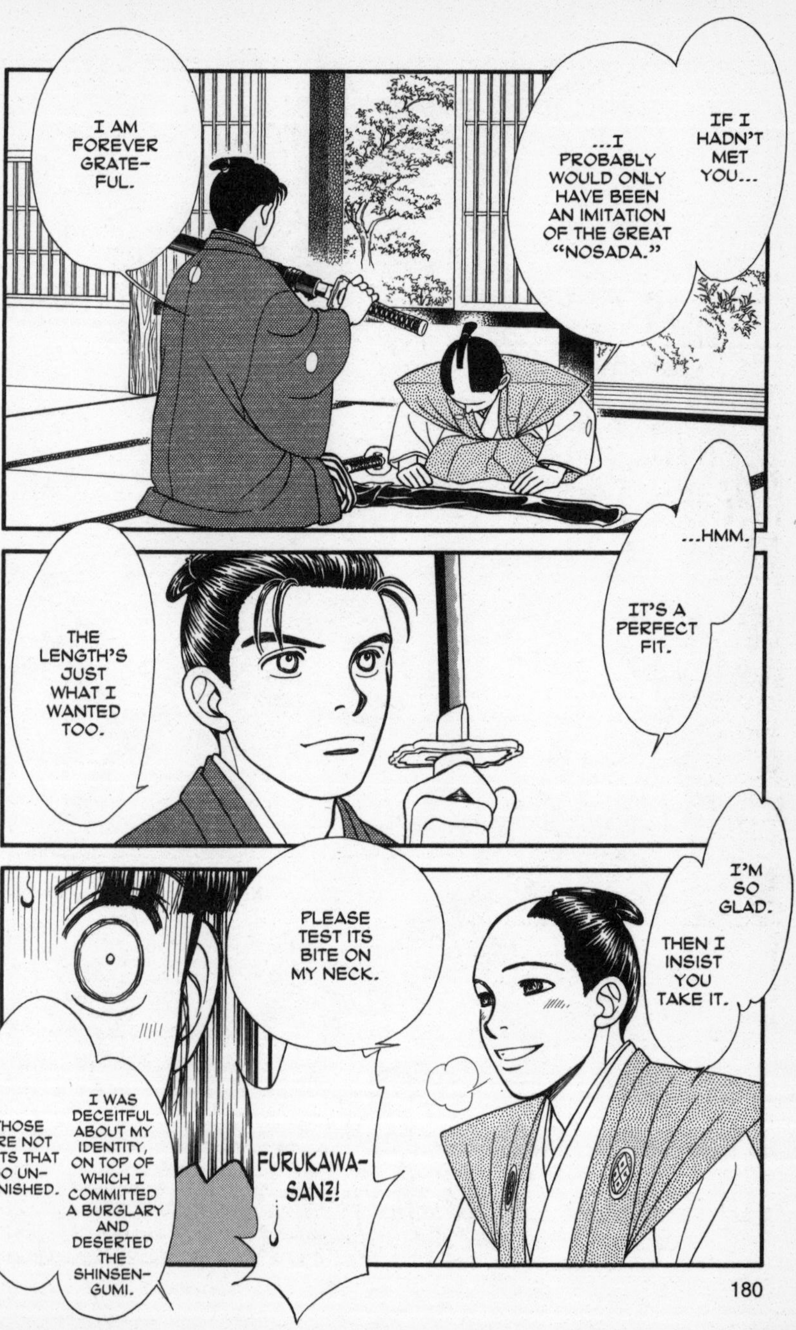
IF I HADN'T MET YOU...
...I PROBABLY WOULD ONLY HAVE BEEN AN IMITATION OF THE GREAT "NOSADA."
I AM FOREVER GRATE-FUL.
...HMM.
IT'S A PERFECT FIT.
THE LENGTH'S JUST WHAT I WANTED TOO.
I'M SO GLAD.
THEN I INSIST YOU TAKE IT.
PLEASE TEST ITS BITE ON MY NECK.
FURUKAWA-SAN?!
I WAS DECEITFUL ABOUT MY IDENTITY, ON TOP OF WHICH I COMMITTED A BURGLARY AND DESERTED THE SHINSEN-GUMI.
THOSE ARE NOT ACTS THAT GO UN-PUNISHED.

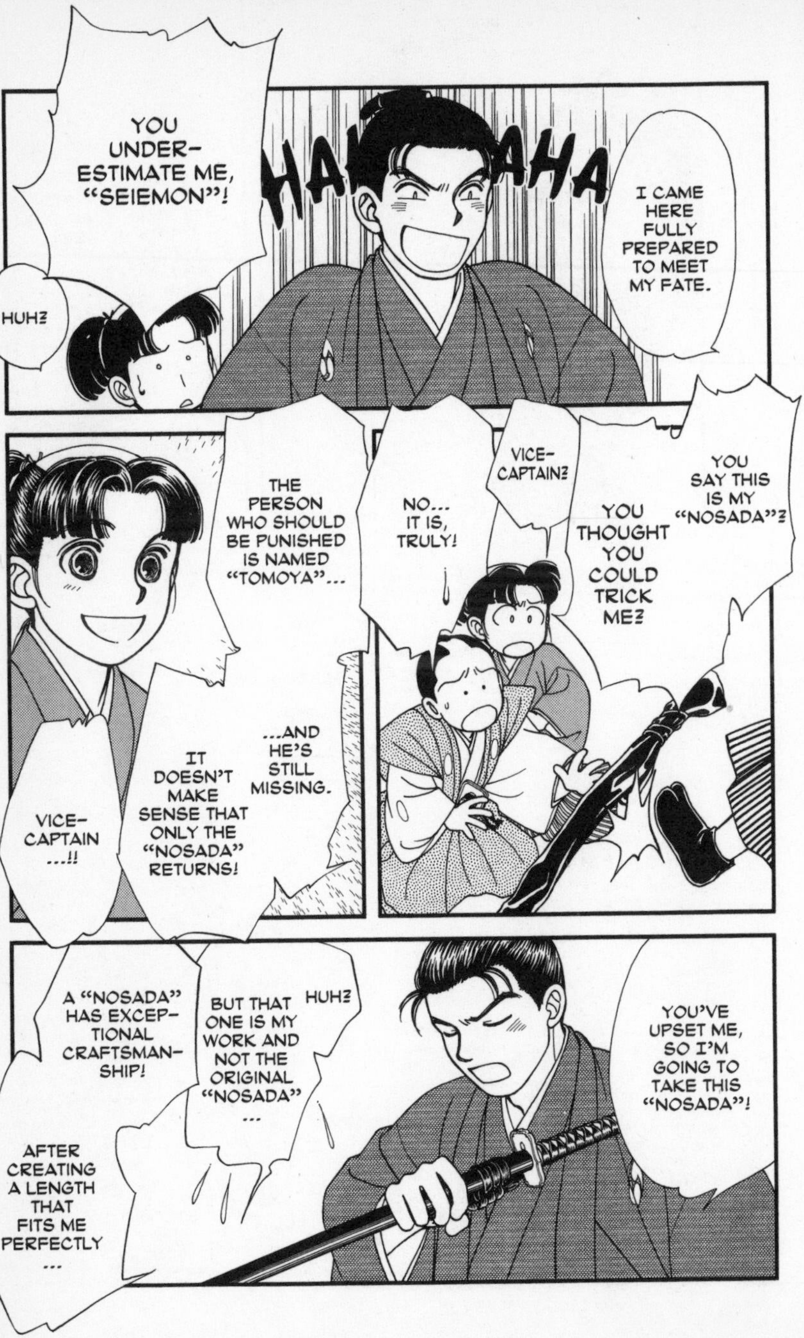
I CAME HERE FULLY PREPARED TO MEET MY FATE.
HAH AHA
YOU UNDER-ESTIMATE ME, "SEIEMON"!
HUH?
YOU SAY THIS IS MY "NOSADA"?
VICE-CAPTAIN?
YOU THOUGHT YOU COULD TRICK ME?
NO... IT IS, TRULY!
THE PERSON WHO SHOULD BE PUNISHED IS NAMED "TOMOYA"...
...AND HE'S STILL MISSING.
IT DOESN'T MAKE SENSE THAT ONLY THE "NOSADA" RETURNS!
VICE-CAPTAIN ...!!
YOU'VE UPSET ME, SO I'M GOING TO TAKE THIS "NOSADA"!
HUH?
BUT THAT ONE IS MY WORK AND NOT THE ORIGINAL "NOSADA"...
A "NOSADA" HAS EXCEP-TIONAL CRAFTSMAN-SHIP!
AFTER CREATING A LENGTH THAT FITS ME PERFECTLY...

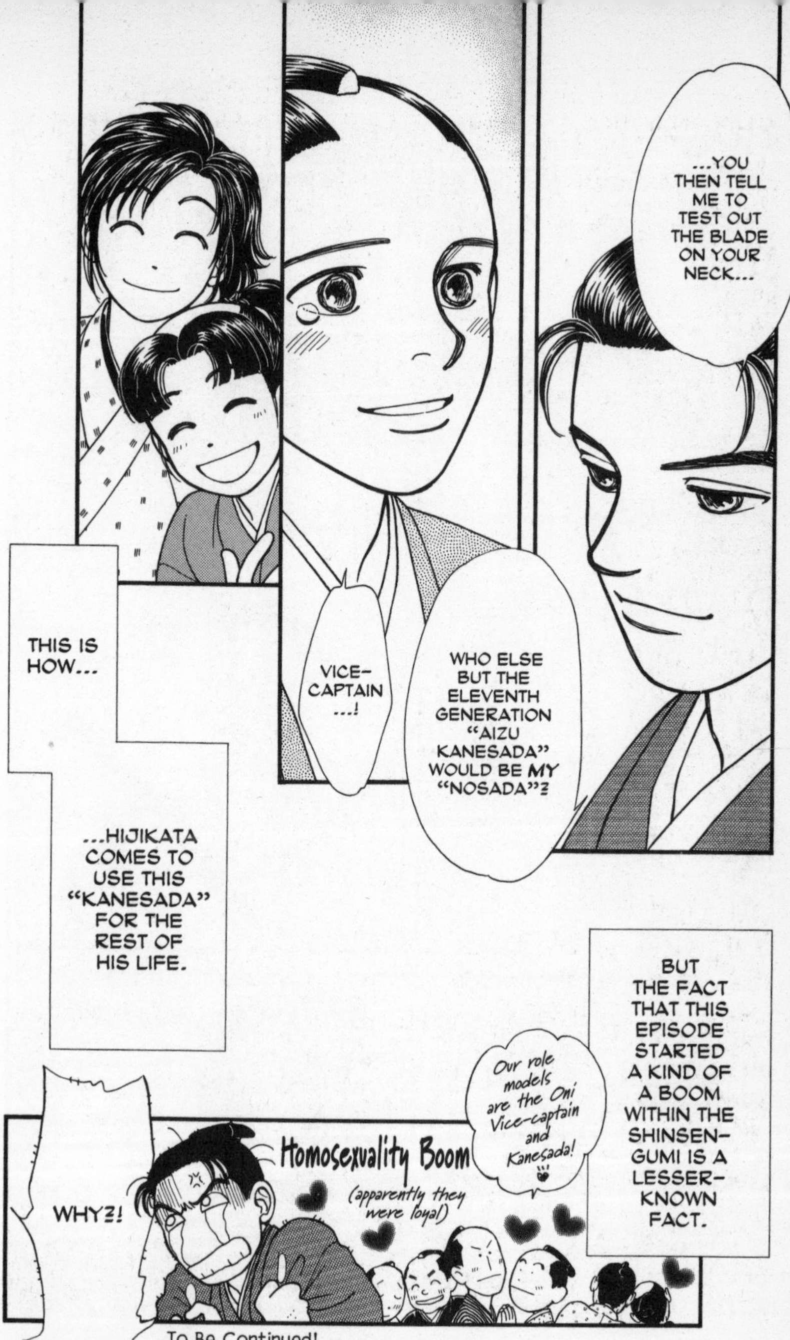
...YOU THEN TELL ME TO TEST OUT THE BLADE ON YOUR NECK...
WHO ELSE BUT THE ELEVENTH GENERATION "AIZU KANESADA" WOULD BE **MY** "NOSADA"?!
VICE-CAPTAIN ...!
THIS IS HOW...
...HIJIKATA COMES TO USE THIS "KANESADA" FOR THE REST OF HIS LIFE.
BUT THE FACT THAT THIS EPISODE STARTED A KIND OF A BOOM WITHIN THE SHINSEN-GUMI IS A LESSER-KNOWN FACT.
Our role models are the Oni Vice-captain and Kanesada!
Homosexuality Boom
(apparently they were loyal)
WHY?!
To Be Continued!

TAEKO WATANABE PRESENTS

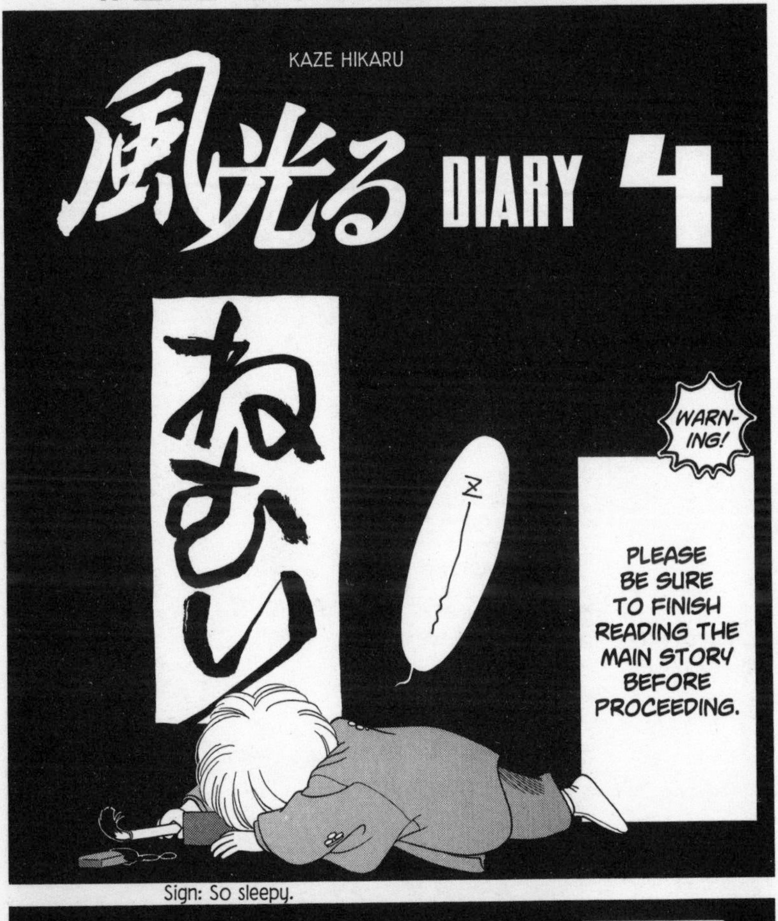
KAZE HIKARU
風光る DIARY 4
WARN-ING!
PLEASE BE SURE TO FINISH READING THE MAIN STORY BEFORE PROCEEDING.
Z
ねむい

Sign: So sleepy.

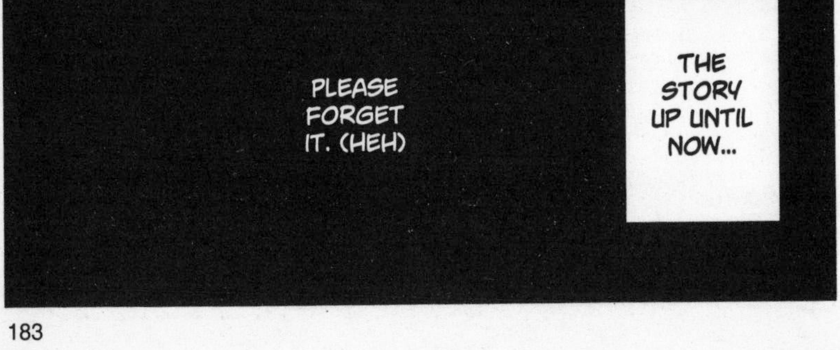
THE STORY UP UNTIL NOW...
PLEASE FORGET IT. (HEH)

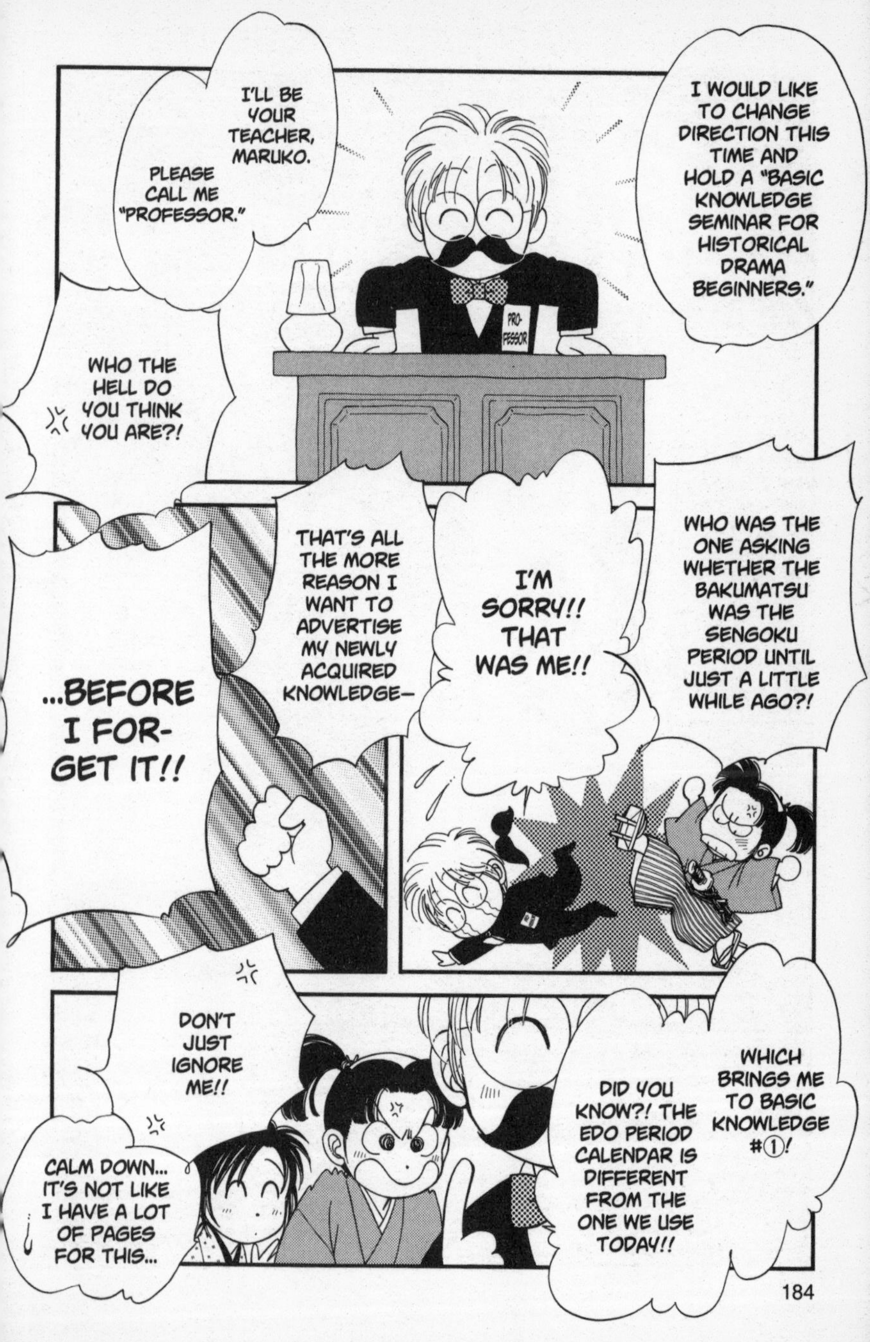
I WOULD LIKE TO CHANGE DIRECTION THIS TIME AND HOLD A "BASIC KNOWLEDGE SEMINAR FOR HISTORICAL DRAMA BEGINNERS."
I'LL BE YOUR TEACHER, MARUKO.
PLEASE CALL ME "PROFESSOR."
PRO-FESSOR
WHO THE HELL DO YOU THINK YOU ARE?!
WHO WAS THE ONE ASKING WHETHER THE BAKUMATSU WAS THE SENGOKU PERIOD UNTIL JUST A LITTLE WHILE AGO?!
I'M SORRY!! THAT WAS ME!!
THAT'S ALL THE MORE REASON I WANT TO ADVERTISE MY NEWLY ACQUIRED KNOWLEDGE—
...BEFORE I FOR-GET IT!!
WHICH BRINGS ME TO BASIC KNOWLEDGE #①!
DID YOU KNOW?! THE EDO PERIOD CALENDAR IS DIFFERENT FROM THE ONE WE USE TODAY!!
DON'T JUST IGNORE ME!!
CALM DOWN... IT'S NOT LIKE I HAVE A LOT OF PAGES FOR THIS...

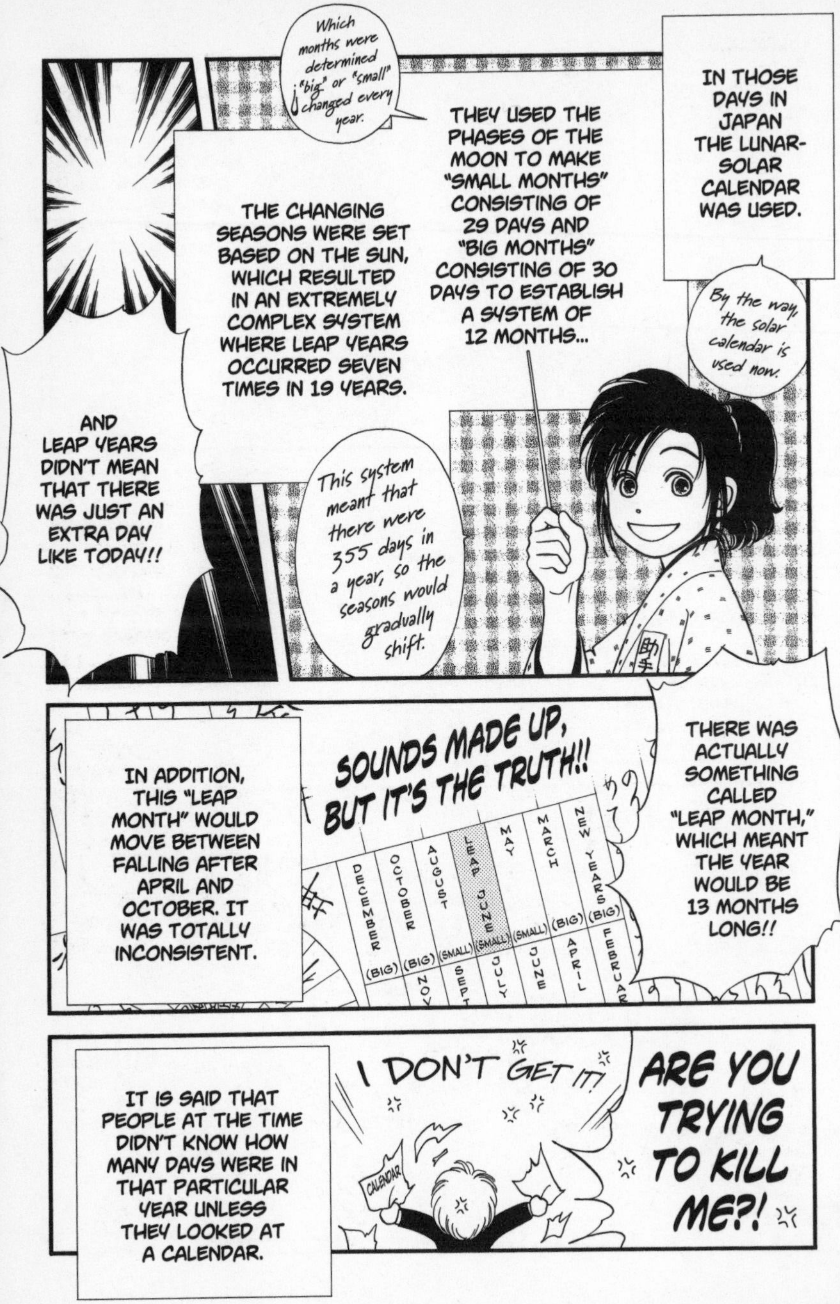
IN THOSE DAYS IN JAPAN THE LUNAR-SOLAR CALENDAR WAS USED.
By the way, the solar calendar is used now.
THEY USED THE PHASES OF THE MOON TO MAKE "SMALL MONTHS" CONSISTING OF 29 DAYS AND "BIG MONTHS" CONSISTING OF 30 DAYS TO ESTABLISH A SYSTEM OF 12 MONTHS...
Which months were determined "big" or "small" changed every year.
THE CHANGING SEASONS WERE SET BASED ON THE SUN, WHICH RESULTED IN AN EXTREMELY COMPLEX SYSTEM WHERE LEAP YEARS OCCURRED SEVEN TIMES IN 19 YEARS.
This system meant that there were 355 days in a year, so the seasons would gradually shift.
AND LEAP YEARS DIDN'T MEAN THAT THERE WAS JUST AN EXTRA DAY LIKE TODAY!!
THERE WAS ACTUALLY SOMETHING CALLED "LEAP MONTH," WHICH MEANT THE YEAR WOULD BE 13 MONTHS LONG!!
SOUNDS MADE UP, BUT IT'S THE TRUTH!!
NEW YEARS (BIG) FEBRUAR
MARCH (BIG) APRIL
MAY (SMALL) JUNE
LEAP JUNE (SMALL) JULY
AUGUST (SMALL) SEPT
OCTOBER (BIG) NOV
DECEMBER (BIG)
IN ADDITION, THIS "LEAP MONTH" WOULD MOVE BETWEEN FALLING AFTER APRIL AND OCTOBER. IT WAS TOTALLY INCONSISTENT.
ARE YOU TRYING TO KILL ME?!
I DON'T GET IT!
CALENDAR
IT IS SAID THAT PEOPLE AT THE TIME DIDN'T KNOW HOW MANY DAYS WERE IN THAT PARTICULAR YEAR UNLESS THEY LOOKED AT A CALENDAR.

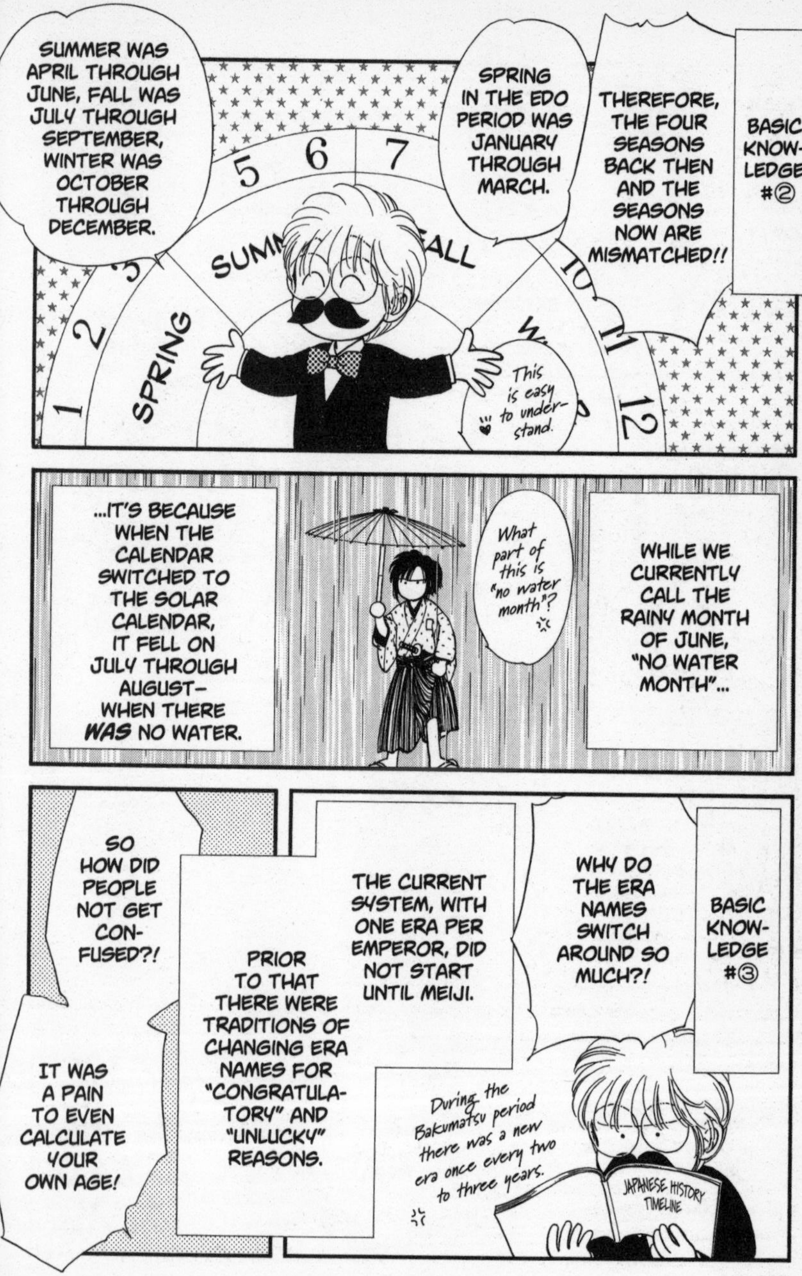
BASIC KNOWLEDGE #②
THEREFORE, THE FOUR SEASONS BACK THEN AND THE SEASONS NOW ARE MISMATCHED!!
SPRING IN THE EDO PERIOD WAS JANUARY THROUGH MARCH.
SUMMER WAS APRIL THROUGH JUNE, FALL WAS JULY THROUGH SEPTEMBER, WINTER WAS OCTOBER THROUGH DECEMBER.
This is easy to under-stand.
WHILE WE CURRENTLY CALL THE RAINY MONTH OF JUNE, "NO WATER MONTH"...
What part of this is "no water month"?
...IT'S BECAUSE WHEN THE CALENDAR SWITCHED TO THE SOLAR CALENDAR, IT FELL ON JULY THROUGH AUGUST—WHEN THERE *WAS* NO WATER.
BASIC KNOW-LEDGE #③
WHY DO THE ERA NAMES SWITCH AROUND SO MUCH?!
THE CURRENT SYSTEM, WITH ONE ERA PER EMPEROR, DID NOT START UNTIL MEIJI.
PRIOR TO THAT THERE WERE TRADITIONS OF CHANGING ERA NAMES FOR "CONGRATULA-TORY" AND "UNLUCKY" REASONS.
During the Bakumatsu period there was a new era once every two to three years.
JAPANESE HISTORY TIMELINE
SO HOW DID PEOPLE NOT GET CON-FUSED?!
IT WAS A PAIN TO EVEN CALCULATE YOUR OWN AGE!

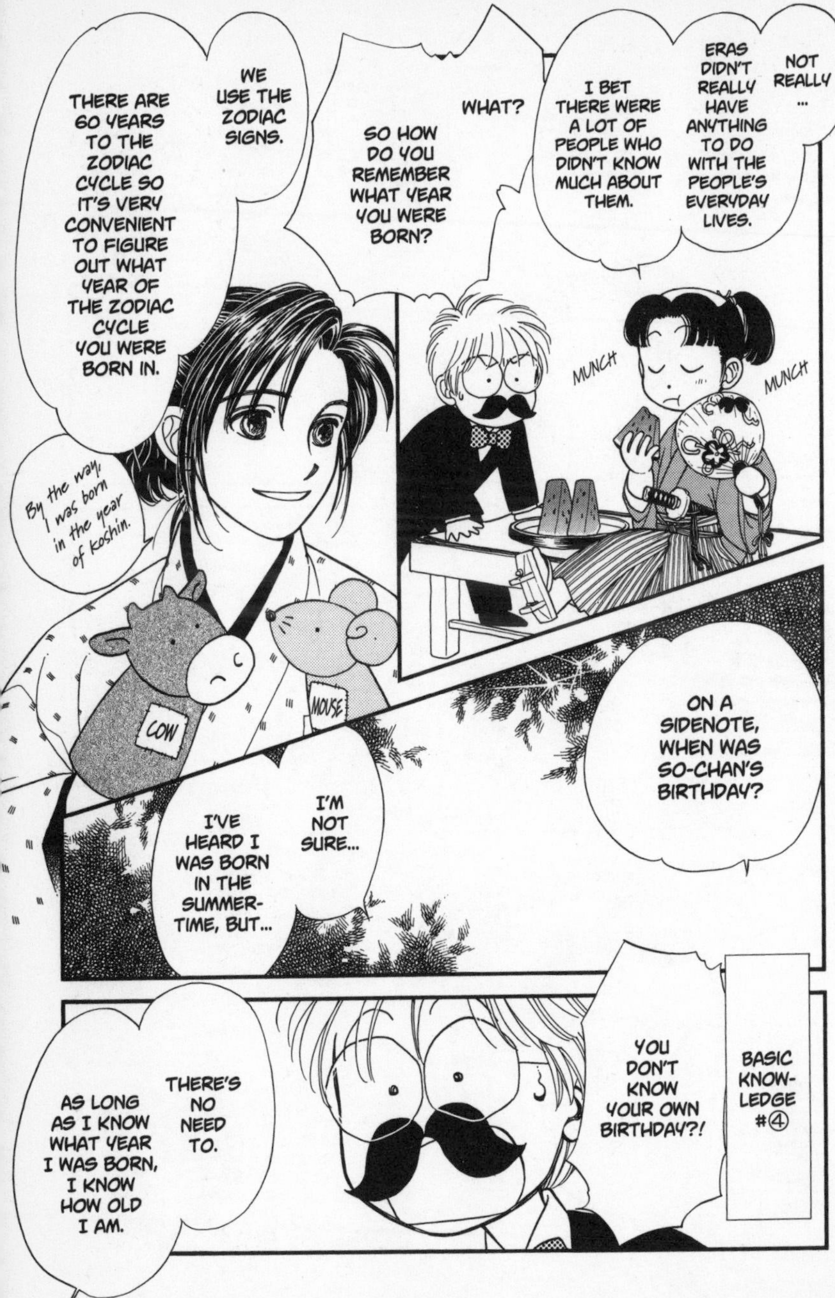
NOT REALLY ...
ERAS DIDN'T REALLY HAVE ANYTHING TO DO WITH THE PEOPLE'S EVERYDAY LIVES.
I BET THERE WERE A LOT OF PEOPLE WHO DIDN'T KNOW MUCH ABOUT THEM.
WHAT?
SO HOW DO YOU REMEMBER WHAT YEAR YOU WERE BORN?
MUNCH
MUNCH
WE USE THE ZODIAC SIGNS.
THERE ARE 60 YEARS TO THE ZODIAC CYCLE SO IT'S VERY CONVENIENT TO FIGURE OUT WHAT YEAR OF THE ZODIAC CYCLE YOU WERE BORN IN.
By the way, I was born in the year of koshin.
MOUSE
COW
ON A SIDENOTE, WHEN WAS SO-CHAN'S BIRTHDAY?
I'M NOT SURE...
I'VE HEARD I WAS BORN IN THE SUMMER-TIME, BUT...
BASIC KNOW-LEDGE #④
YOU DON'T KNOW YOUR OWN BIRTHDAY?!
THERE'S NO NEED TO.
AS LONG AS I KNOW WHAT YEAR I WAS BORN, I KNOW HOW OLD I AM.

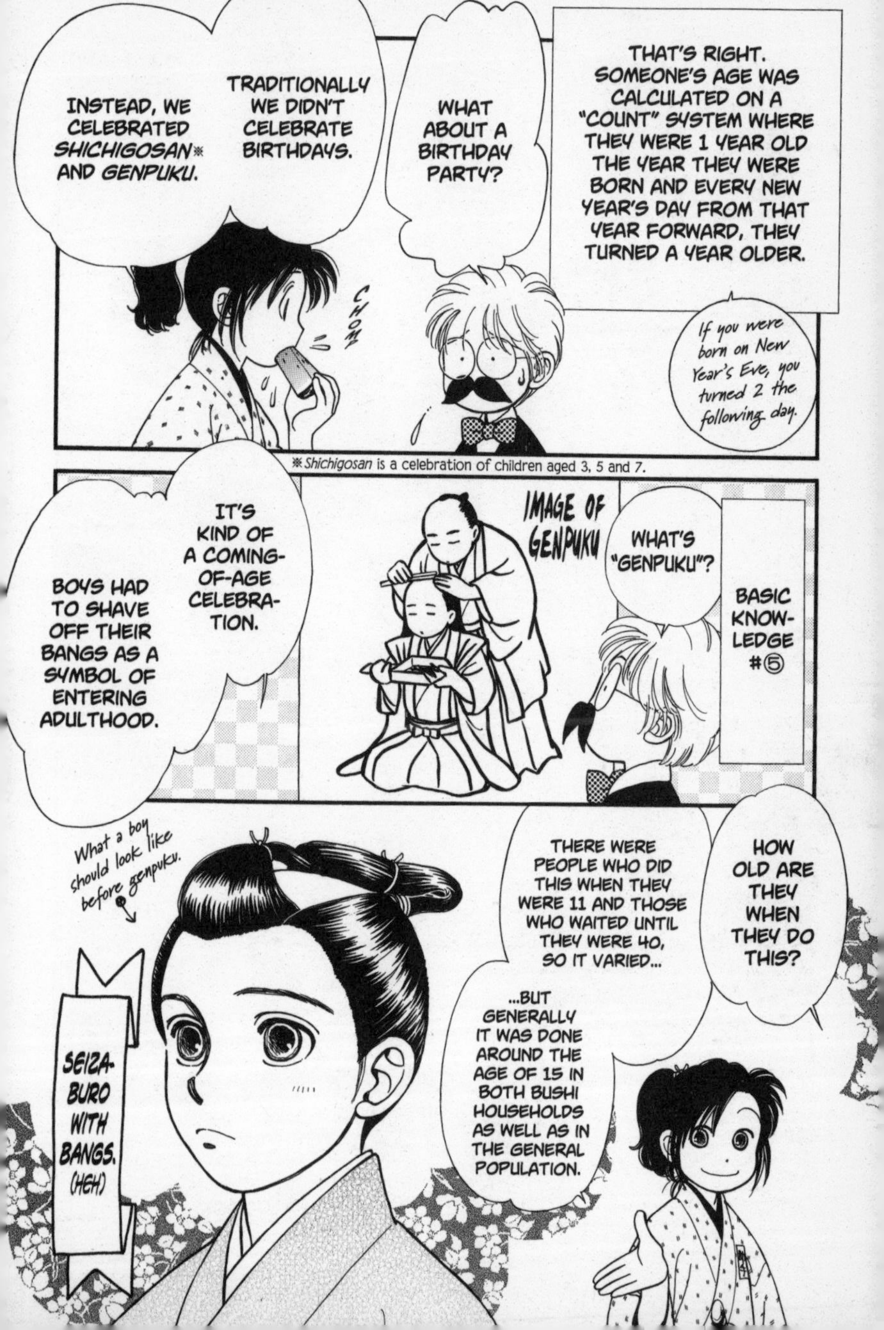
THAT'S RIGHT. SOMEONE'S AGE WAS CALCULATED ON A "COUNT" SYSTEM WHERE THEY WERE 1 YEAR OLD THE YEAR THEY WERE BORN AND EVERY NEW YEAR'S DAY FROM THAT YEAR FORWARD, THEY TURNED A YEAR OLDER.
If you were born on New Year's Eve, you turned 2 the following day.
WHAT ABOUT A BIRTHDAY PARTY?
TRADITIONALLY WE DIDN'T CELEBRATE BIRTHDAYS.
INSTEAD, WE CELEBRATED SHICHIGOSAN※ AND GENPUKU.
CHOMP
※Shichigosan is a celebration of children aged 3, 5 and 7.
BASIC KNOWLEDGE #⑤
WHAT'S "GENPUKU"?
IMAGE OF GENPUKU
IT'S KIND OF A COMING-OF-AGE CELEBRATION.
BOYS HAD TO SHAVE OFF THEIR BANGS AS A SYMBOL OF ENTERING ADULTHOOD.
HOW OLD ARE THEY WHEN THEY DO THIS?
THERE WERE PEOPLE WHO DID THIS WHEN THEY WERE 11 AND THOSE WHO WAITED UNTIL THEY WERE 40, SO IT VARIED...
...BUT GENERALLY IT WAS DONE AROUND THE AGE OF 15 IN BOTH BUSHI HOUSEHOLDS AS WELL AS IN THE GENERAL POPULATION.
What a boy should look like before genpuku.
SEIZABURO WITH BANGS. (HEH)

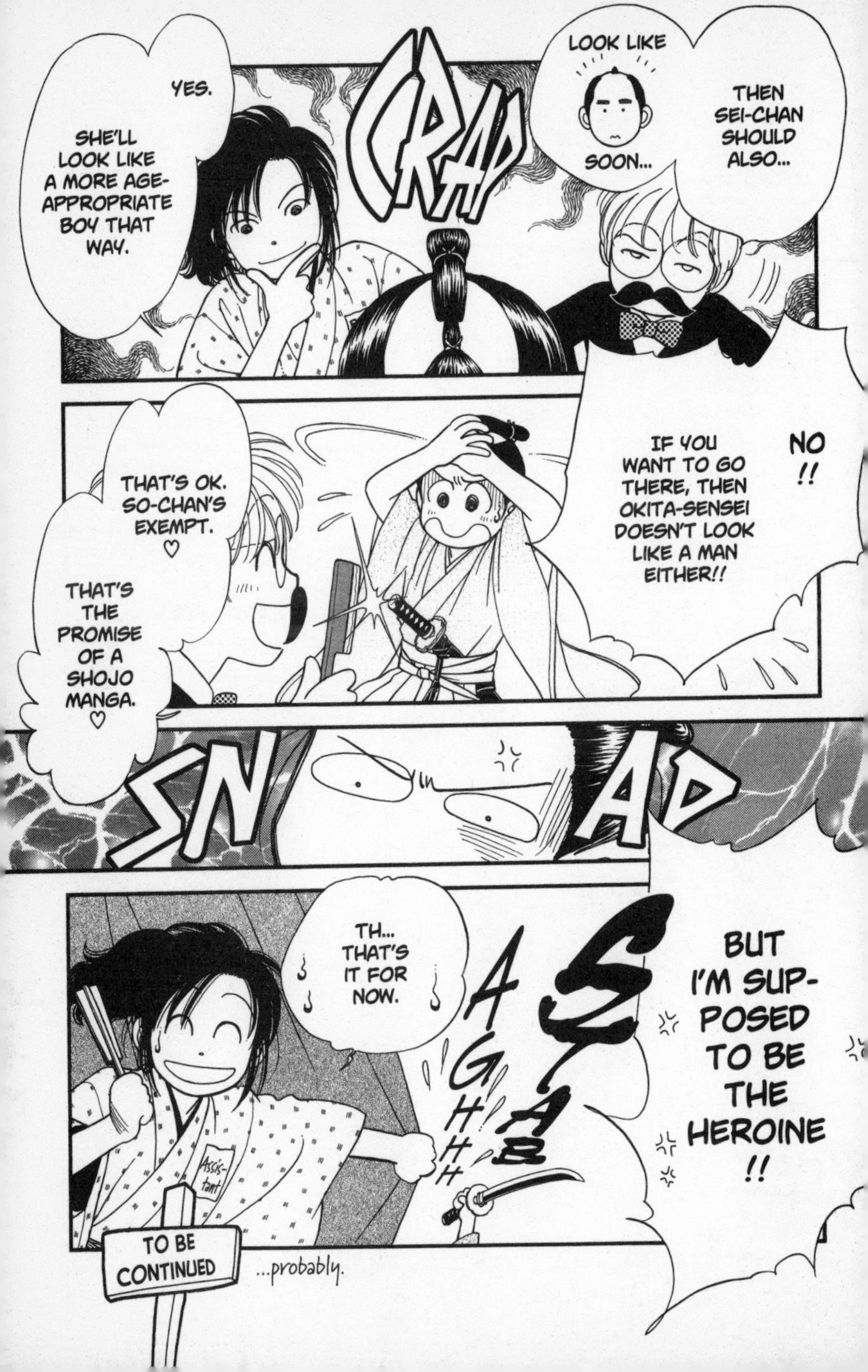
THEN SEI-CHAN SHOULD ALSO...
LOOK LIKE SOON...
CRAP
YES.
SHE'LL LOOK LIKE A MORE AGE-APPROPRIATE BOY THAT WAY.
NO!!
IF YOU WANT TO GO THERE, THEN OKITA-SENSEI DOESN'T LOOK LIKE A MAN EITHER!!
THAT'S OK. SO-CHAN'S EXEMPT. ♡
THAT'S THE PROMISE OF A SHOJO MANGA. ♡
SNAP
BUT I'M SUPPOSED TO BE THE HEROINE!!
AGHHHH
TH... THAT'S IT FOR NOW.
Assis-tant
TO BE CONTINUED
...probably.

Decoding Kaze Hikaru

Kaze Hikaru is a historical drama based in 19th century Japan and thus contains some fairly mystifying terminology. In this glossary we'll break down archaic phrases, terms, and other linguistic curiosities for you so that you can move through life with the smug assurance that you are indeed a know-it-all.

First and foremost, because *Kaze Hikaru* is a period story, we kept all character names in their traditional Japanese form—that is, family name followed by first name. For example, the character Okita Soji's family name is Okita and his personal name is Soji.

AKO-ROSHI:
The ronin (samurai) of Ako; featured in the immortal Kabuki play *Chushingura* (Loyalty), aka *47 Samurai*.

ANI-UE:
Literally, "brother above"; an honorific for an elder male sibling.

BAKUFU:
Literally, "tent government." It is the shogunate—the feudal, military government that dominated Japan for more than 200 years.

BUSHI:
A samurai or warrior (part of the compound word *bushido*, which means "way of the samurai").

CHICHI-UE:
An honorific meaning "father above."

DO:
In kendo (a Japanese fencing sport that uses bamboo swords), this is a short way of describing the offensive single-hit strike to the stomach.

-HAN:

The same as the honorific -SAN, pronounced in the dialect of southern Japan.

-KUN:

An honorific suffix that indicates a difference in rank and title. The use of *kun* is also a way of indicating familiarity and friendliness between students or compatriots.

MEN:

In the context of *Kaze Hikaru*, *men* refers to one of the "points" in kendo. It is a strike to the forehead and is considered a basic move.

MIBU-ROSHI:

A group of warriors who support the Bakufu.

NE'E-SAN:

Can mean "older sister," "ma'am," or "miss."

NI'I-CHAN:

Short for oni'isan or oni'i-chan, meaning older brother.

OKU-SAMA:

This is a polite way to refer to someone's wife. *Oku* means "deep" or "further back," and comes from the fact that wives (in affluent families) stayed hidden away in the back rooms of the house.

ONI:

Literally means "ogre." This is Sei's nickname for Vice Captain Hijikata.

RANPO:

Medical science derived from the Dutch.

RONIN:
Masterless samurai.

RYO:
At the time, one *ryo* and two *bu* (four *bu* equaled roughly one *ryo*) were enough currency to support a family of five for an entire month.

-SAN:
An honorific suffix that carries the meaning of "Mr." or "Ms."

SENSEI:
A teacher, master or instructor.

SEPPUKU:
A ritualistic suicide by disembowlment that was considered a privilege of the nobility and samurai elite.

SONJO-HA:
Those loyal to the emperor and dedicated to the expulsion of foreigners from the country.

TAMEBO:
A short version of the name Tamesaburo.

YUBO:
A short version of the name Yunosuke.

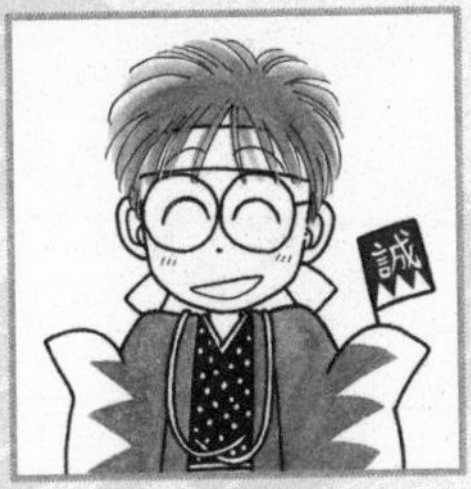
誠

I've completed all four seasons on the covers for volumes 1-4, and now I'm back to spring again for the second time! Yay!! This is so exciting for me, especially because this series was originally supposed to end with volume 2. I didn't think I would be able to get through all four seasons. I had secretly promised myself that if I were able to continue on after that, I would dedicate myself to drawing "the seasons." Yes, as the bushi who must've cherished the seasons, for life was never guaranteed, I decided I would draw their period with care. So, although the cover may merely look like a repeated season at first, I did put a lot of thought into it. I hope my intentions came through.

Taeko Watanabe debuted as a manga artist in 1979 with her story *Waka-chan no Netsuai Jidai* (Love Struck Days of Waka). *Kaze Hikaru* is her longest-running series, but she has created a number of other popular series. Watanabe is a two-time winner of the prestigious Shogakukan Manga Award in the girls category—her manga *Hajime-chan ga Ichiban!* (Hajime-chan Is Number One!) claimed the award in 1991 and *Kaze Hikaru* took it in 2003.

Watanabe read hundreds of historical sources to create *Kaze Hikaru.* She is from Tokyo.

KAZE HIKARU VOL. 5
The Shojo Beat Manga Edition

STORY AND ART BY
TAEKO WATANABE

Translation & English Adaptation/Mai Ihara
Touch-up Art & Lettering/Gia Cam Luc
Cover Design/Courtney Utt
Interior Design/Izumi Evers
Editor/Nancy Thistlethwaite

Managing Editor/Megan Bates
Editorial Director/Elizabeth Kawasaki
Editor in Chief, Books/Alvin Lu
Editor in Chief, Magazines/Marc Weidenbaum
Sr. Director of Acquisitions/Rika Inouye
Sr. VP of Marketing/Liza Coppola
Exec. VP of Sales & Marketing/John Easum
Publisher/Hyoe Narita

Printed in Canada

Published by VIZ Media, LLC
P.O. Box 77010
San Francisco, CA 94107

Shojo Beat Manga Edition
10 9 8 7 6 5 4 3 2 1
First printing, May 2007

www.viz.com

store.viz.com

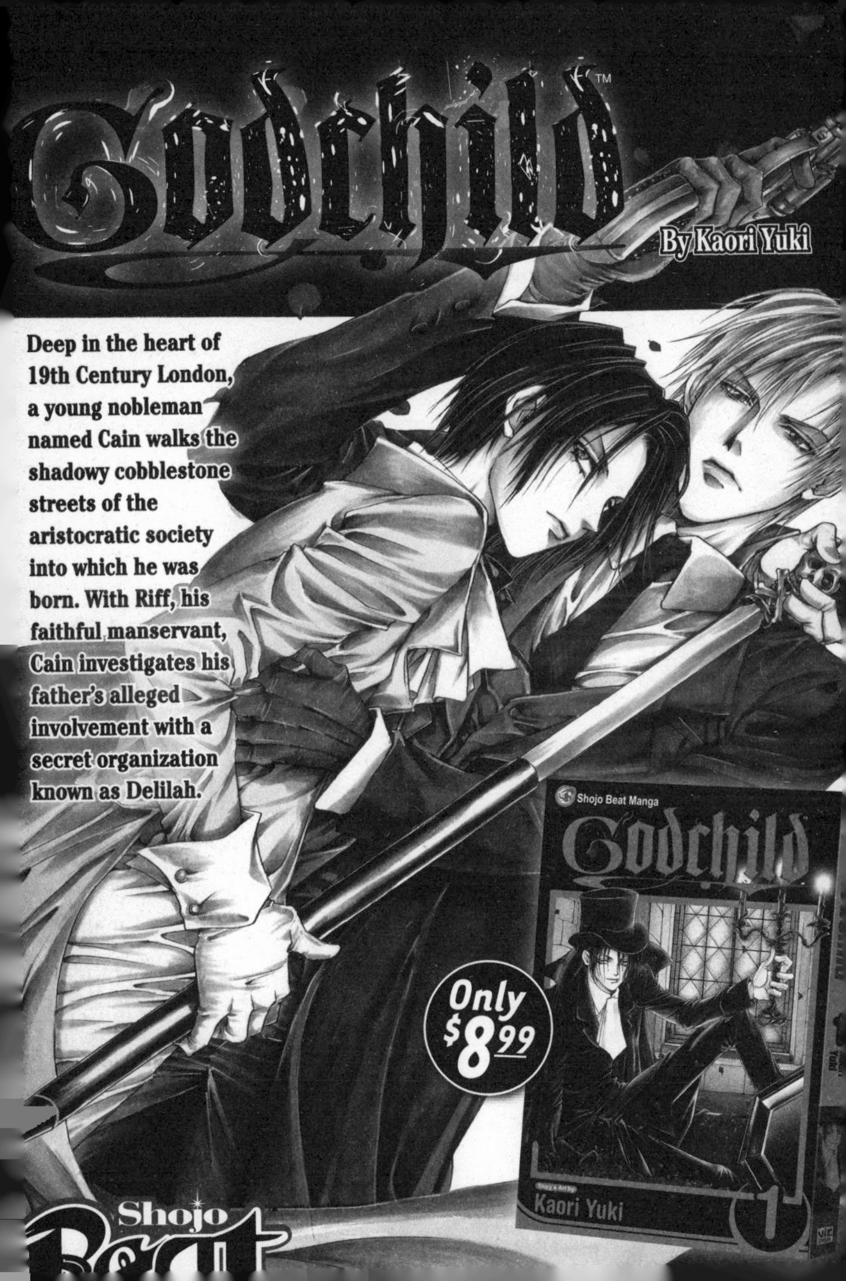
Godchild™
By Kaori Yuki
Deep in the heart of 19th Century London, a young nobleman named Cain walks the shadowy cobblestone streets of the aristocratic society into which he was born. With Riff, his faithful manservant, Cain investigates his father's alleged involvement with a secret organization known as Delilah.
Shojo Beat Manga
Godchild
Kaori Yuki
1
Only $8.99
Shojo

Tell us what you think about Shojo Beat Manga!

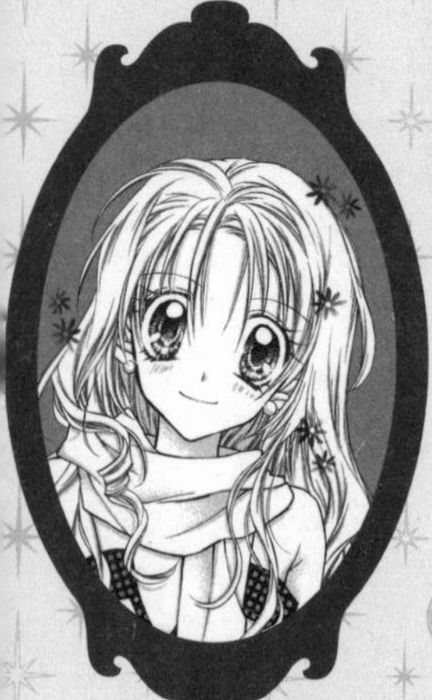

Our survey is now available online. Go to:

shojobeat.com/mangasurvey

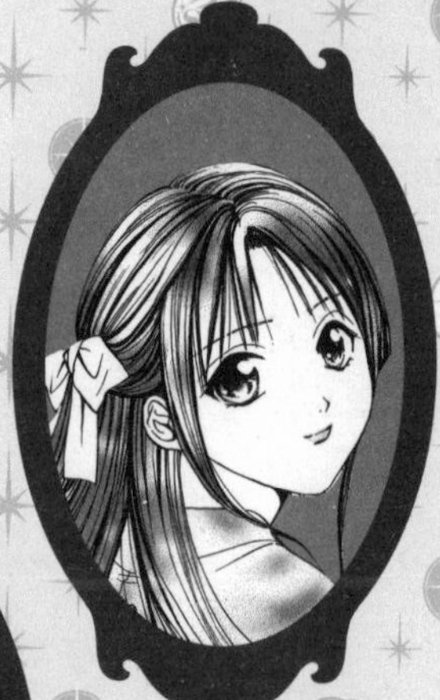

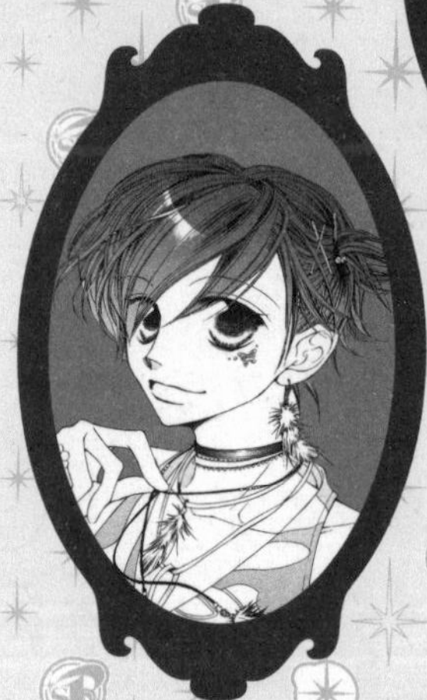

Help us make our product offerings better!

VIZ media

Shojo Beat MANGA from the HEART

THE REAL DRAMA BEGINS IN...

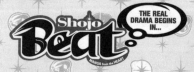

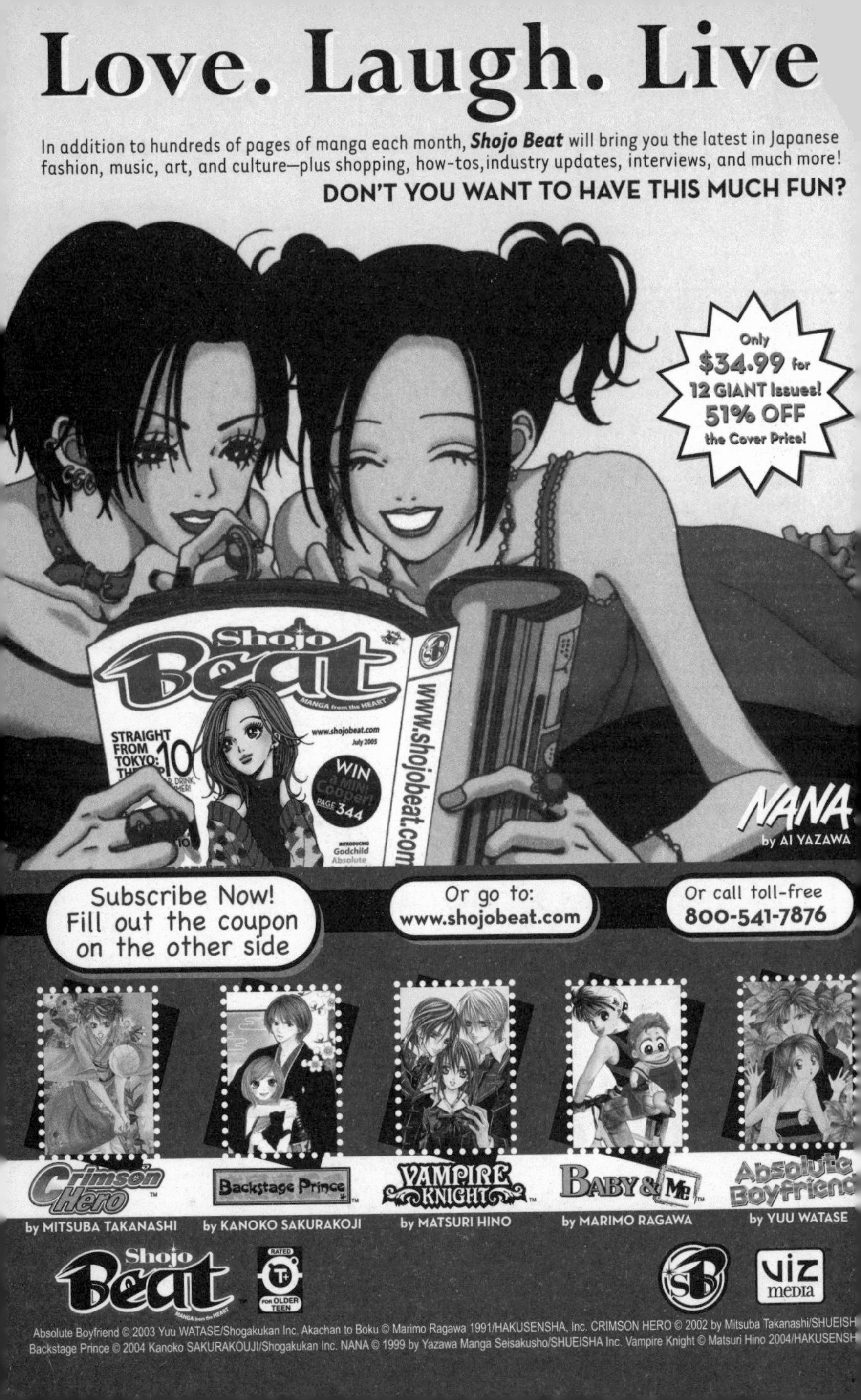
Love. Laugh. Live
In addition to hundreds of pages of manga each month, Shojo Beat will bring you the latest in Japanese fashion, music, art, and culture—plus shopping, how-tos, industry updates, interviews, and much more!
DON'T YOU WANT TO HAVE THIS MUCH FUN?
Only $34.99 for 12 GIANT Issues! 51% OFF the Cover Price!
Shojo Beat
MANGA from the HEART
www.shojobeat.com
July 2005
STRAIGHT FROM TOKYO:
WIN a MINI Cooper! PAGE 344
INTRODUCING Godchild Absolute
www.shojobeat.com
NANA by AI YAZAWA
Subscribe Now! Fill out the coupon on the other side
Or go to: www.shojobeat.com
Or call toll-free 800-541-7876
Crimson Hero by MITSUBA TAKANASHI
Backstage Prince by KANOKO SAKURAKOJI
VAMPIRE KNIGHT by MATSURI HINO
BABY & ME by MARIMO RAGAWA
Absolute Boyfriend by YUU WATASE
Shojo Beat
RATED T+ FOR OLDER TEEN
viz media
Absolute Boyfriend © 2003 Yuu WATASE/Shogakukan Inc. Akachan to Boku © Marimo Ragawa 1991/HAKUSENSHA, Inc. CRIMSON HERO © 2002 by Mitsuba Takanashi/SHUEISH
Backstage Prince © 2004 Kanoko SAKURAKOUJI/Shogakukan Inc. NANA © 1999 by Yazawa Manga Seisakusho/SHUEISHA Inc. Vampire Knight © Matsuri Hino 2004/HAKUSENSH